EVOLVE

STUDENT'S BOOK

Leslie Anne Hendra, Mark Ibbotson,
and Kathryn O'Dell

1A

CAMBRIDGE
UNIVERSITY PRESS

University Printing House, Cambridge CB2 8BS, United Kingdom

One Liberty Plaza, 20th Floor, New York, NY 10006, USA

477 Williamstown Road, Port Melbourne, VIC 3207, Australia

314–321, 3rd Floor, Plot 3, Splendor Forum, Jasola District Centre, New Delhi – 110025, India

79 Anson Road, #06–04/06, Singapore 079906

Cambridge University Press is part of the University of Cambridge.

It furthers the University's mission by disseminating knowledge in the pursuit of education, learning, and research at the highest international levels of excellence.

www.cambridge.org
Information on this title: www.cambridge.org/9781108405034

© Cambridge University Press 2019

This publication is in copyright. Subject to statutory exception and to the provisions of relevant collective licensing agreements, no reproduction of any part may take place without the written permission of Cambridge University Press.

First published 2019

20 19 18 17 16 15 14 13 12 11 10 9 8 7 6 5 4 3 2 1

Printed in Dubai by Oriental Press

A catalogue record for this publication is available from the British Library

ISBN 978-1-108-40521-8 Student's Book
ISBN 978-1-108-40503-4 Student's Book A
ISBN 978-1-108-40914-8 Student's Book B
ISBN 978-1-108-40522-5 Student's Book with Practice Extra
ISBN 978-1-108-40504-1 Student's Book with Practice Extra A
ISBN 978-1-108-40915-5 Student's Book with Practice Extra B
ISBN 978-1-108-40894-3 Workbook with Audio
ISBN 978-1-108-40859-2 Workbook with Audio A
ISBN 978-1-108-41191-2 Workbook with Audio B
ISBN 978-1-108-40512-6 Teacher's Edition with Test Generator
ISBN 978-1-108-41062-5 Presentation Plus
ISBN 978-1-108-41201-8 Class Audio CDs
ISBN 978-1-108-40791-5 Video Resource Book with DVD
ISBN 978-1-108-41200-1 Full Contact with DVD
ISBN 978-1-108-41152-3 Full Contact with DVD A
ISBN 978-1-108-41410-4 Full Contact with DVD B

Additional resources for this publication at www.cambridge.org/evolve

Cambridge University Press has no responsibility for the persistence or accuracy of URLs for external or third-party internet websites referred to in this publication, and does not guarantee that any content on such websites is, or will remain, accurate or appropriate. Information regarding prices, travel timetables, and other factual information given in this work is correct at the time of first printing but Cambridge University Press does not guarantee the accuracy of such information thereafter.

ACKNOWLEDGMENTS

The *Evolve* publishers would like to thank the following individuals and institutions who have contributed their time and insights into the development of the course:

Ivanova Monteros A., **Universidad Tecnológica Equinoccial (UTE)**, Ecuador; Monica Frenzel, **Universidad Andrés Bello**, Chile; Antonio Machuca Montalvo, **Organización The Institute TITUELS, Veracruz**, Mexico; Daniel Martin, **CELLEP**, Brazil; Roberta Freitas, **IBEU**, Brazil; Verónica Nolivos Arellano, Language Coordinator, Quito, Ecuador; Daniel Lowe, **Lowe English Services**, Panama; Maria Araceli Hernández Tovar, **Instituto Tecnológico Superior de San Luis Potosí**, Capital, Mexico; Lenise Butler, **Laureate**, Mexico; Gloria González Meza, **Instituto Politecnico Nacional, ESCA (University)**, Mexico; Miguel Ángel López, **Universidad Europea de Madrid**, Spain; Diego Ribeiro Santos, **Universidade Anhembi Morumbi**, São Paulo, Brazil; Esther Carolina Euceda Garcia, **UNITEC (Universidad Tecnologica Centroamericana)**, Honduras.

To our student cast, who have contributed their ideas and their time, and who appear throughout this book:

Anderson Batista, Brazil; Carolina Nascimento Negrão, Brazil; Felipe Martinez Lopez, Mexico; Jee-Hyo Moon, South Korea ; Jinny Lara, Honduras; Josue Lozano, Honduras; Julieth C. Moreno Delgado, Colombia; Larissa Castro, Honduras.

And special thanks to Katy Simpson, teacher and writer at *myenglishvoice.com*; and Raquel Ribeiro dos Santos, EFL teacher, EdTech researcher, blogger, and lecturer.

Authors' Acknowledgments:

The authors would like to extend their warmest thanks to all of the team at Cambridge University Press who were involved in creating this course. In particular, they would like to thank Ruby Davies and Robert Williams for their kindness, enthusiasm, and encouragement throughout the writing of the A1 level. They would also like to express their appreciation to Caroline Thiriau, whose understanding and support have been of great value. And they would like to thank Katie La Storia for her dedication and enthusiasm throughout the project.

Kathryn O'Dell would like to thank her parents (and grandparents) for passing down a love for words and stories. She also thanks her husband, Kevin Hurdman, for his loving support.

Leslie Anne Hendra would like to thank Michael Stuart Clark, her *sine qua non*, for his support and encouragement during this and other projects.

Mark Ibbotson would like to thank Aimy and Tom for their patience and understanding as family life was bent and squeezed around the project, and – especially – Nathalie, whose energy and creative solutions made it all possible.

The authors and publishers acknowledge the following sources of copyright material and are grateful for the permissions granted. While every effort has been made, it has not always been possible to identify the sources of all the material used, or to trace all copyright holders. If any omissions are brought to our notice, we will be happy to include the appropriate acknowledgements on reprinting and in the next update to the digital edition, as applicable.

Photo:

Key: B = Below, BG = Background, BL = Below Left, BR = Below Right, C = Centre, CL = Centre Left, CR = Centre Right, L = Left, R = Right, TC = Top Centre, TL = Top Left, TR = Top Right.

All images are sourced from Getty Images.

p. xvi (listen): Tara Moore/DigitalVision; p. xvi (say): Tara Moore/The Image Bank; p. xvi (write): Kohei Hara/DigitalVision; p. xvi (watch): Felbert+Eickenberg/Stock4B; p. xvi (students): Klaus Vedfelt/DigitalVision; p. 1, p. 2 (Gabi), p. 8 (CR), p. 14 (L), p. 36 (email): Hero Images; p. 2 (Karina): oscarhdez/iStock/Getty Images Plus; p. 2 (Antonio): Vladimir Godnik; p. 2 (Max): DMEPhotography/iStock/Getty Images Plus; p. 2 (map): Colormos/The Image Bank; p. 2 (network): OktalStudio/DigitalVision Vectors; p. 2 (globe): Image by Catherine MacBride/Moment; p. 4: Tara Moore/Taxi; p. 4, p. 6, p. 22 (living room), p. 24 (lamp), p. 52 (CR), p. xvi (read): Westend61; p. 7: ATGImages/iStock Editorial/Getty Images Plus; p. 8 (1.1a): .shock/iStock/Getty Images Plus; p. 8 (1.1b): Carl Olsson/Folio Images; p. 8 (1.1c): Phil Boorman/Cultura; p. 8 (1.1d), p. 54 (college), p. 62 (photo h): Caiaimage/Sam Edwards; p. 8 (1.1e): Mark Edward Atkinson/Blend Images; p. 8 (1.1f): Thomas Northcut/DigitalVision; p. 8 (1.1g), p. 36 (man), p. 37, p. 49 (CR): Sam Edwards/Caiaimage; p. 8 (1.1h): Glow Images, Inc/Glow; p. 8 (BR): Alistair Berg/DigitalVision; p. 9 (L): ajr_images/iStock/Getty Images Plus; p. 9 (R): Ivan Evgenyev/Blend Images; pp. 10, 20, 30, 42, 52, 62: Tom Merton/Caiaimage; p. 10 (photo a): Georges De Keerle/Hulton Archive; p. 10 (photo b): Monica Schipper/FilmMagic; p. 10 (photo c): DEA/D. DAGLI ORTI/De Agostini; p. 10 (photo d): Scott Gries/Getty Images Entertainment; p. 10 (photo e, i): Bettmann; p. 10 (photo f): Sgranitz/WireImage; p. 10 (photo g): Christopher Furlong/Getty Images News; p. 10 (photo h): Dan Kitwood/Getty Images Entertainment; p. 10 (photo j): ALFREDO ESTRELLA/AFP; p. 11: Thomas Barwick/Stone; p. 13: Paco Navarro/Blend Images; p. 14 (couple), p. 20: Ronnie Kaufman/Larry Hirshowitz/Blend Images; p. 14 (Erika): Tony Anderson/DigitalVision; p. 14 (boy): Flashpop/Stone; p. 14 (woman): aldomurillo/E+; p. 16: Alyson Aliano/Image Source; p. 17: Richard Jung/Photodisc; p. 18: powerofforever/E+; p. 19: Steve Prezant/Image Source; p. 21, p. 30 (chair): Johner Images; p. 22 (bedroom): svetikd/E+; p. 22 (bathroom): JohnnyGreig/E+; p. 24 (bed): Diane Auckland/ArcaidImages; p. 24 (chair): Daniel Grill; p. 24 (table): Steve Gorton/Dorling Kindersley; p. 24 (desk): pbombaert/Moment; p. 24 (bookcase): Andreas von Einsiedel/Corbis Documentary; p. 24 (couch): Fotosearch; p. 24 (shower): RollingEarth/E+; p. 24 (refrigerator): Karen Moskowitz/The Image Bank; p. 24 (TV): Tetra Images; p. 24 (sink): Mark Griffin/EyeEm; p. 24 (rug): Art-Y/E+; p. 25: Hinterhaus Productions/Taxi; p. 26 (coffee): Dobroslav Hadzhiev/iStock/Getty Images Plus; p. 26 (tea): a-poselenov/iStock/Getty Images Plus; p. 26 (sugar): Maximilian Stock Ltd./Photographer's Choice; p. 26 (milk): YelenaYemchuk/iStock/Getty Images Plus; p. 26 (cookie): SvetlanaKoryakova/iStock/Getty Images Plus; p. 27: Shestock/Blend Images; p. 28 (TL): Hinterhaus Productions/DigitalVision; p. 29 (TR): Lilly Bloom/Cultura; p. 30 (TL): PeopleImages/DigitalVision; p. 30 (sofa): jakkapan21/iStock/Getty Images Plus; p. 30 (bookcase): Hany Rizk/EyeEm; p. 30 (couch): Nicholas Eveleigh/Photodisc; p. 30 (bed): Artem Perevozchikov/iStock/Getty Images Plus; p. 30 (desk): tifonimages/iStock/Getty Images Plus; p. 30 (chair): SKrow/iStock/Getty Images Plus; p. 30 (refrigerator): Customdesigner/iStock/Getty Images Plus; p. 30 (TV1): Dovapi/iStock/Getty Images Plus; p. 30 (TV2): Jorg Greuel/Photographer's Choice RF; p. 30 (dining), p. 34 (CR): s-cphoto/E+; p. 30 (frame): Matthias Clamer/Stone; p. 30 (rug): Chaloner Woods/Hulton Archive; p. 30 (lamp): xxmmxx/E+; p. 30 (plant), p. 61 (BG): Dorling Kindersley; p. 33: VCG/Getty Images News; p. 34 (tablet): daboost/iStock/Getty Images Plus; p. 34 (earphone): Dave King/Dorling Kindersleyl; p. 34 (phone): Lonely_/iStock/Getty Images Plus; p. 34 (laptop): scanrail/iStock/Getty Images Plus; p. 34 (smartwatch): Nerthuz/iStock/Getty Images Plus; p. 35: Images By Tang Ming Tung/DigitalVision; p. 36 (cellphone): hocus-focus/iStock/Getty Images Plus; p. 36 (chat): David Malan/The Image Bank; p. 36 (tab, text): ymgerman/iStock Editorial/Getty Images Plus; p. 36 (game): Keith Bell/Hemera/Getty Images Plus; p. 36 (phone): Bloomberg; p. 36 (symbol): jaroszpilewski/iStock/Getty Images Plus; p. 38: ferrantraite/E+; p. 39: John Fedele/Blend Images; p. 41 (C): Adrin Gmez/EyeEm; p. 41 (CR): Tim Hawley/Photographer's Choice RF; p. 42 (TR): Lilly Roadstones/Taxi; p. 42 (BR): Caiaimage/Tom Merton; p. 43: Digital Vision./Photodisc; p. 44 (walk): Inti St Clair/Blend Images; p. 44 (run): JGI/Tom Grill/Blend Images; p. 44 (work): Squaredpixels/E+; p. 44 (study): Geber86/E+; p. 44 (soccer): Thomas Barwick/Taxi; p. 47: David Stuart/Stockbyte; p. 48: Christopher Malcolm/The Image Bank; p. 49 (B): Wavebreakmedia/iStock/Getty Images Plus; p. 51: Juanmonino/E+; p. 52 (man): Jacqueline Veissid/Blend Images; p. 52 (commuters): Ovidio Ferreira/EyeEm; p. 53: David Nunuk/All Canada Photos; p. 54 (mall), p. 62 (photo c): Henglein And Steets/Photolibrary; p. 54 (store): m-imagephotography/iStock/Getty Images Plus; p. 54 (hotel): John Warburton-Lee/AWL Images; p. 54 (school): Robert Daly/Caiaimage; p. 54 (restaurant): Tom Merton/OJO Images; p. 54 (supermarket): David Nevala/Aurora; p. 54 (museum): Eric VANDEVILLE/Gamma-Rapho; p. 54 (hospital), p. 62 (photo g): Steven Frame/Hemera/Getty Images Plus; p. 54 (café): Klaus Vedfelt/Taxi; p. 54 (bookstore): M_a_y_a/E+; p. 54 (thetre), p. 62 (photo e): Clara Li/EyeEm; p. 54 (park), p. 62 (photo a): Eric You/EyeEm; p. 54 (zoo): John Hart/EyeEm; p.55: fotoVoyager/E+; p. 56 (1a): Aimin Tang/Photographer's Choice; p. 56 (1b): Barry Kusuma/Stockbyte; p. 56 (1c): Alan_Lagadu/iStock/Getty Images Plus; p. 56 (1d): swedewah/E+; p. 56 (1e): Witold Skrypczak/Lonely Planet Images; p. 56 (statue): Jeremy Walker/Photographer's Choice; p. 57: cinoby/E+; p. 58: JGI/Jamie Grill/Blend Images; p. 59: Julia Davila-Lampe/Moment Open; p. 60 (BG): Macduff Everton/Iconica; p. 60 (CR): Cesar Okada/E+; p. 60 (TL): Neil Beckerman/The Image Bank; p. 61 (waterfall): Kimie Hishimabukuro/Moment Open; p. 61 (Christ): joSon/The Image Bank; p. 61 (flower): SambaPhoto/Cristiano Burmester/SambaPhotol; p. 61 (monkey): Kryssia Campos/Moment; p. 62 (BG): Planet Observer/UIG/Universal Images Group; p. 62 (photo b): Bernard Jaubert/Canopy; p. 62 (photo d): Caiaimage/Robert Daly/OJO+; p. 62 (photo f): Gary Yeowell/The Image Bank; p. 143 (living room): imagenavi; p. 143 (kitchen): Glasshouse Images/Corbis.

Front cover photography by Arctic-Images/The Image Bank/Getty Images.

Illustrations by: Ana Djordevic (Astound US) p. 5; Alejandro Mila (Sylvie Poggio Artists Agency) pp. 23, 30; Joanna Kerr (New Division) pp. 44, 50; Dusan Lakicevic (Beehive Illustration) pp. 24, 46.

Audio production by CityVox, New York.

EVOLVE

SPEAKING MATTERS

EVOLVE is a six-level American English course for adults and young adults, taking students from beginner to advanced levels (CEFR A1 to C1).

Drawing on insights from language teaching experts and real students, EVOLVE is a general English course that gets students speaking with confidence.

This student-centered course covers all skills and focuses on the most effective and efficient ways to make progress in English.

Confidence in teaching.
Joy in learning.

Better Learning WITH EVOLVE

Better Learning is our simple approach where insights we've gained from research have helped shape content that drives results. Language evolves, and so does the way we learn. This course takes a flexible, student-centered approach to English language teaching.

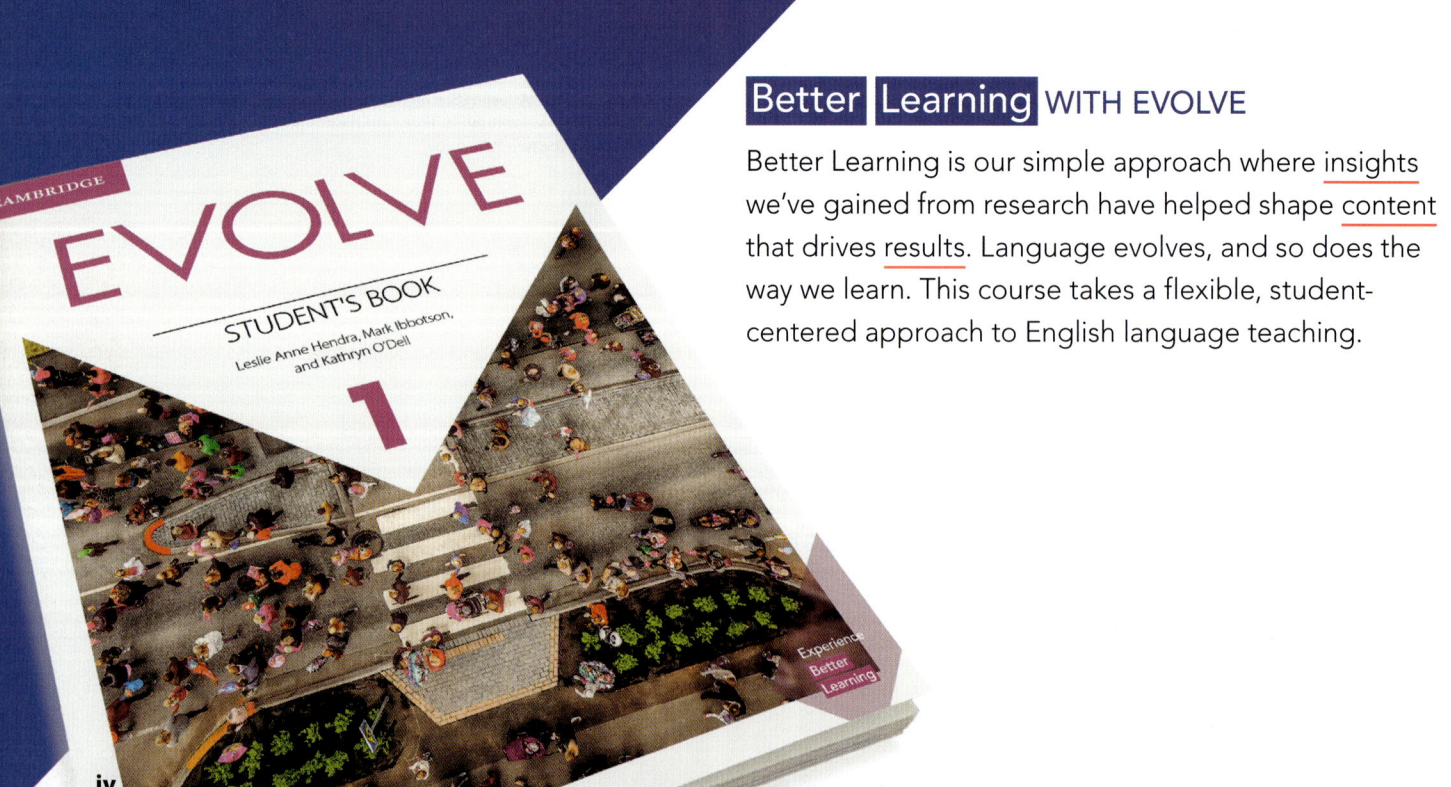

Meet our student contributors

Videos and ideas from real students feature throughout the Student's Book.

Our student contributors describe themselves in three words.

LARISSA CASTRO
Friendly, honest, happy
Mission College, USA

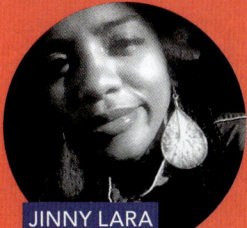
JINNY LARA
Free your mind
Centro Universitario Tecnológico, Honduras

CAROLINA NASCIMENTO NEGRÃO
Nice, determined, hard-working
Universidade Anhembi Morumbi, Brazil

JOSUE LOZANO
Enthusiastic, cheerful, decisive
Centro Universitario Tecnológico, Honduras

JULIETH C. MORENO DELGADO
Decisive, reliable, creative
Fundación Universitaria Monserrate, Colombia

ANDERSON BATISTA
Resilient, happy, dreamer
Universidade Anhembi Morumbi, Brazil

FELIPE MARTINEZ LOPEZ
Reliable, intrepid, sensitive
Universidad del Valle de México, Mexico

JEE-HYO MOON (JUNE)
Organized, passionate, diligent
Mission College, USA

Student-generated content

EVOLVE is the first course of its kind to feature real student-generated content. We spoke to over 2,000 students from all over the world about the topics they would like to discuss in English and in what situations they would like to be able to speak more confidently.

The ideas are included throughout the Student's Book and the students appear in short videos responding to discussion questions.

INSIGHT
Research shows that achievable speaking role models can be a powerful motivator.

CONTENT
Bite-sized videos feature students talking about topics in the Student's Book.

RESULT
Students are motivated to speak and share their ideas.

"It's important to provide learners with interesting or stimulating topics."

Teacher, Mexico (Global Teacher Survey, 2017)

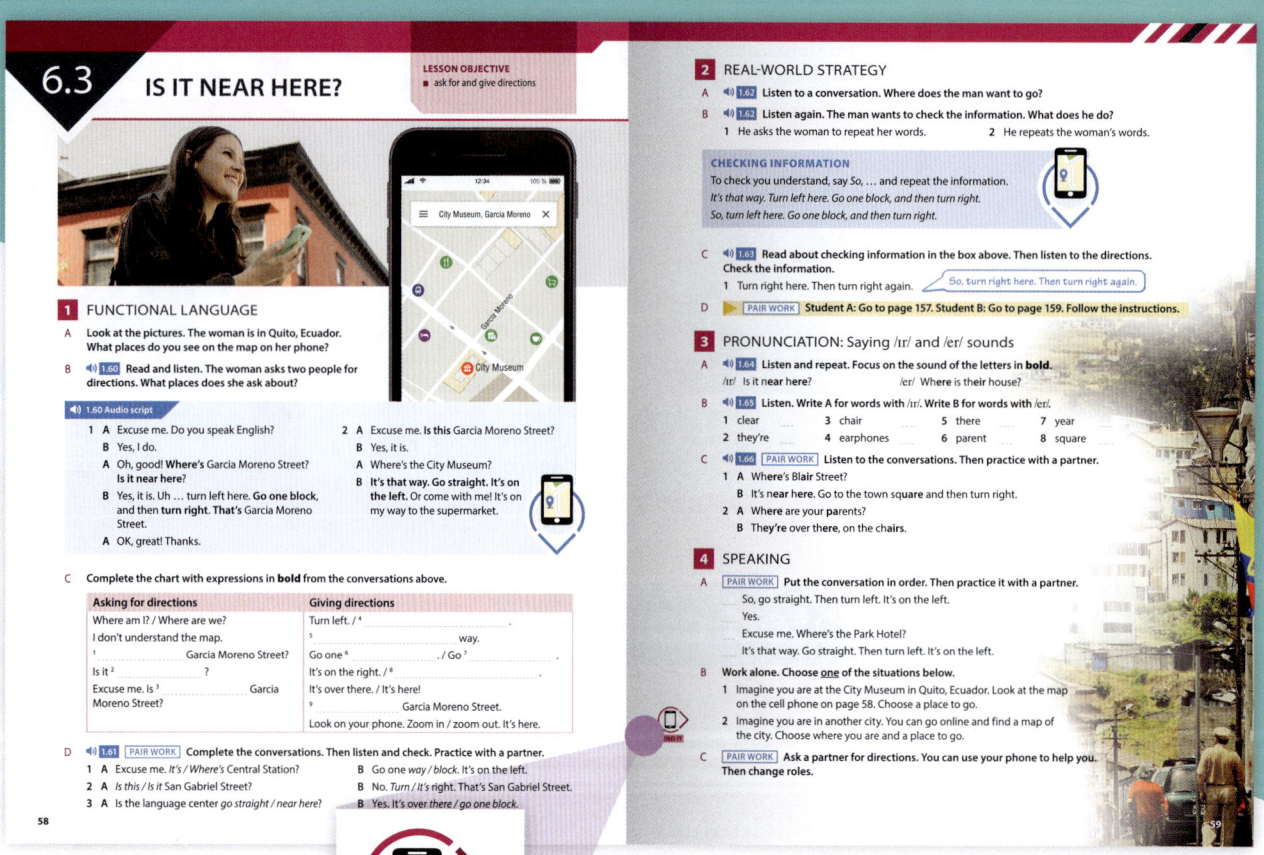

Find it

INSIGHT
Research with hundreds of teachers and students across the globe revealed a desire to expand the classroom and bring the real world in.

CONTENT
Find it are smartphone activities that allow students to bring live content into the class and personalize the learning experience with research and group activities.

RESULT
Students engage in the lesson because it is meaningful to them.

Designed for success

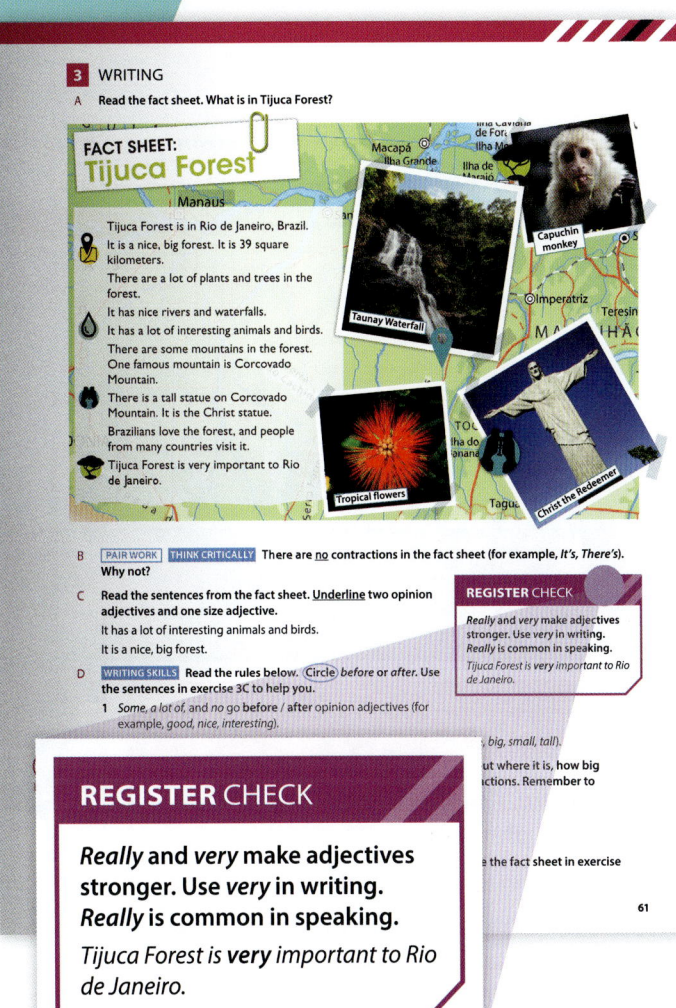

Pronunciation

INSIGHT
Research shows that only certain aspects of pronunciation actually affect comprehensibility and inhibit communication.

CONTENT
EVOLVE focuses on the aspects of pronunciation that most affect communication.

RESULT
Students understand more when listening and can be clearly understood when they speak.

Register check

INSIGHT
Teachers report that their students often struggle to master the differences between written and spoken English.

CONTENT
Register check draws on research into the Cambridge English Corpus and highlights potential problem areas for learners.

RESULT
Students transition confidently between written and spoken English and recognize different levels of formality as well as when to use them appropriately.

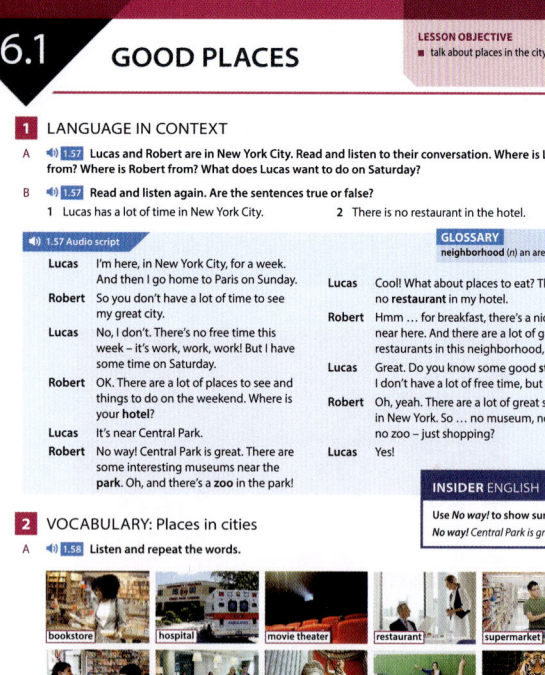

Accuracy check

INSIGHT	CONTENT	RESULT
Some common errors can become fossilized if not addressed early on in the learning process.	*Accuracy check* highlights common learner errors (based on unique research into the Cambridge Learner Corpus) and can be used for self-editing.	Students avoid common errors in their written and spoken English.

"The presentation is very clear and there are plenty of opportunities for student practice and production."

Jason Williams, Teacher, Notre Dame Seishin University, Japan

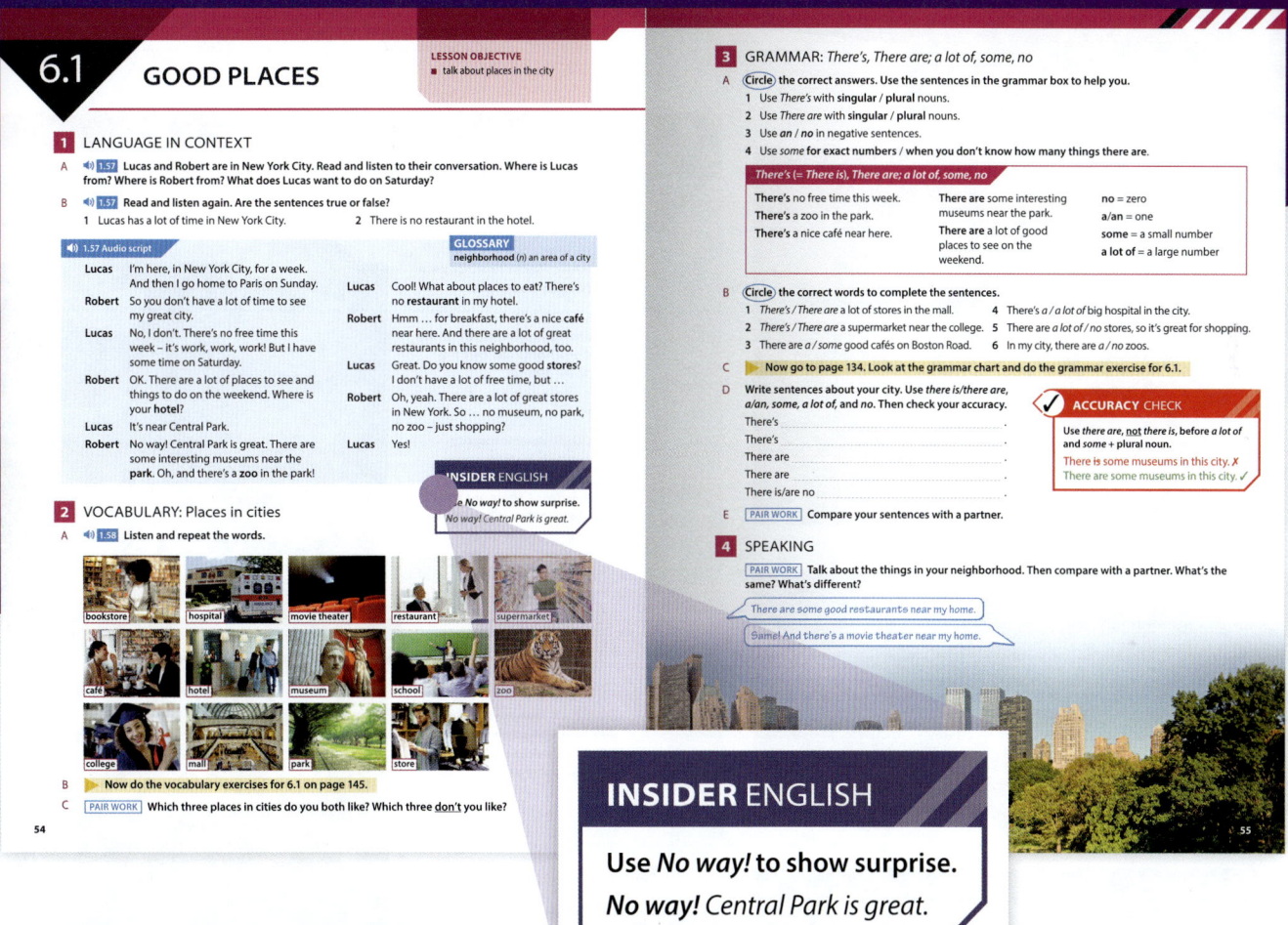

Insider English

INSIGHT
Even in a short exchange, idiomatic language can inhibit understanding.

CONTENT
Insider English focuses on the informal language and colloquial expressions frequently found in everyday situations.

RESULT
Students are confident in the real world.

You spoke. We listened.

Students told us that speaking is the most important skill for them to master, while teachers told us that finding speaking activities which engage their students and work in the classroom can be challenging.

That's why EVOLVE has a whole lesson dedicated to speaking: Lesson 5, *Time to speak*.

Time to speak

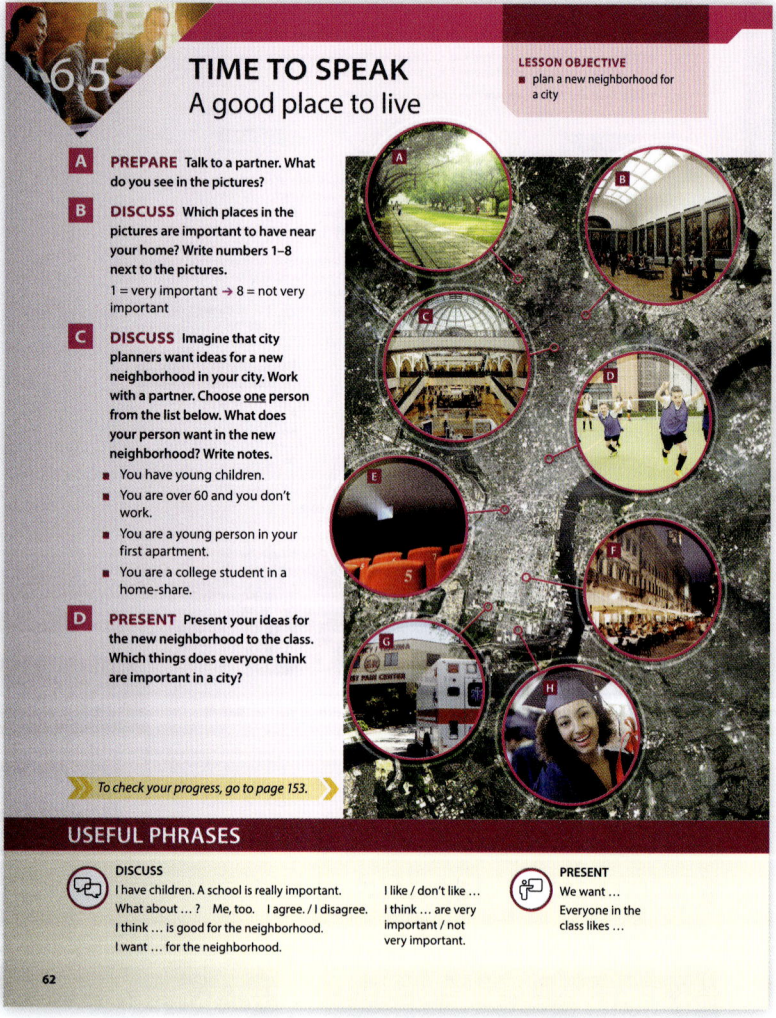

INSIGHT

Speaking ability is how students most commonly measure their own progress, but is also the area where they feel most insecure. To be able to fully exploit speaking opportunities in the classroom, students need a safe speaking environment where they can feel confident, supported, and able to experiment with language.

CONTENT

Time to Speak is a unique lesson dedicated to developing speaking skills and is based around immersive tasks which involve information sharing and decision making.

RESULT

Time to speak lessons create a buzz in the classroom where speaking can really thrive, evolve, and take off, resulting in more confident speakers of English.

Experience Better Learning with EVOLVE: a course that helps both teachers and students on every step of the language learning journey.

Speaking matters. Find out more about creating safe speaking environments in the classroom.

EVOLVE unit structure

Unit opening page
Each unit opening page activates prior knowledge and vocabulary and immediately gets students speaking.

Lessons 1 and 2
These lessons present and practice the unit vocabulary and grammar in context, helping students discover language rules for themselves. Students then have the opportunity to use this language in well-scaffolded, personalized speaking tasks.

Lesson 3
This lesson is built around a functional language dialogue that models and contextualizes useful fixed expressions for managing a particular situation. This is a real world strategy to help students handle unexpected conversational turns.

Lesson 4
This is a combined skills lesson based around an engaging reading or listening text. Each lesson asks students to think critically and ends with a practical writing task.

Lesson 5
Time to speak is an entire lesson dedicated to developing speaking skills. Students work on collaborative, immersive tasks which involve information sharing and decision making.

CONTENTS

	Learning objectives	Grammar	Vocabulary	Pronunciation
Unit 1 I am …	■ Say where you're from ■ Ask for and give personal information ■ Check into a hotel ■ Write a profile ■ Meet new people	■ *I am, you are* ■ *What's … ?; It's …*	■ Countries and nationalities ■ The alphabet ■ Personal information ■ Numbers (1–10) ■ Jobs ■ Greetings, introductions, and goodbyes	■ /ɪ/ and /i/ vowel sounds
Unit 2 Great people	■ Talk about your family ■ Describe friends and family ■ Talk about ages and birthdays ■ Write a post about friends in a photo ■ Compare information about friends and family	■ *is / are* in statements and *yes/no* questions ■ *is not / are not* ■ Prepositions of place	■ Family ■ Numbers (11–100) ■ Adjectives to describe people ■ *really / very* ■ Dates	■ Saying numbers ■ Listening for short forms
Unit 3 Come in	■ Talk about your home ■ Talk about furniture ■ Offer and accept a drink and snack ■ Write an email about a home-share ■ Choose things for a home	■ Possessive adjectives; possessive *'s* and *s'* ■ *It is* (statements and questions with short answers) ■ Information questions with *be*	■ Rooms in a home ■ Furniture ■ Drinks and snacks	■ /k/ at the start of a word

Review 1 (Review of Units 1–3)

	Learning objectives	Grammar	Vocabulary	Pronunciation
Unit 4 I love it	■ Talk about your favorite things ■ Say how you use technology ■ Talk about how you communicate ■ Write product reviews ■ Talk about your favorite music	■ Simple present statements with *I, you, we* ■ Simple present *yes/no* questions with *I, you, we* ■ *a/an*; adjectives before nouns	■ Technology ■ Words for using technology ■ Music	■ Stressed words ■ Listening for the end of a sentence
Unit 5 Mondays and fun days	■ Talk about weekday and weekend activities ■ Tell the time and talk about your routines ■ Show you agree and have things in common ■ Write a report about your activities ■ Compare different work weeks	■ Simple present statements with *he, she, they* ■ Questions in the simple present	■ Days and times of day ■ Everyday activities ■ Telling the time	■ Syllables in words
Unit 6 Zoom in, zoom out	■ Talk about places in the city ■ Talk about nature in your area ■ Ask for and give directions ■ Write a fact sheet about a place in nature ■ Plan a new neighborhood for a city	■ *There's, There are; a lot of, some, no* ■ Count and non-count nouns	■ Places in cities ■ Nature	■ /ɪr/ and /er/ sounds ■ Listening for important words

Review 2 (Review of Units 4–6)

Grammar charts and practice, pages 129–134   Vocabulary exercises, pages 141–146

Functional language	Listening	Reading	Writing	Speaking
■ Check in to a hotel **Real-world strategy** ■ Check spelling		**Meet the artists** ■ Profiles of two artists	**A profile** ■ A personal or work profile ■ Capital letters and periods	■ Introduce yourself ■ Say where you're from ■ Say and spell personal information ■ Arrive at a hotel and check in **Time to speak** ■ Talk to people at a party
■ Ask about and say people's ages and birthdays; give birthday wishes **Real-world strategy** ■ Correct yourself	**Here's my band** ■ A conversation between friends		**A post** ■ A post about friends in a photo ■ *and* to join words and sentences	■ Describe the people in a picture ■ Talk about your family ■ Describe your friends and family ■ Talk about ages and birthdays **Time to speak** ■ Talk about things in common
■ Make and reply to offers **Real-world strategy** ■ Ask about words you don't understand		**A home-share in Burnaby** ■ Emails about a home-share	**An email** ■ An email about a home-share ■ Question marks	■ Describe a house in a picture ■ Talk about rooms in your home ■ Talk about unusual furniture ■ Offer a drink or snack **Time to speak** ■ Discuss what furniture to buy for a new home
■ Ask about a new topic; ask for a response **Real-world strategy** ■ Show you are listening	**Product reviews** ■ A radio program about product reviews		**A review** ■ A product review ■ *but* and *because*	■ Talk about things that you love or like ■ Talk about your favorite technology ■ Discuss what phone plan is good for you ■ Talk about how you communicate with people **Time to speak** ■ Talk about your favorite music
■ Show you agree or have things in common **Real-world strategy** ■ Short answers with adverbs of frequency		**Work, rest and play** ■ An article about work-life balance	**A report** ■ A report about your activities ■ Headings and numbered lists	■ Talk about your fun days ■ Say when and how often you do things ■ Talk about your daily routine ■ Compare information about your activities **Time to speak** ■ Talk about the best week for your body clock
■ Ask for and give directions **Real-world strategy** ■ Check information	**Walk with Yasmin** ■ A podcast about a place in nature		**A fact sheet** ■ A fact sheet ■ Order size and opinion adjectives	■ Describe a picture of a city ■ Talk about good places in your neighborhood ■ Talk about nature in your area ■ Give directions to a visitor **Time to speak** ■ Talk about a good place to live

CLASSROOM LANGUAGE

🔊 **1.02 Get started**
Hi. / Hello.
What's your name?
My name is _____.
This is my class.
This is my partner.
This is my teacher.

Ask for help
I don't understand.
I have a question.
How do you say _____ in English?
What does _____ mean?
How do you spell _____?
Can you repeat that, please?
Sorry, what page?

Your teacher
I'm your teacher.
Open your book.
Close your book.
Go to page _____.
Do you have any questions?

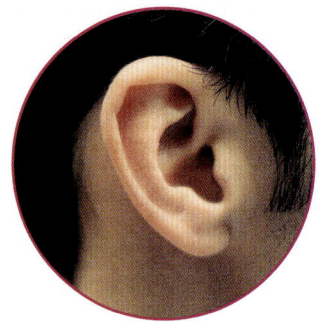
Listen.

Say.

Read.

Write.

Watch.

Work in pairs.

Work in groups.

I AM ...

1

UNIT OBJECTIVES
- say where you're from
- ask for and give personal information
- check into a hotel
- write a profile
- meet new people

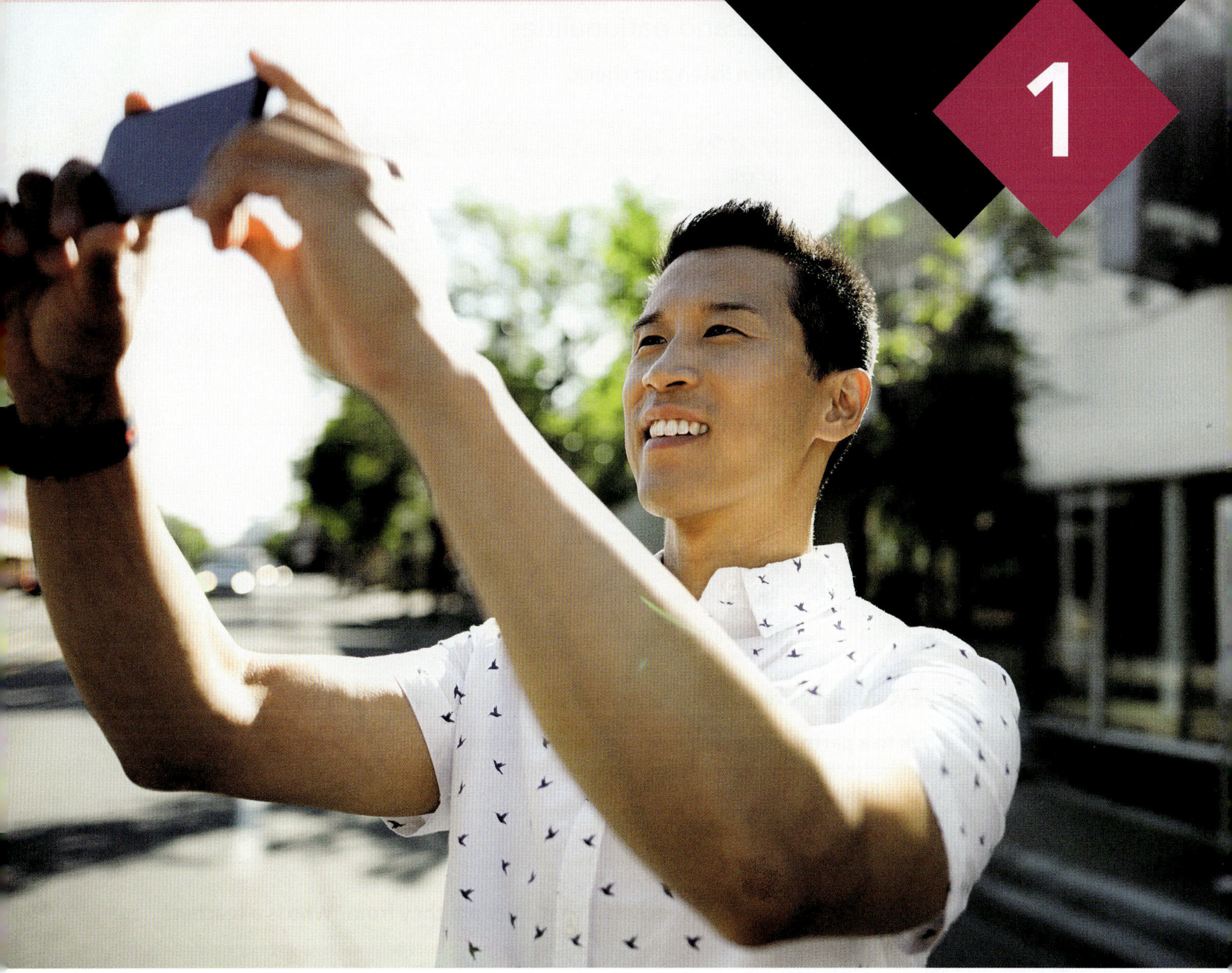

START SPEAKING

CLASS WORK Say your name. Watch Josue for an example.

I am Marco.

I am Anya.

Where is Josue from?

1.1 I'M BRAZILIAN. AND YOU?

LESSON OBJECTIVE
- say where you're from

1 VOCABULARY: Countries and nationalities

A 🔊 1.03 Complete the chart. Then listen and check.

Capital city	Country	Nationality
Brasília	Brazil	1 _____
Santiago	Chile	Chilean
Beijing	China	Chinese
Bogotá	2 _____	Colombian
Quito	Ecuador	Ecuadorian
Paris	France	French
Tegucigalpa	Honduras	Honduran
Tokyo	Japan	Japanese
Mexico City	3 _____	Mexican
Lima	Peru	Peruvian
Moscow	Russia	4 _____
Seoul	South Korea	South Korean
Madrid	Spain	Spanish
Washington, D.C.	the United States	American

B ▶ Now do the vocabulary exercises for 1.1 on page 141.

C **PAIR WORK** Talk to a partner. Say your name, nationality, and city.

> Hi! I'm Yessica. I'm Peruvian, and I'm from Callao.

> Hello! I'm Daniel. I'm from Madrid, in Spain.

2 LANGUAGE IN CONTEXT

A Read the messages from students and teachers. What cities are they from? Who is a teacher?

International school project

- Hi!
- Hi, I'm Gabi. I'm **Brazilian**. I'm from **São Paulo**.
- You're from **Brazil**! Wow! My name is Karina, and I'm from **Colombia**.
- Are you from **Bogotá**?
- No, I'm not. I'm from **Medellín**.

Write a message …

International school project

- My name is Antonio. I'm from **Mexico City** – in **Mexico**!
- Hi, I'm Max. I'm **Russian**. I'm from **Moscow**.
- Hi, Max. Are you a teacher?
- Yes, I am. And you?
- No, I'm not a teacher! I'm a student.

Write a message …

3 GRAMMAR: *I am, you are*

A Circle the correct answers. Use the sentences in the grammar box to help you.
1 For questions (?), say **Are you … ?** / **You are … ?**
2 For affirmative (+) answers, say **Yes, I am.** / **Yes, I'm.**
3 For negative (-) answers, say **No, I not.** / **No, I'm not.**

> **I am (= I'm), you are (= you're)**
>
> **I'm** Brazilian.   **I'm not** from Lima.   **Am I** in room 6B?
> **You're** from Mexico City.   **You're not** from Bogotá.   Yes, **you are**. / No, **you're not**.
>   **Are you** from Tokyo?
>   Yes, **I am**. / No, **I'm not**.

B Complete the sentences.
1 _____ 'm Ecuadorian.
2 Wow! _____ 're from Rio!
3 _____ you from Quito?
4 A Are you American?
   B Yes, I _____ .

C ▶ Now go to page 129. Look at the grammar chart and do the grammar exercise for 1.1.

D Look at the chart. You are Alex. Write four sentences. Then read the information in the Accuracy check box and check your work.

Name	City	Nationality	Country
Alex	Orlando	American	the United States

1 _____
2 _____
3 _____
4 _____

✓ **ACCURACY CHECK**
Use *I* with *am*.
~~Am~~ Spanish. ✗
I'm Spanish. ✓

E **PAIR WORK** Choose a name. Don't tell your partner. Ask and answer questions to find the person.

Harry, student, New York, American
Barbara, student, New York, Brazilian
Mike, student, Chicago, American
Victor, student, Chicago, Brazilian
Kristy, teacher, New York, American
Nayara, teacher, New York, Brazilian
Robert, teacher, Chicago, American
Juliano, teacher, Chicago, Brazilian

– Are you a student?
– Yes, I am.
– Are you from New York?
– No, I'm not. I'm from … .

4 SPEAKING

GROUP WORK Imagine you're a different person. Choose a new name, city, nationality, and country. Talk to other people. Ask questions. For ideas, watch Anderson.

REAL STUDENT
What's Anderson's city, nationality, and country?

1.2 WHAT'S YOUR LAST NAME?

LESSON OBJECTIVE
- ask for and give personal information

1 LANGUAGE IN CONTEXT

A 🔊 **1.04** Rudy and Juana are at a conference. Listen to the conversation. Check (✓) the information they say.

- ☐ college name
- ☐ company name
- ☐ email address
- ☐ first name
- ☐ last name (= family name)

> **INSIDER ENGLISH**
>
> Say *Uh-huh* to show you are listening.
> *My last name is Garcia. G-A-R-C-I-A.*
> *Uh-huh. What's your email address?*

B 🔊 **1.04** Read and listen again. What information do they spell?

🔊 **1.04 Audio script**

Rudy	So, your **first name** is Juana. H-U- …
Juana	No. J-U-A-N-A. My **last name** is Garcia. G-A-R-C-I-A.
Rudy	Uh-huh. What's your **email address**?
Juana	It's juanagarcia@bestmail.com.
Rudy	And what's the name of your **college**?
Juana	It's Garcia College. I'm Juana Garcia from Garcia College!
Rudy	Great! OK, my last name is Jones.
Juana	OK. What's your email address?
Rudy	It's rudythejones@kmail.com.
Juana	Rudy*the*jones! The? T-H-E?
Rudy	Yes. R-U-D-Y-T-H-E-J-O-N-E-S.
Juana	From Jones College?
Rudy	No! From Miami Dade College.

2 VOCABULARY: The alphabet; personal information

A 🔊 **1.05** Read and listen. Then listen again and repeat.

Aa Bb Cc Dd Ee Ff Gg Hh Ii Jj Kk Ll Mm
Nn Oo Pp Qq Rr Ss Tt Uu Vv Ww Xx Yy Zz

B 🔊 **1.06** Listen and (circle) the spelling you hear.

1 first name:	a Raymund	b Raimund	c Raymond
2 last name:	a Cummings	b Cummins	c Comyns
3 email address:	a cb_smith@kmail.com	b cg_smith@kmail.com	c cd_smith@kmail.com
4 college:	a Wallice	b Wallis	c Wallace
5 company:	a Jeferson	b Jefferson	c Jeffersen

C ▶ Now do the vocabulary exercises for 1.2 on page 141.

! In email addresses:
- "." is "dot"
- "@" is "at"
- "_" is "underscore"

D [PAIR WORK] Talk to a partner. Say your first name, last name, email address, and college or company name.

3 GRAMMAR: What's ... ?, It's ...

A (Circle) the correct answers. Use the sentences in the grammar box to help you.
1. For questions, say *What's ... ?* / *It's ...*
2. For answers, say *What's ... ?* / *It's ...*

> **What's ...? (= What is), It's ... (= It is)**
>
> **What's** your first name?   **It's** Juana.
> **What's** the name of your college?   **It's** Garcia College.

✓ ACCURACY CHECK

Use the apostrophe (').
~~Whats~~ your first name? ✗
What's your first name? ✓
~~Its~~ Juana. ✗
It's Juana. ✓

B Write *What's* or *It's* in the spaces. Match the questions (1–3) with the answers (a–c). Then check your accuracy.

1. _____ the name of your company? ___
2. _____ your last name? ___
3. _____ your email address? ___

a _____ luzmendes@xyz.com.
b _____ Mendes.
c _____ Warton Homes.

C ▶ Now go to page 129. Look at the grammar chart and do the grammar exercise for 1.2.

4 SPEAKING

A Look at the information in the box. (Circle) three things to talk about.

| college name | company name | email address | first name | last name |

B [CLASS WORK] Talk to other people. Ask questions about the information in the box.

What's the name of your college?   *It's Wallace College.*

1.3 THIS IS THE KEY

LESSON OBJECTIVE
- check in to a hotel

1 VOCABULARY: Numbers

A 🔊 **1.07** Listen and repeat the numbers.

0 zero	3 three	6 six	9 nine
1 one	4 four	7 seven	10 ten
2 two	5 five	8 eight	

> **INSIDER ENGLISH**
>
> For **0**, say **zero** or **oh**.
> Your room number is two-**zero**-one.
> My address is seven-**oh**-nine …

B **PAIR WORK** Say a number from exercise 1A. Your partner points to the number. Then change roles.

2 FUNCTIONAL LANGUAGE

A 🔊 **1.08** Paulo is at a hotel. Read and listen. Check (✓) the information the hotel clerk asks for.

- ☐ cell phone number
- ☐ company
- ☐ name
- ☐ city
- ☐ email address
- ☐ room number

🔊 **1.08 Audio script**

Clerk	Welcome to New York! What's your name?
Paulo	I'm Paulo Vasques. **I'm here for three nights.**
Clerk	Ah, yes. **What's your cell phone number?**
Paulo	It's (593) 555-2192.
Clerk	Thanks. And what's your email address?
Paulo	It's pvasques89@travelmail.org.
Clerk	Thanks. One moment. **Please sign here. Here's a pen.**
Paulo	OK.
Clerk	Thank you. **This is the key.** It's room 6B.
Paulo	6D. Thanks.
Clerk	No, you're not in 6D. **You're in room 6B.**
Paulo	Oh, OK. Thank you.
Clerk	You're welcome.

B Complete the chart with expressions in **bold** from the conversation above.

Checking in (clerk)		Checking in (Paulo)
What's your ¹_____ number?	Here's a ³_____ .	⁶_____ (593) 555-2192.
Please ²_____ here.	This is the ⁴_____ .	I'm here for three ⁷_____ .
	It's room 6B.	
	⁵_____ room 6B.	

C 🔊 **1.09** Complete the conversations. Then listen and check. Practice with a partner.

1. **A** What's your *email / cell phone* number? **B** *I'm / It's* (593) 555-3194.
2. **A** Please *sign / write* here. **B** OK.
3. **A** Hello. Welcome to the Garden Hotel. **B** Thanks. I'm here for two *mornings / nights*.
4. **A** *This is / It's* the key. You're in room 4D. **B** OK. Thanks.
5. **A** *Here's a / You're* pen. **B** Thank you.

3 REAL-WORLD STRATEGY

A 🔊 **1.10** Listen to a conversation. Circle the correct answers.
1 The woman is at *a hotel / home*.
2 She says her *room number / cell phone number*.

B 🔊 **1.10** Read about checking spelling in the box below. Listen to the conversation again. What does the man ask the woman to spell?

> **CHECKING SPELLING**
> To check spelling, ask *How do you spell your first name / your last name / it?*
> *My name is Paulo Vasques.*
> *How do you spell your last name?*
> *V-A-S-Q-U-E-S.*

C 🔊 **1.11** Listen to the questions. Answer the questions and spell words.
1 How do you spell your last name? — R-I-V-E-R-A.

4 PRONUNCIATION: Saying /ɪ/ and /i/ vowel sounds

A 🔊 **1.12** Listen and repeat the two different vowel sounds.
/ɪ/ six You're in room 6A.   /i/ three You're in room 3A.

B 🔊 **1.13** Look at the underlined letters below. Then listen and repeat. What vowel sounds do you hear? Write A for words with /ɪ/, for example *six*. Write B for words with /i/, for example *three*.

1 ___ email   3 ___ information   5 ___ key
2 ___ is   4 ___ please   6 ___ company

C 🔊 **1.14** PAIR WORK Listen to the conversations. Underline words with the vowel sounds /ɪ/ and /i/. Then practice with a partner.
1 A Is this your key?   B No, it's the key for room three.
2 A What's your company email address? B It's c.b.smith@wallis.com.
3 A What's your Instagram name? B It's SusieSix.

5 SPEAKING

A PAIR WORK Put the conversation in the correct order. Then practice with a partner.

- [7] A Thanks. One moment. Please sign here.
- [5] A Great. Thank you. And what's your email address?
- [ ] B I'm Marie Bernard. I'm here for two nights.
- [ ] B OK.
- [ ] B It's mbernard87@mymail.org.
- [ ] A Ah, yes, two nights. What's your cell phone number?
- [ ] B It's (298) 555-1257.
- [ ] A Thank you. This is the key. It's for room 7C.
- [1] A Hi. Welcome to the Tree House Hotel! What's your name?

B PAIR WORK Choose a hotel in your city. One person is a hotel clerk, and the other person is a visitor. Then change roles.

> Hi. Welcome to the International Hotel. What's your name?

> I'm Jae-hoon Park. I'm here for two nights....

C PAIR WORK Student A: Go to page 156. Student B: Go to page 158. Follow the instructions.

1.4 MY PROFILE

LESSON OBJECTIVE
- write a profile

1 VOCABULARY: Jobs

A 🔊 **1.15** Listen and repeat.

salesperson | artist | teacher | student
hotel clerk | doctor | chef | server

2 READING

A **SCAN** Read the profiles. Circle three job words from exercise 1A.

B **READ FOR DETAILS** Read the profiles again. Complete the chart.

First name	Akemi	
Last name		Silva
City		
Nationality		
Company		
School		

 Use *but* to connect two different ideas.
I'm Peruvian, **but** my home is in the United States.

 People say, *I'm from Paris*. People also say, *I **live** in Paris*. (= Paris is my home now.)

C **PAIR WORK** One person is Akemi. One person is Frank. How are you different?

> I'm Akemi. I'm a student.

> I'm Frank. I'm not a student. I live in Texas ...

STUDIO 10
STORE PROFILES
Meet the artists

ABOUT **AKEMI**

I'm Akemi Tanaka. I live in San Diego, but I'm not American. I'm Japanese. My company is Tanaka Paints. My phone number is (324) 555-6053, and my email is akemit2000@tanakapaints.com. I'm an artist, and I'm a student, too. The name of my school is The Art Institute. It's in California.

ABOUT **FRANK**

My name is Frank Silva. I live in Austin, Texas, in the United States. I'm American and Brazilian. The name of my company is Designs by Frank. It's in my home in Austin. I'm an art teacher, too. The classes are in my home. My phone number is (780) 555-5230, and my email is designsbyfrank@blinknet.com.

3 WRITING

A Read the profiles of two people. Where are they from? Who is a student?

Business Weekly

Meet the **sales team**

Lima, Peru

Hello. My name is Juan Carlos Fernandez. I am Peruvian. I am from Trujillo, but I live in Lima now. I am a salesperson. The name of my company is Omega Sales. My email is jcfernandez_511@omsmail.com, and my cell phone number is (962) 555-3198.

Class Connect – find students around the world

Me, Katya!

Hi! I'm Katya Ivanova. I'm from Russia. My home is in St. Petersburg. It's a great city. I'm an English student. The name of my school is Popov College of English.

@ **email:** kativanova@popovnet.ru
🐦 **Twitter:** katya_ivanova98

B [PAIR WORK] [THINK CRITICALLY] The two profiles are different. Why? Discuss with a partner.

C [WRITING SKILLS] Read the rules. Then find <u>two</u> or more examples for the rules in the profiles.

A B C
Use capital letters (A, B, C …):
- for *I* (*I'm*)
- for names of people
- for names of places, companies, schools
- for nationalities and languages
- at the beginning of sentences

● Use a period (.) at the end of statements.

REGISTER CHECK

Hello, Hi, and *Hey*

Use *hello* in formal writing or speaking, for example at work.
Hello. My name is Juan Carlos Fernandez.

Use *hi* in informal writing or speaking, with friends and family. Use *hey* when you speak to friends and family.
Hi! I'm Katya Ivanova.

 WRITE IT

D Choose a work profile or a personal profile. Then write your profile. Use the profiles in exercise 3A for an example.

E [GROUP WORK] Work in groups. Read other profiles. Are they work profiles or personal profiles? Say why.

9

1.5 TIME TO SPEAK
People from history

LESSON OBJECTIVE
- meet new people

A Who are the people in the pictures? Tell your partner.

B Read the conversations (1–3). Then match them to a–c. Which conversation is with three people?

a an introduction ___
b a greeting ___
c a goodbye ___

1 A Good evening.
   B Hello. How are you?
   A I'm fine, thanks. And you?
   B I'm fine.

2 A Gabi, this is Caio.
   B Hi, Gabi. Nice to meet you.
   C Nice to meet you, Caio.

3 A See you later.
   B Bye.

C PREPARE Practice the conversations from exercise B. Then change roles.

D RESEARCH Imagine you're at a party for people from history. Choose a person. You can go online and find the nationality and home city for your person. Create and write down a cell phone number.

E ROLE PLAY Imagine you're the person from exercise D. Meet other people at the party. Write notes.

F AGREE Say the nationality, city or phone number of a person from the party. Other students say the person.

G DISCUSS Who is your favorite person from the party?

 To check your progress, go to page 152.

USEFUL PHRASES

ROLE PLAY
Are you (American)?
Yes, I am. / No, I'm not. I'm …
I'm from (city).
How do you spell it?
A What's your cell phone number? B It's …

AGREE
The person is from (city). / The phone number is …
It's (name of person).

DISCUSS
My favorite person is …
Me, too.

UNIT OBJECTIVES

- talk about your family
- describe friends and family
- talk about ages and birthdays
- write a post about friends in a photo
- compare information about friends and family

GREAT PEOPLE

2

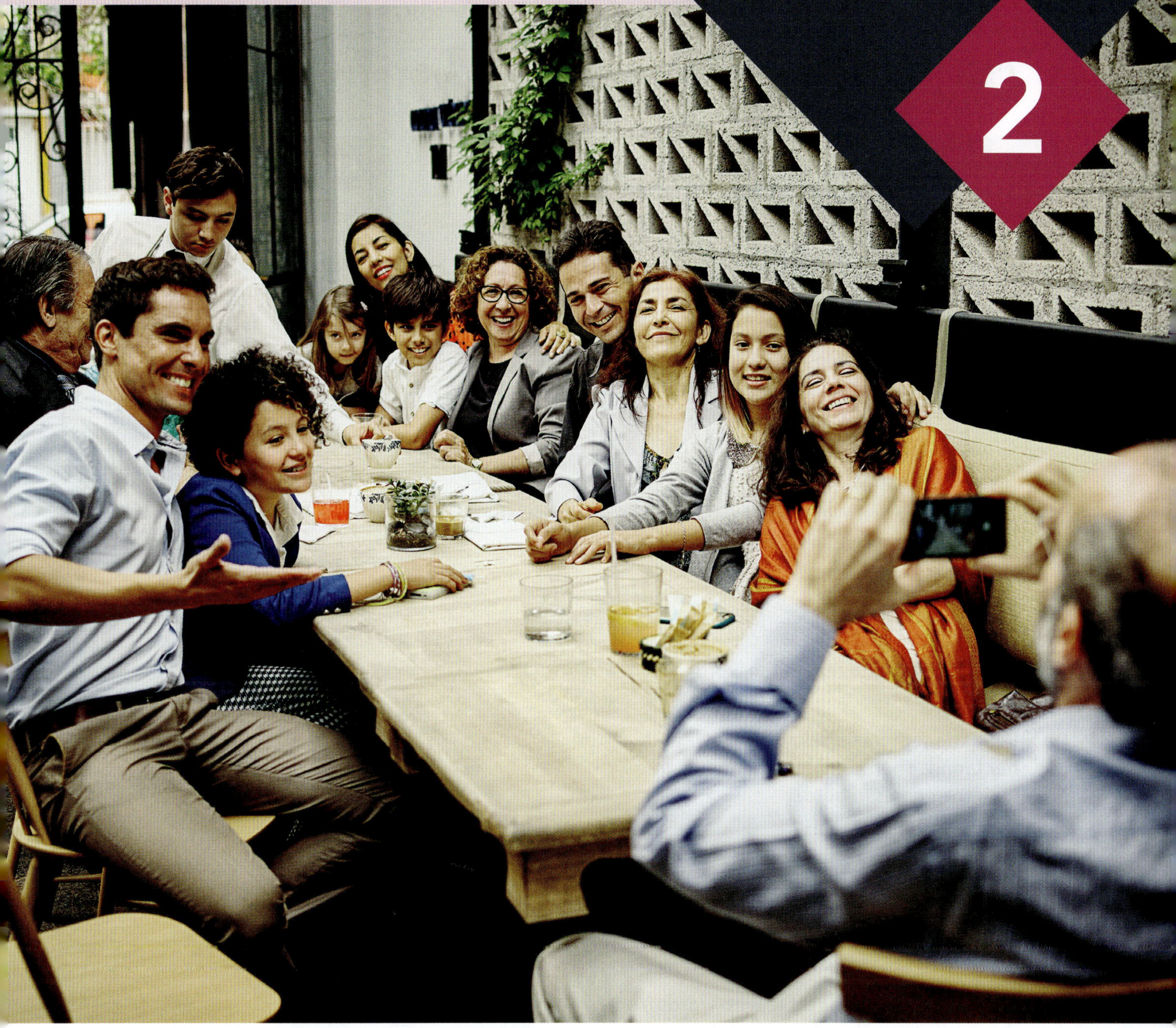

START SPEAKING

Look at the picture. Say words about the people.

Server.

American.

Family.

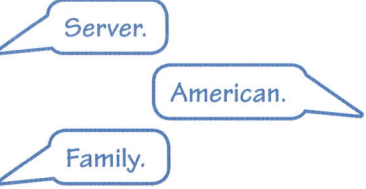

2.1 A FAMILY PARTY

LESSON OBJECTIVE
- talk about your family

1 LANGUAGE IN CONTEXT

A 🔊 **1.16** Sara and Liz are at a party. Read and listen to the conversation. How old are David and Emily? Who are Elizabeth One and Elizabeth Two?

🔊 **1.16 Audio script**

Sara What a great party, Liz! Are your **children** here?
Liz Yes, they are. David … He's my **son**. He's eight. And the girl with him is my daughter Emily. She's ten.
Sara And the man … Is he your **husband**?
Liz No, he's my **brother** Marcus. My husband isn't here.
Sara Oh, OK. Are your **parents** here?
Liz No, they're not. Oh, look. Here's my **grandmother**. She's 86. Grandma, this is my friend Sara.
Grandma Nice to meet you, Sara. I'm Elizabeth.
Sara Nice to meet you. Hey, are you both Elizabeth?
Liz Yes, we are! With friends, I'm Liz. But in my family, she's Elizabeth One, and I'm Elizabeth Two!

REGISTER CHECK

Some words for family are formal and informal. Use formal words at work. Use informal words with friends and family.

Formal	Informal
grandfather	grandpa
grandmother	grandma
father	dad
mother	mom

GLOSSARY
both (det) two people/things

2 VOCABULARY: Family; numbers

A 🔊 **1.17** Listen and repeat the words in the family tree.

B Read the sentences below about Liz and her family. Then complete the family tree with the names in **bold**.
- Liz = sister of **Marcus**.
- **Kyle** = uncle of Liz.
- **Tim** = cousin of Liz.
- **John** = grandfather of Liz.
- Anna = wife of **Paul**.

C 🔊 **1.18** Complete the table with words from the family tree. Then listen and check.

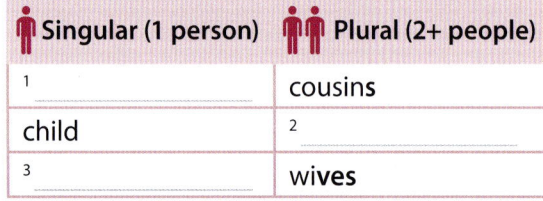

👤 Singular (1 person)	👥 Plural (2+ people)
1 _____	cousin**s**
child	2 _____
3 _____	wi**ves**

D **PAIR WORK** Make three more sentences about the people in the family tree. Then compare with a partner.

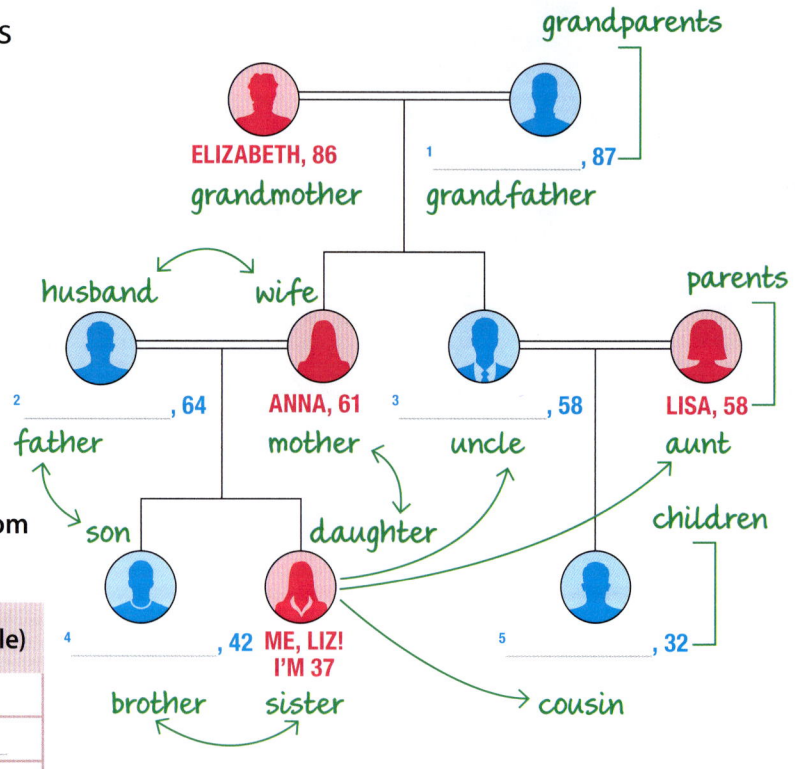

E 🔊 1.19 Write the numbers. Then listen and repeat.

11	eleven	___	sixteen	21	twenty-one	___	sixty
12	twelve	___	seventeen	22	twenty-two	___	seventy
13	thirteen	___	eighteen	30	thirty	___	eighty
___	fourteen	___	nineteen	___	forty	___	ninety
___	fifteen	20	twenty	___	fifty	100	one hundred

F ▶ Now do the vocabulary exercises for 2.1 on page 141.

3 GRAMMAR: *is / are* in statements and *yes/no* questions

A (Circle) the correct answers. Use the sentences in the grammar box to help you.
1 Use *is / are* with *he* and *she*.
2 Use *is / are* with *we*, *you*, and *they*.

> **is / are in statements and yes/no questions**
>
> **Are** your children here?
>   Yes, they **are**.
> He**'s** my son (*'s = is*). He**'s** eight.
> She**'s** my daughter. She**'s ten**.
>
> **Is** he your husband?
>   No, he**'s** my brother Marcus.
> **Are** you both Elizabeth?
>   Yes, we **are**.

B Complete the sentences.
1 This _____ my sister. _____ 23.
2 A _____ your parents Colombian? B Yes, _____ _____ .
3 This _____ my grandfather. _____ 88.
4 A _____ your mother at home? B Yes, _____ _____ .
5 We _____ Russian. We live in Moscow.

C Match the questions with the answers. Then answer the questions so they're true for you.
1 Are your parents American? *b*
2 Are you 21? ___
3 Is your best friend in class? ___
4 Is your teacher Canadian? ___

a Yes. She's from Toronto.
b No. They're Colombian.
c No, he's at work.
d Yes, I am.

D ▶ Now go to page 129. Look at the grammar chart and do the grammar exercise for 2.1.

4 SPEAKING

A **PAIR WORK** Draw a simple family tree. Then talk to a partner about people in your family. Ask and answer questions. For ideas, watch Julieth.

> This is Marcos. He's from Mexico City. He's 25.

> Is he your brother?

REAL STUDENT
Who does Julieth talk about? Is your family tree the same or different?

B **GROUP WORK** Tell your group about three people from your family tree. You can show pictures of the people on your phone.

2.2 THEY'RE REALLY FUNNY!

LESSON OBJECTIVE
- describe friends and family

1 LANGUAGE IN CONTEXT

A   Read the messages. Where is Lara from? Where is she now? Who are the other people in the pictures?

B   Read the messages again. Find the numbers in the messages. What are they?

four   12   19   24   85

Four days with my family

Hi! I'm Lara. I'm 24. I live with my family in Texas, but we're not in Texas now. We're with Grandma Vera at her home in Miami ☀ Here's a picture of me … and here are pictures of my family 🤩

Look at my mom and dad. My parents are both 50 – not **old**, and not **young**! My mom is **short** and my dad is **tall**. They're not **boring**! They're both really **funny**.

This is Erika. She's my sister – and she's my best friend! ❤ She's 19. She's a student, and she's very **smart**. She's **shy**, but she's **friendly**, too.

This is Justin. He's my brother. He's funny. 😂 He's young (12), but he's not short – he's really tall.

This is my grandmother, Grandma Vera. She's old (85!), and she's very **interesting**. She's a good grandma! ❤

2 VOCABULARY: Describing people; really / very

A   🔊 1.20   Listen and repeat the adjectives below. Then find them in the messages. Match the adjectives to the people.

Age	Appearance	Personality		
old	short	boring	funny	shy
young	tall	friendly	interesting	smart

B   (Circle) *really* and *very* in the messages. Do they make the adjectives stronger (++) or weaker (--)?

C Circle the correct word to complete the sentences.

1 A Is he short?
   B No, he's not. He's *tall / shy*.
2 A Is she boring?
   B No! She's really *short / interesting*.
3 A How old is your grandmother?
   B She's 90. She's very *young / old*.
4 A Is Mi-jin a college student?
   B Yes. She's really *smart / short*.
5 A Is your cousin interesting?
   B Yes, and he's *boring / funny*.
6 A Are your children shy?
   B No, they're very *friendly / interesting*.

D ▶ Now do the vocabulary exercises for 2.2 on page 142.

3 GRAMMAR: *is not / are not*

A Circle the correct answers. Use the sentences in the grammar box and the Notice box to help you.
1 For negative (-) statements with *he* and *she*, use *'s not / 're not*.
2 For negative statements with *we*, *you*, and *they*, use *'s not / 're not*.

is not (= 's not) / are not (= 're not)	
He**'s not** short.	They**'re not** boring!
She**'s not** from Miami.	We**'re not** in Texas.
Erika **isn't** old.	My parents **aren't** from Miami.

! After pronouns (*he, she, we, you, they*), use *'s not* and *'re not*.
She**'s not** tall.
You**'re not** from South Korea.
After nouns (people, places, and things), use *isn't* and *aren't*.
Filip **isn't** American.
My friends **aren't** boring.

B Complete the sentences with a subject (*he, she, you, we, they*) and an affirmative (+) or negative (–) verb.
1 _He's not_ old. He's young.
2 She's friendly and really funny. _____ shy.
3 _____ from Brazil. We're not from Argentina.
4 _____ Juliana. She's Camila.
5 _____ my cousins. They're not my brothers.
6 _____ American. You're Canadian.

C ▶ Now go to page 130. Look at the grammar charts and do the grammar exercise for 2.2.

D PAIR WORK Write **two** true sentences and **two** false sentences about a friend or a person in your class. Then exchange sentences with a partner. Correct the false sentences.

> My friend Carina is not tall. She's very funny. She's from Japan. She's smart.

> She is very funny, and she's smart. She's tall, and she's not from Japan.

> Correct!

4 SPEAKING

A Choose four people, for example, family or friends. Write adjectives to describe them. For ideas, watch Larissa.

B GROUP WORK Talk about your people. You can show pictures on your phone. Ask for more information about people, for example, age, nationality, and city.

Are your family or friends the same as Larissa's?

2.3 WHEN IS YOUR BIRTHDAY?

LESSON OBJECTIVE
- talk about ages and birthdays

1 FUNCTIONAL LANGUAGE

A 🔊 1.21 Read and listen. How many parties does Vivian talk about?

1.21 Audio script

Lucas	This is a really great picture!
Vivian	Oh, thanks.
Lucas	Are they your children?
Vivian	Yes. This is Miranda. **She's eight.**
Lucas	Miranda. Nice name.
Vivian	And this is Carlos.
Lucas	How old is he?
Vivian	He's three years old.
Lucas	When's his birthday?
Vivian	It's March 28. **His party is on March 29.**
Lucas	Oh, right. He's four this month!
Vivian	Yeah. And **Miranda's birthday is April 2.**
Lucas	So two birthday parties in five days.
Vivian	Yeah, two parties. No, sorry, three parties! One party for Carlos, one party for Miranda, and then one party with the family.
Lucas	Well, say "**Happy birthday!**" from me!

B Complete the chart with expressions in **bold** from the conversation above.

Asking about ages and birthdays	Saying ages and birthdays	Giving birthday wishes
1 _____ old is he? When's your birthday? 2 _____ 's his birthday? 👨 When's her birthday? 👩	She 3 ___ eight. He's three 4 _____ old. His party is 5 ___ March 29. Miranda's birthday is April 2.	6 _____ birthday!

2 VOCABULARY: Saying dates

A 🔊 1.22 Look at the chart. Listen and repeat the months. What month is your birthday month?

Months					
January	February	March	April	May	June
July	August	September	October	November	December

Dates			
1 first	7 seventh	13 thirteenth	19 nineteenth
2 second	8 eighth	14 fourteenth	20 twentieth
3 third	9 ninth	15 fifteenth	21 twenty-first
4 fourth	10 tenth	16 sixteenth	22 twenty-second
5 fifth	11 eleventh	17 seventeenth	30 thirtieth
6 sixth	12 twelfth	18 eighteenth	31 thirty-first

B 🔊 1.23 **PAIR WORK** Now listen and repeat the dates. Then say the date of your birthday.

> My birthday is February eighth.

C **PAIR WORK** Imagine the dates below are your birthday. Work with a partner. Ask questions and say the birthdays.

1 May 8   3 August 31   5 January 25
2 November 23 4 April 19   6 June 4

When's your birthday?

It's May eighth.

3 REAL-WORLD STRATEGY

A 🔊 **1.24** Listen to a conversation. (Circle) the correct answers.
1 The conversation is about a *wife / child*.
2 The man says an *age / birthday*.

B 🔊 **1.24** Listen again. What number does the man say first? Then what correct number does he say?

> **CORRECTING YOURSELF**
> To correct yourself, say *No, sorry* or *Sorry, I mean …* and say the correct word.
> *He's twenty. No, sorry, twenty-one.*
> *It's March twenty-first. Sorry, I mean May twenty-first.*

C Read the information in the box above about correcting yourself. What does the man say?

D ▶ **PAIR WORK** Student A: Go to page 156. Student B: Go to page 158. Follow the instructions.

4 PRONUNCIATION: Saying numbers

A 🔊 **1.25** Listen and repeat the numbers. Then listen again and underline the stress.

13 thir<u>teen</u> / 30 <u>thir</u>ty   16 sixteen / 60 sixty   18 eighteen / 80 eighty
14 fourteen / 40 forty   17 seventeen / 70 seventy   19 nineteen / 90 ninety
15 fifteen / 50 fifty

B **PAIR WORK** Look at the numbers in the chart. Student A says a number. Student B points to the number. Then change roles.

| 13 | 80 | 40 | 18 | 30 | 60 | 19 |
| 70 | 15 | 17 | 50 | 90 | 14 | 16 |

5 SPEAKING

A **PAIR WORK** Match sentences 1–4 to sentences a–d. Then practice with a partner.

1 How old is your brother? ____   a Happy birthday!
2 When's your birthday? ____   b Say "Happy birthday!" from me.
3 My brother is 30 today. ____   c It's June 18.
4 It's my birthday today. ____   d He's 23.

B **PAIR WORK** Say the name of a friend, then say his/her birthday. Make <u>one</u> mistake. Then correct yourself.

My friend Julia. Her birthday is June fifth. No, sorry, June sixth.

2.4 HERE'S MY BAND

LESSON OBJECTIVE
- write a post about friends in a photo

1 LISTENING

A **PAIR WORK** Talk to a partner. Say what you see in the picture on page 19.

B 🔊 1.26 **LISTEN FOR GIST** Listen to Isabel talk to a friend, Linda. What do they talk about?

C 🔊 1.26 **LISTEN FOR DETAILS** Listen again. Circle the words that Isabel uses to describe the people.

> boring   cool   friendly   funny   interesting   shy   smart

2 GRAMMAR: Prepositions of place

A Look at the picture on page 19 and complete the sentences with the words in the box.

> between   in   ~~in~~   next to   on the left

1 We're not _____in_____ Las Vegas! We're _____ Seattle, at college.
2 This is Joshua, on the right. And this is Nuwa, _____.
3 I'm Isabel. Guy is _____ me.
4 Guy is _____ Nuwa and me.

3 PRONUNCIATION: Listening for short forms

A 🔊 1.27 Listen. Write the words you hear. Then write the full forms.

1 ___Here's___ my band. = ___Here is___
2 _____ in Seattle. = _____
3 _____ really funny. = _____
4 _____ great! = _____

B 🔊 1.28 Complete the conversation with the words in the box. Listen and check.

> I'm   It's   She's   What's   When's

1 Nice to meet you, Sara. _____ Elizabeth.
2 A _____ your birthday?
   B _____ March 14.
3 This is Nuwa. _____ really smart.
4 _____ your name?

4 WRITING

A Read the post. How old are the students?

SOCIALHUB

JING
September 12 at 2:24pm

We're four college students in Seattle, and we're in a band. The name of the band is *JING*. Joshua is on the right. He's 22, and he's from Chicago. He's really friendly and funny. The first letter in *JING* is for Joshua. I'm Isabel. I'm 20, and I'm the "I" in the band name. I'm next to Joshua. Nuwa is on the left. She's 21. She's Chinese, and she's here for school. She's very interesting and smart. She's the "N." Guy is between Nuwa and me. He's 20, and he's the "G." He's shy, so he's the last letter in the name!

👍 Like   💬 Comment   ➡ Share

👍 35   ❤ 35

B PAIR WORK THINK CRITICALLY Why is the name of the band "JING"? Is it a good name?

C WRITING SKILLS Read about two ways to use *and*. Match them (1–2) to the correct example sentence (a–b).

1 Use *and* to connect words. ___
2 Use *and* to connect two sentences and make one long sentence. ___

a We're four college students in Seattle, and we're in a band.
b She's very interesting and smart.

D Read the post again and <u>underline</u> examples of *and*. Does *and* connect words or sentences?

WRITE IT

E Choose a picture of you with three or four people. Write a post about the picture. Say where you are (*in* + city/country). Say where people are in the picture (*next to, on the left/right, between*). Give information about the people. Use *and* to connect words and sentences. Then check your accuracy.

✓ **ACCURACY CHECK**

After prepositions, use *me*, not *I*.

Guy is next to I. ✗
Guy is next to me. ✓
He's between Nuwa and I. ✗
He's between Nuwa and me. ✓

Seattle

2.5 TIME TO SPEAK
True for me

LESSON OBJECTIVE
- compare information about friends and family

A Which family members are in the picture? Compare your ideas with a partner.

B **PREPARE** Complete the sentences so they're true for you.
1. My mom is _____ (nationality).
2. My dad is _____ (age).
3. My grandmother is _____ (name).
4. My grandfather is from _____ (city).
5. My best friend is _____ (personality).
6. My birthday is in _____ (month).

C **DISCUSS** Say your answers from exercise B. Your partner says "True for me" or "Not true for me." Then change roles.

> My mom is Brazilian.

> Not true for me.

> My dad is 50.

> True for me.

D Read the instructions. Then talk to people in your class.

1. Walk around the class. Say hello to someone.
2. Say your answers from exercise B. Your partner says "True for me" or "Not true for me."
3. Change roles.
4. Say goodbye.
5. Talk to a new partner.

E **PRESENT** Who has the same answers? Who has different answers? Tell the class.

▸▸ To check your progress, go to page 152.

USEFUL PHRASES

DISCUSS
Hello./Hi.   My name is …
True for me.   Not true for me.
Really? (for surprise)   Goodbye.

PRESENT
(Name) is the same.
(Name) is different.

UNIT OBJECTIVES
- talk about your home
- talk about furniture
- offer and accept a drink and snack
- write an email about a home-share
- choose things for a home

COME IN

3

START SPEAKING

A   Look at the picture. Where is this house?

B   Who is in the house?

C   What is in the house?

3.1 WELCOME TO MY HOME

LESSON OBJECTIVE
- talk about your home

1 VOCABULARY: Rooms in a home

A 🔊 **1.29** Listen and repeat the words in the pictures. Which words are rooms? Which words are things in rooms?

B **PAIR WORK** Talk to a partner. What's your favorite room in the pictures?

C ▶ Now do the vocabulary exercises for 3.1 on page 142.

2 LANGUAGE IN CONTEXT

A 🔊 **1.30** Alina gives a video tour of her family's home. Listen and read. How many rooms does she talk about?

a six   b seven   c eight

B 🔊 **1.30** Listen again. Answer the questions.
1. What is on the wall?
2. Who is in the kitchen?
3. How many bathrooms are in the apartment?
4. What are the names of the cat and the dog?

C **PAIR WORK** What are your favorite rooms? Talk to a partner. For ideas, watch Felipe's video.

 **REAL STUDENT** *What are Felipe's favorite rooms? Are your favorite rooms the same?*

Hi! Welcome to my new home. I mean, my *family's* new home. We live in an apartment, not a house. OK. First, this is the **living room**, with my mom's favorite **picture** on the **wall**. And this is the **dining area**. It's good for family dinners, or pizza with my friends. And this is the **kitchen**, through the **door**! My mom and her friend are in there now. OK, and this is the **bathroom**, the family bathroom. And here, this is my parents' **bedroom**, with a second bathroom. And this is my bedroom, with two **windows**. Oh! This is Milka. She's our cat. And this is Sergei's room. He's my brother. Hey! T-Rex is on Sergei's bed! Bad dog! On the floor! Now! T-Rex is Sergei's dog. OK, now say "hi" to the camera, T-Rex. Welcome to our apartment!

✓ ACCURACY CHECK

Use *the* when you talk about a specific thing in your home: *the* floor in *the* kitchen, *the* window (in my room), or *the* picture on *the* wall.

3 GRAMMAR: Possessive adjectives; possessive 's and s'

A Circle the correct answers. Use the sentences in the grammar box and the Notice box below to help you.
1. The 's in *Sergei's room* = **possession** / **is**.
2. Possessive adjectives (for example, *my, our, his* …) go **before** / **after** a noun.
3. Add 's to **singular** / **plural** nouns.
4. Add an apostrophe (') after *s* of a **singular** / **plural** noun.

> **Possessive adjectives; possessive 's and s'**
>
> Welcome to **my** home.   This is **your** bedroom.
> This is **her** bedroom.   This is **his** bedroom.
> This is **their** bedroom.   This is my parents' bedroom.
> Milka is **our** cat.   T-Rex is Sergei**'s** dog.
> This is my apartment. **Its** windows are old, but **its** doors are new.

> ! a **noun** = a person or thing, for example, *Katya* or *room*.
> Singular nouns are **1 thing**.
> Plural nouns are **2+ things**.

B Complete the sentences. Use the possessive form of the word in parentheses ( ).
1. Is ___your___ (you) apartment in the city?
2. It's not _____ (my parents) bedroom.
3. What's _____ (John) last name?
4. Maria is _____ (he) wife.
5. _____ (We) home is in Santiago.
6. The _____ (cat) name is Milka.
7. _____ (They) daughter is a college student.
8. What's _____ (she) email address?

C ▶ Now go to page 130. Look at the grammar charts and do the grammar exercise for 3.1.

D [PAIR WORK] Complete the sentences with information about you. Then compare with a partner.

> My *dog's* name is *Friday*.

1. _____ name is _____ .
2. _____ last name is _____ .
3. _____ is my best friend. _____ home is in _____ .
4. My _____ home is great. _____ living room is really interesting.
5. _____ is my cousin. The name of _____ company is _____ .

4 SPEAKING

A Draw a plan of your home, with all the rooms.

B [GROUP WORK] Talk about the rooms in your homes.

> This is my apartment. This is the *door*. And this is the living room, with *two* windows. This is my *bedroom*.

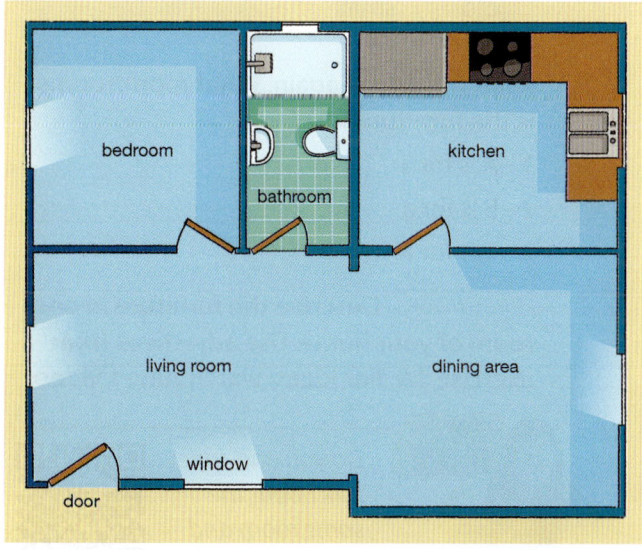

3.2 IS IT REALLY A CHAIR?

LESSON OBJECTIVE
- talk about furniture

1 VOCABULARY: Furniture

A 🔊 **1.31** Listen and repeat the words. Then complete the chart below. Some furniture is in more than one room.

bed | chair | table | desk | bookcase | couch
shower | refrigerator | television/TV | sink | rug | lamp

Bedroom	Living room	Dining area	Kitchen	Bathroom
bed				

B **PAIR WORK** Work with a partner. Say furniture from exercise 1A. Your partner says where it is in his/her home.

> A table.

> In the kitchen. And in the living room.

C ▶ Now do the vocabulary exercises for 3.2 on page 143.

2 LANGUAGE IN CONTEXT

A **PAIR WORK** Choose words to describe the picture in the article.

big	boring	cool	funny
great	interesting	new	nice
old	small		

B Read the article again. What room/rooms is the furniture for?

1 A is for a _____ .
2 B is for a _____ .
3 C is for a _____ .

C **PAIR WORK** Describe the furniture in one room of your home. Use adjectives from exercise 2A. For ideas, watch June's video.

Do you and June talk about the same room and furniture?

NO SPACE? NO PROBLEM!

Is your house or apartment small? Is it *really* small? No space for big furniture? No problem! It's time for smart furniture …

A This **desk** isn't just a desk. It's a desk and a **bed**. It's great for college students.

B Is this one **chair**? Or two chairs? It's both! It's one big chair for you, or it's two small chairs for you and a friend.

C Is your living room small? No dining area in your home? This **couch** and **table** are good for a small space. First, it's a nice table for dinner. Then it's a couch!

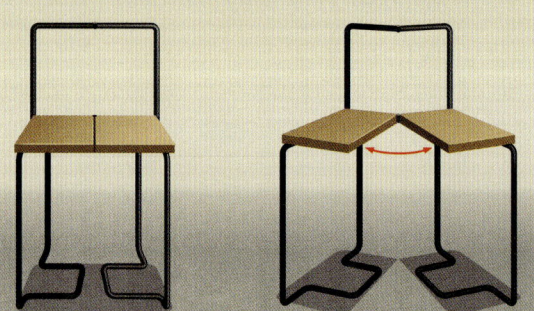

24

3 GRAMMAR: *It is*

A Circle the correct answers. Use the sentences in the grammar box to help you.

1 Use *It's* and *It's not* for a **man or woman / thing**.
2 To make a question with *It is*, say **Is it … ? / It's … ?**

It is in statements and *yes/no* questions	
It's a desk and a bed.	**Is it** *really* small?
It's not one chair, **it's** two chairs!	Yes, **it is**.
	No, it **isn't**.

B Complete the sentences. Then match 1–4 with a–d.

1 A Their house isn't old. _____ new. ___
2 A Where's Toronto? _____ in the United States? ___
3 A We're in your kitchen. _____ really cool. ___
4 A Where's your desk? _____ in your living room? ___

a B Thanks. _____ small, but it's really nice.
b B No, _____ _____ in Canada.
c B No, _____ _____ in my bedroom.
d B Oh. _____ a big or small house?

C ▶ Now go to page 131. Look at the grammar chart and do the grammar exercise for 3.2.

D PAIR WORK Write an affirmative (+) and negative (–) sentence for the rooms and furniture below. Then compare with a partner.

My TV is in my bedroom. It's not new, but it's OK.

1 my TV _____
2 my desk _____
3 my refrigerator _____
4 my bedroom _____
5 my kitchen _____

4 SPEAKING

FIND IT

A Design something for the home. Use the ideas below or your ideas. Draw a picture or find a picture online.

an interesting lamp   a big rug   a great shower   a cool desk   a TV for the wall

B PAIR WORK Look at your partner's picture. Guess what it is. Is it cool? Is it interesting?

Is it a lamp?   Yes, it is.

3.3 COFFEE OR TEA?

LESSON OBJECTIVE
- offer and accept a drink and snack

1 VOCABULARY: Drinks and snacks

A ◆ 1.32 Listen and repeat the words. Which things are drinks? Which thing is a snack?

coffee | milk | sugar | a cookie | tea

2 FUNCTIONAL LANGUAGE

A ◆ 1.33 Adam offers a drink and snack to his friend James. Read and listen. Which drink and snack from exercise 1A does James choose?

> **INSIDER ENGLISH**
>
> Use *sure* in informal speech to say *yes*.
> **Sure**. A cookie, please.
> <u>Don't</u> say *Sure, please*.

◆ 1.33 Audio script

Adam	**Coffee or tea?**
James	**Coffee, please.**
Adam	**With milk?**
James	**No, thanks.**
Adam	OK … Here you are.
James	Thanks. Wow, this is a big cup!
Adam	It is! **Sugar?**
James	**Yes, please.**
Adam	One? Two?
James	In that cup? Six! No. Two, please.
Adam	Just two. And …
James	Ah! Cookies! Hmm …
Adam	They *are* small!
James	Next to the big cup, yeah – they're really small! But sure. **A cookie, please.**
Adam	Here you are!
James	Thank you.

B Complete the chart with expressions in **bold** from the conversation above.

Making offers	Replying to offers
Coffee ¹_____ tea?	Coffee, ³_____.
²_____ milk?	⁴_____, thanks.
Sugar?	⁵_____, please.

3 REAL-WORLD STRATEGY

A 🔊 1.34 Listen to a conversation. What does the man want?

coffee ☐   tea ☐   milk ☐   sugar ☐   a cookie ☐

B 🔊 1.34 Listen again. Circle the word the man doesn't understand. What does it mean?

> biscuit   coffee   cookie   tea

> **ASKING ABOUT WORDS YOU DON'T UNDERSTAND**
> To ask about a word, say *Sorry, I don't understand. What's a (word)?*
> *Sorry, I don't understand. What's a biscuit?*

C Read the information on asking about words you don't understand in the box above. Answer the questions.
1. What does the man say when he doesn't understand?
2. How does he ask about the word?

4 PRONUNCIATION: Saying /k/ at the start of a word

A 🔊 1.35 Listen and repeat. Focus on the /k/ sound.
1. **C**offee or tea?
2. This is a big **c**up!
3. A **c**ookie, please.

B 🔊 1.36 Listen. Which speaker (A or B) says the /k/ sound? Write A or B.
1. coffee ___
2. cookie ___
3. kitchen ___
4. cup ___
5. couch ___
6. cool ___

C [PAIR WORK] Work with a partner. Say the words in exercise 4B. Does your partner say the English /k/ sound?

5 SPEAKING

[PAIR WORK] Work with a partner. One person is A. The other person is B. Then change roles.

A Offer your partner a drink/snack from exercise 1A.
B Ask about a word: "Sorry, I don't understand. What's (a) … ?"
A Point to a picture of the word on page 26: "This is (a) … ."
B Say "Yes, please." or "No, thanks."

3.4 HOME-SHARE

LESSON OBJECTIVE
- write an email about a home-share

1 READING

A **SCAN** Francisco is a student. He's in Burnaby in Canada for a year. He wants a room in a home-share. Scan the ad. Who is the owner of the house?

B **READ FOR MAIN IDEAS** Read the emails. What does Francisco ask questions about?

Home-share in Burnaby « Back to results

One bedroom, with furniture, in a five-bedroom house. Great for a student. Fifteen minutes from Morden College. No pets. From March 1. $650 a month. Contact: John Redmond at jredmond@bestmail.com

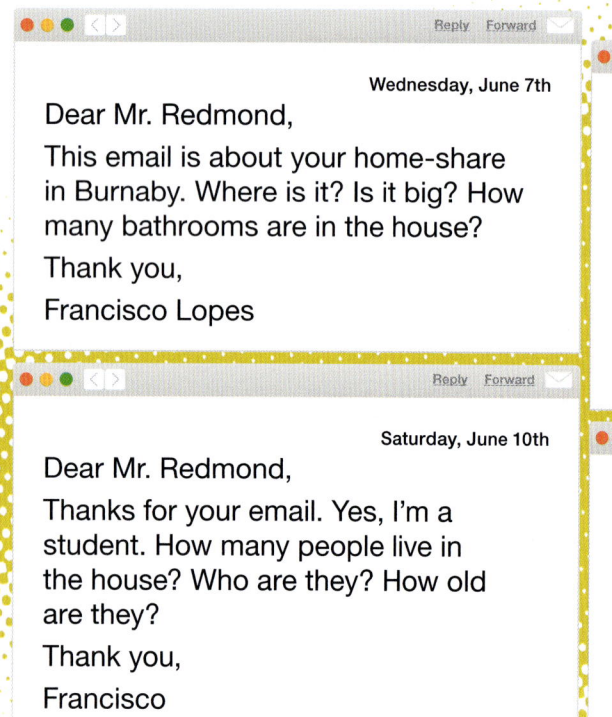

Wednesday, June 7th

Dear Mr. Redmond,

This email is about your home-share in Burnaby. Where is it? Is it big? How many bathrooms are in the house?

Thank you,

Francisco Lopes

Friday, June 9th

Dear Mr. Lopes,

The house is on Grafton Street in Burnaby. It's very big, with two bathrooms. One bathroom is next to the kitchen and one bathroom is next to the bedroom in my ad. Are you a student?

Sincerely,

John Redmond

Saturday, June 10th

Dear Mr. Redmond,

Thanks for your email. Yes, I'm a student. How many people live in the house? Who are they? How old are they?

Thank you,

Francisco

Sunday, June 11th

Dear Mr. Lopes,

Four people live in the house now. Two are students. They are 20 and 22 years old. Two are not students. Mr. Johnson is 36 years old, and Mrs. Smith is 71. She is my wife's mother.

Sincerely,

John

2 GRAMMAR: Information questions with *be*

A **PAIR WORK** Complete the questions with question words from the emails in exercise 1B. Then find John's answers to the questions. Use the questions and answers to have a conversation with a partner.

1. _____ is it?
2. _____ bathrooms are in the house?
3. _____ people live in the house?
4. _____ are they?
5. _____ are they?

B ▶ Now go to page 131. Look at the grammar chart and do the grammar exercise for 3.4.

C **PAIR WORK** **THINK CRITICALLY** Is this a good place for Francisco to live? Why or why not?

28

Home-share on **BOND STREET**

✉ Contact owner

3 WRITING

A Francisco writes to the owner of a second home-share. Read the emails. Answer the questions.

1. Is the owner a woman or a man?
2. How many questions are about the house? the people?
3. Look at the pictures above. Which rooms do you see? Which room is in the email but isn't in the pictures?
4. Is it a good place for Francisco? Why or why not?

Dear Mrs. Hyland,

This email is about your home-share in Burnaby. Where is it? How many bedrooms and bathrooms are in it? How many people are in the house? Are they students? I'm a student at Morden College, and I'm 22.

Thank you,

Francisco Lopes

Dear Mr. Lopes,

Thank you for your email. The house is on Bond Street. It's big, with four bedrooms, three bathrooms, and a big kitchen. Three people live in the house now. They are students at Morden College. They are your age – 22.

Sincerely,

Emma Hyland

B **WRITING SKILLS** (Circle) the question marks (?) in Francisco's email, above. Then (circle) the correct answer in the rules, below.

1. Use **one question mark** / **two question marks** for each question.
2. The question mark is at **the end** / **the beginning** of each question.

REGISTER CHECK

Formal, polite emails and informal, friendly emails use different words.

Formal	Informal
Dear	Hello / Hi
Thank you	Thanks
Sincerely	Love

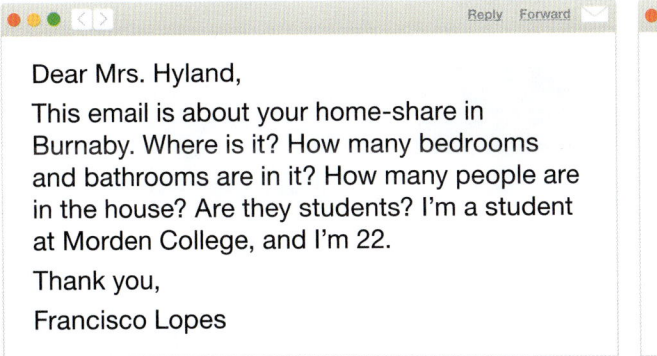

C Write an email to the owner of a home-share. Start with: *This email is about …* Ask questions about the house and the people.

D PAIR WORK Exchange emails with a partner. Write a reply to your partner. Write about a bad place or a good place.

E PAIR WORK Read your partner's reply. Is it a good place or a bad place?

3.5 TIME TO SPEAK
A new home

LESSON OBJECTIVE
- choose things for a home

> Hi, I'm Jason. I'm 25 years old. I'm single, and I'm a student. I ♥ soccer and parties. This is my new apartment!

A DISCUSS Talk about Jason's new home with a partner. Say the rooms you see. Is it a good home for him?

B PREPARE Talk about the things in the pictures. Which rooms are good places for them?

A $120
B $180
C $150
D $80
E $30
F $60
G $280
H $330
I $80
J $120
K $20
L $60
M $10
N $10
O $10

C DECIDE With a partner, make a list of things to buy for Jason's new home. You have $1,000.

D PRESENT Compare your lists. Which list is the class' favorite?

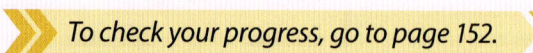
To check your progress, go to page 152.

USEFUL PHRASES

DISCUSS
This is the (kitchen/…)
It's good for him. / It's not good for him.

PREPARE
Where's a good place for a (couch/…)?
In the living room?

DECIDE
What's important for Jason?
This is a big/small (TV).
It's $180 ($ = dollars).
It's expensive. ($$$)
It's cheap. ($)

What about this (TV/…)?
This TV is good for Jason.
I agree. / I don't agree.
Good idea!

REVIEW 1 (UNITS 1–3)

1 VOCABULARY

A **Write the words in the correct place in the chart.**

artist	chef	French	Mexico	server
bookcase	Colombia	Honduran	parents	South Korea
~~Brazil~~	cousin	hotel clerk	Peruvian	table
brother	desk	Japanese	refrigerator	wife

Countries	Nationalities	Jobs	Family	Furniture
Brazil				

B **Write one more word for the categories in exercise 1A.**

2 GRAMMAR

A **Complete the sentences with the words in the box.**

| 're not | 's | 's | Are | I'm not | Is | isn't | it is |

1 Loretta _____ friendly. She's nice, too.
2 A _____ you shy? B No, _____.
3 Donna _____ 14. She's only 13.
4 What _____ your last name?
5 They _____ from Chicago. They're from Dallas.
6 A _____ your company in China? B Yes, _____.

B **Circle the correct answers.**

¹ *My / I* name is Sam, and this is Vic. We're brothers. This is ² *their / our* apartment. ³ *Vic / Vic's* room is big. ⁴ *My / His* room is small, but it's OK. It's next to the kitchen! We're in apartment 22B. ⁵ *We / Our* sister and ⁶ *her / his* husband are in apartment 23B.

C **Write five things about your home and family. Use possessive adjectives and possessive 's/s'.**

3 SPEAKING

A **PAIR WORK** Think of a person you and your partner know. Think about the person's job, age, nationality, and other information. Describe the person. Your partner guesses the person. Then change roles.

> She's a student. She's 21. She's our friend. She's Peruvian. She's very funny.

> Is it Alessa?

B **Write two sentences about your partner's person.**

4 FUNCTIONAL LANGUAGE

A Circle the correct answers to complete the conversation.

Teacher Welcome to the college language center. What's your name?
Sabrina It's Sabrina Calvo.
Teacher How do you ¹ *spell / mean* your last name?
Sabrina C-A-L-V-O.
Teacher Thank you. OK. ² *How / When* old are you, and ³ *how's / when's* your birthday?
Sabrina I'm ⁴ *21 / 21st*. My birthday ⁵ *is / are* August 2.
Teacher OK. You're ⁶ *on / in* room 6C. Sorry, I ⁷ *spell / mean* room 6D. It's next to the library.
Sabrina Sorry, I don't ⁸ *understand / mean*. ⁹ *Where's / What's* a library?
Teacher It's a room with books.
Sabrina OK. Thank you.

B Complete the conversation with the words in the box. There is **one** extra word.

| milk | please | tea | thanks | yes |

Server Coffee or ¹ _____ ?
Ivan   Tea, ² _____ .
Server OK. With ³ _____ ?
Ivan   No, ⁴ _____ .

5 SPEAKING

A **PAIR WORK** Choose **one** of the situations below. Talk to a partner. Have a conversation.

1 You are at a hotel. A clerk asks for your personal information. Answer the questions. Look at page 6 for useful language.

> Good evening. Welcome to Hotel 24. What's your name?

2 You ask a friend about his/her family's ages and birthdays. Your friend answers your questions. Look at page 16 for useful language.

> Is this your daughter? How old is she?

3 A friend is at your home. Offer him or her a drink and a snack. Look at page 26 for useful language.

> Coffee or tea?

B **PAIR WORK** Change roles and repeat the situation.

UNIT OBJECTIVES
- talk about your favorite things
- say how you use technology
- talk about how you communicate
- write product reviews
- talk about your favorite music

I LOVE IT

4

START SPEAKING

A Look at the people in the picture. Where are they? Why are they here?

B Talk about things you like 😊 or love ❤. For ideas, watch the video with June and Felipe.

 **REAL STUDENTS** *What do June and Felipe like or love?*

4.1 FAVORITE THINGS

LESSON OBJECTIVE
- talk about your favorite things

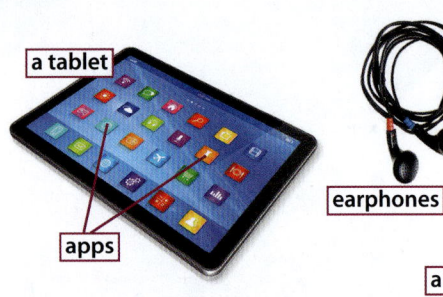
a tablet
apps

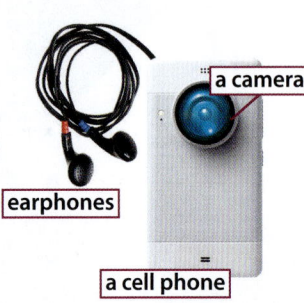
a camera
earphones
a cell phone

a game
a laptop

a smartwatch

1 VOCABULARY: Technology

! A **laptop** is a **computer**.

A 🔊 1.37 Look at the pictures above. Listen and repeat the words.

B PAIR WORK Look at the pictures again. Which things do you like? Which things <u>don't</u> you like? Tell a partner.

😊 I like this.   ☹ I don't like this.

C ▶ Now do the vocabulary exercises for 4.1 on page 143.

2 LANGUAGE IN CONTEXT

A Read the webpage. What things from exercise 1A do the people talk about? Which thing on the webpage isn't in the pictures above?

zozo **I love my refrigerator. Am I OK?**

COMMENTS

JJ You love a refrigerator! No, you're not OK! We love people – we don't love things.

erico-hello I don't agree, JJ! I love my family ... and I love my smartwatch. We love people, *and* we love things.

vera True. I love my cell phone and the apps on it. I don't have a tablet, but I really want an iPad. Yes, it's OK to love things. But a *refrigerator*? I have a nice refrigerator. I *like* it, but I don't *love* it.

stee33 I don't love my refrigerator, but I love the things in it! 😋

B Read the webpage again. Are sentences 1–6 true or false for the people? Circle the correct answer.

1. I have a refrigerator. For zozo, this is *true / false*.
2. I love things. For erico-hello, this is *true / false*.
3. I have a tablet. For vera, this is *true / false*.
4. I want a tablet. For vera, this is *true / false*.
5. I have a cell phone with apps. For vera, this is *true / false*.
6. I love my refrigerator. For stee33, this is *true / false*.

3 GRAMMAR: Simple present statements with *I*, *you*, *we*

A Circle the correct answers. Use the sentences in the grammar box to help you.
1. Use the simple present for things that are **generally true** / **finished**.
2. Use *I, you,* or *we* / *I'm, you're,* or *we're* with present simple verbs.
3. Use *don't* in **affirmative** / **negative** simple present statements.
4. Simple present verbs have **the same** / **different** spelling after *I*, *you*, and *we*.

Simple present statements with *I, you, we*	
I **love** my watch.	I **don't love** my refrigerator.
I **have** a cell phone.	I **don't have** a tablet.
You **want** a tablet.	You **don't want** a watch.
We **love** our family.	We **don't love** things.

B Complete the sentences with the words in the box.

> don't have   don't like   don't want   have   love   want

1. My new smartwatch is cool. I _____ it!
2. I _____ my earphones. They aren't very good.
3. I _____ 85 apps on my cell phone.
4. We _____ games on our cell phones. We don't like them.
5. I don't like tablets. I don't have a tablet, and I _____ a tablet.
6. Your laptop is really old. You _____ a new laptop.

C ▶ Now go to page 131. Look at the grammar chart and do the grammar exercise for 4.1.

D [PAIR WORK] Complete the sentences. Make them true for you. Then compare with a partner.
1. I _____ a smartwatch.
2. I _____ my cell phone.
3. I _____ games on my cell phone.
4. I _____ tablets.
5. I _____ a new computer.

4 SPEAKING

[PAIR WORK] What technology do you have? What do you love? What don't you like? Tell your partner. For ideas, watch Anderson's video.

> I have a good app. It's KickMap. I love it.

> I like iPhones. I want a …

Do you have the same things?

4.2 MY PHONE IS MY WORLD

LESSON OBJECTIVE
- say how you use technology

1 LANGUAGE IN CONTEXT

A 🔊 1.38 Read and listen. Olivia is at a phone store, TechUBuy. Circle the things she talks about.

family   friends   her laptop   her phone   school   work

GLOSSARY
phone plan (n) a service you pay for to make calls, send messages, and use the internet on your cell phone

🔊 1.38 Audio script

Clerk	Welcome to TechUBuy!
Olivia	Hi! I want a new phone plan. I love my phone. It's my world! But my plan is expensive.
Clerk	Do you know which plan you want?
Olivia	No. I have no idea.
Clerk	OK. First, I have some questions. What do you do on your phone? Do you **call** your friends?
Olivia	No. I **chat** with my friends, but I don't *call* them. We **send messages**. And we **leave voice messages**.
Clerk	Ah, yes. And do you **send emails**?
Olivia	Yes. I **read emails** on my phone – from friends and for work.
Clerk	And what else? Do you **listen to music** on your phone?
Olivia	Yes, I do, and I **watch videos**. I also **use social media** – I **post photos**, **leave comments**, …
Clerk	OK. Your phone really *is* your world! So, we have three phone plans …

2 VOCABULARY: Using technology

A Read the chart. Which verbs are <u>not</u> in the conversation in exercise 1A?

INSIDER ENGLISH

Say *What else?* to ask for more information about a topic.
And what else? Do you listen to music on your phone?

verbs + nouns		
buy apps / games / music / movies	**play** games	**leave** voice messages / comments
call friends / family	**post** photos / comments	**use** apps / social media / technology
chat with friends / family	**read** emails / messages	
listen to music	**send** emails / (text) messages	**watch** movies / videos / TV
… on the internet … on my computer / laptop … on my cell phone / tablet … on my smartwatch		

I call family on my cell phone.

I listen to music on my phone.

I chat with friends on the internet.

I use apps on my cell phone and tablet.

I play games on my computer.

I read emails on my tablet.

I send text messages on my phone.

I post photos on the internet.

B 🔊 1.39 Look at the pictures. Listen and repeat. Then say <u>three</u> things you do.

C ▶ Now do the vocabulary exercises for 4.2 on page 144.

3 GRAMMAR: Simple present yes/no questions with I, you, we

A Circle the correct answers. Use the sentences in the grammar box to help you.
1. To make simple present questions, use **Do** / **Are** + the subject (for example, *I* or *we*) + a verb.
2. To make negative short answers, use **do** / **don't**.

Simple present yes/no questions with *I, you, we*	
Do I **post** good photos?	Yes, you **do.** / No, you **don't.**
Do you **use** social media?	Yes, I **do.** / No, I **don't.**
Do you **know** which plan you want?	Yes, I **do.** / No, I **don't.**
Do you and your friends **send** emails?	Yes, we **do.** / No, we **don't.**

B Complete the *yes/no* questions. Use the words in parentheses ( ).
1. _____ on your computer? (*you, listen to music*)
2. _____ on your phone? (*you, play games*)
3. _____ to your teachers? (*you and your friends, send text messages*)
4. _____ on social media? (*you, post comments*)
5. _____ on your laptop? (*you, watch videos*)

C PAIR WORK Ask and answer the questions so they are true for you. Say *"Yes, I do."* or *"No, I don't."*

D ▶ Now go to page 132. Look at the grammar chart and do the grammar exercise for 4.2.

4 SPEAKING

A PAIR WORK What do you do on your phone and the internet? Compare with a partner.

B PAIR WORK Look at the cell phone plans. Which plan is good for you? Why? Ask and answer questions with a partner. Use the conversation on page 36 to help you.

> Do you play games on your phone?

>> No, I don't. I call friends and family, and I send text messages. I don't use social media on my phone. Plan 1 is good for me.

Plan 1 — $10 / month
- 2 GB data
- 100 minutes of talk time
- 100 text messages
- Music app

Plan 2 — $15 / month
- 5 GB data
- 50 minutes of talk time
- 200 text messages
- Photo app

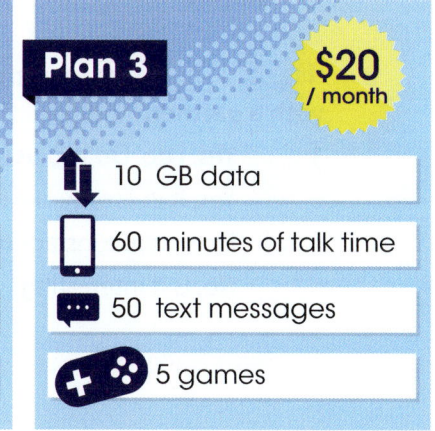

Plan 3 — $20 / month
- 10 GB data
- 60 minutes of talk time
- 50 text messages
- 5 games

4.3 WHAT ABOUT YOU?

LESSON OBJECTIVE
- talk about how you communicate

1 FUNCTIONAL LANGUAGE

A PAIR WORK How do you communicate with family and friends? Check (✓) the things you use. Then compare with your partner.

- ☐ cards
- ☐ email
- ☐ letter
- ☐ phone
- ☐ social media
- ☐ video chat

B 🔊 1.40 Rocío, a college student in Los Angeles, talks to her new friend Jeff. Read and listen. How do they communicate with family and friends?

🔊 1.40 Audio script

Jeff	So, you're from Chile. Does your family live in Chile, too?
Rocío	Yes, but LA is my home now! I use technology to chat with my family. I call my parents on my phone, and I send messages to my brothers. It's really nice.
Jeff	Right. **What about email?**
Rocío	Yeah. I send emails to my friends in Chile. **How about you?**
Jeff	I like email, but I use Facebook, too.
Rocío	OK. I like Instagram.
Jeff	Oh, yeah? **Do you post photos?**
Rocío	Yes, photos of LA. My family and friends really like them. **Do you post photos, too?**
Jeff	No, but I post comments on other people's photos.
Rocío	Nice comments?
Jeff	Yes, of course!

C Complete the chart with expressions in **bold** from the conversation above.

Asking about a new topic	Asking for a response
1 _____ email?	3 _____ post photos,
2 _____ post photos?	4 _____ ?
Do you send cards? / use social media?	5 _____ about you?
	What about you?
	And you?

D 🔊 1.41 PAIR WORK Put the conversations in the correct order. Listen and check. Then practice with a partner.

1. ___ Yes, I do. Do you use it, too?
   ___ Yes, it is. I really like it.
   _1_ Do you use Instagram?
   ___ No. Is it interesting?

2. ___ No, but I send birthday messages.
   ___ Yes, to my family and friends. What about you?
   ___ Hmm … birthday messages are OK, but I like cards.
   _1_ Do you send birthday cards to your family?

38

2 REAL-WORLD STRATEGY

> **SHOWING YOU ARE LISTENING**
> To show you are listening, say *Right*, *Yeah*, or *OK*.
> Jeff   I use Facebook, too.
> Rocío OK. I like Instagram.

A Read about how to show you are listening in the box above. What does Rocío say?

B 🔊 1.42 Listen to a conversation. How does the man communicate with his family?

C 🔊 1.42 Listen again. What does the woman say to show she's listening?

D ▶ PAIR WORK Student A: Go to page 156. Student B: Go to page 159. Follow the instructions.

3 PRONUNCIATION: Saying stressed words

A 🔊 1.43 Listen and repeat the questions. Which words are stressed? Why are they stressed?
   1 What about email?   2 How about you?   3 Do you post photos?

B 🔊 1.44 Listen and <u>underline</u> the stressed words in the questions.
   A Do you use Facebook? (1 word)
   B Yeah. How about you? (1 word)
   A Me, too. I post photos and comments.
   B Do you post videos? (2 words)
   A No, but I send videos on WhatsApp.
   B Do you use video chat? (2 words)
   A Yeah, video chat is great.

C PAIR WORK Practice the conversation in exercise 3B. Does your partner use stressed words?

4 SPEAKING

A Think about ways to communicate with people. Which ways do you use? Write a list.

B PAIR WORK Talk to a partner about how you communicate. Ask questions to start a new topic. Show you are listening.

> I use Instagram. It's great.
>
> Yeah.
>
> Do you use Instagram, too?
>
> Yes, and I use Snapchat. What about you?
>
> I don't use Snapchat.

4.4 GREAT! FIVE STARS

LESSON OBJECTIVE
- write product reviews

1 LISTENING

A **PAIR WORK** Read the definition of "product review." Then answer the questions with a partner.

GLOSSARY
product review (n) people's opinions and comments about things they buy

1. Do you buy things on the internet?
2. Do you look at or write product reviews?

B 🔊 1.45 **LISTEN FOR GIST** Listen to product reviews from three vloggers. Match the reviews (1, 2, and 3) to the products below.

an app ___   a TV ___   a tablet ___

C 🔊 1.45 **LISTEN FOR MAIN IDEAS** Listen again. How many stars do you think the vloggers give? Circle your answer. Then compare with a partner.

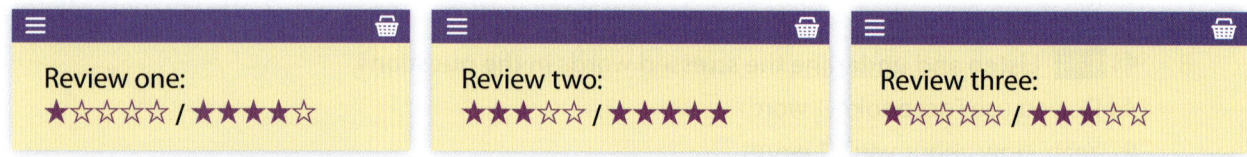

Review one: ★☆☆☆☆ / ★★★★☆
Review two: ★★☆☆☆ / ★★★★★
Review three: ★☆☆☆☆ / ★★★☆☆

D **PAIR WORK** **THINK CRITICALLY** Talk to a partner. Which review is useful to you?

2 GRAMMAR: *a/an*; adjectives before nouns

A Circle the correct answers. Use the sentences in the grammar box to help you.

1. Use *a* or *an* with a **singular** / **plural** noun.
2. Use *a* / *an* before most vowel sounds (*a, e, i, o, u*).
3. Use *a* / *an* before a consonant sound (*b, c, d, …*).
4. **Use** / **Don't use** *a* or *an* with plural nouns.

a/an; adjectives before nouns

a/an	no *a/an*
You take **a photo**.	You take **photos**. (plural nouns)
A tablet is expensive.	**This tablet** is expensive. (*this* + noun)
I have **an uncle**.	I have **two uncles**. (number + noun)
We live in **a house**.	**Our house** is small. (possessive adjectives)
You have **a new phone**.	His phone **is new**. (*be* + adjective)

B Use the words to make sentences. Then check your accuracy.

1. a / cell phone. / I / new / want _____
2. two / We / in / TVs / our house. / have _____
3. app / really / This / interesting. / is _____
4. you / an / Do / iPad? / have _____
5. like / tablets? / Do / you _____

 ACCURACY CHECK

Don't use *a/an* with a plural noun.

We have computers at work. ✓
We have a computers at work. ✗

C ▶ Now go to page 132. Look at the grammar chart and do the grammar exercise for 4.4.

3 PRONUNCIATION: Listening for the end of a sentence

A 🔊 **1.46** Listen. Which sentence do you hear: A or B? Which speaker is finished?

1. A I love games. ↗
   B I love games. ↘

2. A This tablet is great for games. ↗
   B This tablet is great for games. ↘

B 🔊 **1.47** Listen. Draw one ↗ and one ↘ for each sentence.

1. I like it because it's small.
2. It's cheap, but it's nice.
3. It's really fast, and it has a nice design.
4. It's expensive because it's a great product.

4 WRITING

A **PAIR WORK** Read the product reviews. What are the products? Do you like them? Do you want them?

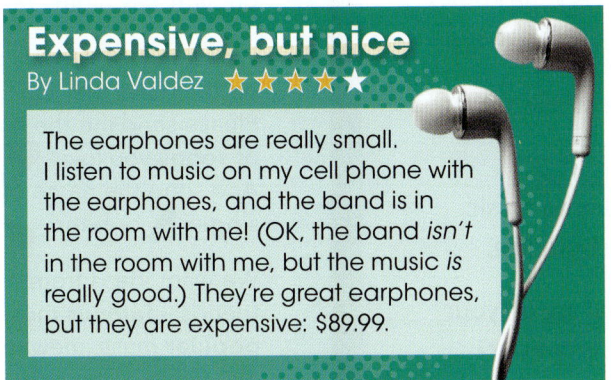

Expensive, but nice
By Linda Valdez ★★★★☆

The earphones are really small. I listen to music on my cell phone with the earphones, and the band is in the room with me! (OK, the band *isn't* in the room with me, but the music *is* really good.) They're great earphones, but they are expensive: $89.99.

A cheap chair!
By Carl Rogers ★★☆☆☆

This chair is cheap. It's $29.50. I have two chairs – one chair for me, and one chair for my wife. We sit in them and watch TV. I don't like it because it's small, and I'm a big man. I don't sit *in* the chair. I sit *on* it! Is it comfortable? NO!

GLOSSARY
comfortable (*adj*) good to sit on

B Read the reviews again. Complete the chart.

	Earphones	Chair
Title	Expensive, but nice	
Number of stars		
Price ($)		
Good or bad product?		

FIND IT

C Choose a product you know or find a product on the internet. Find the information in exercise 4B.

D **WRITING SKILLS** (Circle) the words *but* and *because* in the reviews above. Then (circle) the correct answer in the rules.

1. Use *but* to add an idea that is **the same / different**.
2. Use *because* to **give a reason / ask a question**.

REGISTER CHECK

In informal writing, use exclamation points (!) after funny sentences or after words and sentences with a strong feeling, for example, with *love*, *like*, or *don't like*.

I don't sit in the chair. I sit on it!
Is it comfortable? NO!

WRITE IT

E Write reviews for a good product <u>and</u> a bad product. Use the products below or your own ideas. Write a title, number of stars, and the price.

| an app | a camera | a desk | a game | a lamp | a tablet | a watch |

F **PAIR WORK** Read a partner's reviews. Do you like their products? Do you want them?

4.5 TIME TO SPEAK
Playlists

LESSON OBJECTIVE
- talk about your favorite music

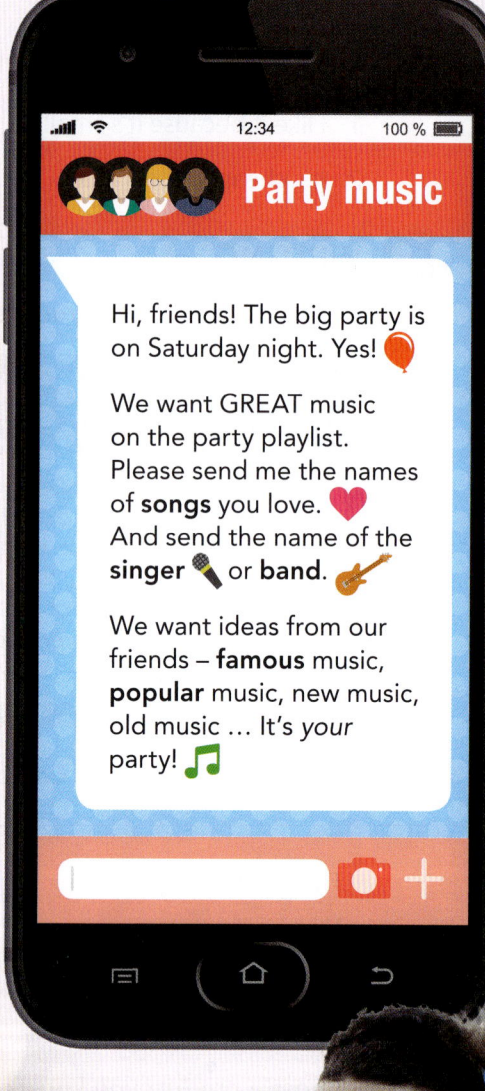

A Read the text message. What is the message about?

B 🔊 1.48 Use words from the message to complete the definitions (1–5). Then listen and check.
1. A playlist is a list of your favorite s_____.
2. People in a b_____ play music or sing.
3. A s_____ is a person in a band. He or she sings the words in a song.
4. F_____ music is music that everyone knows.
5. P_____ music is music that everyone likes.

C **PREPARE** Talk to a partner. Say the name of one singer, one band, and one song you like.

D **DISCUSS** Tell your partner about your favorite music. Make a list of singers, bands, and songs you both like.

E **AGREE** Find singers, bands, and songs that are on your list and on other people's lists. Which music is famous? Which music is popular?

F **DECIDE** Imagine you're going to the party in the text message. Talk to people in your group. Find songs that everyone likes. Then choose ten songs for the party playlist.

>> To check your progress, go to page 153.

USEFUL PHRASES

DISCUSS
This song is my favorite.
Me, too!
I don't like this song.

AGREE
What music do you have on your list?
I have (song/singer/band) on my list.
Let's have this song on the list.
I don't want this song on the list.
What do you think?

DECIDE
Do we want (song/singer/band) or (song/singer/band)?
Here are our ten songs for the party playlist.

UNIT OBJECTIVES
- talk about weekday and weekend activities
- tell the time and talk about your routines
- show you agree and have things in common
- write a report about your activities
- compare different work weeks

MONDAYS AND FUN DAYS

5

START SPEAKING

A Look at the picture and describe the people. Who are they? Where are they?

B Are they happy? Is it a fun day?

C For you, what is a fun day?

43

5.1 PLAY OR FAST-FORWARD?

LESSON OBJECTIVE
- talk about weekday and weekend activities

1 VOCABULARY: Days and times of day; everyday activities

A 🔊 1.49 Listen and repeat. What's your favorite day? What's your favorite time of day?

weekdays					weekend	
Monday	Tuesday	Wednesday	Thursday	Friday	Saturday	Sunday

Times of day: morning, afternoon, evening, night

B 🔊 1.50 Listen and repeat the sentences.

1. I go out in the evening.

2. I run on Monday and Friday.

3. I work on the weekend.

4. I study in the morning.

5. I don't play soccer.

C PAIR WORK Which sentences in exercise 1B are true for you? Tell your partner. Then say <u>two</u> more true sentences about your activities.

D ▶ Now do the vocabulary exercises for 5.1 on page 144.

2 LANGUAGE IN CONTEXT

A Read the article. Who are Sam and Justine? What activities does Sam do on weekdays?

GLOSSARY
after (*adv*) he works, then he plays soccer
before (*adv*) he runs, then he goes to work
every (*det*) 100% (of days / evenings)
way of life (*phrase*) how you live your life

PLAY ▶ or FAST-FORWARD? ⏩

By Matt Newman

Weekdays = **work** or **study**. **Weekends** = fun. Right? Not for my brother, Sam! For Sam, *every* day is a fun day! He works from **Monday morning** to **Friday afternoon**, but he usually **runs** in the morning before work. On Monday and **Thursday**, he **plays soccer** after work, and he **goes out** with friends on **Wednesday**. He doesn't go out *every* evening – on **Tuesdays** he stays home and watches TV. His way of life is ▶ "play now."

My sister, Justine, is very different. She has fun, but not every day. From Monday to Friday, she works. She doesn't have time for sports, and she hardly ever goes out! It's OK because Justine has free time on the weekend. She chats with family in the afternoon and then goes out with friends at night. Her way of life is work, work, work, and ⏩ "fast-forward to the weekend."

😊😊 Sam and Justine are both happy people, but their ways of life are *very* different. What about you? What's *your* way of life?

B   What's Sam's way of life: "play now", or "fast-forward"? What's Justine's way of life?

C   **PAIR WORK** What's your way of life: "play now" or "fast-forward to the weekend"? Tell your partner. For ideas, watch June's video.

Are you the same as June?

3   GRAMMAR: Simple present statements with *he*, *she*, *they*

A   Circle the correct answers. Use the sentences in the grammar box to help you.
1   In affirmative statements with **he and she** / **they**, most simple present verbs end in -s.
2   The verb *have* is irregular. In affirmative statements with *he* and *she*, use **have** / **has**.
3   To make negative statements with *he* and *she*, use **don't** / **doesn't** + verb.

> **Simple present statements with *he*, *she*, *they***
>
> He **works** Monday to Friday.   She **doesn't have** time for sports.
> She **chats** with family in the afternoon.   They **don't go out** every evening.
> She **has** fun, but not every day.   My dad **doesn't play** soccer.
> They **have** fun on the weekend.

B   Complete the sentences with the words in the box.

| doesn't | don't | has | have | play | plays |

1   My friends _____ video games every weekday evening.
2   On weekdays, my sister _____ go out in the evening.
3   Every day, my sister and her husband _____ tea in the morning.
4   Pedro _____ soccer on his college team, but not in every game.
5   My mom _____ a tablet, but she doesn't use it.
6   My grandparents _____ work, so from Monday to Friday they're at home.

C   Look at the sentences in exercise 3B and the adverbs of frequency chart. Then circle the correct answers.
1   My friends *often* / *hardly ever* / *never* play video games.
2   On weekdays, my sister is *always* / *sometimes* / *never* at home in the evening.
3   My sister and her husband *always* / *hardly ever* / *never* drink tea in the morning.
4   Pedro *always* / *sometimes* / *never* plays in his college soccer games.
5   My mom *always* / *often* / *never* uses her tablet.
6   My grandparents are *usually* / *hardly ever* / *never* at home on weekdays.

Adverbs of frequency
always   100%
usually
often
sometimes
hardly ever
never   0%

D   ▶ Now go to page 133. Look at the grammar chart and do the grammar exercise for 5.1.

4   SPEAKING

A   Look at the activities in exercise 1B on page 44. What activities do your family or friends do? When do they do them? Write a list. Use adverbs of frequency.

B   **PAIR WORK** Talk to a partner about your family and friends' activities. Who is "play now"? Who is "fast-forward"?

> My sister is "play now." She often goes out in the evening …

5.2 LISTEN TO YOUR BODY CLOCK

LESSON OBJECTIVE
- tell the time and talk about your routines

1 VOCABULARY: Telling the time

A 🔊 1.51 [PAIR WORK] Listen and repeat the times. Then point to a picture and ask *"What time is it?"* Your partner says the time.

It's eight **o'clock**.

It's five-fifteen.
It's **(a) quarter after** five.

It's three-thirty.

It's ten forty-five.
It's **(a) quarter to** eleven.

It's nine-oh-five.
It's five **after** nine.

It's six-fifty.
It's ten **to** seven.

It's **12:00 p.m.** / It's **noon**.
It's **12.00 a.m.** / It's **midnight**.

a.m. = before 12 noon
p.m. = after 12 noon
to = before

B ▶ Now do the first vocabulary exercise for 5.2 on page 145.

GLOSSARY
routine (*n*) the things you do every day at the same time
tired (*adj*) you are sleepy
late (*adj*) toward the end of the morning or evening

2 LANGUAGE IN CONTEXT

A 🔊 1.52 Read and listen. Alex talks to his doctor. What is Alex's problem? What is your "body clock"?

🔊 **1.52 Audio script**

Alex	I'm always so tired.
Doctor	Tell me about your routine, Alex. What time do you **get up**?
Alex	On weekdays, I usually get up at **7:45**, and I go to class at **8:30**.
Doctor	Do you **eat breakfast**?
Alex	No, I don't. But I **drink coffee**.
Doctor	When do you eat?
Alex	At noon. Then I **go to class** again in the afternoon. I usually **have dinner** at **9:00**. My parents don't like that.
Doctor	Well, it is very late. Do they have dinner before you?
Alex	Yes, they do. Usually at **6:00**.
Doctor	Does your mom make dinner for you?
Alex	No, she doesn't. I make it.
Doctor	OK. What do you do on weekends?
Alex	On Friday and Saturday, I go out with friends. I usually **go to bed** at **2:00** or **3:00** a.m. And on Sunday, I get up really late and watch TV.
Doctor	Alex, it's time to listen to your body clock!

B 🔊 1.52 [PAIR WORK] Listen again. Write notes about Alex's routine. Compare with a partner.

He doesn't eat breakfast. He drinks coffee.

C ▶ Now do the second vocabulary exercise for 5.2 on page 145.

D [PAIR WORK] Is your routine the same as or different from Alex's? Tell your partner. For ideas, watch Josue's video.

REAL STUDENT

Is your routine different from Josue's, or the same?

3 GRAMMAR: Questions in the simple present

A Circle the correct answers. Use the sentences in the grammar box to help you.
1. With the pronouns *I*, *you*, *we*, and *they*, use **Do** / *Does*.
2. With the pronouns *he*, *she*, and *it*, use *Do* / **Does**.
3. In yes/no questions, the word order is *Do or Does* + **person or thing** + **verb** / *Do or Does* + *verb* + *person or thing*.
4. In information questions, put the question word(s) (for example, *Where* or *What time*) **before** / *after* *do* and *does*.

Questions in the simple present

Yes/no questions
Do I **have** class today?
Do you **go out** with friends?
Does he **go** to classes every day?
Does it **have** good apps?
Do they **have** dinner before you?

Information questions
How **do** I **get** to class?
What time **do** you **go out** with friends?
When **does** he **go** to classes?
What **does** it **have**?
Where **do** they **eat** dinner?

B PAIR WORK Complete the conversations. Use the audio script on page 46 to help you. Then practice them with a partner.

1. A _____ _____ do you go to work?
   B I _____ to work at 7:00.
   A Wow! _____ do you go to bed?
   B I usually go to bed after midnight. I'm always tired!
2. A _____ they play soccer?
   B _____, they do. What about you?
   A No, I _____.

3. A _____ Martin have a new job?
   B Yes, he _____.
   A _____ does he work?
   B He _____ in an office.

C ▶ Now go to page 133. Look at the grammar charts and do the grammar exercise for 5.2.

D Write **three** questions about your partner's routine. Use the words in the box to start your questions. Then check your accuracy.

> Do … ?   What … ?   What time … ?
> When … ?   Where … ?

✓ **ACCURACY CHECK**

Use *do* or *does* with information questions in the simple present.
Where Margaret work? ✗
Where does Margaret work? ✓

E PAIR WORK Ask and answer the questions from exercise 3D with a partner.

4 SPEAKING

A Think about your routines and your family's routines. What do you do? When do you do it?

B PAIR WORK Ask your partner about their routines and their family's routines. Do they listen to their body clock?

> When do you get up?
>
> I usually get up at 7:30, but my sister gets up at 5:00!

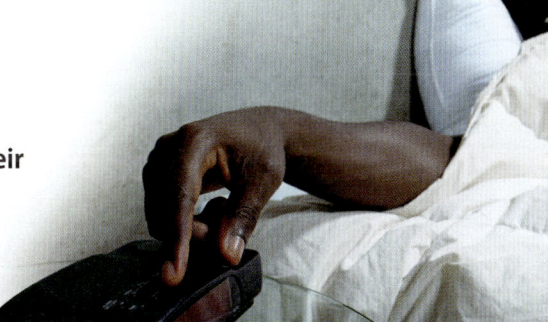

5.3 ME, TOO

LESSON OBJECTIVE
- show you agree and have things in common

1 FUNCTIONAL LANGUAGE

A 🔊 1.53 The men are at work. Read and listen to their conversation. What do both the men do?

> 🔊 **1.53 Audio script**
>
> A Do you always run at lunchtime?
> B Yeah, I usually run for about 30 minutes.
> A That's cool. It's good to go out.
> B **I agree.** And what about you? Do you run?
> A Hardly ever. Well, I play basketball.
> B So you run a lot!
> A **That's true.** But I don't have the ball a lot! I'm not very good.
> B **Me, neither.** But basketball is fun.
> A **Yeah, I know.**
> B I play with friends.
> A **Me, too.** Hey, we have a game on Thursday after work. Play with us!
> B Thursday. Um … yeah, OK.
> A Great! Now I'm not the only bad player.
> B Very funny!

B Complete the chart with expressions in **bold** from the conversations above.

Showing you agree	Showing you have things in common
I ¹_____. That's ²_____. / That's right. ³_____, I know.	⁴_____, neither. (-) Me, ⁵_____. (+)

C Choose the correct answers to complete the conversations. Then practice with a partner.

1. A I play basketball on the weekend.
   B *Me, too / Me, neither*. I play on Sunday.
2. A Soccer is great.
   B *I agree / right*. Do you play?
3. A This game is boring.
   B *Yeah, I know / Me, neither*. The team isn't very good.
4. A I don't get up late on Saturday.
   B *Me, too / Me, neither*. I get up at 8.

48

2 REAL-WORLD STRATEGY

SHORT ANSWERS WITH ADVERBS OF FREQUENCY
People sometimes answer questions with adverbs of frequency, not complete sentences.
A Do you always run at lunch?
B Usually. And what about you? Do you run?
A Hardly ever.

A Read about short answers with adverbs of frequency in the box above. Who runs a lot: A or B? Who doesn't run a lot?

B 🔊 1.54 Listen to a conversation. Who gets up early on the weekend: the man, the woman, or both of them?

C 🔊 1.54 Listen again. What one-word answer does the man say? What one-word answer does the woman say?

D ▶ PAIR WORK Student A: Go to page 157. Student B: Go to page 159. Follow the instructions.

3 PRONUNCIATION: Saying syllables in words

A 🔊 1.55 Listen. How many syllables do you hear? Write 1, 2, or 3.
1 run ___   2 basketball ___   3 soccer ___

B 🔊 1.56 Say the words. How many syllables are there? Write 1, 2, or 3. Listen and check.
1 weekend ___   3 usually ___   5 sport ___
2 Wednesday ___   4 chat ___   6 morning ___

C Look at the audio script on page 48. Find more examples of words with one or two syllables.

4 SPEAKING

A Write a list of things you do often. Write how you feel about the activities.
chat with friends online – fun
watch TV – interesting

B PAIR WORK Tell your partner what you do and how you feel about the activities. Your partner says when he/she agrees and when you have things in common. Then change roles and repeat.

On weekdays, I watch TV in the evening.
Me, too.
It's sometimes interesting.
Yeah, I know.

5.4 A HAPPY LIFE

LESSON OBJECTIVE
- write a report about your activities

1 READING

A **SKIM** Look at the picture and the title. What is the magazine article about?

WORK, REST, and PLAY = The WRAP test

Doctors always say, for a happy life, **work**, **rest**, and **play**! OK, but it isn't always easy. What about *your* life? Do you **work**, **rest**, and **play**? Do you **work**, **rest**, and **play**? Or do you **work**, **rest**, and **play**?

Look at Cheryl.

She's very busy. She's a salesperson. She works at a store Monday to Friday from 10:00 a.m. to 5:30 p.m. She has a French class in the evening on Tuesdays and Thursdays. After class, she listens to music or watches TV. Then she does her homework. On the weekend, she has free time. She plays soccer with her friends. She often goes out with her sister on Saturday night. On Sunday, she studies French for her class. Then she sometimes plays the guitar.

What is Cheryl's WRAP?
What about you? To find out, take the WRAP test …

B **READ FOR DETAILS** Read the article again. Complete the chart with the correct verbs.

Work		Rest		Play	
works	at a store		music		soccer
	a French class		TV		with her sister
	her homework				the guitar
	French				

C **PAIR WORK** **THINK CRITICALLY** Which WRAP result is true for Cheryl?

1 **work**, rest, and play   2 **work**, rest, and **play**   3 work, **rest**, and **play**

2 WRITING

A Read Andre's WRAP report. What does he do on weekdays? What does he do on the weekend?

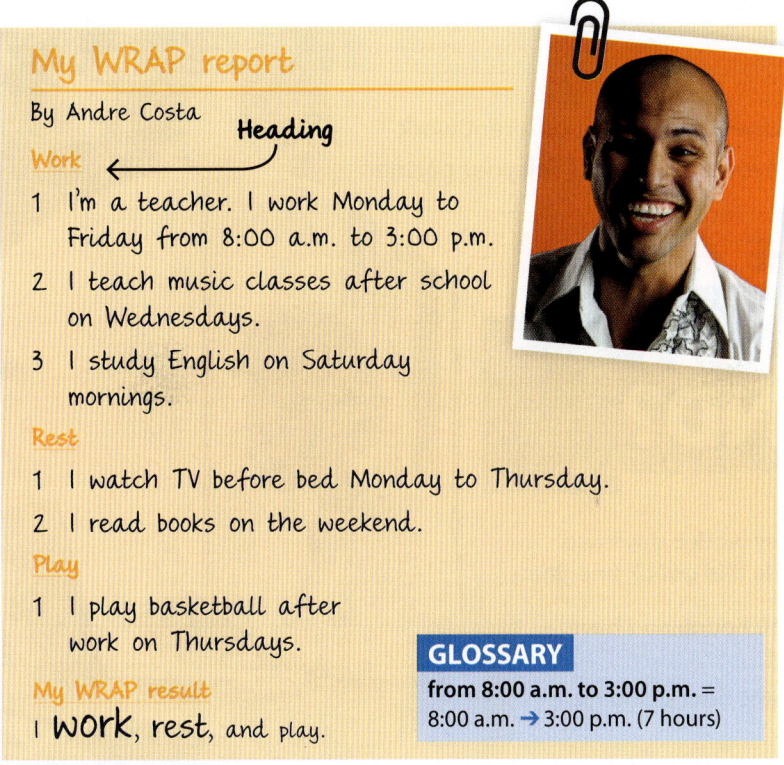

My WRAP report
By Andre Costa
Work ← Heading
1 I'm a teacher. I work Monday to Friday from 8:00 a.m. to 3:00 p.m.
2 I teach music classes after school on Wednesdays.
3 I study English on Saturday mornings.
Rest
1 I watch TV before bed Monday to Thursday.
2 I read books on the weekend.
Play
1 I play basketball after work on Thursdays.
My WRAP result
I **work**, **rest**, and **play**.

GLOSSARY
from 8:00 a.m. to 3:00 p.m. =
8:00 a.m. → 3:00 p.m. (7 hours)

REGISTER CHECK

Write *a.m.* and *p.m.* after times.
I work Monday to Friday from 8:00 a.m. to 3:00 p.m.

Say *in the morning*, *in the afternoon*, or *at night* after times.
Andre says, "I sometimes go to bed at 1:30 in the morning."

B **WRITING SKILLS** Look at the heading "Work." Circle the other headings in the report. What do they show?
 a days and times in the report
 b different sports in each part of the report
 c the different topics in the report

C Look at the numbered lists in the report above. What do the lists show?
 a Andre's test results (= answers)
 b Andre's activities
 c Andre's classes

D Write notes in the chart below with your information. Use the chart in exercise 1B for an example.

Work	Rest	Play

WRITE IT

E Write your WRAP report. Use headings and numbered lists. Include activities, times, and days.

F  Work with a partner. Read your partner's report. What's his/her WRAP result?

G **GROUP WORK** Compare reports in your group. Tell the group about your partner.

> Sora works at a restaurant on the weekend. She …

5.5 TIME TO SPEAK
Life = 5 + 2

LESSON OBJECTIVE
- compare different work weeks

A **PREPARE** Read the magazine article about different work weeks. Which week is your favorite: A, B, or C? Tell your partner.

END OF THE TWO-DAY WEEKEND?

For a lot of people, life = 5 + 2. They work 5 days and have 2 days for the weekend. But is this good? Imagine:

Week A	We work 4 long days (10 hours) and have 3 days for the weekend.
Week B	We work 6 short days (6½ hours) and have 1 day for the weekend.
Week C	We work 7 very short days (5½ hours) and don't have a weekend.

B **DISCUSS** Imagine you have a "week A" life. Talk to a partner. Describe your routine. What do you do, and when do you do it? Then talk about week B and week C.

C **DECIDE** Which week is good for your body clock: A, B, C, or "5 + 2"? Why?

D **AGREE** Tell the class which week is your favorite. Which week does everyone like? Which week does no one like?

▶▶ To check your progress, go to page 153.

USEFUL PHRASES

PREPARE
Which week is your favorite?
Week ... is my favorite.

DISCUSS
I have a week A/B/C life.
I get up / have breakfast at ...
I work from ... to ...
Before/After work, I ...
I have free time from ... to ...

DECIDE
Week ... is good for me because ...
I like / don't like week ... because ...
I want free time on the weekends / in the evenings.
I like long /short work days.

UNIT OBJECTIVES
- talk about places in the city
- talk about nature in your area
- ask for and give directions
- write a fact sheet about a place in nature
- plan a new neighborhood for a city

ZOOM IN, ZOOM OUT

6

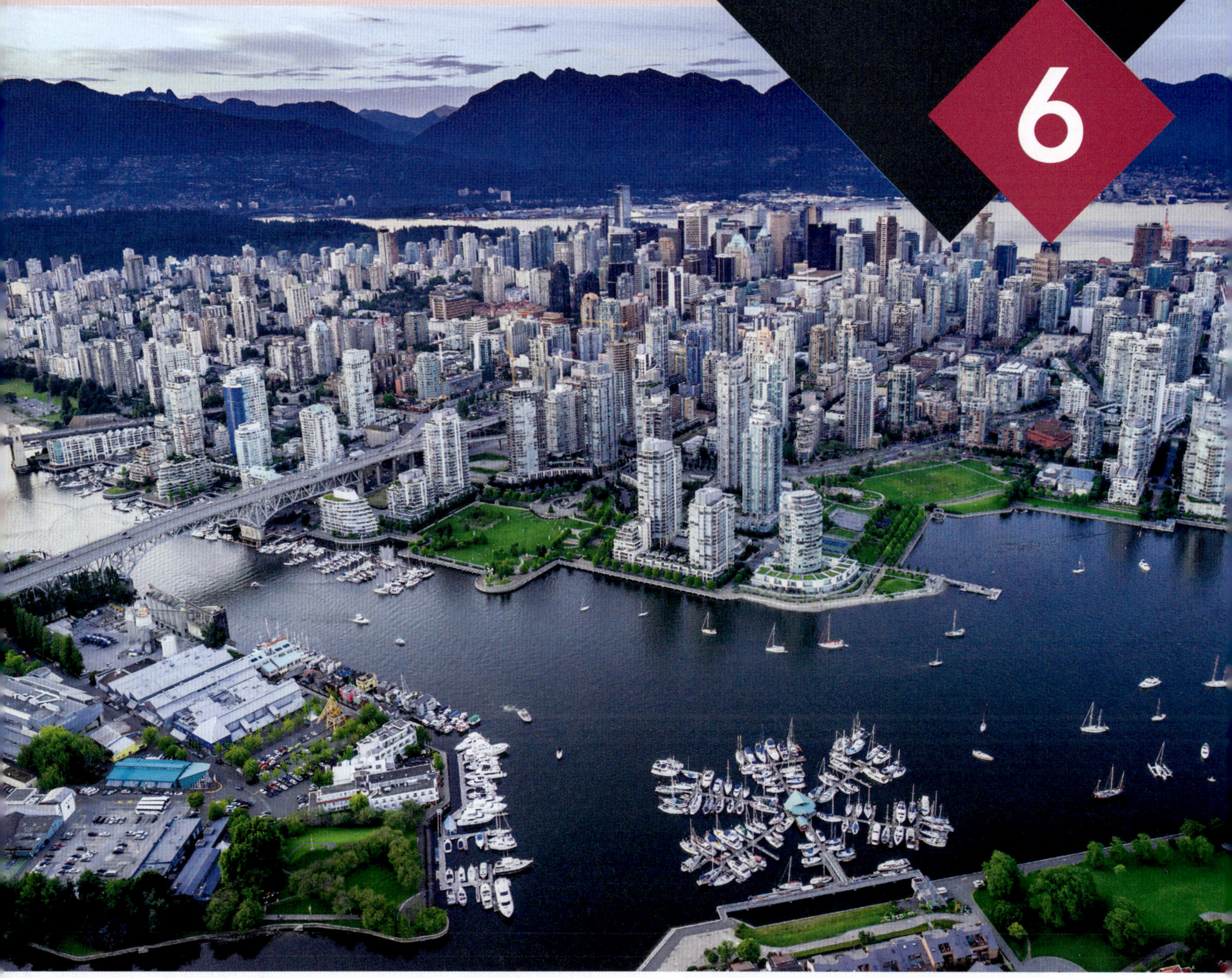

START SPEAKING

A Say things you see in the picture. For ideas, watch Julieth's video.

B Do you want to go here? Why or why not?

C Do you like cities? Do you like places in nature? Which is your favorite?

Do you see the same things as Julieth?

53

6.1 GOOD PLACES

LESSON OBJECTIVE
- talk about places in the city

1 LANGUAGE IN CONTEXT

A 🔊 1.57 Lucas and Robert are in New York City. Read and listen to their conversation. Where is Lucas from? Where is Robert from? What does Lucas want to do on Saturday?

B 🔊 1.57 Read and listen again. Are the sentences true or false?
1 Lucas has a lot of time in New York City.
2 There is no restaurant in the hotel.

🔊 1.57 Audio script

Lucas I'm here, in New York City, for a week. And then I go home to Paris on Sunday.
Robert So you don't have a lot of time to see my great city.
Lucas No, I don't. There's no free time this week – it's work, work, work! But I have some time on Saturday.
Robert OK. There are a lot of places to see and things to do on the weekend. Where is your **hotel**?
Lucas It's near Central Park.
Robert No way! Central Park is great. There are some interesting museums near the **park**. Oh, and there's a **zoo** in the park!
Lucas Cool! What about places to eat? There's no **restaurant** in my hotel.
Robert Hmm … for breakfast, there's a nice **café** near here. And there are a lot of great restaurants in this neighborhood, too.
Lucas Great. Do you know some good **stores**? I don't have a lot of free time, but …
Robert Oh, yeah. There are a lot of great stores in New York. So … no museum, no park, no zoo – just shopping?
Lucas Yes!

GLOSSARY
neighborhood (*n*) an area of a city

INSIDER ENGLISH
Use *No way!* to show surprise.
No way! Central Park is great.

2 VOCABULARY: Places in cities

A 🔊 1.58 Listen and repeat the words.

 bookstore
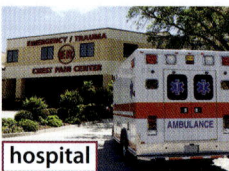 hospital
 movie theater
 restaurant
 supermarket
 café
 hotel
 museum
 school
 zoo
 college
 mall
 park
 store

B ▶ Now do the vocabulary exercises for 6.1 on page 145.

C **PAIR WORK** Which three places in cities do you both like? Which three <u>don't</u> you like?

3 GRAMMAR: *There's, There are; a lot of, some, no*

A Circle the correct answers. Use the sentences in the grammar box to help you.
1 Use *There's* with **singular** / **plural** nouns.
2 Use *There are* with **singular** / **plural** nouns.
3 Use *an* / *no* in negative sentences.
4 Use *some* **for exact numbers** / **when you don't know how many things there are**.

There's (= There is), There are; a lot of, some, no

There's no free time this week.
There's a zoo in the park.
There's a nice café near here.

There are some interesting museums near the park.
There are a lot of good places to see on the weekend.

no = zero
a/an = one
some = a small number
a lot of = a large number

B Circle the correct words to complete the sentences.
1 *There's / There are* a lot of stores in the mall.
2 *There's / There are* a supermarket near the college.
3 There are *a / some* good cafés on Boston Road.
4 There's *a / a lot of* big hospital in the city.
5 There are *a lot of / no* stores, so it's great for shopping.
6 In my city, there are *a / no* zoos.

C ▶ Now go to page 134. Look at the grammar chart and do the grammar exercise for 6.1.

D Write sentences about your city. Use *there is/there are*, *a/an*, *some*, *a lot of*, and *no*. Then check your accuracy.

There's _____.
There's _____.
There are _____.
There are _____.
There is/are no _____.

ACCURACY CHECK

Use *there are*, <u>not</u> *there is*, before *a lot of* and *some* + plural noun.
There ~~is~~ some museums in this city. ✗
There are some museums in this city. ✓

E PAIR WORK Compare your sentences with a partner.

4 SPEAKING

PAIR WORK Talk about the things in your neighborhood. Then compare with a partner. What's the same? What's different?

> There are some good restaurants near my home.

> Samel And there's a movie theater near my home.

6.2 CITY LIFE, WILD LIFE

LESSON OBJECTIVE
- talk about nature in your area

1 VOCABULARY: Nature

A 🔊 1.59 Listen and repeat the words. Which picture is your favorite? Which words describe water?

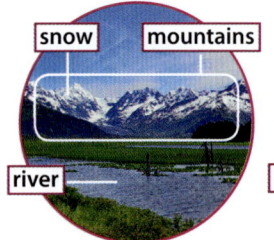
snow, mountains, river

island, beach, ocean

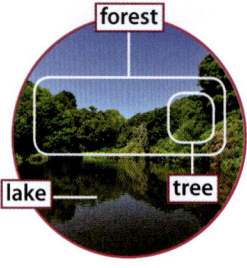
forest, lake, tree

flower, grass, plants

hill, desert

B Cross out the word that does not belong.
1 lake   ~~flower~~   ocean
2 plants   trees   snow
3 river   desert   lake
4 grass   beach   ocean
5 forest   ocean   trees
6 mountain   hill   island

C ▶ Now do the vocabulary exercises for 6.2 on page 146.

2 LANGUAGE IN CONTEXT

A Read the article. Choose a good title.
1 What's your favorite city?
2 Are you close to nature?
3 Do you like nature?

B **PAIR WORK** Take the test. Then compare your answers with a partner.

Do I like nature? Sure. We all love flowers and trees. But I live in a big city, so I don't live close to nature … Or do I? What about you? Take the test. For each sentence, (circle) all the answers that are true for you.

	In your neighborhood	In your city (e.g., in a park)	1–3 hours from your city	Not near your city
There's a lot of **grass**.	A	B	C	D
There are a lot of **flowers**.	A	B	C	D
There are some **trees**.	A	B	C	D
There's a **river**.	A	B	C	D
There's a **lake**.	A	B	C	D
There's a **forest**.	A	B	C	D
There are some **mountains** and **hills**.	A	B	C	D
There's a **beach**.	A	B	C	D
There's an **ocean**.	A	B	C	D
There are a lot of **plants**.	A	B	C	D

♡ 21   💬 25   ↻ 14

A = 3 points,   **B** = 2 points,   **C** = 1 point,   **D** = 0 points

Are you close to nature?
45–60 points
Nature is everywhere!
30–44 points
There's a lot of nature near you.
15–29 points
There's some nature near you.
1–14 points
There isn't a lot of nature near you.
0 points
You only see nature on TV!

C **PAIR WORK** Give examples of nature in your city. For ideas, watch Larissa's video.

REAL STUDENT

Are your answers the same as Larissa's?

3 GRAMMAR: Count and non-count nouns

A Circle the correct answers. Use the sentences in the grammar box to help you.
1 Count nouns have **plural and singular forms** / **no singular or plural form**.
2 Use *a/an* with **singular** / **plural** count nouns.
3 Use ***There's*** / ***There are*** with plural count nouns.
4 Use ***There's*** / ***There are*** with singular count nouns and non-count nouns.

Count and non-count nouns

Singular	Plural	No singular or plural form
There's a **river** in my city.	There are two **rivers**.	There's no / some / a lot of **grass**.
There's an **ocean** near here.	There are no **oceans** near here.	There's no / some / a lot of **water** in the ocean.
	There are some **plants**.	
	There are a lot of **flowers**.	

B Complete the sentences with the correct form of the nouns in parentheses ( ).
1 There are no ____trees____ (tree) in my neighborhood.
2 There's an _____ (ocean) three hours from my city.
3 There's a lot of _____ (nature) in this city.
4 There are some _____ (restaurant) on my street.
5 There is no _____ (grass) near my house.
6 There are a lot of _____ (hotel) in my city.

C ▶ Now go to page 134. Look at the grammar chart and do the grammar exercise for 6.2.

D **PAIR WORK** Change the sentences in exercise 3B so they're true for you and your city. Compare your sentences with a partner.

> There are some trees in my neighborhood.

4 SPEAKING

A Choose a city in your country or in a different country. Think about the nature there.

B **PAIR WORK** Work with a partner. Tell your partner about the place. Does your partner know the place?

> There's a beach in the city.
> There are no hills or mountains.
> There are a lot of trees …

> I know! It's Tampa, in the U.S.!

6.3 IS IT NEAR HERE?

LESSON OBJECTIVE
- ask for and give directions

1 FUNCTIONAL LANGUAGE

A Look at the pictures. The woman is in Quito, Ecuador. What places do you see on the map on her phone?

B  1.60 Read and listen. The woman asks two people for directions. What places does she ask about?

1.60 Audio script

1 **A** Excuse me. Do you speak English?
   B Yes, I do.
   A Oh, good! **Where's** Garcia Moreno Street? **Is it near here?**
   B Yes, it is. Uh … turn left here. **Go one block**, and then **turn right**. That's Garcia Moreno Street.
   A OK, great! Thanks.

2 **A** Excuse me. **Is this** Garcia Moreno Street?
   B Yes, it is.
   A Where's the City Museum?
   B **It's that way. Go straight. It's on the left.** Or come with me! It's on my way to the supermarket.

C Complete the chart with expressions in **bold** from the conversations above.

Asking for directions	Giving directions
Where am I? / Where are we?	Turn left. / 4 _____ .
I don't understand the map.	5 _____ way.
1 _____ Garcia Moreno Street?	Go one 6 _____ . / Go 7 _____ .
Is it 2 _____ ?	It's on the right. / 8 _____ .
Excuse me. Is 3 _____ Garcia Moreno Street?	It's over there. / It's here!
	9 _____ Garcia Moreno Street.
	Look on your phone. Zoom in / zoom out. It's here.

D 🔊 1.61 **PAIR WORK** Complete the conversations. Then listen and check. Practice with a partner.

1 **A** Excuse me. *It's / Where's* Central Station? **B** Go one *way / block*. It's on the left.
2 **A** *Is this / Is it* San Gabriel Street? **B** No. *Turn / It's* right. That's San Gabriel Street.
3 **A** Is the language center *go straight / near here*? **B** Yes. It's over *there / go one block*.

2 REAL-WORLD STRATEGY

A 🔊 1.62 Listen to a conversation. Where does the man want to go?

B 🔊 1.62 Listen again. The man wants to check the information. What does he do?
1 He asks the woman to repeat her words.
2 He repeats the woman's words.

CHECKING INFORMATION
To check you understand, say *So, …* and repeat the information.
It's that way. Turn left here. Go one block, and then turn right.
So, turn left here. Go one block, and then turn right.

C 🔊 1.63 Read about checking information in the box above. Then listen to the directions. Check the information.
1 Turn right here. Then turn right again. — So, turn right here. Then turn right again.

D ▶ PAIR WORK Student A: Go to page 157. Student B: Go to page 159. Follow the instructions.

3 PRONUNCIATION: Saying /ɪr/ and /er/ sounds

A 🔊 1.64 Listen and repeat. Focus on the sound of the letters in **bold**.
/ɪr/ Is it n**ear** h**ere**?   /er/ Wh**ere** is th**eir** house?

B 🔊 1.65 Listen. Write A for words with /ɪr/. Write B for words with /er/.
1 clear ___   3 chair ___   5 there ___   7 year ___
2 they're ___   4 earphones ___   6 parent ___   8 square ___

C 🔊 1.66 PAIR WORK Listen to the conversations. Then practice with a partner.
1 A Wh**ere**'s Bl**air** Street?
   B It's n**ear** h**ere**. Go to the town sq**uare** and then turn right.
2 A Wh**ere** are your p**ar**ents?
   B Th**ey**'re over th**ere**, on the ch**airs**.

4 SPEAKING

A PAIR WORK Put the conversation in order. Then practice it with a partner.
___ So, go straight. Then turn left. It's on the left.
___ Yes.
___ Excuse me. Where's the Park Hotel?
___ It's that way. Go straight. Then turn left. It's on the left.

B Work alone. Choose <u>one</u> of the situations below.
1 Imagine you are at the City Museum in Quito, Ecuador. Look at the map on the cell phone on page 58. Choose a place to go.
2 Imagine you are in another city. You can go online and find a map of the city. Choose where you are and a place to go.

FIND IT

C PAIR WORK Ask a partner for directions. You can use your phone to help you. Then change roles.

6.4 A FOREST IN THE CITY

LESSON OBJECTIVE
- write a fact sheet about a place in nature

1 LISTENING

A Look at the pictures. Where is the woman? What do you see?

B 🔊 1.67 **LISTEN FOR DETAILS** Listen to the podcast *Walk with Yasmin*. Where is the forest?

C 🔊 1.67 **LISTEN FOR EXAMPLES** Listen again. Check (✓) the words Yasmin says.

Forest
- ☐ animals
- ☐ grass
- ☐ an ocean
- ☐ a river
- ☐ flowers
- ☐ a mountain
- ☐ plants
- ☐ trees

City
- ☐ hospitals
- ☐ museums
- ☐ restaurants
- ☐ stores
- ☐ hotels
- ☐ people
- ☐ schools
- ☐ zoos

2 PRONUNCIATION: Listening for important words

A 🔊 1.68 Read the sentences below. Focus on the underlined words. Then listen. Which sentence do you hear, A or B?

A There <u>are</u> some tall trees <u>and</u> a lot <u>of</u> big plants here.

B There are some <u>tall trees</u> and a <u>lot</u> of <u>big plants</u> here.

B 🔊 1.69 <u>Underline</u> the important words in each sentence. Listen and check.

1. There's a river near me. (1 word)
2. There are a lot of interesting animals here. (3 words)
3. I'm on a mountain in a forest. (2 words)
4. There's an ocean and some beautiful beaches. (3 words)

3 WRITING

A Read the fact sheet. What is in Tijuca Forest?

FACT SHEET: Tijuca Forest

- Tijuca Forest is in Rio de Janeiro, Brazil.
- It is a nice, big forest. It is 39 square kilometers.
- There are a lot of plants and trees in the forest.
- It has nice rivers and waterfalls.
- It has a lot of interesting animals and birds.
- There are some mountains in the forest. One famous mountain is Corcovado Mountain.
- There is a tall statue on Corcovado Mountain. It is the Christ statue.
- Brazilians love the forest, and people from many countries visit it.
- Tijuca Forest is very important to Rio de Janeiro.

Capuchin monkey

Taunay Waterfall

Tropical flowers

Christ the Redeemer

B PAIR WORK | THINK CRITICALLY There are **no** contractions in the fact sheet (for example, *It's, There's*). Why not?

C Read the sentences from the fact sheet. Underline two opinion adjectives and one size adjective.

It has a lot of interesting animals and birds.

It is a nice, big forest.

REGISTER CHECK

Really and *very* make adjectives stronger. Use *very* in writing. *Really* is common in speaking.

Tijuca Forest is **very** important to Rio de Janeiro.

D WRITING SKILLS Read the rules below. (Circle) *before* or *after*. Use the sentences in exercise 3C to help you.

1 *Some*, *a lot of*, and *no* go **before** / **after** opinion adjectives (for example, *good, nice, interesting*).

2 Opinion adjectives usually go **before** / **after** size adjectives (for example, *big, small, tall*).

E Choose a natural area to write about. You can go online to find facts about where it is, how big it is, what nature is there, and who goes to it. Use *very*. Do **not** use contractions. Remember to write adjectives in the correct order.

F Write a fact sheet about a place in nature. Write five or six sentences. Use the fact sheet in exercise 3A for an example.

6.5 TIME TO SPEAK
A good place to live

LESSON OBJECTIVE
- plan a new neighborhood for a city

A PREPARE Talk to a partner. What do you see in the pictures?

B DISCUSS Which places in the pictures are important to have near your home? Write numbers 1–8 next to the pictures.

1 = very important ➔ 8 = not very important

C DISCUSS Imagine that city planners want ideas for a new neighborhood in your city. Work with a partner. Choose <u>one</u> person from the list below. What does your person want in the new neighborhood? Write notes.

- You have young children.
- You are over 60 and you don't work.
- You are a young person in your first apartment.
- You are a college student in a home-share.

D PRESENT Present your ideas for the new neighborhood to the class. Which things does everyone think are important in a city?

▶ To check your progress, go to page 153.

USEFUL PHRASES

DISCUSS
I have children. A school is really important.
What about … ?   Me, too.   I agree. / I disagree.
I think … is good for the neighborhood.
I want … for the neighborhood.

I like / don't like …
I think … are very important / not very important.

PRESENT
We want …
Everyone in the class likes …

REVIEW 2 (UNITS 4–6)

1 VOCABULARY

A Look at the groups of words in 1–6. In each group, circle the word that does not belong. Then match the groups with the categories (a–f).

1	grass	mountain	river	song	tree	___	a	technology
2	call friends	get up	hill	play soccer	work	___	b	music
3	album	band	camera	playlist	singer	___	c	places in cities
4	afternoon	hotel	Monday	morning	night	___	d	nature
5	app	laptop	morning	phone	tablet	___	e	things we do
6	café	hospital	restaurant	run	store	___	f	days and times of day

B Match each word you circled in 1–6 to a different category (a–f). Then add <u>one</u> extra word to the categories.

2 GRAMMAR

A Make questions and answers. Use the words in parentheses ( ) and *do/does/don't/doesn't*.

1. **A** _____ you _____ video games?
   B Yes, I sometimes _____ games on my cell phone. (play)
2. **A** Where _____ you _____ at lunchtime?
   B I usually _____ at home. (eat)
3. **A** _____ your grandfather _____ ?
   B Yes, he _____ at the hospital. (work)
4. **A** _____ you and your family _____ soccer?
   B No, we _____ it. (like)
5. **A** What _____ your parents _____ on TV?
   B Not a lot! They _____ usually _____ TV. (watch)
6. **A** _____ your children _____ phones?
   B My daughter has a cell phone, but my son _____ one. (have)

B **PAIR WORK** Ask and answer <u>five</u> questions about things you and your family do.

C Circle the correct answers.

I ¹*work / works* in a hotel. It's an expensive hotel with ²*a / some* really nice rooms. It's next to a big park. ³*There's / There are* a lot of trees, and ⁴*there's / there are* a lake, too. It's really nice in the park, so I ⁵*often / never* go at lunchtime, and I ⁶*have / has* lunch near the lake.

D Write a description of a nice place. Write how often you go there.

3 SPEAKING

A **PAIR WORK** Talk about a place. Describe it or say what you do there. Your partner guesses the place. Then change roles.

> There's a couch, and there are some chairs. I often watch TV in the evening.

> It's your living room.

B Write three sentences to describe a place from exercise 3A. Then compare with a partner.

4 FUNCTIONAL LANGUAGE

A Circle the correct answers.

Felix Your photos are great.
Maya Thanks. My phone has a good camera.
Felix ¹*See / So*, all the pictures are from the camera on your cell phone.
Maya Yes, that's ²*fine / right*. I always use my cell phone camera.
Felix ³*Hey. / Yeah*.
Maya ⁴*What / Where* about you?
Felix I always use my phone, too. I don't have a different camera.
Maya ⁵*Me, / My* neither. I don't want a different camera. They're really big …
Felix Yeah, I ⁶*know / do*. And they're expensive.
Maya ⁷*That's / There's* true.

B Complete the conversation with the words in the box. There are <u>two</u> extra words.

| turn | way | to | me | you | near |

A Excuse ¹_____. Where's the zoo?
B The zoo?
A Yes. Is it ²_____ here?
B Yes. It's that ³_____. Go one block, and then ⁴_____ left.

5 SPEAKING

A PAIR WORK Choose <u>one</u> of the conversations below. Ask and answer the questions with a partner.

1 What technology do you have? How often do you use it?

> I have a laptop, a phone, and a TV. I use my laptop every day. I send emails, and I …

2 What do you on weekdays? When do you do fun things?

> On weekdays, I go to work. I get up at 7:00 a.m., and then I …

3 What's a good place to go to in or near your city? Where is it?

> There's a new Chinese restaurant near here. It's really good.

> Yeah. Where is it?

B PAIR WORK Change roles and repeat the conversation.

GRAMMAR REFERENCE AND PRACTICE

1.1 *I AM*, *YOU ARE* (page 3)

I am (= I'm), you are (= you're)				
	Affirmative (+)	**Negative (-)**	**Question**	**Short answers**
I	I'm from Lima.	I'm not from Mexico City.	Am I in room 6B?	Yes, **you are.** / No, **you're not.**
You	You're from Paris.	You're not from Bogotá.	Are you from Tokyo?	Yes, **I am.** / No, **I'm not.**

A Match 1–6 to a–f to make sentences.

1 I'm   a not.   4 Are you   d am.
2 I'm from   b Mexican.   5 Yes, I   e Brazil?
3 No, I'm   c Honduras.   6 Are you from   f Chinese?

1.2 *WHAT'S ... ?*, *IT'S ...* (page 5)

What's ... ? (= What is)	**It's ... (= It is)**
What's your first name?	**It's** Juana.
What's the name of your college?	**It's** Garcia College.
What's your email address?	**It's** juanagarcia@bestmail.com.

> **!** Don't repeat the subject of the question:
> ~~The name of my company is~~
> It's Dallas Sales.

A Put the words in order to make sentences.

1 first / is / My / Ruby. / name
2 is / address / My / dfox@kmail.com. / email
3 Green College. / my college / of / The name / is
4 my company / Dallas Sales. / The name / is / of

2.1 *IS* / *ARE* IN STATEMENTS AND *YES/NO* QUESTIONS (page 13)

***is / are* in statements and *yes/no* questions**			
	Affirmative	**Question**	**Short answers**
He / She / It	**'s** ten. (*'s = is*)	**Is** he your husband? **Is** she your friend?	Yes, he **is.** / No, he**'s not.** Yes, she **is.** / No, she**'s not.**
You / We / They	**'re** cousins. (*'re = are*)	**Are** you brothers? **Are** they your children?	Yes, we **are.** / No, we**'re not.** Yes, they **are.** / No, they**'re not.**

A Write sentences and questions with *is* and *are*.

1 she / 22   *She's 22.*
2 they / your cousins   ?
3 he / 18   ?
4 my grandparents / Brazilian   .
5 we / in Room 5B   ?
6 no, you / not   .

129

2.2 IS NOT / ARE NOT (page 15)

is not (= 's not) / are not (= 're not)	
He / She / It	**'s not** in Rio de Janeiro.
You / We / They	**'re not** shy.

isn't (= is not) / aren't (= are not)		
Jack	**isn't**	boring.
The students	**aren't**	in the class room.

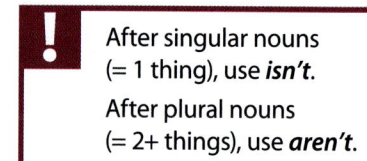

After singular nouns (= 1 thing), use **isn't**.
After plural nouns (= 2+ things), use **aren't**.

A Circle the correct words to complete the sentences.

1. Jan *is / isn't* from New York City. He's from Miami.
2. *She's / She's not* 18. She's not 20.
3. Daniel is in Moscow. *He's / He's not* in St. Petersburg.
4. You're not shy. *You're / You're not* really friendly!
5. My cousins are in Japan. *They're / They're not* in the U.S.
6. *We're / We're not* sisters. We're friends.

3.1 POSSESSIVE ADJECTIVES; POSSESSIVE 'S AND S' (page 23)

Possessive adjectives	
I → **my**	This is **my** apartment.
he → **his**	**His** name is Sergei.
she → **her**	It's **her** favorite picture.w
it → **its**	Nice cat! What's **its** name?
you → **your**	Is this **your** room?
we → **our**	**Our** home is in La Paz.
they → **their**	Rita is **their** daughter.

Possessive 's and s'
Add possessive **'s** to a singular noun. (= 1 thing)
This is Sergei**'s** room.
My mother**'s** name is Kate.
Add possessive **'** after the *s* of a plural noun. (= 2+ things)
This is his parents**'** house.
My cousins**'** house is in Rio.

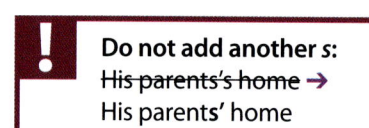

Do not add another *s*:
His parents's home →
His parents**'** home

A Circle the correct words to complete the sentences.

1. *My / I* email address is sky121@bestmail.com.
2. My *friends / friend's* name is Ramona.
3. This is *his / he's* hotel room.
4. Excuse me. What's *you / your* name?
5. This is my *parents's / parents'* new car.
6. David is *our / we* son.
7. The name of *Ann's / Anns'* company is Mason Sales.
8. What's *they're / their* telephone number?

3.2 IT IS (page 25)

> ❗ *It* is a pronoun. *It* is always singular. Use *it* for things. For example, *the house = it*.
> Use *isn't* after nouns. Use *'s not* after pronouns.

It is in statements and yes/no questions

	Affirmative	Negative	Question	Short answers
The house	**is** small.	**isn't** small. (*isn't = is not*)	**Is it** small?	Yes, **it is**.
It's (= *it is*)	small.	**not** small.		No, **it's not**.

A Answer the questions so they're true for you. Write statements. Use *It's* and *It's not* to give more information.

1. Is your home an apartment? — My home isn't an apartment. It's a house.
2. Is your bedroom cool?
3. Is your kitchen big?
4. Is your parents' house old?
5. Is your friend's TV new?
6. Is your refrigerator tall?

3.4 INFORMATION QUESTIONS WITH BE (page 28)

Question word		be	
What		is	your name?
Where		is	the house?
How old		are	they?
Who		are	they?
How many	people	are	in the house?
How many	rooms	are	in it?

> ❗ Information questions ask for information about, for example, people, places, age, time, and quantity. Don't answer information questions with *yes/no* answers.
> Use *is* to talk about 1 thing. Use *are* to talk about 2+ things. Use a noun after *How many …?*

A Put the words in the correct order to make questions.

1. is / Who / brother? / your — Who is your brother?
2. you? / How / are / old
3. her / is / college? / Where
4. email / is / What / address? / your
5. many / are / people / How / the house? / in
6. apartment? / is / his / Where

4.1 SIMPLE PRESENT STATEMENTS WITH I, YOU, WE (page 35)

Simple present statements with *I, you, we*

	Affirmative	Negative
I / You / We	**have** a smartwatch.	**don't have** a smartwatch.
	like my phone.	**don't like** my phone.
	love games.	**don't love** games.
	want a tablet.	**don't want** a tablet.

A Put the words in order to make sentences.
1. games. / like / I
2. your / I / smartwatch. / love
3. don't / I / a / laptop. / have
4. a / tablet. / want / We
5. like / don't / laptops. / You
6. camera. / want / I / don't / a

4.2 SIMPLE PRESENT YES/NO QUESTIONS WITH I, YOU, WE (page 37)

Simple present yes/no questions with *I, you, we*	
yes/no questions	Short answers
Do I **send** nice emails?	Yes, you **do.** / No, you **don't.**
Do we **post** good photos?	Yes, you **do.** / No, you **don't.**
Do you **use** social media?	Yes, I **do.** / No, I **don't.**
Do you **and your friends play** games?	Yes, we **do.** / No, we **don't.**

A Write questions. Then answer the questions so they're true for you.
1. you / call your family / on the weekends — *Do you call your family on the weekends* ? *Yes, I do* .
2. you / post comments / on Twitter ? .
3. you / send text messages / to your parents ? .
4. you and your friends / watch movies / on TV ? .

4.4 A/AN; ADJECTIVES BEFORE NOUNS (page 40)

a/an	adjectives before nouns

Use *a/an* with singular nouns. It means "one."
     Do you have **a** laptop? (= 1 laptop)
     This is **an** app for photos. (= 1 app)
 Use *a* before consonant sounds (for example, b, c, d, f, …): **a** tablet, **a** cookie
 Use *an* before vowel sounds (a, e, i, o, u): **an** app, **an** apartment
	Adjectives go before a noun:
	 You have a **nice** home. ✓
	 You have a ~~home nice~~. ✗
	 It's an **expensive** laptop. This is a **new** apartment.
	 I post **interesting** photos.
	 The ending of an adjective is the same for singular and plural nouns. Do <u>not</u> add *s* to an adjective.
	 I like **small** TVs. ✓
	 I like ~~smalls~~ TVs. ✗

Don't use *a/an* with:	
1 plural nouns: I like **photos**. 2 *this* + noun: **This tablet** is nice.	3 numbers + noun: I have **one son** and **two daughters**. 4 possessive adjectives + noun: **My phone** is really old.

A (Circle) the correct words to complete the sentences.
1. Do you have *a camera / an camera*?
2. We don't want *a new TV / new a TV*.
3. *Your an apartment / Your apartment* is very nice.
4. I want coffee and *a cookie / a one cookie*.
5. *A game / This game* is really boring.
6. We have *a children / three children*.
7. I don't like *computers / computer*.
8. Do you live in *a apartment / an apartment*?

5.1 SIMPLE PRESENT STATEMENTS WITH *HE, SHE, THEY* (page 45)

Simple present statements with *he, she, they*		
	Affirmative	Negative
He / She	**plays** basketball. **goes out** every evening. **watches** TV a lot. **studies** on the weekend. **has** a big house.	**doesn't play** basketball. **doesn't go out** every evening. **doesn't watch** TV a lot. **doesn't study** on weekends. **doesn't have** a big house.
They	**play** soccer. **have** a big house.	**don't play** soccer. **don't have** a big house.

! Use *in* to talk about times of day: *I run in the morning.*
Use *on* to talk about days: *I play soccer on Saturdays.*

! Use adverbs of frequency say *how often* you do things.
100%   always   usually   often   sometimes   hardly ever   never   0%
Put adverbs of frequency <u>before</u> the verb: *She **sometimes** works on Saturday.*
With pronouns + *be*, adverbs of frequency go <u>after</u> the verb: *I'm **usually** at home in the evening.*

A (Circle) the correct words to complete the sentences.
1 My sister often *watch / watches* basketball on TV.
2 I don't like coffee, so I *usually / never* drink it.
3 My laptop is old and slow. I *always / hardly ever* use it.
4 My grandma *don't / doesn't* have a cell phone. She *always / hardly ever* calls me from home.
5 My friends are usually at work on Saturday and Sunday. They *have / don't have* free time on the weekend.

5.2 QUESTIONS IN THE SIMPLE PRESENT (page 47)

Simple present: *yes/no* questions				Short answers
Yes/no questions				
Do	I/we	**work** on the weekend?		Yes, I **do**. / No, we **don't**.
Do	you	**eat** breakfast?		Yes, I **do**. / No, I **don't**.
Does	she/he	**study** in the evening?		Yes, she **does**. / No, he **doesn't**.
Does	it	**have** two bedrooms?		Yes, it **does**. / No, it **doesn't**.
Do	they	**go** to class on Monday?		Yes, they **do**. / No, they **don't**.

Simple present: information questions				
I / You / We / They	Where	do	I / we	**go** every day?
	What time	do	you	**get up**?
	What	do	they	**do** on Saturday?
He / She / It	Where	does	he	**live**?
	When	does	she	**meet** her friends?
	What time	does	it	**open**?

! *What time ... ?* and *When ... ?*
A *What time is it?*
B *It's 1.30.*
A *When does he study?*
B *He studies in the evening.*

A Put the words in the correct order to make questions.
1 lunch? / eat / does / he / Where
2 to / she / go / Does / this school?
3 their / do / meet / friends? / When / they
4 do / work? / you / What / go / to / time
5 soccer / your friends / after work? / play / Do

133

6.1 THERE'S, THERE ARE; A LOT OF, SOME, NO (page 55)

There's (= there is), there are; a lot, some, no

Singular (= 1 thing)		Plural (= 2+ things)	
		There are **no** stores on our street.	= zero
There's **a** restaurant near the hotel.	= one	There are **three** bedrooms in the house.	= an exact number
There's **no** shower in the bathroom.	= zero	There are **some** chairs in the kitchen.	= a small number
		There are **a lot of** apps on my phone.	= a big number

A Look at the words in parentheses ( ). Then complete the sentences with the words in the box.

> There's a   There's no   There are no   There are a lot of   There are some

1. _____ parks in the city. (zero)
2. _____ people in the café. (a big number)
3. _____ great stores on Pacific Street. (a small number)
4. _____ park next to the hospital. (one)
5. _____ restaurant in this museum. (zero)

6.2 COUNT AND NON-COUNT NOUNS (page 57)

Count nouns (nouns with a singular and plural form)

Singular	Plural
Use *There is* with *a* or *an*.	Use *There are* with *no*, *some*, *a lot of*, or a number.
There's **a plant**.	There are **no plants**. There are **some plants**.
	There are **a lot of plants**. There are **two plants**.

Non-count nouns (nouns with no singular or plural form)

Use *There is* with *no*, *some*, or *a lot of*. Do <u>not</u> use *a*, *an*, or a number.
There's **no grass**.   There's **some grass**.   There's **a lot of grass**.   ~~There's three grass.~~

A Write sentences with *There's* or *There are*. Make some nouns plural.

1. no / milk / in the refrigerator — *There's no milk in the refrigerator.*
2. a lot of / plant / in my house
3. a / restaurant / in the museum
4. some / sugar / on the table
5. some / small hotel / near here

VOCABULARY PRACTICE

1.1 COUNTRIES AND NATIONALITIES (page 2)

A Write the country or the nationality.

1. Are you _Russian_ ? (Russia)
2. I'm from _____. (Mexican)
3. I'm _____. (Ecuador)
4. You're from _____. (Chilean)
5. Are you _____? (Japan)
6. Are you from _____? (Brazilian)
7. I'm not _____. (South Korea)
8. I'm from Madrid. I'm _____. (Spain)

B Underline two correct answers for each sentence.

1. Are you from <u>Russia</u> / Chilean / <u>South Korea</u>?
2. I'm from American / Mexico / Japan.
3. You're not French / Peru / Colombian.
4. Are you from New York / Chicago / American?
5. I'm not Mexico / Brazilian / Chinese.
6. You are Peruvian / French / Chile.
7. Are you Peruvian / Japan / South Korean?
8. I'm from Ecuadorian / Lima / Germany.

1.2 THE ALPHABET; PERSONAL INFORMATION (page 5)

A Add <u>five</u> missing letters to the alphabet, in order.

1. A B C ^D/ E F G H I J L M O P Q R T U V W X Z
2. a c d e g h j k l m n o q r s t v w x y z

B Complete the sentences with the words in the box.

| College   company   email address   first name   last name |

1. The name of my _____ is Home Sales, Inc.
2. A What's your _____? B It's jenatkins@abc.net.
3. A Hey, Ana. What's your _____? B It's Gomez. Ana Gomez.
4. I'm a student at Hunter _____ in New York City.
5. A Hi, Susie Ball. How do you spell your _____? B S-U-S-I-E.

2.1 FAMILY; NUMBERS (page 13)

A Write the words in the chart.

| ~~aunt~~   child   daughter   grandfather   husband   parent   son   wife |
| brother   cousin   father   grandmother   mother   sister   uncle |

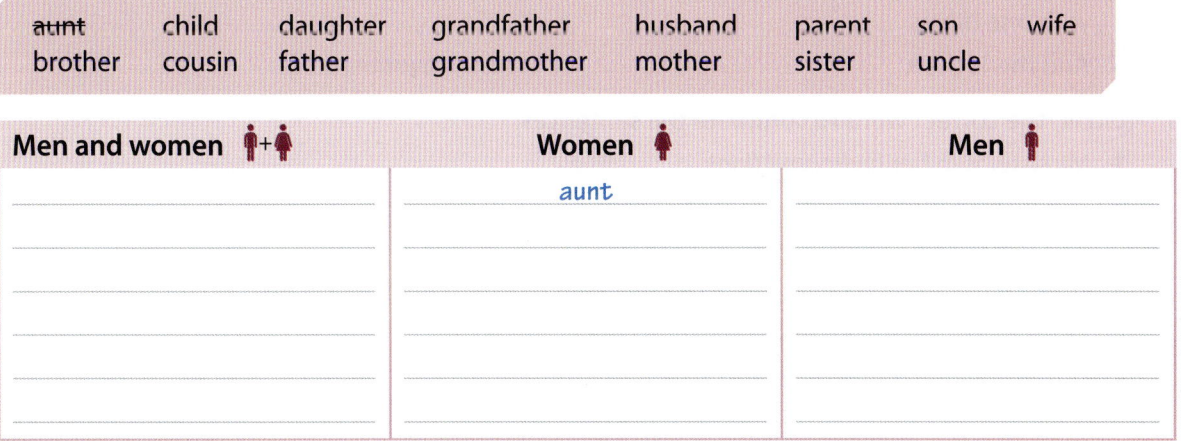

B Write the numbers.
1 twenty-two   22
2 fifty-one   ___
3 thirty-nine   ___
4 eighty-three   ___
5 forty-six   ___
6 sixty-seven   ___
7 thirty-eight   ___
8 seventy-four   ___
9 ninety-five   ___
10 twenty-six   ___

2.2 DESCRIBING PEOPLE; REALLY / VERY (page 14)

A Complete the sentences with the words in the box. You won't use all the words.

| friendly | interesting | old | really | short |
| shy | smart | boring | tall | young |

1 Carrie is two. She's really _____.
2 He's a college student. He's _____.
3 My father is 190 cm. He's very _____.
4 He's not interesting. He's _____.
5 My friend Georgio is _____ funny!
6 Ariana is 95. She's very _____.

B Unscramble the letters in parentheses ( ). Write the adjectives.
1 Susana is ___interesting___ and really _____.   (nteisreignt) / (tlal)
2 My son is _____ and _____.   (mtras) / (ynufn)
3 My grandfather is _____ and _____.   (dlo) / (rosth)
4 The child is very _____ and _____.   (ynugo) / (ysh)
5 They're _____ and not _____.   (fienrdyl) / (bgrion)

3.1 ROOMS IN A HOME (page 22)

A Read the sentences and complete the words.
1 This is our d_____ a_____,
   with a p_____ on the w_____.
2 This is my sister's b_____. It's next to the b_____.
3 This is our dog, Jack. He's on the f_____.
4 This is the d_____ of our house.
5 This is the l_____ r_____,
   with one big w_____.
6 And this is the k_____. It's my favorite room.

B (Circle) the correct word to complete the sentences.
1 My sister is in her *bedroom* / *floor*.
2 This is the bathroom, with one *wall* / *window*.
3 This is the *dining area* / *door* to the kitchen.
4 My family is in the *living room* / *bathroom* now.
5 The *picture* / *kitchen* on the wall is interesting.
6 Our cats are on the *door* / *floor*.

3.2 FURNITURE (page 24)

A Match the words to the things in the picture.

| chair | ~~couch~~ | refrigerator | rug | sink | table | television |

1 _couch_   2 _____   3 _____   4 _____

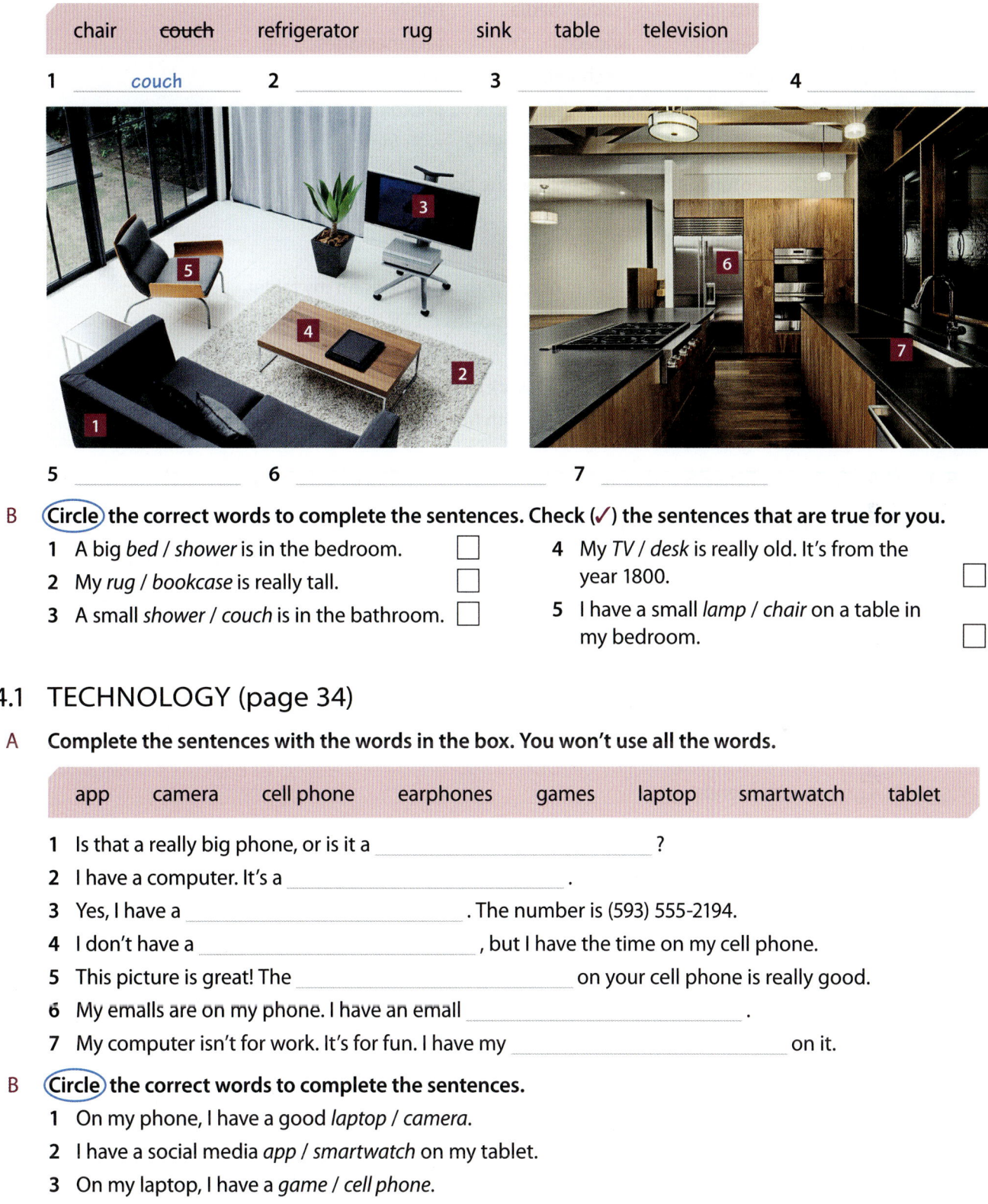

5 _____   6 _____   7 _____

B Circle the correct words to complete the sentences. Check (✓) the sentences that are true for you.
1 A big *bed / shower* is in the bedroom. ☐
2 My *rug / bookcase* is really tall. ☐
3 A small *shower / couch* is in the bathroom. ☐
4 My *TV / desk* is really old. It's from the year 1800. ☐
5 I have a small *lamp / chair* on a table in my bedroom. ☐

4.1 TECHNOLOGY (page 34)

A Complete the sentences with the words in the box. You won't use all the words.

| app | camera | cell phone | earphones | games | laptop | smartwatch | tablet |

1 Is that a really big phone, or is it a _____?
2 I have a computer. It's a _____.
3 Yes, I have a _____. The number is (593) 555-2194.
4 I don't have a _____, but I have the time on my cell phone.
5 This picture is great! The _____ on your cell phone is really good.
6 My emails are on my phone. I have an email _____.
7 My computer isn't for work. It's for fun. I have my _____ on it.

B Circle the correct words to complete the sentences.
1 On my phone, I have a good *laptop / camera*.
2 I have a social media *app / smartwatch* on my tablet.
3 On my laptop, I have a *game / cell phone*.

4.2 USING TECHNOLOGY (page 36)

A Cross out the word that doesn't belong with each verb.

1	call	friends	social media	family
2	watch	movies	videos	text messages
3	use	music	technology	apps
4	post	cell phone	comments	photos
5	send	text messages	email	with friends

B Complete the sentences with the words in the box.

> chat   listen   play   read   watch

1 I _____ to music with earphones on my tablet.
2 We don't _____ movies on TV.
3 My brother and I _____ games on our tablets.
4 I don't _____ work emails at home.
5 Do you _____ with friends on the internet?

5.1 DAYS AND TIMES OF DAY; EVERYDAY ACTIVITIES (page 44)

A Read the days and times of day (a–j). Then put them in the correct order (1–10).

a on Thursday, in the morning   ___
b on Tuesday, in the afternoon   ___
c on Thursday, in the evening   ___
d on Monday, at night   1
e on Sunday, in the morning   ___
f on Saturday, in the evening   ___
g on Wednesday, in the morning   ___
h on Friday, in the afternoon   ___
i on Tuesday, in the evening   ___
j on Saturday, in the afternoon   ___

B Use phrases from exercise A to complete the sentences so they're true for you. Write an X if you never do the activity.

1 I go out with friends _____.
2 I watch TV _____.
3 I study _____.
4 I run _____.
5 I play soccer _____.
6 I read _____.
7 I work _____.
8 I'm in bed _____.

5.2 TELLING THE TIME (page 46)

A Look at the times (1–8). Then circle the correct sentence.

1. 3:40   a It's twenty to four.   b It's forty to three.
2. 12:30   a It's twenty thirty.   b It's twelve thirty.
3. 6:15   a It's a quarter after six.   b It's a quarter to six.
4. 12:00 a.m.   a It's midnight.   b It's noon.
5. 1:45   a It's a quarter to one.   b It's one forty-five.
6. 8:07   a It's seven to eight.   b It's eight-oh-seven.
7. 9:15   a It's nine fifteen.   b It's nine fifty.
8. 4:52   a It's five forty-two.   b It's four fifty-two.

B <u>Underline</u> the correct words to complete the paragraph.

Carmen *gets up / goes to* bed at 7:15 a.m. She eats *lunch / breakfast* at 7:45. Then she *goes to work / gets up*. She usually has *dinner / lunch* at 12:30 p.m. She drinks *coffee / class* in the afternoon. On Tuesday, she goes to *class / lunch* after work – she studies English. She usually eats *dinner / coffee* at 7:00. She goes to *bed / class* at 11 p.m.

6.1 PLACES IN CITIES (page 54)

A Complete the sentences with the words in the box.

> café   college   hotel   museum   park   school   mall   zoo

1. We often eat breakfast in a _____.
2. I sometimes run in the _____.
3. The _____ has hundreds of old pictures and a lot of art.
4. The _____ in my neighborhood has 160 children.
5. The students at the _____ are 18 to 22 years old.
6. This is a great _____. It has a lot of my favorite stores.
7. The rooms in the _____ have bathrooms with showers.
8. The _____ in my city has 20 elephants.

B Cross out <u>one</u> word that does not complete each sentence.

1. We have lunch in a _____ on Saturdays.   restaurant   store   park
2. We learn about things at a _____.   school   restaurant   museum
3. We shop at the _____ every weekend.   mall   hospital   supermarket
4. The _____ has a big TV.   park   hotel   restaurant
5. She studies English in _____.   school   college   a movie theater

6.2 NATURE (page 56)

A Complete the email with the words in the box.

> flowers   lake   mountain   snow   trees

Hi Julia,

How are you? I'm great! My new town is *really* cool. I like nature, and there's a lot of nature here! There's a big, tall ¹_____ near my house. There's a forest on the mountain, with a lot of ²_____. There's ³_____ on top of the mountain in January and February. There's a small ⁴_____ in my neighborhood, and I run next to the water in the morning. There are no ⁵_____ now because it's January.

I love this town. Please visit soon!

Your friend,

Marisa

B Circle the correct word to complete the sentences.

1. My house is on the *beach / forest* next to the ocean.
2. There is a lot of *ocean / grass* in the park.
3. There are a lot of plants and flowers in the *forest / lake*.
4. There's a lot of water in the *river / desert*.
5. My grandma and grandpa live near the *ocean / flowers*.
6. A lot of animals eat *plants / mountains*.
7. Donna lives on a small *island / desert* in the Atlantic Ocean.
8. There are a lot of small *grass / hills* here, but there are no mountains.

This page is intentionally left blank

PROGRESS CHECK

Can you do these things? Check (✓) what you can do. Then write your answers in your notebook.

UNIT 1

Now I can …	Prove it
☐ say countries and nationalities.	Write your country and your nationality.
☐ use *I am*.	Write two sentences about you. Use *I'm* and *I'm from*.
☐ use the alphabet to spell words.	Spell your first name and your last name. Spell your email address.
☐ ask and answer questions with *What's … ?* and *It's …* .	Write a question and answer about personal information. Use *What's* and *It's*.
☐ check into a hotel.	Write two questions you hear at a hotel. Write answers to the questions.
☐ write a profile.	Read your profile from lesson 1.4. Find a way to improve it. Use the Accuracy check, Register check, and the new language from this unit.

UNIT 2

Now I can …	Prove it
☐ say family names and numbers.	Write the names and ages of four members of your family. Write the numbers in words.
☐ use *is* and *are*.	Write four sentences with *is* and *are*. Write about you or your family and friends.
☐ use adjectives to describe people.	Complete the sentences with adjectives. *My parents are … My best friend is …*
☐ use *is not* and *are not*.	Make the three sentences negative. *She's tall. We're from Seoul. They're funny.*
☐ talk about ages and birthdays.	When's your birthday? How old is your best friend? Write answers in full sentences.
☐ write a post about friends in a photo.	Read your post about friends from lesson 2.4. Find a way to improve it. Use the Accuracy check, Register check, and the new language from this unit.

UNIT 3

Now I can …	Prove it
☐ talk about rooms in my home.	Write five rooms and five things in rooms.
☐ use possessive adjectives, *'s* and *s'*.	Change the words in parentheses ( ) to possessives. *This is my (brother) bedroom. (He) bedroom is between (I) bedroom and (we) (parents) bedroom.*
☐ talk about furniture.	Write five or more words for furniture.
☐ use *it is*.	Complete the questions. Then answer with your own information. _____ your home big? _____ near your school?
☐ offer and accept a drink and snack.	Someone says, "Coffee?" Write two different answers.
☐ write an email about a home-share.	Read your email from lesson 3.4. Find a way to improve it. Use the Accuracy check, Register check, and the new language from this unit.

PROGRESS CHECK

Can you do these things? Check (✓) what you can do. Then write your answers in your notebook.

Now I can …	Prove it	UNIT 4
☐ talk about my favorite things.	Write about five things you like, love, or want.	
☐ use the simple present.	Write about a thing you have and a thing you don't have.	
☐ say how you use technology.	Write about three ways you use your phone.	
☐ use *yes/no* questions in the simple present.	Complete the questions. Then write the answers with your own information. _____ you use apps on your phone? _____ you and your parents chat online?	
☐ ask questions to develop a conversation.	Complete the conversation. A _____ social media? B Yes, I do. _____ ?	
☐ write product reviews.	Read your product reviews from lesson 4.4. Find a way to improve them. Use the Accuracy check, Register check, and the new language from this unit.	

Now I can …	Prove it	UNIT 5
☐ use days and times of days with everyday activities.	Write two things you do on weekdays in the morning. Write two things you do on Saturday.	
☐ use the simple present and adverbs of frequency.	Complete the sentences. Write about your friends. _____ *always* _____ *on the weekend*. _____ *and* _____ *never* _____ *in the evening*.	
☐ tell the time and talk about routines.	What time is it now? When do you get up on weekdays? What time do you usually have dinner? Write answers in full sentences.	
☐ ask *yes/no* and information questions in the simple present.	Complete the questions with *do* or *does*. Then write your answers. *What time* _____ *you get up on Saturday? Where* _____ *you and your friends eat lunch on Monday?* _____ *your teacher have lunch at school?*	
☐ show you agree or have things in common.	Read the statements. Write responses that are true for you. *Soccer is fun.* *I never run.*	
☐ write a report.	Read your WRAP report from lesson 5.4. Find a way to improve it. Use the Accuracy check, Register check, and the new language from this unit.	

Now I can …	Prove it	UNIT 6
☐ use words for places in a city.	Write about six places in a city.	
☐ use *there's / there are* with *a/an, some, a lot of, no*.	Write four true sentences for your city. Use the sentences below. *There are* _____ *in my city. / There's* _____ *in my neighborhood*.	
☐ use words for places in nature.	Write about six places in nature.	
☐ use count and non-count nouns.	Write about the plants, trees, and grass in your neighborhood.	
☐ ask for and give simple directions.	Write one way to ask for directions and one way to give directions.	
☐ write a fact sheet.	Read your fact sheet from lesson 6.4. Find a way to improve it. Use the Accuracy check, Register check, and the new language from this unit.	

PAIR WORK PRACTICE (STUDENT A)

1.3 EXERCISE 5C   STUDENT A

1   You are Sandra, the visitor. Give your information to your partner.
2   You are the hotel clerk. Ask for your partner's information. Complete the hotel card.

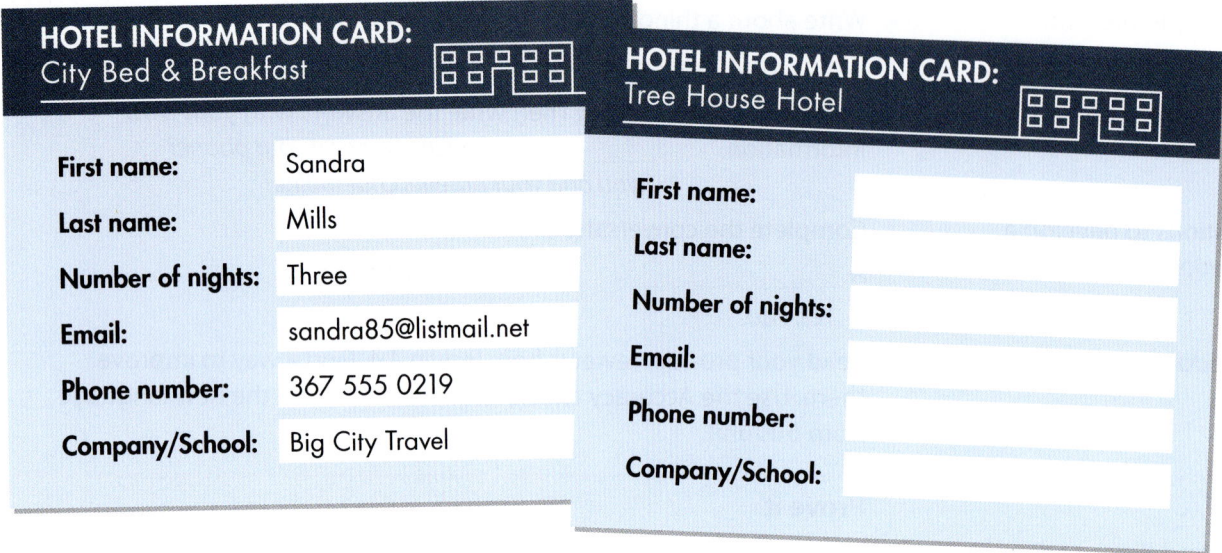

HOTEL INFORMATION CARD: City Bed & Breakfast

First name:	Sandra
Last name:	Mills
Number of nights:	Three
Email:	sandra85@listmail.net
Phone number:	367 555 0219
Company/School:	Big City Travel

HOTEL INFORMATION CARD: Tree House Hotel

First name:	
Last name:	
Number of nights:	
Email:	
Phone number:	
Company/School:	

2.3 EXERCISE 3D   STUDENT A

1   Say a person from the table. Say the incorrect birthday. Then correct yourself.

> Anna. Her birthday is August 15. No, sorry, August **13**.

Person	Anna	Martin	Paulo	Rosa	Jacob
Incorrect birthday	August 15	December 2	June 5	October 21	April 12
Correct birthday	August **13**	December **3**	**July** 5	October **31**	April **20**

2   Listen to your partner. Write the correct birthday. Circle the correction (the number or the month).

Person	Gloria	Larry	Helena	Susan	Bruno
Incorrect birthday	September 13	November 6	May 9	February 30	January 25
Correct birthday					

4.3 EXERCISE 2D   STUDENT A

1   Follow the flow chart. Use the topics in the box or your own ideas. Talk about two or three topics.

> laptops   music videos
> social media   video chat

2   Follow the flow chart. Talk about the topics your partner chooses.

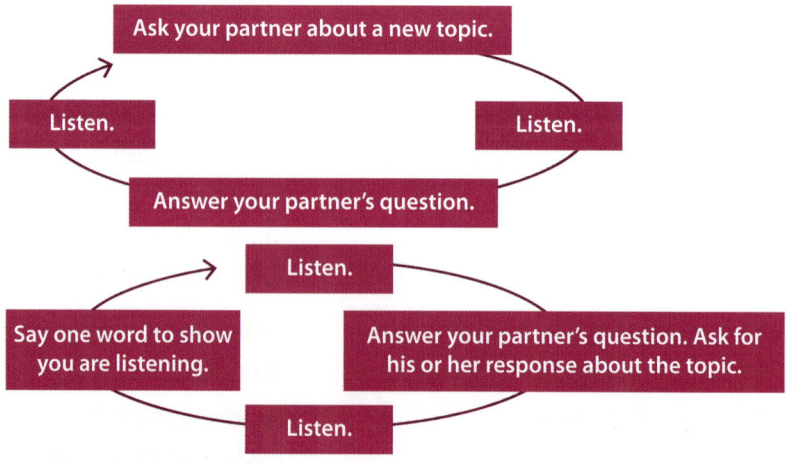

5.3 EXERCISE 2D   STUDENT A

1 **Choose <u>one</u> of the jobs in the box. <u>Don't</u> tell your partner. Then complete the sentences about the job with** *always, usually, often, sometimes, hardly ever,* **or** *never*.

| doctor | hotel clerk | server | student |

1 I _____ get up early.
2 I _____ eat at home.
3 I _____ have free time.
4 I _____ work with friends.
5 I _____ read books.
6 I _____ send emails for work.
7 I _____ go to bed late.
8 I _____ work on the weekend.

2 **Your partner is a teacher, salesperson, chef, or artist. Ask questions and guess the job.**

3 **Your partner asks you questions. Answer with <u>one or two</u> words. Your partner guesses your job.**

6.3 EXERCISE 2D   STUDENT A

Give the directions below to Student B. Student B repeats and you listen. Is it correct?

1 Turn left here. Then go straight. It's on the left.
2 It's over there. Go two blocks. Turn right. Then turn right again.
3 Turn left here. Then turn left again. It's on the right.

PAIR WORK PRACTICE (STUDENT B)

1.3 EXERCISE 5C   STUDENT B

1. You are the hotel clerk. Ask for your partner's information. Complete the hotel card.
2. You are Tom, the visitor. Give your information to your partner.

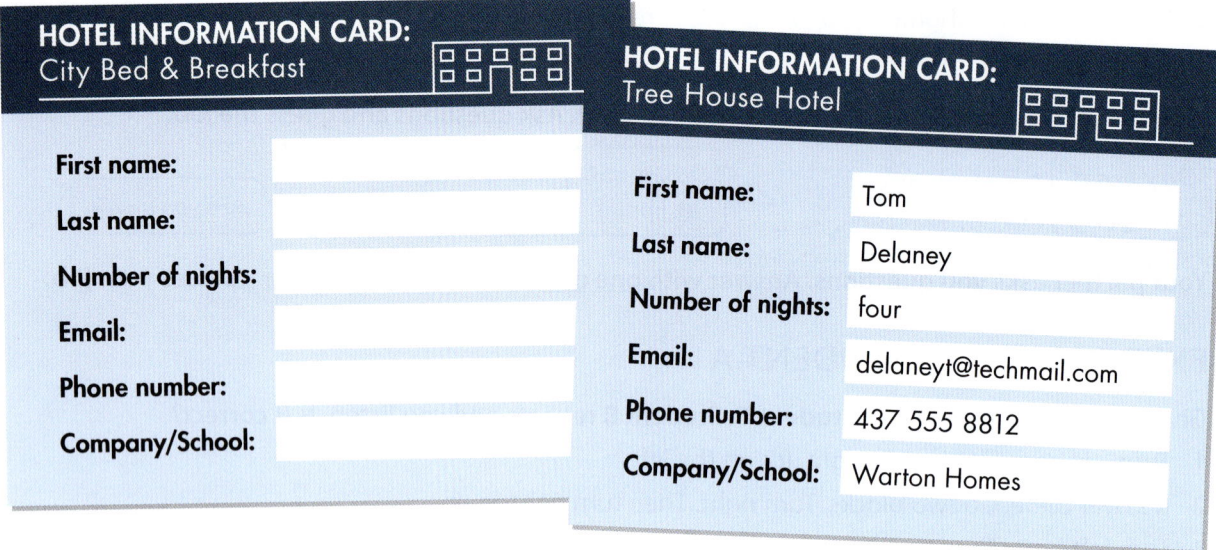

HOTEL INFORMATION CARD: City Bed & Breakfast

- First name:
- Last name:
- Number of nights:
- Email:
- Phone number:
- Company/School:

HOTEL INFORMATION CARD: Tree House Hotel

- First name: Tom
- Last name: Delaney
- Number of nights: four
- Email: delaneyt@techmail.com
- Phone number: 437 555 8812
- Company/School: Warton Homes

2.3 EXERCISE 3D   STUDENT B

1. Listen to your partner say the incorrect birthdays, and then the correct birthdays. Write the correct birthday. <u>Underline</u> the correction (the number or the month).

Person	Anna	Martin	Paulo	Rosa	Jacob
Incorrect birthday	August 15	December 2	June 5	October 21	April 12
Correct birthday					

2. Say a person from the table. Say the incorrect birthday. Then correct yourself.

> Gloria. Her birthday is September 13. No, sorry, September 30.

Person	Gloria	Larry	Helena	Susan	Bruno
Incorrect birthday	September 13	November 6	May 9	February 30	January 25
Correct birthday	September <u>30</u>	November <u>16</u>	<u>March</u> 9	February <u>20</u>	January 2<u>4</u>

4.3 EXERCISE 2D   STUDENT B

1 Follow the flow chart. Talk about the topics your partner chooses.

2 Follow the flow chart. Use the topics in the box or your own ideas. Talk about two or three topics.

> laptops   music videos
> social media   video chat

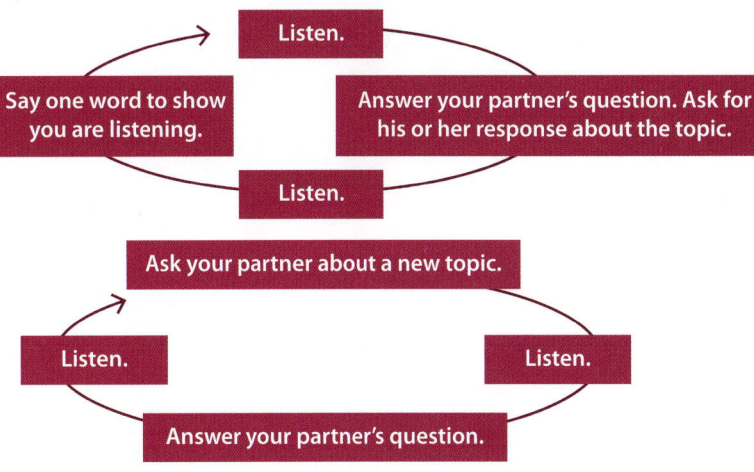

5.3 EXERCISE 2D   STUDENT B

1 Choose <u>one</u> of the jobs in the box. <u>Don't</u> tell your partner. Then complete the sentences about the job with *always*, *usually*, *often*, *sometimes*, *hardly ever*, or *never*.

> artist   chef   salesperson   teacher

1 I _____ get up early.
2 I _____ eat at home.
3 I _____ have free time.
4 I _____ work with friends.
5 I _____ read books.
6 I _____ send emails for work.
7 I _____ go to bed late.
8 I _____ work on the weekend.

2 Your partner asks you questions. Answer with <u>one or two</u> words. Your partner guesses your job.

3 Your partner is a student, doctor, server, or hotel clerk. Ask questions and guess the job.

6.3 EXERCISE 2D   STUDENT B

Give the directions below to Student A. Student A repeats and you listen. Is it correct?

1 Turn left. Go straight. That's San Gabriel Street.
2 Go straight. Then turn right. It's on the right.
3 Turn right here. Turn right again. Then turn left. It's on the right.

This page is intentionally left blank

This page is intentionally left blank

This page is intentionally left blank

This page is intentionally left blank

This page is intentionally left blank

This page is intentionally left blank

This page is intentionally left blank

VAULT DWELLERS

Designer
James Sheahan

'Parzival and the Wasteland Knights'
Jim Johnson

Additional Material
James Barry, Richard L. Gale, Jim Johnson, Ryan Schoon, Federico Sohns, Jon Webb, and Sam Webb

Line Development
James Barry and Sam Webb

Editing
Mike Brunton

Proof Reading
Virginia Page, Federico Sohns, Charlie Perkins, Richard L. Gale, and James Barry

Art Direction
Chris Birch and Jon Webb

Photography and Video
Salwa Azar and Steve Daldry

Photo Retouching
Rocío Martín Pérez

Graphic Design
Michal E. Cross and Stephanie Toro

Layout
Richard L. Gale

Sculpt Art Direction
James Barry and Jon Webb

Head of 3D Art
Jonny La Trobe-Lewis

Staff 3D Artists
Chris "Chrispy" Peacey, Domingo Díaz Fermín, and Alex Gargett

Freelance 3D Artists
Roy Gabriel, M. Mar García, Gael Goumon, Tobias Kornemann, Jamie Phipps, Ana Román Peña, Romeo Salbatecu, Luigi Terzi, and Ben Wolseley-Charles

Painters
Lewis Collins, Adam Huenecke, Jon Webb

Scenery
Dreamspirit Studio, Matt Sonnati

Development Team
Javier Angeriz-Caburrasi, James Barry, Stefano Guerriero, Virginia Page, James Sheahan, Katya Thomas, Jon Webb, and Sam Webb

Playtesters
Adam Brown, Costin Becheanu, Troels Rohde Hansen, Ian Henderson, Clive Oldfield, Christoph Krumm, Project Pipewrench

Publisher
Chris Birch

Executive Assistant and Social Media Manager
Salwa Azar

Production Management
Steve Daldry and Peter Grochulski

Community Support
Lloyd Gyan and Shaun Hocking

Sales Manager
Rhys Knight

Sales and Retailer Manager
Cole Leadon

Thanks to
Mike Kockis and his design team, all at Bethesda, Rita Birch and the operations team, Jason Enos and the Wargames team, Matt Timm and the RPG Team, Gavin Dady and Rob Harris

MODIPHIUS™ ENTERTAINMENT

Modiphius Entertainment, 39 Harwood Road, London, SW6 4QP, United Kingdom

© 2019 Bethesda Softworks LLC. FALLOUT and related logos are trademarks or registered trademarks of ZeniMax Media Inc. or its affiliates in the U.S. and/or other countries. All Rights Reserved. The Modiphius Entertainment logo is TM of Modiphius Entertainment. All rights reserved to their respective owners.

Any unauthorised use of copyrighted material is illegal. Any trademarked names are used in a fictional manner; no infringement is intended. This is a work of fiction. Any similarity with actual people and events, past or present, is purely coincidental and unintentional except for those people and events described in an historical context.

Modiphius Entertainment Product Number: MUH051778
ISBN: 978-1-912743-27-8
Printed by Standartų Spaustuvė, UAB, Vilnius, Lithuania.

Fallout: Wasteland Warfare
Roleplaying Game

CONTENTS

SECTION 1 – INTRODUCTION
1.1	What is a Roleplaying Game?	2

SECTION 2 – THE WORLD OF THE WASTELAND
2.1	The Wasteland	4
2.2	Survivors	7
2.3	The Brotherhood of Steel	9
2.4	Raiders	11
2.5	Super Mutants	13
2.6	The Enclave	15
2.7	The Institute	17

SECTION 3 – CREATING A CHARACTER
3.1	Characters	20
3.2	Creating a Player Character	21
3.3	Skill List	24
3.4	Gifts and Scars	28
3.5	Perks	30
3.6	Specialist Characters	34
3.7	Luck	35
3.8	Experience & Progression	36
3.9	Archetype Cards	38

SECTION 4 – RULES OF PLAY
4.1	Skill Tests	42
4.2	Special Effects	50
4.3	Action Play	51
4.4	Action: Move	53
4.5	Action: Charge	54
4.6	Action: Shoot	55
4.7	Action: Throw	57
4.8	Action: Close Combat	57
4.9	Action: Use Expertise	59
4.10	Action: Prepare	59
4.11	Quick Actions	61
4.12	Minor Activities	62
4.13	Damage	63
4.14	Armor	64
4.15	Health	65
4.16	Criticals	66
4.17	Conditions	67
4.18	Advanced Combat and Weapons	69
4.19	Items	73

SECTION 5 – THE OVERSEER
5.1	The Role of the Overseer	80
5.2	Adjudicating Skill Tests	81
5.3	Other Adjudications	86
5.4	Non-Player Characters	88
5.5	The Covert Approach	88
5.6	Chase Scenes	92
5.7	Scavenging	93
5.8	Items and Costs	94
5.9	Settlements	95
5.10	Crafting	98
5.11	Reference: Special Effect Dice	99
5.12	Playing in Conjunction with F:WW	100

SECTION 6 – INTRODUCTORY CAMPAIGN: PARZIVAL AND THE WASTELAND KNIGHTS
6.1	Summary	102
6.2	Part One: Mister Parzival	103
6.3	Part Two: The Quest	114
6.4	Part Three: Kameloth	123
6.5	Conclusion	129

APPENDICES
A1	Miniatures Gallery	130
A2	Icons Index	135
A3	Index	136

A PALADIN FENDS OFF DEADLY ASSAULTRONS

FOWW RPG-001-111 — SECTION 1

WHAT IS A ROLEPLAYING GAME?

In the *Fallout: Wasteland Warfare Roleplaying Game*, you explore the world of *Fallout* by taking on the role of one character in a story "told" by all the Players plus an Overseer, who runs the game. This expansion to *Fallout: Wasteland Warfare* allows you to create your own character, deciding everything from their personality and backstory to their S.P.E.C.I.A.L. attributes and skills.

Using your character, you'll make decisions about how they behave and react, working together with the other Player Characters to complete tasks, and even speaking as them in certain situations.

By using the game's rules, you and your fellow Players will take their characters on quests, scavenging, discovering, fighting, and possibly even surviving, with the Overseer narrating the plot and describing the effects of your actions. Doing so shapes the story as you play, as well as providing a fun and immersive game set in the Wasteland of the *Fallout* universe.

WHAT YOU NEED

Players and Characters

To play this roleplaying expansion, you'll need several players – usually between one and five – each controlling a **Player Character** (**PC**). Your character is like a heroic model in *Fallout: Wasteland Warfare*, acting independently in Free Play, or taking turns in Action Play (which includes combat).

Your character's details are recorded on a Character Mat found on page 40 (also available from the Modiphius website), on which you place an Archetype card (see page 38) and Equipment cards, and record Expertise Skills. To generate your own character, follow the steps in 'Creating a Player Character', p.21.

When you make decisions for your character and attempt to achieve goals, you'll roll dice to determine if they complete that action successfully – just like you would using Expertise in *Fallout: Wasteland Warfare*. You'll use the character's S.P.E.C.I.A.L. attributes and Skills to determine their ability at the task they're attempting, and the dice rolled give you a result that depends on those values.

An Overseer

To play the game, the group needs an Overseer, someone who adjudicates the rules and dice results, and describes the scenes in the game. Instead of taking one character, they play the allies and enemies of the Player Characters. The role of the Overseer is vital, with advice and guidance found in the Overseer chapter, starting on p.80.

Dice

Fallout: Wasteland Warfare and this roleplaying expansion use custom dice to resolve most characters' actions. More details can be found on pp.42-44, and the dice you need are available from the Modiphius online store and friendly local gaming stores.

PLAYING THE GAME

The rules for playing the *Fallout: Wasteland Warfare RPG* start on p.20, and cover everything you need to know to fully engage in your and the Overseer's story. You may want to start with the core rules for resolving a Skill Test (p.42) or, if you're interested in seeing what characters will look like, the 'Creating a Character' chapter starts on p.20.

Running the Game

Overseers should give themselves a good grounding in the rules by reading through the core rules from p.42, and then reading the 'Overseer' chapter which follows it (p.80). You'll also need to be familiar with character creation (p.20), though. Looking up rules during the game is fine too, by the way!

MINIATURES

It's not necessary to use miniatures with the *Fallout: Wasteland Warfare RPG*, but using them for combat makes keeping track of where all the characters are much easier. A whole range of *Fallout* miniatures are available from the Modiphius online store, and from friendly local gaming stores.

SECTION 02
THE WORLD OF THE WASTELAND

FOWW RPG-001-111

FOWW RPG-001-111 — SECTION 2.1

THE WASTELAND

War. War never changes. The United States of America is no more. It was destroyed when the world's nuclear warheads were launched. The ensuing apocalypse brought an end to both the Great War and the civilized world. In its place exists the Wasteland, an irradiated landscape pockmarked by ruined cities, decaying civilizations, and pockets of desperate survivors. It is inhabited by a variety of mutated creatures, horrific beasts, and undying ghouls. The radiation from the detonations spread quickly. Everything that wasn't killed immediately was irradiated, and most of the country's diverse plant and animal life was wiped out.

Survivors work to reclaim what little they can and salvage what they cannot rebuild. Civilization is starting to take root again and certain areas of the country have reached a level of stability that might even be called comfortable, at least for the rich and powerful. The coasts have been the easiest to reclaim, and many of the cities on the Eastern Seaboard have been re-inhabited. Among these are the Capital Wasteland and the Commonwealth, which exist in the ruins of Washington D.C. and Boston, respectively.

Disparate factions have begun to split off as these communities have grown. Each faction looks to make its own way and some are far more dangerous than others. By far the most dangerous are the Raiders. They place no value on any Human life but their own. Yet civilization has begun to flourish, despite the opposition. Trade, economy, and even government

> ### A note from your friendly Vault-Tec™ Representative
> #### WELCOME TO YOUR NEW HOME!
> Welcome to post-vault America! As you explore your new home and the wonders and opportunities available to you, Vault-Tec™ is here to help! Here we've presented a handy guide to the new landscape you now find yourself in; some may call it a wasteland, but in reality it's the gateway to your new and vibrant life. Think of the possibilities!

have begun in some areas of the Wasteland. Each community adapts or adjusts its own governmental system according to its needs. Merchants travel protected routes, trading at cities across the Wasteland. The merchants have created a new currency in the form of bottlecaps ('Caps'). These old metal caps once topped Nuka-Cola bottles, but are now backed as a currency by the Hub in New California.

Life in the Wasteland is harsh. The sun beats down hard and the radiation is intense. Clean water and food are rarities. Most survivors have been forced to adapt to dirty water and irradiated food. Surviving alone in the Wasteland is difficult at best, but living in a community comes with its own struggles.

AREAS OF THE WASTELAND

New California

New California grew from the ruined shell of Los Angeles and began to spread along the western coast. It is the birthplace of both the Brotherhood of Steel and the New California Republic. LA itself is a mess of twisted skyscrapers and collapsed buildings and is now known as "The Boneyard." It is dangerous to live near the Boneyard but the remains provide valuable artifacts and tech that can be traded for much-needed Caps. The area has been taken over and is now run by the New California Republic. They keep a presence in most cities, including The Hub, which is the largest, most functional city in the Wasteland.

The Capital Wasteland

The Capital Wasteland is the given name for what was Washington D.C. and the surrounding areas. D.C. was targeted directly by the nuclear assault that ended the Great War, and the White House is nothing more than a glassy crater. The remains of the Capitol Building, Museum of Technology, and other structures around the Mall still exist, but are inhabited by ruthless Super Mutants. Smaller cities have begun to grow on the outskirts of the capital as survivors band together and try to take back the area. The largest of

>
> ### A note from your friendly Vault-Tec™ Representative
> #### WHEREVER YOU GO...
> You may find yourself in any of these locations, or completely different areas altogether. Vault-Tec™ prides itself on having 'branches' in all areas of the country, from the picturesque Blue Ridge Mountains to the more adventurous areas of wartorn Anchorage itself; wherever you go, we're there for you and your survival bunker needs. Just remember as you venture out into these new environs that, while they may not be as deluxe as a vault, so long as you keep your spirits up and some heavy weaponry to hand, there's nothing you can't do. No matter where you make your home, always carry the values of Vault-Tec™ with you!

THE BROTHERHOOD HAS ITS WORK CUT OUT CLEANSING THE WASTELAND

these, Rivet City, exists within the shell of a wrecked aircraft carrier.

The Commonwealth

The Commonwealth covers most of what was Massachusetts, including the city of Boston, and it is home to the enigmatic Institute. The Institute rose from within the Commonwealth Institute of Technology to bring Synth AI technology to the world. The Commonwealth has been a hotbed of controversy since the arrival of the Synths. Some organizations, such as the Brotherhood of Steel, attempted to eradicate the Synths, while the Railroad attempted to save them from the Institute's slavery. The largest city in the Commonwealth is Diamond City. It is built within and around the remains of the city's baseball stadium.

CREATURES OF THE WASTELAND

Brahmin are cows that have been exposed to radiation. They have mutated to have two heads and a giant set of udders. Brahmin are generally peaceful animals, and survivors have taken to raising them as cattle. They are used to produce safe, fresh meat, pull carts like oxen, or carry goods like pack mules. They are one of the main domesticated work animals of the Wasteland.

Deathclaws are by far the most dangerous creatures to roam the Wasteland. Rumor has it that they are the product of the evil experiments to create some kind of apex predator, chameleons mutated into terrifying monsters, and Deathclaws have become a legendary threat.

Ghouls are the survivors of the atomic blasts and radiation that created the Wasteland. Those who didn't die instantly were slowly mutated into zombie-like creatures called Ghouls. Most manage to maintain their personalities and memories from before the Great War. While Ghouls aren't necessarily dangerous, some non-Ghouls harbor prejudices against them. Ghouls live together in strongholds such as the Necropolis in New California, or Underworld in the Capital Wasteland.

Mirelurk is a generally accepted term for the mutated water creatures that are also able to survive on land. They can take the shape of crabs, turtles, or other aquatic animals and emerge from lakes, rivers,

A note from your friendly Vault-Tec™ Representative
RED IN TOOTH AND CLAW

When greeting the colorful creatures and rusty robot inhabitants of the Wasteland, be aware that not all of them will welcome you with a happy tune and a winning smile. There's a good chance you may be stung, nipped, clawed, bitten, burned (with acid or flame), electrocuted, gnawed on, chomped, slashed, skewered, drained dry, or drooled on. Try not to let it get you down! Apply a stimpak to the affected area, collect any appendages that may have been detached, and carry on with your exploration.

and the sea to hunt on land. Mirelurks are a reliable source of meat, but it is usually tainted and will most likely cause radiation sickness if consumed.

Mole rats are another product of pre-war genetic mutation. Mole rats are incredibly common right across the Wasteland and rapidly reproduce. They often hunt in packs and can be incredibly dangerous, burrowing under the ground and resurfacing to bite and claw at their prey.

Radroaches and **Radscorpions** are normal pests that have been exposed to far too much radiation. They have become a bigger, deadlier, more poisonous version of their ancestors. They are a common scourge in the Wasteland and far more dangerous when they attack in numbers. It is best to keep a far distance as their blood can be very poisonous.

AUTOMATONS OF THE WASTELAND

Assaultrons were RobCo's primary weapons-grade robot, and were deployed to the front lines by the United States Army during the war. They are quick, nimble, and customizable, with a variety of weaponry such as lasers and razor-sharp claws. An Assaultron will not stop until its core is damaged: even after losing limbs and pieces of machinery, it continues to fight on. Some Assaultrons are equipped with bombs set to detonate if they are destroyed.

Eyebots are the watchful eye of the Enclave across the Wasteland, and controlled by the mysterious head of the Enclave, President John Henry Eden. They are used to control the population and spout propaganda to keep the Wasteland loyal to the Enclave. Eyebots have been hijacked by other organizations and modified to spy for them instead of the Enclave.

Protectrons were created by the robotics company RobCo. They were designed to perform manual labor or serve as greeters or database managers. Many of these robots are still following their original programming and can be found across the Wasteland. Some have been reprogrammed to act as bodyguards or escorts, while others have gone haywire over time, and will randomly attack any target they see. Protectrons come in a variety of different styles and loadouts.

Sentry Bots are large and tank-like. Slow moving and heavily armored, they carry top-grade weaponry, and are often used to guard high-profile fixed locations such as Brotherhood bunkers or Enclave facilities. Sentry Bots should NOT be underestimated, as they are incredibly difficult to take down.

Utility Robots serve a variety of mundane tasks such as cooking, cleaning, and tailoring. Before the War they were incredibly common and almost every household had a Utility Robot. These come in three main types. The Mr. Handy is used for general maintenance and construction; its many hands come equipped with buzz saws, flamethrowers, and other construction tools that can easily serve as weapons. Mr. Gutsy is a personal protection automaton, and comes equipped with heavier armor than most Utility Robots. It also carries a plasma weapon to be used in defense. The third most common is Miss Nanny, a utility bot designed to care for and raise newborns; these were incredibly useful in the vaults as there were many children in need of care after the war.

FOWW RPG-001-111 — **SECTION 2.2**

SURVIVORS

Survivors are working to rebuild the old world while facing all of the threats that come with life in the Wasteland. Most of these came from inside vaults: large, self-contained structures built underground to protect Humanity in case of nuclear disaster. The vaults around the world only began to open when the air was deemed safe from radiation. This allowed survivors access to the new world, and they emerged with the tools and supplies to rebuild. Vaults did not open at the same time, and some survivors were left locked in for decades while the world outside advanced. Other vaults malfunctioned and the people inside mutated or died. Some vaults were attacked and plundered by Raiders. In some cases, vault members became Raiders themselves. They decided against contributing to the world and instead take whatever they can. The lucky percentage of the population who managed to survive in the vaults were then given the burdensome task of rebuilding the shattered world.

Some survived outside of the vaults. They took cover in underground labs, sewers, or even their own personal bomb shelters. These makeshift bunkers lacked the vaults' sustainability and offered limited protection. Most of these survivors turned into Ghouls due to radiation exposure, but even Ghouls contribute to rebuilding society.

The early survivors who left their vaults within the first few years of the Great War, and those who were never in vaults, didn't find much waiting for them. These survivors founded the first cities of the Wasteland, and civilization slowly began to reform. Larger cities, like Megaton, Rivet City, and the Hub, were founded and run by natural leaders who had the charisma and willpower to lead their people. No central government has formed within the Wasteland, and many cities and territories have their own ruling bodies and leadership structures. Some factions, like the Brotherhood of Steel and the Institute, have a codified organizational structure that resembles a government.

The most structured civilization in the Wasteland is that of the New California Republic. The NCR is fighting to bring democracy back to the world while also establishing trade routes, an economy, and a set of laws. Most of the West is under the control of the NCR and they are the closest thing to a stable "force for good" in the Wasteland.

The daily life of a survivor is much like a pioneer in the early days of America. Their concerns are based around gathering, building, and providing for their families. Farms are not plentiful in the Wasteland but some do exist. Each farmer must do their part to provide for the budding civilizations. Other survivors take on trade jobs such as blacksmiths, merchants, construction workers, or hired muscle. There is still room for high level professions like scientists and engineers, and most of these skilled individuals get recruited by the Brotherhood or the Institute.

SURVIVORS SHELTER BEHIND HASTILY ERECTED JUNK BARRICADES

A note from your friendly
Vault-Tec™ Representative

SURVIVING TOGETHER (WHERE POSSIBLE)

You may encounter other vault dwellers who have emerged from the safety of their vault recently, or even some who have prematurely emerged against company policy. For the most part they will be friendly and outgoing; your Vault suit and Pip-Boy will be your ticket to warm food, a comfortable bed and all the hospitality you've come to expect from the Vault-Tec™ family.

On rare occasions this may not be forthcoming. At this point you have many options – using the new 'Caps' currency to ease your way, appealing to their common Humanity with inspiring words, or appealing to their common Humanity with inspiring weaponry.

NOTABLE SETTLEMENTS

Acadia
Acadia is built into the remains of an old observatory at Far Harbor, and has become home to runaway Synths who fled the Institute. Humans and Synths are able to coexist within its borders.

Broken Hills
Broken Hills was founded by Super Mutants as a place for the mutants to coexist with both Humans and Ghouls. The city itself is built into a mine where the Super Mutants work to extract uranium. The intense radiation doesn't have much of an effect on them.

Diamond City
Diamond City is the largest settlement in all of the Commonwealth. It is built into the remains of Fenway Park, which was once a notable landmark. The city is incredibly prosperous and has grown to bursting over the years. It features restaurants, hotels, clubs, a radio station, and even has its own newspaper. It is as close to pre-war "normal" as things can get in the Commonwealth.

The Hub
The Hub is one of the largest cities on the West Coast and is the central state of the New California Republic. The Hub is built into a pre-war city that managed to survive most of the damage of the war, and most of the old buildings within the Hub are still intact. Life there is reminiscent of life before the war. The Hub is home to many of the merchant groups in the Wasteland and it has its own functional police and a variety of trade guilds and criminal organizations.

Junction City
Junction City is one of very few cities known to exist in the desolate Midwest, existing in the ruins of what was once Kansas City. It is constantly under attack from Raider gangs and has its own army of enforcers to protect it. Junction City is self-sufficient and does not need to beg for help from bigger factions like the Brotherhood of Steel.

Megaton
Megaton is one of the largest cities in the Capital Wasteland. It was built around a Megaton bomb that failed to detonate. The city exists in the crater made when a bomber plane crashed, and is mostly built from parts salvaged from that aircraft in the early days. The Megaton bomb itself is still active and could go off at any time. The people of Megaton have made peace with that and there are some that even worship the bomb.

Sandy Shores
This city was once called Shady Sands but its name changed after it became the capital city of the New California Republic. It is the largest city in the Republic and one of the largest cities in the entire Wasteland. It is a large farming community that grows crops and tends to large herds of Brahmin.

Rivet City
Rivet City is a thriving community built within and around the remains of a United States Navy aircraft carrier. It is one of the most secure places to live in the Wasteland outside of the hidden Institute. There are so many rooms built into the carrier that most families are able to afford a room to themselves. The large common area within the ship was turned into a bustling market.

The Underworld
Hidden inside the Museum of History within the Capital Wasteland exists a community of Ghouls, banding together to survive. These refugees have come from all across the Wasteland, enticed by the promise of a safe haven. Humans are allowed in the Underworld, as long as they don't cause any trouble.

Vault-Tec™ Vaults
Vault-Tec™ was responsible for the creation of the vaults used to protect Humanity in the case of nuclear war. These vaults were meant to safeguard the last survivors so they could rebuild the world. Or so Vault-Tec™ says. In reality, many of the vaults were laboratories, where Vault-Tec™ could carry out dangerous and illegal experiments. The Super Mutants and many of the Raider gangs were created due to the interference of Vault-Tec™ in their vaults.

A note from your friendly
Vault-Tec™ Representative

VAULT-TEC™ – BY YOUR SIDE

Despite what you may have heard, read or possibly experienced, Vault-Tec™ always has your best interests at heart. In the topsy-turvy world of the great war and the post nuclear wasteland, who's to say what may or may not be illegal, immoral, or ideologically dubious? Take it from us: any trials and tribulations you've gone through have made you stronger, better adapted and better able to survive in the Wasteland. All thanks to your faith in the Vault-Tec™ family. You're welcome!

THE BROTHERHOOD OF STEEL

The Brotherhood of Steel is the most widely spread faction in the Wasteland. It has chapters on the west and east coasts, and even in the Midwest. The original founding chapter grew out of the remains of the United States military and many of the military's structures, organization, and tactics seeped into the Brotherhood.

THE HISTORY OF THE BROTHERHOOD

Roger Maxson, the Brotherhood's founder, was a Captain in the United States Army just before the start of the Great War. His unit was stationed at Mariposa Military Base, which was the site of Human testing for the government's Forced Evolutionary Virus. The FEV was responsible for creating Super Mutants in an attempt to build new soldiers for the United States. Maxson discovered what was happening at the base in the early days of the Great War and executed the scientists responsible. He shut down the project and took control of Mariposa for himself. He tried to cut off all ties to the military and government after seeing what horrors they had allowed, but it was too late. The Great War had come.

Maxson sensed the impending danger of the war and opened the doors of Mariposa to the surrounding towns and tried to protect as many as he could. The military base survived the initial bombing, but Mariposa was not built to sustain a large population for any amount of time. The world outside was already a Wasteland and provisions were running low. Maxson was forced to lead the people to safety.

Maxson led his people to the nearby fallout shelter of Lost Hills in what became known as "The Exodus." This is where he eventually settled his budding organization and it became the first headquarters of the Brotherhood of Steel. Maxson vowed to use his power to help rebuild civilization and bring order to the Wasteland.

The influence of the Brotherhood began to grow over time, and new leadership took over and influenced the organization. It retained its strict military code and the faction gained a dedicated group of followers. Eventually, the motivation of the group changed from rebuilding civilization to controlling it.

It became an imperative of the Brotherhood to steal and hoard all pre-war technology. This was both to "protect" the people from its dangers and also to ensure the Brotherhood remained the most technologically advanced faction in the Wasteland. This desire led to its war with the Enclave, another faction that had been gaining technological power

> **A note from your friendly Vault-Tec™ Representative**
>
> **AD VICTORIAM?**
>
> The Brotherhood of Steel name is well earned – they are a wall of solid armor and heavy weaponry. You should be aware that they are not always as beneficent as they first appear; many call them the Brotherhood of Steal instead, and with good reason! While they can be a powerful ally, you shouldn't let their supposedly lofty ideals get in the way of your success. Husband your advanced equipment carefully, just in case they decide you aren't worthy of their technocratic tyranny!

in the Wasteland and directly competing with the Brotherhood. Their war took a heavy toll on both sides but the Enclave was scattered in the conflict.

The Brotherhood continued to grow for years after the war and many smaller chapters broke off to stake a claim in new lands, such as the Capital Wasteland and The Pitt. Meanwhile, the **West Coast Brotherhood** continued to gain power. This growth brought it into an inevitable conflict with the New California Republic.

While the West Coast Brotherhood expanded, the **East Coast Brotherhood** also grew in power under the leadership of Arthur Maxson – direct descendant of the Brotherhood's founder. It has an established foothold in the Capital Wasteland, the Citadel, a secret bunker hidden beneath the Pentagon. The Brotherhood has been able to continue its mission from within the Citadel and gather more valuable pre-war technology. The organisation has also made serious technological advances of its own, including the *Prydwen*, a mobile airship fortress that has been dispatched north to the Commonwealth.

Other splinter groups of the Brotherhood exist across the Wasteland, such as the **Midwest Brotherhood**.

ORGANIZATION STRUCTURE

The Brotherhood is organized as a mixture of a military force and a religious order. It uses a similar chain of command to the military, and uses military tactics and bases to carry out its operations. However, internally, it is structured more like a religious organization: its ranks range from Initiate to Paladin. Recruits begin their lives in the Brotherhood as **Initiates** who serve to assist Paladins, Knights, and other ranking members of the Brotherhood until a time they are deemed worthy to join the actual ranks. From there, Initiates will be separated into two groups, based on their abilities. These two groups are "The Scribes" and "The Knights."

The **Scribes** serve the day-to-day needs of the Brotherhood inside their protected bunkers. They study pre-war technology, attempt to understand it, and are fundamental in producing new technologies.

Meanwhile, the **Knights** don their iconic Power Armor and assert the Brotherhood's authority in the outside world. Knights who perform admirably over the years are promoted to the much-coveted rank of **Paladin**. Paladins are the Brotherhood's elite operatives and fight on the front lines of the Brotherhood's wars. Paladins can eventually retire and be promoted to serve on the Brotherhood's Council of Elders – if they survive that long. Paladins are also granted the best Power Armor and weapons the Brotherhood can provide.

CONFLICTS

The Brotherhood of Steel is a large, aggressive entity and cannot peacefully coexist with other organizations. They have fought wars across the Wasteland and will fight many wars to come.

The Enclave
The West Coast Brotherhood was successful in its campaign against the Enclave, but the rival organization still exists and is gaining strength along the eastern coast. They still view the Brotherhood as an enemy and are willing to fight it openly in the streets of the Capital Wasteland and Commonwealth.

The Institute
The Institute is run by some of the Commonwealth's most brilliant scientists. Their combined genius has finally created true artificial intelligence in the form of robotic beings known as the Synth. The Brotherhood sees the creation of these robots as unethical and does not view them as Human. It has adopted a goal of shutting down the Institute and destroying any Synths that its forces come across.

The New California Republic
The New California Republic defeated the Brotherhood in the west and forced it into hiding, but conflict still erupts whenever they meet. The NCR still has the numbers it needs to quash any possible rebellion and the West Coast Brotherhood resorts to guerilla tactics to fight back against the larger NCR army. Much time has passed since the war and the West Coast Brotherhood has nearly rebuilt to a point where it can strike back.

Brotherhood Tactics
The Brotherhood operate like a military unit, with its own divisions and unit rankings. When it performs an operation in hostile territory, it does so with the support of a Vertibird and several Paladins equipped with a variety of artillery and laser weapons. The East Coast Brotherhood watches from the skies within their airship, the *Prydwen*, and dispatches Vertibirds filled with troops when it sees conflict down below. This is especially true when that conflict is with the Super Mutants. The Brotherhood is generally protective of Human life and will not put innocents at risk.

KNIGHT CAPTAIN CADE PREPARES A SORTIE

FOWW RPG-001-111 — SECTION 2.4

RAIDERS

The term "Raider" is a general classification for survivors who have chosen to turn on mankind. They resort to violence and aggression to secure their needs. There are many different types and styles of Raiders but they all have one thing in common: they cannot be trusted. A Raider would just as soon turn on a fellow soldier as they would an enemy if they thought they could benefit from the betrayal. Some factions of Raiders are more organized than others and have their own camps, bases, and leadership structures. Others have devolved into nomadic gangs that move from place to place and pillage whatever they can.

Travelers passing through the Wasteland always need to be wary of Raider ambush. The merchant caravans that travel across the country are often the target of their raids. Many merchants have taken to bringing armed guards on their trips or enlisting the help of the NCR or Brotherhood of Steel to protect trade routes.

Raiders are scavengers, and they build weapons and armor out of whatever they can find in the wreckage of the old world. Occasionally they stumble onto a piece of pre-war technology, such as laser weapons or Power Armor, allowing them to rise above being a normal Raider squad.

> **A note from your friendly Vault-Tec™ Representative**
>
> **A CHEMICAL ROMANCE**
>
> While out and about in the Wasteland, you may find yourself face to face with unsavory characters or the more militant groups of survivors know as Raiders. Do not be afraid! While they have made some questionable choices in the face of nuclear annihilation, they may also be your best route to success in this inhospitable environment. Don't write off these possible new friends because of an addiction or two, especially when using their 'resources' to your own benefit.

RAIDER TACTICS

Raiders aren't known for their subtlety and will usually attack directly, with a complete disregard for Human life. They have no qualms about operating in public or in broad daylight. Often employing superior numbers, they can easily overwhelm opponents, but will flee if they feel they are outnumbered, or when faced with dangerous opponents like Super Mutants. Raiders don't usually carry powerful weapons, and a well-equipped survivor can deal with an individual Raider with relative ease. Most Raiders carry simple Melee Weapons like clubs and axes, so are especially vulnerable to long-range weapons.

RAIDER TERRITORIES

Raiders claim territory with no regard for the original owners. They will build makeshift walls around the territory they claim, even if it exists in the middle of a settlement or city. Their walls are usually decorated with enemy bodies, brightly colored profanities, and graffiti showing their Raider gang signs. These makeshift walls are used as a warning to keep outsiders away, but they offer little actual protection.

RAIDER FACTIONS

Disciples
Leader: Nisha
Main Camp: Fizztop Mountain, Nuka-World
Area of Operation: Nuka-World, The Commonwealth

The Disciples are a wild and bloodthirsty gang, and are far more sadistic than your average group of Raiders. They kill just for the thrill of it and take pleasure in torture. Nisha does not keep strict control of the Disciples, and allows them to do whatever they want as long as the gang's actions don't bring trouble to their doorstep.

Forged
Leader: Slag
Main Camp: Saugus Ironworks
Area of Operation: The Commonwealth

Slag's Forged are an exclusive group of Raiders. Their initiates are forced through many deadly trials before finally joining the gang. Slag uses his position within the Ironworks to harness the power of fire and keep his Raiders well equipped and armored. The Forged worship fire and look to "the Forge" itself as if it were a god. Initiates must change their names to something that champions the Forge, such as "Flare" or "Spark" upon joining the gang.

groups. They hide out within the abandoned theme park Nuka-World and use that as their base to carry out operations. They have large plans for expansion after they take complete control over the old park.

The Pack
Leader: Mason
Main Camp: Bradberton Amphitheater, Nuka-World
Area of Operation: Nuka-World, The Commonwealth

The Pack is the third Raider gang vying for control of the old Nuka-World amusement park. The savage, animalistic Pack don bright makeup in animal patterns and wear colorful masks that make them stand out. Their hierarchy is based on that of an animal pack, with their leader known as the 'Alpha.' Lower members of the gang are able to challenge the Alpha for the title at any time.

The Pitt Raiders
Leader: Lord Ashur
Main Camp: Haven
Area of Operation: The Pitt

Paladin Owyn Lyons led a force to the remains of Pittsburgh during the early days of the Brotherhood of Steel's expansion. His mission was to bring order to this area which had become known as "The Pitt." During the cleansing of the Pitt, an operation referred to as the Scourge, Paladin Ashur was left behind and presumed dead after an explosion. After the Scourge, Ashur was discovered alive and still in his functional Power Armor by a group of Raiders, who looked up to him as a god. Paladin Ashur took advantage of their faith, and brought the Pitt Raiders to his side. He organized them into a gang and used them to take control of the criminal element within the Pitt. The Pitt Raiders operate as slave traders, buying from Capital Wasteland slavers.

Rust Devils
Leader: Ivey
Main Camp: Fort Hagen
Area of Operation: The Commonwealth

The Rust Devils are more technologically advanced than the average Raider gang, and often use robots to fight their battles. They try to scavenge and reprogram robots before the Brotherhood of Steel can claim them. The Rust Devils also experiment with Human and robot augmentation. They use Human brains and tissue to control robotic bodies with mixed, and often terrifying, results.

ACK-ACK AND SINJIN PILLAGE THE AREA

The New Khans
Leader: Darion
Main Camp: Vault 15
Area of Operation: New California

The Khans are a gang modeled after the great Mongolian Khans of old, and they ravage the countryside of New California. They roam the Wasteland, pillaging and burning everything they cannot take with them. The Khans originated in Vault 15 after the survivors there turned on each other and formed many different gangs. The Khans grew to be the most powerful of these under the leadership of Garl Death-Hand. Garl was killed during an attempt to capture the future President of New California, and another Raider, Darion, was forced to take over. Darion led the retreat back to the safety of Vault 15, and used the vault's protection to safely harass the NCR and then train a new generation of Khans to return to their Mongol ways.

Operators
Leaders: Mags and William Black
Main Camp: The Parlor, Nuka-World
Area of Operation: Nuka-World, The Commonwealth

The Operators function more as an underworld crime family than as a pack of bloodthirsty Raiders. They keep their business quiet, for the most part, and dress in casual, everyday clothing. This makes them harder to distinguish than most Raider

SUPER MUTANTS

FOWW RPG-001-111 — SECTION 2.5

Super Mutants are the byproduct of Human experimentation carried out by the United States Government in the days before the Great War. The government had labs spread out across the country, and each was working on their own version of the Forced Evolutionary Virus (FEV), a genetic manipulator that gave birth to the Super Mutants. Each of these labs failed during the Great War, the Super Mutants escaped during the collapse, and they began to populate the world. Each lab had been designing their own strain of the FEV, and so there are several different varieties of Super Mutants spread across the Wasteland.

The FEV increased the size and strength of its subjects while also disfiguring them and changing the color of their skin. The exact coloration, abilities, and attributes of the resulting mutants varies based on which part of the world the Super Mutants originate from, but they are still easily recognizable. The FEV strains also had differing effects on the Super Mutants' intelligence. Some groups were made incredibly intelligent and thus able to integrate into a society, while others are little more than animals acting on instinct.

WEST COAST MUTANTS

The Super Mutants of New California originated at Mariposa Military Base. The base was shut down by Roger Maxson, the founder of the Brotherhood of Steel, but the damage had been done long before he discovered it. That same facility was later discovered by the scientist Richard Grey. Stumbling upon a pure FEV solution while exploring, he was instantly mutated into a more powerful version of a Super Mutant. His strength and intelligence were both increased dramatically, and he obtained psychic powers that allowed him to control the Super Mutants he created. He changed his name to "The Master" and sent his Super Mutants out into New California. After the Master was defeated, the Enclave recovered the FEV and continued his work to create more Super Mutants in the area.

These West Coast Super Mutants are more intelligent than most, and some even seek to reintegrate with the population. There is a settlement in New California, Broken Hills, where rehabilitated Super Mutants work hand in hand with Humans. The rest have formed their own gangs and factions, which are more likely to fight against each other than to fight side by side.

EAST COAST MUTANTS

The Mutants that plague the East Coast came from a variety of sources, one of them being the FEV testing program in Huntersville, West Virginia. The West Tek science group decided to field test FEV in the Appalachian Mountains by infecting the local drinking supply with the virus. The rest of the Super Mutants in the area were created by government scientists secluded in Vault 87. The Institute also experimented with their own version of the FEV.

These Super Mutants were designed to be less intelligent and more aggressive than their West Coast counterparts. Some Super Mutants from New California can still be found along the East Coast, and it is easy to confuse the two groups. East Coast mutants were designed to be bigger and stronger, with unlimited growth potential. These grow larger as they grow older, eventually towering to the size of buildings as a mighty Behemoth.

The version of FEV created by Vault 87 had a few unintentional side-effects. Many of their subjects turned into wild animals that were unable to think or

SLEDGEHAMMERS: WHEN LOCKPICKS JUST WON'T DO

reason. These Super Mutants are the most dangerous type and will attack and kill without thought.

The East Coast Super Mutants still organize into loose groups and display a sense of cohesion in their efforts to find more FEV and use it to increase their numbers. Either by design, or by happy accident, Super Mutants are sterile and cannot reproduce.

Their only hope to increase their numbers is to infect Humans with FEV and turn them into fresh Super Mutants.

There is evidence that the FEV can be cured, and that Super Mutants can be returned to their original, Human forms. The formulation and location of this serum is a mystery.

SUPER MUTANT TACTICS

Any Super Mutant group encountered in the wild should be considered hostile. It is always best to observe a group before attacking as the tactics and effectiveness of each group will vary greatly. Most Super Mutants have crude weapons in the form of clubs, lengths of wooden two-by-four, or hammers. More advanced groups can carry laser weapons and wear heavy armor. These are far more dangerous groups, as advanced weapon use is usually a sign of advanced intelligence. Intelligent Super Mutants will also work together more cohesively than your average group.

Savage Super Mutants will simply rush in and attack, without any real tactics or teamwork. They are easy to outsmart, but the ferocity with which they attack can be surprising, and some survivors aren't prepared for that level of aggression.

Super Mutants have also domesticated mutated animals that they use in their hunting parties. The most common of these are the **Centaurs**, horrible, nightmare creatures that were created when the FEV didn't take. They are an amalgamation of disfigured, mutated body parts that crawl around on all fours.

When centaurs are not available, Super Mutants have been known to use **Mutant Hounds** to hunt instead, letting them roam to bring down their prey.

ON OCCASION EVEN MR. HANDY BACKUP DOESN'T HELP...

VARIETIES OF SUPER MUTANTS

Super Mutants have been categorized based on shared characteristics to make their countless variations easier to recognize and label in the field.

Basic Super Mutants are the common, aggressive Super Mutants that are most widely seen in the Wasteland. They generally rush in with Melee Weapons, or attack with crude hunting rifles. They have a low technology level.

Behemoth Super Mutants are the rarest form of Super Mutant; with no check on their growth they have been known to tower 20 feet high or more. They have lost most remnants of their intelligence or Humanity, and are nothing more than beasts. Luckily, there are only a few Behemoths. They cause great destruction wherever they go.

Huntersville Super Mutants were the results of experiments performed in the Appalachian Mountains. These Mutants share a common ancestry with the Vault 87 Super Mutants but are slightly smarter and able to adapt to life in the mountains. They rarely make permanent strongholds, but will do so occasionally.

Initiate Super Mutants are much larger, muscular, and more athletic than other Super Mutants. These Mutants are also highly intelligent and have a working knowledge of technology that they use to build advanced weapons and armor. They are known to carry gauss rifles and laser weapons into battle.

A note from your friendly **Vault-Tec™ Representative**

VAULT-TEC™ AND A BETTER YOU

Any reference to Vault 87 'experimenting' on or 'creating' Super Mutants in any way is of course completely untrue. Vaults are safe areas in which to wait out the nuclear warfare raging above, and not a series of confined spaces in which to test new, fun theories on social interaction and Human experimentation.

It is a matter of record that the residents of Vault 87 are almost all entirely immune to radiation – what better way to prepare for the post-nuclear landscape! Always remember: Anything Vault-Tec™ does is with you in mind and providing you with the best chance of success in the Wasteland.

Mariposa Super Mutants are more cultured and civilized than the rest of their brethren. They broke free from the Master's control after he was killed, and decided they had a choice to make. Many of these Super Mutants allied with civilization and are not aggressive at all. These Super Mutants are more common on the West Coast, though many clusters have migrated to the Capital Wasteland and Commonwealth.

Vault 87 Super Mutants possess almost no intelligence. They are tough to kill, impossible to reason with, and incredibly resistant to attacks and radiation. They can speak, but their vocabulary is limited.

FOWW RPG-001-111 — SECTION 2.6

THE ENCLAVE

The Enclave is all that remains of the former government of the United States of America. The Enclave claims to have always been the power behind the politics, and their membership is made up of brilliant scientists, tactically astute generals, cunning politicians, and charismatic influencers. They are still running the show from within their secret bunkers and claim to have the descendants of many powerful figures among their membership, including the last President of the United States. The power they wield includes technological advances that outshine both the Brotherhood of Steel and the Institute. This makes their claims more believable.

The Enclave operate in secret and their membership is exclusive. They only accept what they consider "pure" Humans. These are Humans that have not suffered from radiation, genetic mutation, Forced Evolutionary Virus infection, or other prolonged Wasteland effects. They believe this purity makes them better than those outside their organization. They look at most Wastelanders as inferior and less than Human.

HISTORY OF THE ENCLAVE

The Enclave always knew that nuclear war would come. They saw the path that the world was on and followed it to an inevitable conclusion. They knew they couldn't do anything to stop it but they could at least prepare for it. They made back-room deals with companies like Vault-Tec™ to provide special bunkers to protect the Enclave when the world ended. They built a hidden command center into one of their Pacific oil rigs, and when the Great War finally began, it became the Enclave's central hub. This hub was originally designed to continue America's war with China but in the face of widespread extinction, the Enclave turned its efforts toward rebuilding the country.

They spent their time watching the world from the shadows while perfecting technologies such as the Power Armor and Vertibirds that would eventually end up in the hands of the Brotherhood of Steel. They finally decided it was time to reclaim their country after decades consolidating power. They captured the fallen Mariposa Research Lab and continued the FEV experiments that once took place there. They engineered the chemical into a weapon that could wipe out all life on the mainland.

The Enclave was stopped, and the Brotherhood of Steel and New California Republic waged wars against the Enclave that nearly destroyed them. The Enclave was forced to abandon their rig and most of their holdings in the West as a result of the war. The survivors were called to retreat east by the new president of the Enclave, John Henry Eden, and so they made the trek across country to start again in the Capital Wasteland.

The old Enclave bunkers in Washington D.C. were still functional, and the Enclave's leadership had access to the old systems and an artificial intelligence named ZAX, the computer left in charge of running the Enclave's systems. When they arrived, they discovered that John Henry Eden was a creation of the ZAX system, while had developed the persona to instill patriotism and obedience across the Capital Wasteland. The Enclave had doubts about the AI's behavior, but the persona of President Eden was obviously working, and so they let ZAX continue the facade.

The Enclave made it a priority to strengthen their position in the Capital Wasteland. They then returned to their plan to use the FEV to wipe out Humanity in order to take complete control of the world. The Enclave once again found resistance from the Brotherhood of Steel, which again fought to protect the world from the Enclave's designs, and shattered them in the process. The Enclave's East Coast contingent splintered even further and disappeared back into the shadows.

The Enclave is greatly diminished in power, yet has still managed to survive. Its influence still stretches across the country, and there are still many hidden Enclave bunkers positioned throughout the Wasteland.

ORGANIZATION STRUCTURE

The Enclave is divided up into three distinct departments, with each carrying out a specific function in the Wasteland.

Department of the Army

This is the technologically advanced military force that the Enclave uses to carry out its operations in the Wasteland. They were, at one time, the most advanced fighting force on this planet with their soldiers in Power Armor wielding energy weapons. The Department of the Army also fields an Air Force made up of Vertibirds and a Navy comprised of a few ancient battleships from the pre-war era. The Army operates in squads and uses advanced military tactics and gear, including sentry drones that can protect their flanks. The Army can also dispatch an elite black-ops unit, the deadly Sigma Squad, to deal with particularly dangerous threats.

Research and Development

This branch has been responsible for the Enclave's amazing technological advancements, and is run by some of the most brilliant minds in the Wasteland. They designed the advanced Power Armor that is able to keep the Enclave soldiers safe from radiation. These scientists are rarely seen in the field. When they are, they are wearing heavy environmental protection suits.

Peacekeeping and Recovery

This department maintains bases around the Wasteland under the guise of "protecting" the citizens. They actually exist to keep an eye on the population and quietly remove anyone who the Enclave considers "non-compliant."

ENCLAVE TACTICS

The Enclave no longer has the numbers or power it once had, and its old tactics no longer work. The Brotherhood of Steel has matched them in technology and the New California Republic has them beaten for numbers. The Enclave now relies on small, heavily armed squads, with the best possible weapons and equipment, instead of dispatching a large contingent of troops. These small groups, like Sigma Squad, can be mustered and sent in to perform tasks quietly. These new tactics make the Enclave much more dangerous because it is difficult to ascertain where they might be operating. An air fleet of Vertibirds is highly visible, but a squad of black-ops veterans can easily approach undetected.

The Enclave can still come out in full force, but resources are stretched thin and the army cannot be dispatched as often. If the Enclave ever feels its existence is being threatened, or if they feel the risk is worth the gain, they will not hesitate to unleash their full force.

FOWW RPG-001-111 — SECTION 2.7

THE INSTITUTE

The Institute is a collective made up of scientists, engineers, and great thinkers that was founded in the basement of the Commonwealth Institute of Technology. The Institute is now developing technology far beyond what the Enclave or Brotherhood of Steel have ever been able to produce, their greatest triumph being the creation of synthetic Humans, called "Synths." The creation of Synths has put the Institute at odds with the people of the Commonwealth, who misunderstand and fear the Synths.

The Institute operates in secret, and few really know how to find their base of operations or know what happens inside its walls.

THE HISTORY OF THE INSTITUTE

When the Great War came, and the warheads began to drop, the students and faculty of the Commonwealth Institute of Technology (CIT) took shelter in the sturdy basement of the technology building. The students who survived the fallout took stock of the world around them and decided they could use their knowledge to rebuild society. They began to operate out of the ruins of the CIT and dedicated themselves to their Synth project. Their goal was to build new workers to help supplement the Wasteland's fallen population.

The people of the Wasteland were originally grateful for the Institute's help. They shared in the technological advances and built settlements, yet the Wastelanders were wary of the early-model Synths and did not fully trust the Institute. In return, the Institute's members felt that they were in danger around the outsiders. These factors combined to drive the Institute into hiding and, at that point, they decided the people of the Wasteland were on their own. The Institute would do nothing to help them. Instead, the Institute would prepare for the future. They work toward sustainable technologies that will allow them to one day regrow the world, even if Humanity dies off around them.

The Institute built a teleportation device, the Molecular Ray, and used it to teleport themselves deep below the surface, to a place no one could possibly reach them. They left their Synths on the surface to provide menial labor, scavenge for parts, and carry out surface tasks for them.

Over time, the Institute was able to perfect their Synth technology. By using the DNA of a cryogenically frozen newborn baby from the pre-war era, the Institute was able to create Synths that were completely undetectable. These 3rd Generation Synths could be slipped into Wasteland civilization without anyone ever knowing. Once there, they could gain positions of power or replace powerful figures with Synthetic versions and help control the Wasteland from afar.

The plan worked flawlessly for quite some time until a Synth in Diamond City went haywire, exposing its artificial nature and attacking the residents before being put down. Stories of the Institute and their Synths were still at the back of people's minds. A sense of paranoia grew, and measures were put into place to detect and eliminate these Synths. The Brotherhood of Steel sprang into action and branded the existence of these Synths as an immoral use of technology. They have launched a campaign against the Institute and attempt to destroy them once and for all.

Meanwhile, another group was formed to fight the Institute and its works. This new group, the Railroad, believes that Synths are fully cognizant and should be recognized as Humans and given the same rights. They agree with the Brotherhood that the Institute must be destroyed, but they do not believe that Synths should be eliminated. The Railroad tries to free Synths from the Institute's control by giving them new lives and identities. They are constantly searching for a way to reach the Institute's base, start a revolution from within, and free the Synths that are being used as slaves.

A note from your friendly
Vault-Tec™ Representative

YOU, ROBOT?

Anything that can give you an edge in the new, irradiated world can be turned to your advantage. Palling-up with these new, cyborg-like bully boys might be your best option in a pinch — always think about your quickest and best route to survival in a post-emergence world.

That said, Vault-Tec™ does not overtly condone replacing parts of yourself with new, tougher, better materials that shine in the light with the glorious chrome color of polished aluminum. Not at all.

ORGANIZATION STRUCTURE

The Institute is divided into several divisions, and each has its own division head that reports back to the mysterious Director. The Institute recruits externally and only brings in new blood after they have gone through rigorous testing. The process is hard, but new members are welcomed openly and treated fairly by the Institute.

The Advanced Systems Division
Division Head: Madison Li

This division was responsible for creating the teleporter that the Institute uses to get in and out of their facility. They are also responsible for the advanced weapons and armor that the Synths and Institute members wear on their trips to the surface world. They run the robotics lab, which produces new Synths.

The Bioscience Division
Division Head: Clayton Holdren

This division is responsible for all biotech advancements, including crop production, pharmaceuticals, and genetic engineering. They also hold samples of the Forced Evolutionary Virus, which was responsible for creating Super Mutants. Rumor has it that they are working on a way to reverse engineer the virus to create a cure.

The Facilities Division
Division Head: Allie Filmore

Facilities makes sure the Institute stays operational. It performs daily tasks like servicing the life support systems, ventilation, and the power network.

The Synth Retention Bureau
Division Head: Justin Ayo

The SRB was designed to perform one task: it tracks down and returns rogue Synths to the Institute. To do this, the Institute created a specific Synth model called the **Courser**. Coursers have their personality levels tweaked to ensure they won't rebel, while their combat abilities have been vastly improved over other models. Other divisions within the Institute fear the SRB, as they have a hit squad of Coursers under their command and they are very effective in their role. The SRB also works to hunt down Railroad members so they can shut down the rebel organization once and for all. The SRB also employs a murder, or flock, of "**Watchers**", synthetic crows with built in monitoring devices.

INSTITUTE TACTICS

The Institute has a nearly limitless army in its Synths. Rarely will an Institute member travel to the surface to perform a combat operation since they can send Synths by the dozen through the teleporter. These Synths are equipped with top-of-the-line armor and laser weapons, and usually operate in small squads. These squads patrol the Wasteland or guard targets that the Institute considers valuable. When a precision specialist is needed, the Institute will dispatch a Courser, even if the target is not a Synth. Coursers are incredibly difficult to defeat, and so it usually takes only one Courser to finish a job.

SOMETIMES A 'TACTICAL WITHDRAWAL' IS CALLED FOR

SECTION 03

CREATING A CHARACTER

FOWW RPG-001-111

FOWW RPG-001-111 — SECTION 3.1

CHARACTERS

S.P.E.C.I.A.L. ATTRIBUTES

In the world of *Fallout: Wasteland Warfare*, each character from the distinguished Elder Maxson of the Brotherhood of Steel to the lowliest Radroach has a set of attributes and information on their unit card. These attributes – their initials spell out S.P.E.C.I.A.L. – indicate how good a character is in combat, how tough they are, and how well they interact with other characters, enemies and objects. Every character's card includes 'S.P.E.C.I.A.L.' attributes, with separate values for Strength, Perception, Endurance, Charisma, Intelligence, Agility, and Luck.

Strength (STR)
Strength is often used to show how good a character is at Close Combat, and their ability with a Melee Weapon, one specifically designed for close or hand-to-hand combat.

Perception (PER)
Perception is often used to show a character's ability with a Ranged Weapon. It also indicates how easily they can detect dangers and react to enemy activity.

Endurance (END)
Endurance is the attribute that shows a character's toughness and usually how much damage they can take before dying. It sometimes indicates a character's ability with a Thrown Weapon.

Charisma (CHA)
Charisma is used for a variety of Skill Tests and shows how charming, intimidating, or cunning a character can be.

Intelligence (INT)
Intelligence is used for interacting with computer terminals, lock picking and in many other Skill Tests.

Agility (AGI)
Agility shows a character's nimbleness. It is often used for Thrown Weapons, and sometimes for Close Combat or Shooting.

Luck (LUC)
Especially heroic characters may use Luck to change near-miss attacks to hits or to dodge potentially fatal damage.

While the examples above show the most common uses of S.P.E.C.I.A.L. attributes, this is only a broad guide. Different characters and factions in games may use different attributes for Skill Tests. For example, most characters will use Strength for Close Combat, but others may use Agility or even Perception instead.

> THROUGHOUT THE FOLLOWING THREE CHAPTERS, RELEVANT CARD ICONS ARE HIGHLIGHTED IN THE SIDEBARS. A FULL INDEX OF CARD ICONS CAN BE FOUND ON P.135.

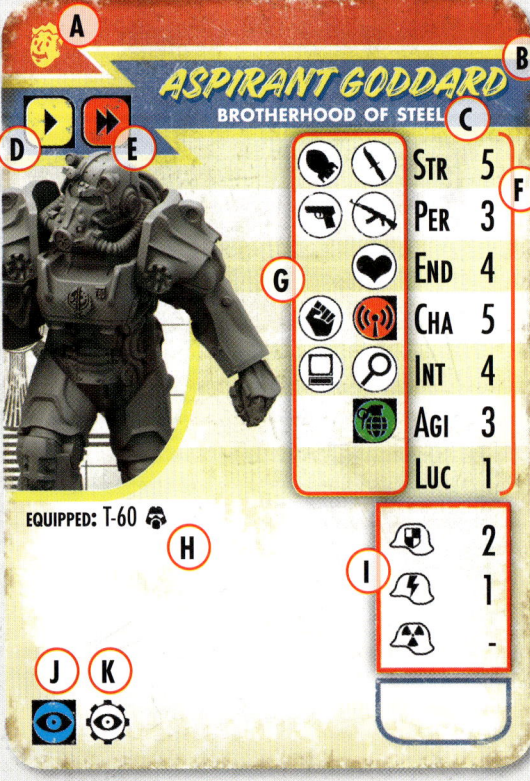

ANATOMY OF A UNIT/ARCHETYPE CARD

The **archetype cards** used for Player Characters in the *Fallout: Wasteland Warfare RPG* have the same layout as unit cards used in *Fallout: Wasteland Warfare*. Archetype cards are, in effect, a type of unit card (see page 38).

A. Unique unit (feature of *Fallout: Wasteland Warfare*).
B. Unit name.
C. Faction (see p.34).
D. Move distance (range by color) (see pp.52-3).
E. Charge distance (range by color) (see pp.52 and 54).
F. S.P.E.C.I.A.L. attribute values (see above).
G. Skills (see pages 10, 24-27).
H. Specialities panel.
I. Armor Ratings (physical, energy, and radiation) (see p.64).
J. Awareness range (by color) (see p.52).
K. Capacity to use Quick Actions, Critical Points or Luck Points may be shown in the lower left corner of the card.

FOWW RPG-001-111 — SECTION 3.2

CREATING A PLAYER CHARACTER

1. **Choose a starting archetype card** (which can be found on pages 38-39)

   Gain any **items** shown as EQUIPPED on the archetype card.

2. Gain the **Expertise Skills** mentioned in 'Starting Character Archetypes' (pp.22-23) for free.

3. Decide on the character's **backstory**.

4. **Add 2 Gifts**, which are positive abilities from the character's past (see pp.28-29).

5. **Add 2 Scars**, which are negative outcomes from the character's past (see pp.29-30).

6. **Spend 5 Experience Points** (**XPs**) on the archetype card (see 'Spending Experience Points', p.36).

   - You must buy **at least 1 Perk** with XP. Perks that increase an attribute may not be bought.
   - **At least 1 Speciality** must be bought (p.36).
   - Each Expertise Skill may be bought only once (in addition to any free Expertise Skills on the card).

7. Place the archetype/unit card on a **Character Mat** and fill in the spaces on the **Health Track** greater than the character's full Health.

   If the attribute on which the starting Character's Health is based is 5 or less, their starting Health is increased to 6. If a starting Character's Health is 6, make it 7. This does not alter the attribute the character's Health is based upon.

8. If the archetype/unit card has '**Super Mutant**' written below their character profile's name, the character is affected by some extra rules for Super Mutants (see 'Super Mutants', p.34).

9. If the archetype/unit card shows the **Robot Type** icon , the character is affected by some extra rules for Robots (see 'Robots', p.34).

10. **Spend 100 Caps** on equipment.

IF YOU OWN *FALLOUT: WASTELAND WARFARE* AND USE YOUR RPG CHARACTER IN THE WARGAME, THE HEALTH IS JUST WHAT IS ON THE CARD LIKE OTHER UNIT CARDS. YOUR CHARACTER DOES NOT GAIN THE EXTRA STARTING HEALTH MENTIONED HERE.

ROBOT TYPE ICON

EXISTING FALLOUT CHARACTERS

If a Player wants to use a unit card from *Fallout: Wasteland Warfare* for their character, they can do so at the Overseer's discretion. The Overseer and Player determine any free starting Expertise skills, Perks, Gifts and Scars. In some cases, the Overseer may wish to tailor some of the character's abilities such as placing usage limits on X6-88's Stealth Boy, or altering their abilities to match the scenario's difficulty and other Player Characters' capabilities.

HEROIC

All Player Characters are Heroic, which awards them the icons shown above the archetype card or unit card on the Character Mat.

The icons on the Heroic bar give a character:

- V.A.T.S.   see 'V.A.T.S.', p.61.
- Critical icon   see 'Criticals', p.66.
- Luck icon   see 'Luck', p.35.
- Action Point Use Icons see 'Using APs', p.61.

HEROIC CARD ICON

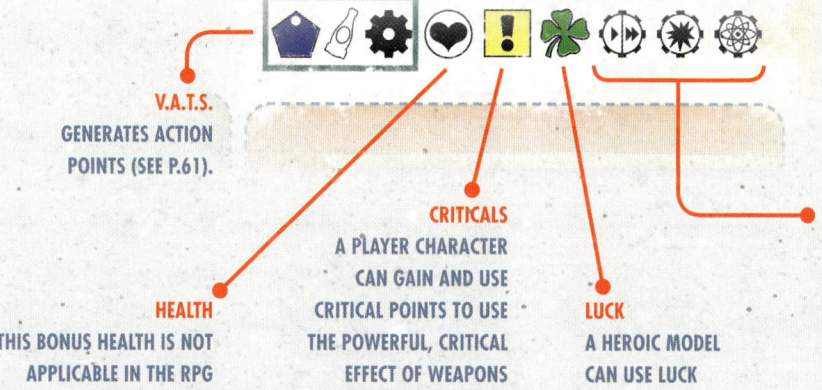

V.A.T.S. GENERATES ACTION POINTS (SEE P.61).

HEALTH THIS BONUS HEALTH IS NOT APPLICABLE IN THE RPG VARIANT OF THE GAME.

CRITICALS A PLAYER CHARACTER CAN GAIN AND USE CRITICAL POINTS TO USE THE POWERFUL, CRITICAL EFFECT OF WEAPONS (SEE 'CRITICALS', P.66).

LUCK A HEROIC MODEL CAN USE LUCK (SEE LUCK, P.35).

ACTION POINT USE A PLAYER CHARACTER CAN SPEND ACTION POINTS TO PERFORM THESE QUICK ACTIONS IN ADDITION TO THEIR USUAL TWO ACTIONS PER ROUND. (SEE 'ACTION POINTS', P.61).

IF YOU OWN *FALLOUT: WASTELAND WARFARE*, NOTE THAT 'HEROIC' DOES NOT ADD ANY EXTRA HEALTH IN THE RPG.

THE CHARACTER MAT

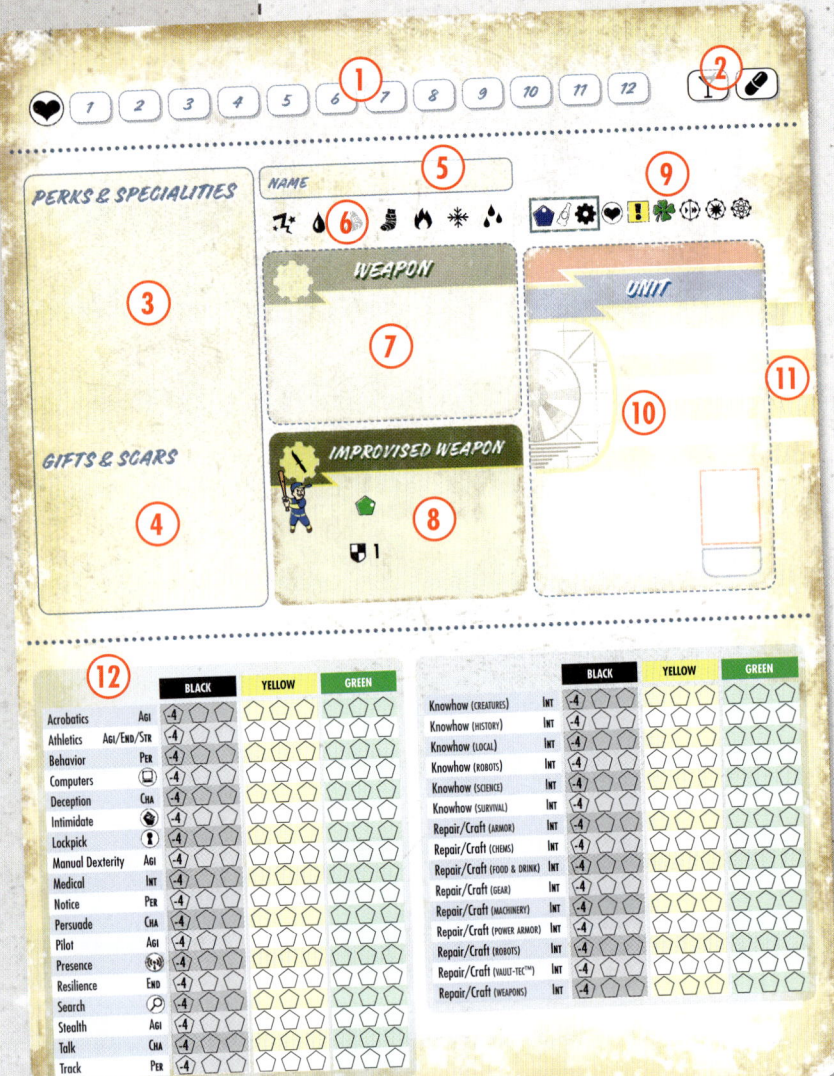

The Character Mat shows the character's archetype or unit card as well as other information such as their Expertise Skills, Health Track where damage is recorded, the Improvised Weapon that all characters have available, conditions, etc.

① Health Track.
② Addiction boxes (if this has a cross in when an Addiction Test fails, the character becomes addicted).
③ Space for writing Perks and Specialities.
④ Space for writing Gifts and Scars.
⑤ Character Name.
⑥ Conditions (circle the icon when the character suffers from a condition) – Stun, Poison, Injured Arm, Injured Leg, On Fire, Frozen, Bleeding.
⑦ Space for weapon card(s).
⑧ Default Improvised Weapon (still usable if a weapon card is placed on the Character Mat).
⑨ Heroic abilities: V.A.T.S., Criticals, Luck, Action Point Use (Move, Attack, Expertise).
⑩ Space for the archetype or unit card.
⑪ Space to write any adjustments to S.P.E.C.I.A.L. attributes, e.g. if a Perk gives Agi +1.
⑫ Skills List and Effect Dice.

GHOULS

If a character is not a Super Mutant or Robot, a Player can opt for their character to be a Ghoul instead of a Human. Reviled by some, Ghouls are Humans deeply affected by the radiation of the Wasteland. One day they may become feral but until then they inhabit the Wasteland like others do. A Ghoul receives the Lead Belly Perk for free and their Radiation Armor is set to 'X', granting them immunity. This kind of character will meet groups and people who will be hostile to, or suspicious of them purely because they are a Ghoul.

STARTING CHARACTER ARCHETYPES

Characters in the Wasteland come from all sorts of backgrounds and survive all kinds of journey. These starting character archetypes are just the beginning of a character's story in this RPG. Below are short descriptions of each that include any free Expertise Skills and Perks they start with. The archetype cards can be found on pages 38-39.

Bandit

Limited resources in the Wasteland mean one person's gain is another person's loss. The Bandit is no stranger to gaining resources without permission. Why work at something when you can take it from someone else who has already done the work? Survival is survival, and the Bandit is used to a fight to secure it.

Expertise Skills: Acrobatics, Knowhow (Survival), Knowhow (Local).

Chem Maker

Chems are a valuable commodity but require detailed knowledge to manufacture. Often working with gangs, Chem Makers are able to make and sell chems of various types. They also know how to defend themselves and what's theirs as a result.

Expertise Skills: Persuade, Talk, Deception, Repair & Craft (Chems), Medical.

Defender

The Defender is used to being part of a settlement, often mounting patrols and defending the settlement against invaders and thieves using a broad range of combat capabilities.

Expertise Skills: Behavior, Knowhow (Local), Medical, Repair & Craft (Armor).

Fixer
The Fixer has built a good rapport with many types of Wastelanders. Their extended lifespan has given them the chance to build a wide network of contacts, and develop their powers of persuasion.

Expertise Skills: *Persuade, Talk, Behavior, Knowhow (Local), Manual Dexterity.*

Forager
Finding junk, food, and information in the Wasteland is an important task and one where the Forager excels. Whether for themselves or part of a settlement, the Forager can survive in the wild and will usually bring back something of value.

Expertise Skills: *Stealth, Track, Knowhow (Creatures), Repair & Craft (Food & Drink).*

Handyman
Basic technology like power generators, water pumps and weapons need maintaining. A good Handyman is a valuable asset for any settlement or group, and they are usually good at protecting what they've created and repaired too.

Expertise Skills: *Resilience, Medical, Repair & Craft (Machinery), Repair & Craft (Weapons).*

Heavy (Super Mutant)
Super Mutants are known for their unsubtle and bellicose manner. The Heavy's first instinct is to solve every problem with a fight, and why not? They are exceptionally strong and dangerous.

Expertise Skills: *Intimidate, Athletics.*

Hunter (Super Mutant)
The Hunter is a Super Mutant used to finding and catching meals. Relatively skilled with Ranged Weapons (especially for a Super Mutant), the Hunter is used to being away from their camp to find food.

Expertise Skills: *Track, Intimidate, Knowhow (Creatures), Knowhow (Local).*
Speciality: *Track: Humans.*

Infantry
These are members of the front-line military, and solid fighters trained in all weapon types. Infantry were possibly trained by the Brotherhood of Steel, the Minutemen, or some other organisation.

Expertise Skills: *Notice, Resilience, Knowhow (Local), Repair & Craft (Weapons), Repair & Craft (Armor).*

Mr. Handy Type-I (Robot)
The Mr. Handy robot series served many functions. With three multi-functional arms, three separate eyes and a hover thruster for swift movement, a Mr. Handy could assist with almost any programmed task.

Expertise Skills: *Notice, Resilience, Any 3 Knowhow skills.*

Pilot
Not many in the Wasteland get to travel in vehicles, let alone fly them. The Pilot is used to spotting things others might not spot, and has broad experience with most types of weapons, but has not had the need to use them too often.

Expertise Skills: *Pilot, Notice, Track, Athletics, Resilience, Knowhow (Survival), Repair & Craft (Machinery).*

Researcher
Gathering information is a luxury for many in the Wasteland, but knowledge can really pay off. By rifling through old buildings or computer files in the field, or learning from books, the Researcher can find information of great value.

Expertise Skills: *Talk, Knowhow (Science), Knowhow (History), Repair & Craft (Gear).*

Scout
Often part of a larger group, the Scout is commonly used as an outrider or look-out. They are good at detecting trouble or danger and often put an end to it before it can become a more significant threat.

Expertise Skills: *Notice, Behavior, Knowhow (Survival).*

Sniper
Fast and light, the Sniper is probably from a military background, having been taught how to remain unnoticed. Whilst comfortable attacking from a distance, skills in Computers and Lockpicking mean they can usually get to where they need to be.

Expertise Skills: *Stealth, Notice, Athletics.*

Technician
Often with a military-style background, the Technician has spent much hands-on time around technology many never see. Ready to defend themselves if necessary, the Technician's speed and knowledge are their key weapons for survival.

Expertise Skills: *Knowhow (Robots), Knowhow (Science), Any 2 Repair & Craft, Any 1 Repair & Craft Speciality.*

Thug
The Thug likes a fight, usually toe-to-toe or at close range, without concern for their own safety. Preferring not to wear extra armor to remain fast-moving, a Thug is an unpredictable combatant first and foremost. Gathering resources is someone else's job.

Expertise Skills: *Acrobatics, Deception, Repair & Craft (Weapons), Repair & Craft (Armor).*

FOWW RPG-001-111 — SECTION 3.3

EXPERTISE SKILLS

Archetype/unit cards also show a character's Expertise Skills. These are used to make Skill Tests easier and/or succeed with a greater/better effect. See 'Spending Experience Points', p.36 for more on how to gain skills.

When making an Expertise Skill Test, a character with the matching skill receives any Effect Dice due to having that skill. Just having the skill grants the character a **black Effect Dice** (and they won't suffer the Unskilled penalty). They may have gained further Effect Dice if they have gained the skill multiple times (see 'Gaining Expertise Skills', p.36).

Advice for Overseers describing how different Effect Dice may affect Skill Tests can be found on p.81.

The Expertise Skills are summarized in the table below (full descriptions begin on p.25). The Attribute column (and attribute name shown in brackets after the skill name in the descriptions) shows the attribute used to set the Skill Value when making a Skill Test (unless the Overseer chooses otherwise, based on circumstances). Where an icon is shown in the Attribute column, use the attribute next to that icon on the archetype or unit card.

EXPERTISE SKILLS		
EXPERTISE SKILL NAME	**SOME AREAS THE SKILL INCLUDES**	**ATTRIBUTE**
Acrobatics	Climb, jump, and ride	AGI
Athletics	Swimming and long-distance running	AGI/END/STR (see p.25)
Behavior	Perceive unusual behavior and get a sense of someone's (or something's) intent	PER
Computers	Accessing, using, and hacking computers	💻
Deception	Bluff, lie, and disguise	CHA
Intimidate	Hostile persuasion	✊
Knowhow: Creatures	Creatures' lifestyles and habits	INT
Knowhow: History	Past events, places, and people	INT
Knowhow: Local	In-depth knowledge of an area the character knows	INT
Knowhow: Robots	Robot makes, models, and capabilities	INT
Knowhow: Science	Technically advanced devices, principles, and theories	INT
Knowhow: Survival	Bushcraft and wilderness navigation	INT
Lockpick	Includes fine mechanical devices like traps	🔑
Manual Dexterity	Pickpocket, escapology, and sleight of hand	AGI
Medical	Performing first aid and diagnosing injuries	INT
Notice	Perceive motion, sounds, smells, or things out of the ordinary (this is not the same as Search)	PER
Persuade	Persuade, negotiate, bargain in an affable manner	CHA
Pilot	Control vehicles of all types	AGI
Presence	Leadership, authority, stage presence	📡
Repair & Craft: Armor	Unpowered Armor, and clothing	INT
Repair & Craft: Chems	Chemical protective equipment, laboratory equipment, machinery that uses chemicals (such as purifiers)	INT
Repair & Craft: Food & Drink	Includes tending crops	INT
Repair & Craft: Gear	Survival equipment, tools, and everyday items for living.	INT
Repair & Craft: Machinery	Generators, lights, water pumps, engines	INT
Repair & Craft: Power Armor	Powered Armor	INT
Repair & Craft: Robots	Robots, and immobile AI-driven machinery	INT
Repair & Craft: Vault-Tec™	Items created by Vault-Tec™	INT
Repair & Craft: Weapons	Weapons of all kinds, and simple tools	INT
Resilience	Endure pain, stay awake, and hold breath	END
Search	Finding item/info by manual searching or looking	🔍
Stealth	Move undetected and hide	AGI
Talk	Gather information and make contacts	CHA
Track	Find and understand tracks	PER

SKILL LIST

The following briefly describes each skill, and offers some examples of **Specialities** within that skill. The Specialities are examples of the first ones a character could take within a skill, but they can gain a Speciality within a Speciality, which are not described in the examples. (See *Gaining Specialities*, p.36.)

Acrobatics (AGI)

A character with **Acrobatics** has excellent physical control and co-ordination, and is skilled at performing activities involving bursts of action and speed, including climbing, jumping, and riding.

Speciality examples: *Climb/Ride.*

Athletics (Relevant AGI/END/STR attribute)

A character with **Athletics** has excellent physical control and co-ordination, and can perform activities requiring long periods of steady activity such as swimming, lifting, long-distance running, and manual labor. The attribute used for the Skill Value depends on the specific activity being performed.

Speciality examples: *Long distance running/Swimming.*

Behavior (PER)

A character with **Behavior** is able to perceive small signs in another's behavior and get a sense of their intent. It only gives subtle indications, so can be considered the character's "gut feel", and it is not mind-reading or a lie detector.

Speciality examples: *Raiders/Sense hostile intent.*

Computers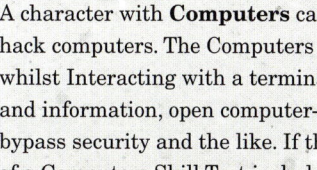

A character with **Computers** can access, use, and hack computers. The Computers skill may be used whilst Interacting with a terminal to gain access and information, open computer-controlled safes, bypass security and the like. If the Skill Dice result of a Computers Skill Test includes an icon, the Complication (see 'Complications', p.46) is often that the terminal is locked for a short period (the remainder of the round during Action Play), during which time no other Use Computers attempts can be made on that terminal. This is in addition to any other failure outcomes caused, such as setting off an alarm.

Speciality examples: *Find data/Gain access/Password.*

Deception (CHA)

A character with **Deception** is good at getting people to believe false information and selling a lie. This may be through direct lies and bluffing, actions like misdirection and cheating, and other acts such as disguise and mimicry.

Speciality examples: *Disguise/Impersonate.*

Intimidate

A character with **Intimidate** is good at persuading others to act even though it is against the will of the target. This is done through hostile persuasion, manipulation, and physical presence, but without resorting to open violence. The target is inspired to comply due to some level of fear for themselves or others.

Speciality examples: *Extortion/Intimidating dialogue.*

Knowhow: Creatures/History/Local/Robots/Science/Survival (INT)

A character with a **Knowhow** skill has a lot of general knowledge about that specific subject area. It is broad knowledge rather than encyclopedic, but much greater than the average person's knowledge of the area.

- **Creatures** covers the Wasteland's animals, and insects of all sizes.

    Speciality examples: *Mirelurks/Plains terrain.*

- **History** covers knowledge of past events, places and people.

    Speciality examples: *Brotherhood of Steel/Corporations/Vault-Tec™ vaults.*

- **Local** covers knowledge of a specific area which the character knows inside out. A character must choose a relevant area when first gaining the skill.

    Speciality examples: *A neighborhood within local area/The geography and layout of the area.*

- **Robots** covers all common types of robots (primarily current robots).

    Speciality examples: *Assaultrons/Robots of the Great War.*

- **Science** covers knowledge of technically advanced devices, principles and theories.

    Speciality examples: *Advanced weapons and armor/Chemistry.*

- **Survival** covers a wide array of bushcraft skills such as survival in the wild, building shelters and fires, navigation and foraging for natural foods and water.

    Speciality examples: *Caves and subterranean areas/Finding food/Navigation/Snare building.*

Lockpick

A character with **Lockpick** can unlock and lock mechanical locks, and other mechanical devices such as traps. The Lockpick skill may be used whilst Interacting with a lock. If the Skill Dice result of a Lockpick Skill Test includes an icon, the Complication (see 'Complications', p.46) is often that

INTIMIDATE SKILL ICON

COMPUTER SKILL ICON

LOCKPICK SKILL ICON

AURA ABILITY ICON

a lockpick tool breaks and no other Use Lockpick attempts can be made on the mechanism for a short period (the remainder of the round during Action Play). This is in addition to any other failed outcomes such as setting off a trap.

Speciality examples: Door locks/Locks on Containers/Padlocks/Traps.

Manual Dexterity (AGI)

A character with **Manual Dexterity** can perform subtle manual tasks, sometimes clandestine, including activities such as pickpocketing, sleight of hand and escapology.

Speciality examples: Close-up magic/Drawing/Pickpocketing.

Medical (INT)

A character with **Medical** skill can perform first aid as well as diagnose injuries, common diseases, and sicknesses. With the right resources, they can attempt to treat common diseases, but they are not a doctor or surgeon.

Speciality examples: Diseases/First Aid.

Notice (PER)

A character with **Notice** discerns more about the world than others using their senses to perceive motion, sounds, smells, or things out of the ordinary. It is often used passively but a character can actively use the Notice skill to detect things too. This is not the same as **Search**.

Speciality examples: Hearing/Seeing/Smelling.

Persuade (CHA)

A character with **Persuade** is great at bringing others round to their way of thinking in a sociable and affable way. They are skilled at negotiation, bargaining, and brokering deals which use the Persuade skill, and it is often used to get better prices when buying or selling. Persuade is not hostile or threatening, which would require the **Intimidate** skill instead. Persuade does not make a character a good liar; the **Deception** skill is required to lie convincingly.

Speciality examples: Bartering in a specific geographic area/Buying junk/Selling junk/Super Mutants.

Pilot (AGI)

A character with **Pilot** can fly, drive and control vehicles of all types at a basic level.

Speciality examples: Tracked vehicles/Vertibird.

Presence

A character with **Presence** is gifted with an air of leadership and non-hostile authority, an aura that can bring comfort to others and rally people together, and the ability to be noticed and hold an audience's attention with superior stage-presence. Note that the color of the Presence skill icon sets the maximum distance at which a character's Aura abilities (see page 68) have influence, if any.

Speciality examples: Act/Rally.

Repair & Craft: Armor/Chems/Food & Drink/Gear/Machinery/Power Armor/Robots/Vault-Tec™/Weapons (INT)

A character with a **Repair & Craft** skill has practical ability to mend things in the selected field. They know how to make things, fix things, and know what makes those things tick. They can create Mods of the type matching their skill (see 'Crafting', p.98), and repair items (see 'Repairing Items', p.98). They do need an appropriate Workbench or Workstation (see 'Settlements', p.95) and the relevant materials or resources.

- **Armor** covers all armor except Power Armor.

  Speciality examples: Combat Armor/Mods.

- **Chems** covers all types of Chems.

  Speciality examples: Healing chems/Time-slowing chems.

- **Food & Drink** covers all type of foodstuffs and cooking.

  Speciality examples: Alcohol/Cooking/Growing crops/Nuka-Cola.

- **Gear** covers all types of gadgets and gizmos such as Stealth Boy, Fire Extinguishers, smoke grenades, signal flares (see 'Gear', p.73).

  Speciality examples: Stealth Boy/Traps.

- **Machinery** covers all types of basic machinery such as generators, production lines, lighting, radio beacons, water pumps, engines, etc.

  Speciality examples: Communications/Factory and production lines/Settlement machinery.

- **Power Armor** covers all types of Power Armor.

  Speciality examples: Mods/T-45/T-60.

- **Robots** covers all types of robots.

  Speciality examples: Mr Handy series/Mods/Assaultron series.

- **Vault-Tec™** primarily covers the systems within vaults but also includes any items created by Vault-Tec™ such as Pip-Boys.

  Speciality examples: Pip-Boy/Vault security systems.

- **Weapons** covers all type of weapons.

  Speciality examples: Energy weapons/Rifles/Mods.

PRESENCE SKILL ICON

Resilience (END)

A character with **Resilience** has learnt some control over their body. They are better at enduring pain, staying awake, holding their breath, and even resisting disease.

Speciality examples: Hold breath/Staying calm.

Search

SEARCH SKILL ICON

A character with **Search** is great at finding things via manual searching, looking and/or other means. They have a knack for finding things faster than others or finding things others may miss. Searches may find an item in a pile of trash or rubble, information in a library or a pile of paperwork, locate valuable items in a room, discover hidden compartments, etc.

The Search skill may be used to find objects, notice recent tracks, etc. If the Skill Dice result of a Search Skill Test includes an /X/ icon, the Complication (see 'Complications', p.46) may be that the Search takes longer, more noise than expected is made, the character's clothing gets snagged, etc. – this is in addition to any other outcomes failure causes.

Speciality examples: Information finding/Search dwellings.

Stealth (AGI)

A character with **Stealth** can move and hide with a reduced chance of being noticed or detected by someone else. Not only do they know how to move covertly but they also know how to use the environment to their advantage.

Speciality examples: Night-time/Urban environments/Hiding.

Talk (CHA)

A character with **Talk** is great at making a connection with others to find out information, rumors and gossip. Gaining information is often much better when it is two-way, and so Talk can be used to both gather and spread information. Talk does not allow a character to be a good liar, which is the work of the **Deception** skill.

Speciality examples: Local politics/Make new contacts/Ghouls.

Track (PER)

A character with **Track** is able to find, read, and follow people, creatures, and robots via signs of their passage. Tracks on the ground are a primary means, but other indications play a part, such as broken branches, discarded litter, and so on. The difficulty can be affected by the type of terrain, amount of light, weather, speed, etc.

Speciality examples: Deathclaws/Mountainous terrain.

NOTHING SCREAMS INTIMIDATION LOUDER THAN 'I MEAN IT, BUDDY – THIS THING'S LOADED!'

FOWW RPG-001-111 — SECTION 3.4
GIFTS AND SCARS

Gifts and **Scars** are traits, behaviors and abilities that have been gained by a character due to their background and upbringing. Some Gifts and Scars have defined rule effects and some do not. Players should incorporate the effects of their Gifts and Scars into their characters' actions, attitudes and behaviors. For example, Arrogant characters receive a -2 penalty to all social CHA Tests, but should also be keen to be the first to charge into a room, or more likely to volunteer to be Deathclaw bait!

Gifts and Scars *cannot* be bought using XP. When selecting Gifts and Scars, Gifts should not be selected that counter the character's Scars, and vice versa. Players and the Overseer can agree new Gifts and Scars not on the list. Note that Gifts and Scars should be capabilities that are different to Perks.

Gifts benefit a character but only in specific moments and/or never so much that they give a major advantage.

As with Gifts, **Scars** should be limited in their application and effects.

GIFTS	
GIFT NAME	**EFFECT**
Alert	You gain a +2 bonus to PER-based Skill Tests
Ally	You have a friend in a position of power or influence that can help you in key ways. This assistance is of a different level or nature than a Contact could provide.
Ambidextrous	You can use either hand to perform tests (your character must have at least AGI 4), and can avoid penalties for having injured hands or arms.
Average Joe/Jane	Your plain appearance makes you blend into crowds and become harder to spot. Add several bonuses at the Overseer's discretion.
Benefactor	A public or secret benefactor (Overseer's choice) gives you a gift of gear, Caps, or a resource.
Big-Boned	Your character gains +1 STR.
Big-Brained	Your character gains +1 INT.
Blends In	You receive a +2 bonus to using cover or when sneaking around.
Bold	You get an improved benefit when spending Luck Points (at the Overseer's discretion).
Bright-Eyed	Your character gains +1 PER.
Bug Free	Your character is less likely to suffer effects of any disease (Overseer's discretion depending on the disease in question).
Charmed Life	Your character gains +1 LUC.
Competitive	You gain a +2 bonus to Opposed Tests.
Confident	You receive a +2 bonus to specific CHA Tests, as long as your character has at least CHA 4.
Contact	You have a contact in a faction, location, or group of some kind who can give you information or assistance that the Overseer thinks appropriate. This is a lesser kind of help than that from an Ally.
Dead Aim	When Shooting, you may ignore one item of cover.
Dodge	Your character is better at getting out of the way (Overseer's discretion, depending on circumstances).
Eidetic Memory	Your character doesn't forget details. Most easy INT tasks are automatically successful and other INT Tests that are memory-based are easier (at the Overseer's discretion).
Eyes like a Radowl	Your character can see better in the dark, and suffers no penalty due to low-light conditions.
Famous	You're well known within a region for some specific feat, which you should weave into your backstory. This may pay off in favors or prestige.
Far-sighted	You've got the eyes of an eagle. You get a +2 bonus when aiming at or interacting with things at Awareness color range or greater.
Fast Healer	You recover Health more quickly (in favorable circumstances and at the Overseer's discretion).
Fleet of Foot	Your character gains +1 AGI.
Gift of Gab	Your character gains +1 CHA.
Go for the Vitals	You benefit when targeting specific parts of the body during attacks.
Healthy	Your character suffers a one-time permanent +1 to Health.

Inheritance	You receive a one-time gift of gear, Caps, or a resource. The source of the inheritance is either known to you, or can be a mystery to unravel (Overseer's choice).
Iron Stomach	You are more difficult to poison.
Lead Skin	You are more resistant to the effects of radiation. Add several bonuses at the Overseer's discretion.
Lungs like a Brahmin	Your character gains +1 END.
Natural Leader	You gain +2 bonus to specific CHA Tests, but must have at least CHA 5.
Patron	Either a public or secret patron gives you gear, Caps, or resources in exchange for a regular favors or things. Effectively, a patron gives you stuff and you return with regular stories of your exploits, or trinkets from your victories, etc.
Quick Draw	Your character takes less time to pull out a sheathed or holstered weapon.
Situational Awareness	Your characrer may go before all other characters in the first round of combat. After this, combat continues as usual. (Overseer chooses who goes first if more than one character has this gift.)
Sense of Direction	You instinctively know which way is north, or know the right way through a location.
Sense of Time	You have an instinct as to time: you know how long things take and, if knocked out, you know how much time has passed (with a 10% margin of error).
Tech Wizard / Gearhead	Your gain a +2 bonus to specific INT Tests, specifically related to computers, tech, machinery, etc.
Wealthy	You come from a wealthy background and get a one-time windfall of 25 Caps.

SCARS

SCAR NAME	EFFECT
Addiction	You are addicted to a substance that you must have once a day, or you will suffer a -2 penalty to all tests or -3 to specific attributes. You can 'buy' this Scar twice for a serious addiction that requires a double dose per day with higher penalties (set by your Overseer).
Amputee	You are missing one or more limbs, either as partial amputations like a hand or forearm or foot, or the full amputation of a leg or an arm. You may have a prosthetic that gives you a -2 to tests related to the missing limb. If you lose, damage, or never had such a prosthetic, you will be prevented from completing some tasks.
Arrogant	You have a -2 penalty to all social CHA Tests.
Cursed	Your character loses -1 LUC.
Deaf	You cannot hear. At the Overseer's discretion this may mean that you are unaware of enemies outside your Line of Sight.
Devotion	You are related to someone – a child, family member, lover, etc. – that frequently gets into trouble, and you are often pulled into their dramas.
Diseased	Your character suffers a one-time permanent -1 to Health.
Dullard	Your character loses -1 INT.
Favor Owed/ Indebted	You owe someone a favor, and they'll collect payment at a really inconvenient time.
Flat-footed	You suffer a -2 penalty to AGI Tests involving running, climbing, dancing, etc.
Fragile	Your character loses -1 STR.
Fumble-fingered	You have a -2 penalty to AGI, particularly in fine motor skills such as Lockpicking.
Gullible	You suffer a -2 penalty to social tests.
Hatred	You hate a particular faction, race or species, such as Ghouls, Robots, Super Mutants, the Brotherhood of Steel, etc. You will immediately enter social or physical conflict with them unless you pass an INT or CHA Test.
Hemophiliac	You bleed more easily than normal, and as a result your wounds heal more slowly. You must rest for 2 hours to remove 1 point of damage, instead of 1 hour.
Hidden Shame	There is a deep secret about you that you protect at all costs. Any revelation might ruin you!
Hit Every Branch on the Way Down	Your character loses -1 CHA.
Hunted	Someone or something is seeking you out. There is a chance every adventure for a creature with a vendetta to appear (as determined by the Overseer).
I Know Something	You know something terrible about your faction, an ally, or an important person that would cause major problems if it became public knowledge.

SECTION 3 – CREATING A CHARACTER

SCARS (CONTINUED)	
SCAR NAME	EFFECT
Indifferent	You just kind of don't care about people or their problems. Your character suffers a -2 penalty to social tests.
Infamous	You have a reputation throughout the Wasteland for an action or deed in your past, and you can't shake this notoriety. Whenever you're in a social situation, and get noticed, you'll be the center of attention for good or ill.
Intolerant	You don't like a particular faction, race, or species such as Ghouls, robots, Super Mutants, the Brotherhood of Steel, or whatever. You get a -2 penalty to all social tests in relation to those you do not tolerate.
Mute	You cannot speak. You may have developed a sign language, have a mechanical device attached to your vocal cords, or may simply be unable to speak at all.
Myopic	Your character goes after all other characters in the first round of combat. After this, combat continues as usual. (Overseer chooses who goes last if more than one character has this scar.)
Narrow Vision	Your character loses -1 PER.
Near-sighted	You can't see clearly at any distance. You suffer a -2 penalty when attempting a test with an object at Awareness color range or greater, and cannot shoot or interact with things at Awareness color range.
Night Blind	You have trouble seeing in low-light conditions, and have a -2 penalty to tests conducted at night or in low-light conditions.
One-eyed	You've lost the use of one of your eyes and possibly the eye itself. You suffer a -2 penalty to most PER Tests.
Rival	A former friend, a rival suitor, a schoolmate, or a friend from work is highly competitive with you. Whenever you meet, they immediately attempt to one-up you.
Secretly a Synth	You don't realize it yet, but you are actually a Synth.
Two Left Feet	Your character loses -1 AGI.
Wanted	Someone has put a bounty on your head. There is a percentage chance every adventure that a bounty hunter will appear to capture you (as determined by the Overseer).
Weak Lungs	Your character loses -1 END.

FOWW RPG-001-111 — **SECTION 3.5**

PERKS

IF YOU OWN *FALLOUT: WASTELAND WARFARE*, NOTE THAT THE PERKS GUN NUT (ALL TYPES), BLACKSMITH, AND ARMORER ARE NOT USED IN THE RPG. THE REPAIR & CRAFT SKILLS SERVE THE SAME FUNCTION (SEE CRAFTING, P.98).

Characters can have one or more **Perks**, which add or increase their abilities. Player Characters gain Perks as they gain experience by spending Experience Points. Perks that may be gained multiple times are indicated by 'Y' in the 'Multi' column in the Perks table, below.

Only Perks listed in the table below can be used in the RPG. Perks that can be used in the RPG *only* (not in *Fallout: Wasteland Warfare*) are indicated by 'Y' in the 'RPG only' column. Perks that are *not* RPG-only exist on unit cards in *Fallout: Wasteland Warfare*.

Characters may not benefit from the same Perk from different sources – ie from their own Perk and by being in the aura of another character's Perk.

The icons in the following table are explained later in this book, and have their own Icon Index on page 135.

PERKS				
PERK NAME	XP	EFFECT	MULTI	RPG ONLY
Acrobatic Dodge	2	Once per battle, you can Test AGI. If successful, ignore all damage from a single attack.	–	Y
Action Boy/Girl	3	⬟☆⚙. A character cannot use this in addition to V.A.T.S. during an activation. (Note: this is not useful to Player Characters who automatically get V.A.T.S.).	–	–
Agile	Varies	You gain +1 AGI.	Y	–
Aquaboy/Aquagirl	2	You can hold your breath underwater for long periods and do not take radiation damage when swimming.	–	Y
Armor Knowledge	2	For 🛡, 1 ⬟ treated as 🎯.	–	Y
Artillerist	3	☀🛡⊗ 1 color shorter (minimum Orange).	–	Y

PERKS (CONTINUED)

PERK NAME	XP	EFFECT	MULTI	RPG ONLY
Attack Dog	3	☀: Dog attacks get ☆ 🧦	–	–
Basher	2	When using a Ranged Weapon in Close Combat, ignore the extra Armor Rating it gives your target. The -2 penalty to skill is still applied.	–	–
Battle Experience	2	☀ During turn when the character is activated, may swap 1 ⬟/⬟/⬟ for 1 ⬟.	–	Y
Big Leagues	3	Re-roll 1 blank result on ⬟ in an attack with 🗡.	–	–
Blitz	3	One 🗡 attack per activation can be made at Orange range. It still uses the 🗡 skill but is resolved as a Shooting attack. Push Back can still occur but with no follow-up. If you are engaged with an enemy, you may still use this to attack a target with which you are not engaged.	–	–
Bloody Mess	2	When an enemy character will be incapacitated due to an attack by you, make a 50:50 roll (see page 35). If successful, the gruesome wound unnerves nearby enemies. Each enemy character within Yellow of the character to be incapacitated receives a -2 penalty which they lose after their next Action (including Reactions).	–	–
Brave	2	☀ Other characters may use your ✊.	–	Y
Bushcraft	3	You use the cooked effect of food.	–	Y
Cannibal	3	If you eat a portion of Human flesh, remove 2 regular damage.	–	Y
Cap Collector	3	Prices when buying are lower for you.	–	Y
Careful	4	When shooting into Close Combat, the intended target is always affected – no need to randomize.	–	Y
Charismatic	Varies	You gain +1 CHA.	Y	–
Chem Resistant	2	Once per day, you may re-roll an Addiction Test (see page 74).	–	–
Chemist	2	Chems last one extra round for you.	–	–
Concentrated Fire		When shooting at a target which you shot at with your previous Action, you gain a +2 bonus to 🔫/🔫/🔫. This can be used a maximum of once per activation.	–	–
Critical Banker	4	You may have up to double the number of Critical Points usually allowed on a weapon.	–	–
Demolition Expert	3	You may re-roll 1 blank result on ⬟ in an attack when using 💣.	–	–
Distracting	4	Once during an activation, you may spend an Action to allocate a penalty of -2 to one opposing character within 📡. If you are engaged, you must be engaged with the opposing character. This penalty is removed when you next activate. The Action spent counts as a Move for Triggers but you do not move.	–	Y
Dog Handler	3	☀ 🐾 can 🔍 using PER. At start of their activation, nearby dogs are Heroic for that activation.	–	–
Enduring	Varies	You gain +1 END.	Y	–
Fist	3	This counts as an Improvised Weapon, +1 base damage.	–	Y
Fortune Finder	3	You find more Caps than most people (Overseer's discretion as to the extra amount you find).	–	Y
Genius	2	You are never locked out of 💻.	–	Y
Ghoulish	4	Radiation damage counts as healing. Many Wasteland inhabitants will treat you differently or negatively because of your strange metabolism.	–	–
Gunslinger	3	You may re-roll a blank result on 1 ⬟ in an attack with 🔫.	–	–

DAMAGE EFFECT DICE

ACCURACY EFFECT DICE

ARMOR REDUCTION EFFECT DICE

SPECIAL EFFECT DICE

TO HELP COLOR BLIND PLAYERS IDENTIFY WHICH DICE ARE BEING REFERENCED ON CARDS, THE ICONS FOR EFFECT DICE HAVE DOTS IN DIFFERING CORNERS.

PERKS (CONTINUED)

PERK NAME	XP	EFFECT	MULTI	RPG ONLY
Hacker	2	🖥️ +2. If your character has no 🖥️ skill, this Perk gives your character 🖥️ 2.	–	–
Hammer Time	3	You can choose 🟡 for Charge bonus instead of ⬟/🟢.	–	Y
Heavy Gunner	3	Your may re-roll 1 blank result on ⬟ in an attack with 🔫.	–	–
Huntsman	3	Before making any dice rolls for any shot, you can choose to replace damage caused by 🏹 with: 1 🛡️/⚡🔵☆🧦. The type of damage matches the type usually dealt by the weapon. This cannot be used with ☢️ weapons.	–	–
Intelligent	Varies	You gain +1 INT.	Y	–
Lead Belly	3	You may ignore any radiation damage from consuming food and drink.	–	–
Life Giver	Varies	You gain ❤️ +1. The XP cost is your new Health number minus 3 (but a minimum XP cost of 1), e.g. increasing Health from 4 to 5 would cost 5–3=2 XP.	Y	–
Locksmith	2	You gain 🔑 +2. If your character has no 🔑 skill, this Perk gives your character 🔑 2.	–	–
Lone Wanderer	4	When not within Presence of any friendly character (excluding dogs), you gain: +1 🛡️; +1 ⚡; +1 ☢️; +1 🟡 for 🔫 and 🔫; and ❤️ +2.	–	–
Look Out!	3	If unengaged and before any Armor Dice roll, you may take weapon damage suffered by a friendly character within Orange and LoS. This may be used once between activations.	–	Y
Lucky	Varies	You gain +2 LUC.	Y	–
Medic	2	Stimpaks remove 1 additional 💥; RadAway removes 1 additional ☢️.	–	–
Moving Target	3	If 2 Actions (not Quick Actions) are spent Moving and/or Charging during an activation, ranged attacks against you suffer a -2 penalty. This benefit ends: at the start of your next activation; if you are engaged at any time; at the start of performing a Reaction; when suffering from Push Back; or when taking damage.	–	–
Mysterious Stranger	4	If ☢️ is rolled during a V.A.T.S. roll, Mysterious Stranger attacks your nearest unengaged enemy in LoS. This is your choice, if tied. Auto-hit: Resolve 2 plus 🛡️ + ⬟. This attack is optional.	–	–
Mysterious Stranger II	3	Requires: Mysterious Stranger Perk. If ★/☢️ rolled during V.A.T.S. roll, Mysterious Stranger appears up to Red away. Auto-hit on any character in LoS: Resolve 3 🛡️ + 🟡. This attack is optional and there is a maximum of one Mysterious Stranger Perk per activation.	–	–
Mysterious Stranger III	3	Requires: Mysterious Stranger II Perk. As Mysterious Stranger II, but when Mysterious Stranger's appears, either immediately resolve Mysterious Stranger's attack OR Mysterious Stranger can use a Reaction with 👁️ to attack later. There is a maximum of one Mysterious Stranger Perk per activation.	–	–
Nerd Rage	3	You may, when on 1 or 2 ❤️ gain: +1 ⚙️; Strong Armor Rating +1; or +⬟ on 🗡️ attacks. This is usable once per battle. ⏱️ 1	Y	–
Newshound	2	You gain 💥 +2 🔍. If your character has no 🔍 you get 🔍 2 instead.	–	Y
Nimble	2	You can break engagement using Slide.	–	Y
Ninja	3	If no-one has LoS to you (other than your target), shots at long range add 1 🟢.	–	–

PERKS (CONTINUED)

PERK NAME	XP	EFFECT	MULTI	RPG ONLY
Orders	3	When you activate, you can make 1 Unready Non-Player Character within Yellow Ready.	–	Y
Pack Leader	2	This perk cannot be equipped by Dogs, Creatures, or Robots. The character gains the Dog Handler (🐕) ability. If they already have (🐕), you affect one additional dog. This Perk can be equipped multiple times. DOG HANDLER ☀: (🐾) can (🔍) using PER. If Dog Handler character is Heroic, nearby (🐾) also Heroic for their activation.	Y	–
Pain Train	4	Whilst you are wearing (🎭) and performing a Charge Action you can immediately roll 1 (⬟) and the target resolves Damage icons (and makes their usual armor roll) instead of gaining a Charge Bonus. This is part of the Charge Action.	–	–
Party Boy/Party Girl	3	You will never become addicted.	–	–
Perceptive	Varies	You gain +1 PER.	Y	–
Purpose	2	You are resistant to 💤.	–	Y
Rad Resistant	3	Your ☢ is increased by 1.	–	–
Refractor	3	Your ⚡ is increased by 1.	–	–
Rifleman	3	You may re-roll blank result on 1 (⬟) during attack with (🔫).	–	–
Robotics Expert	2	This Perk allows you to attach Mods which display (🤖) to Robots which display (🤖), but no more than 2 Mods per Robot unit card. You require the Mods to attach and must be using a Robot Workbench. This Perk also allows you to equip Robots with Robot weapons that are not standard for that Robot type.	–	–
Rooted	2	You cannot be Pushed Back unless willing to be pushed.	–	–
Rousing	2	You may remove 💤 from 1 other character within (📶).	–	Y
Scrapper	2	Scrapping items generates more resources than usual but of the same type as normally generated (Overseer decides what materials you salvage, and the quantity of each).	–	Y
Scrounger	3	You find more ammunition than most people (extra amount at Overseer's discretion).	–	Y
Sharpshoot	4	When Shooting, you ignore one item of cover.	–	Y
Sneak	4	Movement and Melee attacks are not Triggers outside one range ruler distance.	–	–
Steady Aim	3	You may re-roll 1 (⬟) in attacks made with (🔫)/(🔫).	–	Y
Strong	Varies	You gain +1 STR.	Y	–
Strong Back	2	Being Encumbered has no effect. Instead, being Over-Encumbered has the effect of being Encumbered.	–	Y
Toughness	3	Your (🛡) is increased by 1.	–	–
Unarmed	3	When you are using an Improvised Weapon, you receive +(⬟) and (👊)(①) = (🌀).	–	Y
Urban	2	You automatically succeed at your first Climb Test during a climb. At the starting of a fall, you may Test AGI to grab any appropriate handhold to prevent falling.	–	Y
Weak Point		You treat (🔫) 1 (⬟) as (⬢).	–	Y
Wild	3	☀ When using (🗡) you may swap 1 (⬟)/(⬟) for 1 (⬟).	–	Y
Wasteland Whisperer	3	If unengaged, you may make an Opposed CHA Test versus one Creature that is weaker than you (as determined by the Overseer). If successful, that Creature will not attack you. This effect ends if you attack the Creature or leave its Presence.	–	Y

FOWW RPG-001-111 — SECTION 3.6

SPECIALIST CHARACTERS

LEADERS

Leaders are titles that some characters may have, each title giving the character one or more extra abilities. Player Characters do not automatically receive Leader abilities, but may earn them if the Overseer feels it is appropriate as part of their progression. A character may have a maximum of one Leader title at any time.

Beneficial effects of the abilities from a Leader's title affect friendly characters, although the Leader character can choose to withhold this benefit. Benefiting from a Leader's ability requires a good connection between the characters and the Overseer can deem the connection between characters too weak for the benefit to have any effect.

LEADER CARD ICON

TYPES

Some characters are of a specific type (such as a Dog, Robot or Creature) and this may add some specific rules. Each type has an icon to identify it.

Robots

- Robots can only use cards which show the (🤖) icon, or cards that specifically state they can be used by Robots, or are equipped by the character's card.
- Robots are immune to Poison and radiation damage.
- Robots can have damage removed using a Robot Repair Kit.
- A Robot may equip a total of 2 Robot Weapons, 2 Robot Mods and 1 non-Weapon Robot item.
- If a Robot has Weapons named on its archetype or unit card, those are the only Weapons it may equip unless a character with the Robotics Expert perk changes them.

Creatures

- Creatures can only use cards which show the (🐾) icon, or specifically state can be used by Creatures on the cards, or are equipped by the Unit's card.
- Creatures cannot use Power Armor, Armor, Clothing, Food and Drink, Alcohol, Chems, Perks, Mods or Weapons unless this is specifically stated on the relevant cards, or is equipped by the Creature's unit card.
- A Creature may equip a total of 2 Creature Weapons, 2 Creature Mods and 1 non-Weapon item.
- A Creature type cannot be run as a PC.

ROBOT TYPE ICON

CREATURE TYPE ICON

DOG TYPE ICON

DOG HANDLER ICON

Dogs

- Dogs cannot use Power Armor, Armor, Clothing, Alcohol, Chems, Perks, Mods or Weapons unless specifically stated on the cards in question, or the items are equipped by the Dog's unit card.
- Dogs can use Food and Drink.
- A Dog type cannot be run as a PC.

Dog Handler

Dog Handler is an aura ability (see 'Aura Abilities and Effects', p.68) that some characters possess. One Dog that starts its activation within the aura of a Dog Handler character with whom they are familiar gains the following benefits during its activation:

1. The Dog character may use the Search skill, based on its own PER.
2. If the Dog Handler character is a Player Character or a Major NPC (see p.88) then the Dog character is Heroic (see 'Heroic', p.21).

These benefits only last for the Dog's activation, and do not affect the Dog's Reaction, if it has one (it isn't necessary to remember whether a Dog was Heroic during its activation). The first time a Dog gains the Luck ability, it gains Luck Points (see p.35) equal to its LUC. These can only be used when a Dog is Heroic, and the pool it starts with does not increase even if it starts its activation in the Dog Handler's aura in later rounds. When a Dog is Heroic, Critical Points (see p.66) are gained by a relevant weapon card as usual, and the Critical Effect of a fully charged weapon may only be used by a Dog while it is Heroic.

FACTIONS

In *Fallout: Wasteland Warfare*, characters are often part of a wider group, such as Super Mutants or the Brotherhood of Steel. In the RPG, the character's faction is determined by the Overseer (regardless of what is shown under the title of their unit card). A character can change factions during games, and can occasionally belong to more than one faction. A character's faction may affect situations during games as determined by the Overseer. It's quite possible for characters' lives to be affected by inter-factional rivalries, for example.

Super Mutants

Whether a Player Character or not, Super Mutants are subject to the following rules:

- Super Mutants use the (🗡) skill for Skill Tests when using a Ranged Weapon in Close Combat.
- They cannot wear Power Armor (☢).
- They are Immune to radiation (☢) damage.
- Food always counts as cooked when eaten.

FOWW RPG-001-111 — SECTION 3.7

LUCK

Characters with the Luck icon can use Luck to improve their fate. Having multiple Luck icons gives no extra benefit.

When created, a character starts with a number of Luck Points equal to their LUC attribute. Once spent, these can be regained as determined by the Overseer. A character can never have more Luck Points than their LUC attribute.

LUCK ICON

Luck Points can be used for different effects depending upon the situation. When a character spends a Luck Point, they declare what they are using it for and make a **50:50 Luck Test** (see the 'Randomizing' sidebar, below). If successful, the effect occurs; if not, the effect doesn't happen, but either way, the Luck Point is spent.

USES FOR LUCK POINTS

A Luck Point can be used to:

Enhance a Skill Test
Prior to rolling the dice for a Skill Test, a character can spend **1 Luck Point** to **add 1 black, yellow, or green Effect Dice** to the roll.

Multiple Luck Points can be used on a single Skill Test with each adding one Effect Dice of any type. The usual maximums apply, but note that a blue Effect Dice cannot be added this way.

Improve a Skill Test
After an unsuccessful Skill Test has been rolled for a character, the Player can declare their use of a Luck Point. If their 50:50 Luck Test is successful, the Skill Dice result receives a **-2 modifier**, perhaps changing a narrow failure to a success. Note that Luck cannot be used if the original test was successful. Also, the ⓧ result on Skill Dice is not a number, so it cannot be altered by Luck. Only one Luck Point can be used in this way for any one Skill Test.

Worsen a Skill Test (by Someone Else)
If a character is the target of a successful Skill Test, they have an opportunity to use Luck to turn the other party's success into a failure: that is, turn a successful attack into a miss. After a successful Skill Test has been rolled, even if Luck was used to make it succeed, but before the effect is known, the character declares if they will use a Luck Point. If their 50:50 Luck Test is successful, the Skill Dice receives a **+2 modifier**, perhaps changing the success into a failure. Criticals automatically succeed, so Luck cannot change them. Note that after a target has used Luck to make a Skill Test into a failure, the character performing that Skill Test cannot use Luck if they did not already do so after making their roll.

Reduce Damage
After damage has been caused to a character, but before it is applied, the Player declares if they will spend a Luck Point to attempt to **reduce the damage by 1**. If their 50:50 Luck Test is successful, the damage is reduced by 1 and then any remainder applied. Luck spent this way is done after any relevant armor roll has been made. Only one Luck Point can be used on any one application of damage.

Generate Additional Critical Point
After a successful attack, the attacking character declares if they will spend a Luck Point to gain one additional Critical Point. If their 50:50 Luck Test is successful, **1 CP is added** to the weapon used. This is in addition to any CPs the attack roll generated, and happens if the target was hit, regardless of what actual damage was caused. Only one Luck Point can be used to gain a Critical Point on any one attack. A character must be able to use Criticals to use Luck this way.

Using Multiple Luck Points
A character may use multiple Luck Points on the same test, but may not use more than one on a single application of Luck: i.e. a character cannot use two Luck Points to try to worsen the same Skill Test result twice or reduce damage twice, but they could spend a Luck Point to worsen the Skill Test and another Luck Point to reduce the damage.

RANDOMIZING

To decide a **50:50**, roll the black Damage Dice:

| Outcome A | Any damage (single or double) |
| Outcome B | Anything not a single or double damage |

To determine a random **1 in 3 chance**, roll the blue Special Effect Dice:

Outcome A	Any Single Bottle
Outcome B	Any Single Star or Blast
Outcome C	Any two icons

To determine a random **1 in 4 chance**, split the 4 outcomes into pairs and use 50:50 to decide the pair, then 50:50 to decide which of that pair is the outcome.

FOWW RPG-001-111 — SECTION 3.8

EXPERIENCE & PROGRESSION

Players can develop their characters in almost any direction they wish, but it is the Overseer who determines if something can be learned or improved. A character needs to have had an appropriate experience to learn from, or have access to books or a teacher, or to have equipment on which to train. For example, a character that has never met or seen the tracks of, say, a Deathclaw would need a book or teacher to learn about tracking Deathclaws. They couldn't just suddenly know how to do it.

Gaining Experience Points

After making progress in a scenario, or after significant encounters, the Overseer may award **Experience Points** (**XP**) to the Player Characters which can then be spent on improving the character.

Spending Experience Points

A Player may spend their character's XP to gain or improve skills, attributes, and abilities. The Player can spend them at any time the Overseer feels is appropriate: some new skills may only be learned with a relevant period of practice, whilst others may be new knowledge gained during a scenario.

The amount of XP an improvement costs depends on the improvement, and is sometimes based on existing improvements too.

HOW TO INCREASE COMBAT SKILLS

A character cannot purchase Combat Skills in the same way that Expertise Skills can be purchased. A character looking to improve their combat Skill Tests purchases Specialities in specific weapons that they want to use more effectively, adds Mods to their weapons, and/or purchases a Perk to improve results in combat.

BROAD INCREASES VERSUS SPECIALISATION

A character can concentrate their abilities in areas by purchasing Specialities that give a good boost to the chances of success, but in a narrow field. Broader than Specialities is purchasing Expertise Skills multiple times, which give extra Effect Dice for all Skill Tests made using that skill. Even broader, but usually most costly, is purchasing Perks that increase an attribute which, as a consequence, increase the Skill Value for all skills associated with that attribute.

EXPERIENCE POINT SPENDS	
XP	**GAIN**
1+	**Expertise Skill** ■ 1 XP for a new non-Combat Skill. ■ If the character already possesses the skill, the cost is an extra 2 XP per Effect Dice the character already receives for having the skill.
2	**Speciality for a Skill** ■ The Overseer may allow a Player to purchase a very narrow Speciality for 1 XP.
2–4	**Perk** ■ Some Perks can be bought multiple times. ■ Perks which improve Attributes (i.e. Strong gives +1 STR) cost XP equal to the new attribute value minus 4 (a minimum of 1 XP). For example, increasing STR from 6 to 7 costs 7 – 4 = 3 XP. ■ Costs are shown in the Perks table (see Perks, pp.30-33)

Gaining Expertise Skills

A character may purchase skills from the Expertise Skills table (see p.24). However, a character may not purchase any new skill represented by an icon (i.e. Computers, Lockpick) which is not shown on their archetype or unit card (unless through very special circumstances determined by the Overseer).

The first time a character gains an Expertise skill, they gain a black Effect Dice when making Skill Tests of that type. They no longer have the Unskilled penalty (see p.85). Each time a character gains an Expertise skill they already possess, the character gains a further black, yellow or green Effect Dice. They choose which color they want when they gain the skill. When making Skill Tests, a character uses all the Effect Dice they have gained.

> *Example: A Raider has the Track skill so rolls a black Effect Dice when making Track Skill Tests. The Raider then purchases the Track skill again and decides that this time they will add a green Effect Dice. When the Raider makes a Track Skill Test from now on, they will roll both a black and green Effect Dice.*

When a skill is gained, color in the relevant outline in the Skills area of the Character Mat to record what color dice was gained.

Gaining Specialities

A character can only gain **Specialities** within Skills they already possess, and each Speciality must be a specific subsection of their skill: a Speciality of Rifle could be using a Bolt-Action Pipe Rifle (as long as the character already has the Rifle skill); a Speciality of

EXPERTISE INCREASES SUIT SOME CAMPAIGNS; FOR OTHERS, EXTRA HEALTH MAY BE NEEDED TO MAKE IT TO THE END

Medical could be First Aid. The choice and scope of the Speciality's focus is up to the Player and Overseer. For example, a Speciality in Track could be to Track Super Mutants, or it could be to track anything (but only) in mountainous regions. Some examples of potential Specialities within each Skill are shown in the Skill List (pp.25-27).

A character can have multiple Specialities within a skill: Rifle Specialities for both Bolt-Action Pipe Rifle and for Gauss Rifle, so they gain +2 for Rifle Skill Tests with either of these weapons.

A character may gain a **Speciality within a Speciality** and the bonuses for them accumulate.

Example: a character with Repair & Craft: Weapons could take the Speciality of Energy Weapons (giving them **+2** for any repair or crafting of an energy weapon), and then take a further Speciality within Energy Weapons of Plasma Rifle (giving them **+4** for any repair or crafting of Plasma Rifles). A character with Knowhow: Creatures could take a Speciality in Mirelurks and then a Speciality within that of Mirelurk Queens, and so on.

Specialities within Combat Skills are always for one specific weapon: a Speciality of Rifle can be Laser Rifle but cannot be energy weapons generally. Combat skill Specialities cannot have nested Specialities within them.

A character may not gain the exact same Speciality multiple times. Some Specialities may overlap and accumulate: for example, a character who has Specialities in Track for Deathclaws and for mountainous regions gains +4 when tracking Deathclaws in mountainous regions. The Overseer may limit these overlaps as they see fit.

Gaining Health
Extra Health can be gained via the Life Giver Perk. This can be bought multiple times "within reason" – which actually means at the Overseer's discretion for your particular campaign!

FOWW RPG-001-111 — SECTION 3.9

ARCHETYPE CARDS

These **archetype cards** are examples specifically created for this expansion. They are designed to give you a taste of the game, and show you how character cards interact in the game. The cards cover a range of character pre-gens, giving Players easy options to use and a fast way to get into the game. Later you may want to use different cards chosen from the main *Fallout: Wasteland Warfare* game itself, or create your own to fit with your character choices.

The archetype cards shown here can also be used in your home games of *Fallout: Wasteland Warfare*. Please note that these cards are not tournament or organised-play legal. They are instead a fun addition for Players to homebrew ideas, campaigns, and new situations and scenarios in their own homes and gaming groups.

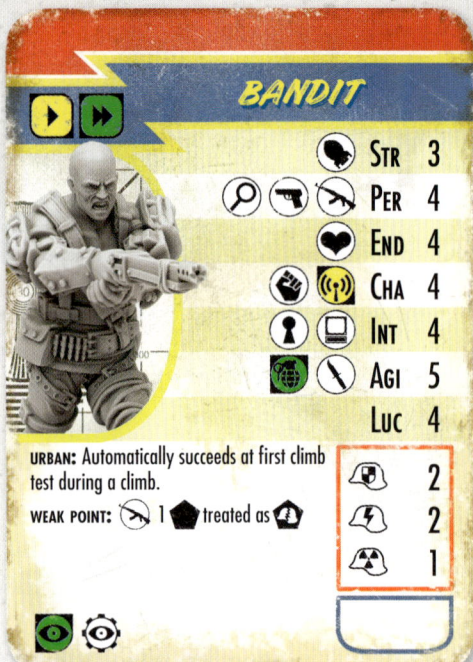

HUNTER
SUPER MUTANT

- Str 6
- Per 5
- End 6
- Cha 3
- Int 2
- Agi 5
- Luc 2

- 🪖 2
- ⚡ 1
- ☢ X

INFANTRY

- Str 5
- Per 4
- End 5
- Cha 3
- Int 3
- Agi 4
- Luc 2

ARMOR KNOWLEDGE: Combat tests: 1 ⬠ treated as ⬢

- 🪖 2
- ⚡ 2
- ☢ -

MR HANDY TYPE-1

- Str 3
- Per 5
- End 6
- Cha 5
- Int 6
- Agi 4
- Luc 2

EQUIPPED: Mr. Handy Buzzsaw and Mr. Handy Flamer.

- 🪖 3
- ⚡ 1
- ☢ X

PILOT

- Str 3
- Per 5
- End 4
- Cha 4
- Int 5
- Agi 3
- Luc 2

- 🪖 1
- ⚡ 2
- ☢ -

RESEARCHER

- Str 2
- Per 4
- End 4
- Cha 4
- Int 7
- Agi 3
- Luc 4

WELL-READ: Does not suffer the Unskilled penalty for any Knowhow skill.

- 🪖 1
- ⚡ 1
- ☢ -

SCOUT

- Str 4
- Per 6
- End 5
- Cha 3
- Int 5
- Agi 4
- Luc 3

URBAN: Automatically succeeds at first climb test during a climb.
SHOOT TO STUN:

- 🪖 3
- ⚡ 1
- ☢ 1

SNIPER

- Str 3
- Per 6
- End 4
- Cha 5
- Int 3
- Agi 6
- Luc 3

SHARPSHOOT: When shooting, ignore one item of cover.
CAREFUL: Shooting into close combat always affects intended target.

- 🪖 2
- ⚡ 1
- ☢ -

TECHNICIAN

- Str 2
- Per 3
- End 4
- Cha 3
- Int 7
- Agi 4
- Luc 4

GENIUS: Never locked out of 💻

- 🪖 1
- ⚡ 1
- ☢ -

THUG

- Str 3
- Per 5
- End 5
- Cha 3
- Int 3
- Agi 7
- Luc 2

LIGHT ARMORED: Movements are one color shorter if 🛡/🎒 equipped. Can not use 😷.
URBAN: Automatically succeeds at first climb test during a climb.

- 🪖 2
- ⚡ 1
- ☢ 1

Character Sheet

♥ 1 2 3 4 5 6 7 8 9 10 11 12 🍸 💊

PERKS & SPECIALITIES

NAME

GIFTS & SCARS

WEAPON

IMPROVISED WEAPON
🛡 1

UNIT

Skill	Attribute	BLACK	YELLOW	GREEN
Acrobatics	Agi	-4		
Athletics	Agi/End/Str	-4		
Behavior	Per	-4		
Computers	💻	-4		
Deception	Cha	-4		
Intimidate	✊	-4		
Lockpick	🔑	-4		
Manual Dexterity	Agi	-4		
Medical	Int	-4		
Notice	Per	-4		
Persuade	Cha	-4		
Pilot	Agi	-4		
Presence	📡	-4		
Resilience	End	-4		
Search	🔍	-4		
Stealth	Agi	-4		
Talk	Cha	-4		
Track	Per	-4		

Skill	Attribute	BLACK	YELLOW	GREEN
Knowhow (CREATURES)	Int	-4		
Knowhow (HISTORY)	Int	-4		
Knowhow (LOCAL)	Int	-4		
Knowhow (ROBOTS)	Int	-4		
Knowhow (SCIENCE)	Int	-4		
Knowhow (SURVIVAL)	Int	-4		
Repair/Craft (ARMOR)	Int	-4		
Repair/Craft (CHEMS)	Int	-4		
Repair/Craft (FOOD & DRINK)	Int	-4		
Repair/Craft (GEAR)	Int	-4		
Repair/Craft (MACHINERY)	Int	-4		
Repair/Craft (POWER ARMOR)	Int	-4		
Repair/Craft (ROBOTS)	Int	-4		
Repair/Craft (VAULT-TEC™)	Int	-4		
Repair/Craft (WEAPONS)	Int	-4		

Modiphius Entertainment gives their express permission for this page to be copied for personal use.

SECTION 04
RULES OF PLAY

FOWW RPG-001-111

FOWW RPG-001-111 — SECTION 4.1

SKILL TESTS

SKILL TESTS

During a game of the *Fallout: Wasteland Warfare RPG*, characters attempt activities such as shooting, lockpicking, and persuading. When a character attempts an activity whose outcome is not certain, the actual result is determined by a **Skill Test**. Skill Tests are only required for activities that have uncertain outcomes: a healthy person jumping across a three-foot gap between buildings is unlikely to require a test; leaping the same gap whilst carrying lots of gear with a wounded leg would require a test. So, for example, would leaping a ten-foot gap. Skill Tests require rolling the Skill Dice (often with some Effect Dice) and the resulting throw is compared to the character's **Skill Value** to see if it was a success and then the effect.

Some skills each have a specific icon displayed inside a circle and shown on a unit card. The Skill Value used for tests of these skills is based on the attribute number next to the matching icon. The same skill icon can appear next to different attributes depending on the character: for example, a Super Mutant's Melee skill is based on their Strength while Dogmeat's Melee skill is based on Agility. Note that Health has an icon in a circle, but it is not a skill (See 'Health', pp.65-66).

All other skills do not have specific icons, and the Skill Value used is based on an Attribute that depends on the skill and the character. For example, Perception might be used for a Notice Test to observe a figure watching from the distance, Intelligence for a Knowledge Test to understand factory schematics, or Charisma used for a Persuade Test so that a farmer lets the characters shelter in a barn while a storm passes. Guidance on skills and the attributes on which to base them is given in 'Adjudicating Skill Tests', p.81.

Skills fall into one of two main categories: **Combat Skills** and **Expertise Skills** (see table, above right).

Characters may attempt actions for which they do not possess skills, but suffer the **'Unskilled'** penalty

COMBAT SKILLS	EXPERTISE SKILLS
Rifle	Search
Pistol	Lockpick
Thrown	Computers
Melee	Presence
Heavy Weapon	Plus, ALL skills without specific icons. (See p.24 for the full list)
Battle Cry	

(see 'Unskilled Tests', p.85). Sometimes the Overseer will determine that a Skill Test cannot be attempted at all if the skill in question needs specific training or experience, e.g. repairing a complex engine.

Characters with an Expertise Skill do not suffer the Unskilled penalty, and they also add **Effect Dice** (see 'Effect Dice', p.44) when using that skill. This means a character can succeed at more difficult tests and/or have a better quality of success (see 'Resolving Expertise Tests', p.45). These bonus Effect Dice only apply to Expertise Skills, not to Combat Skills.

The *Fallout: Wasteland Warfare RPG* has a list of Expertise skills which covers many activities and defines attributes which relate to skills (see 'Expertise Skills', p.24). However, Expertise Skills can cover any subject or activity, so Players and the Overseer can co-operate to create any skill they wish. See 'Experience and Progression', p.36, for more information.

Sometimes tests are based directly on attributes: lifting a heavy object requires a **Str Test**, and holding that heavy object for a prolonged period might then require an **End Test**. These tests are treated just like Expertise Skill Tests, but without a bonus Effect Dice for having a skill. Such tests are usually written with the three-letter abbreviation for the attribute, and sometimes followed by a modifier (see 'Penalties and Bonuses', p.46); For example, "Test Per -2" means Test Perception with a -2 penalty to the Skill Value.

MAKING A SKILL TEST

To make a Skill Test, the Player rolls the **Skill Dice**, a twenty-sided dice with numbers and icons, and usually one or more **Effect Dice**, twelve-sided dice which come in a variety of colors.

For a Skill Test to succeed, the result (after any modifications) must be **equal to or lower than a relevant Skill Value** for the test. Bonuses and penalties can adjust the Skill Value before the roll. All modifiers, bonuses and penalties, are totalled before being applied to the Skill Value being used. If a ⓧ is rolled on the Skill Dice, the Skill Test is always a failure and cannot be adjusted by numerical bonuses to make it a success. The chances of success for each Skill Value are:

SKILL VALUE	1	2	3	4	5	6	7	8	9	10+
Chance of Success	25%	30%	35%	40%	45%	55%	65%	75%	80%	85%

Str 6
Per 7
End 5
Cha 6
Int 6
Agi 7
Luc 4

THE SKILL ICONS SHOWN WITHIN CIRCLES ON A CHARACTER'S CARD HAVE A VALUE EQUAL TO THE ATTRIBUTE WITH WHICH THEY SHARE A LINE. IN THE EXAMPLE ABOVE, THE RIFLE SKILL FOR THIS CHARACTER IS SHOWN NEXT TO THEIR PERCEPTION, WHICH IS 7, SO THEIR RIFLE SKILL IS ALSO 7.

> "WELL, YOU COULD BLAST IT, BUT MY COMPUTER SKILLS WOULD BE A MIGHT FASTER... AND QUIETER."

Example of a Skill Test: A Paladin using a weapon with a Comfort Grip modification is firing at a target and receives a **+2 bonus** to their Skill Value for that modification. However, at the time of the shot it is dark and raining heavily, so the Overseer rules that the test has a penalty of **-4**. Therefore, a total modifier of **+2 – 4 = -2**, applied to the **Skill Value of 7** for an **adjusted Skill Value of 5**. The Paladin needs to make a roll of **5 or lower** on the Skill Dice to be successful and hit their target.

SKILL DICE

The **Skill Dice** is a white, twenty-sided dice with numbered faces showing values from 2 to 10, and other faces which bear icons as shown in the table below:

If a Skill Test fails, none of its Effect icons count, apart from any **Action Point** icon on the Skill Dice which are still available for use. Action Points are discussed later, on p.61.

The Overseer may also add penalties for Skill Tests based on many factors, and add bonuses by either increasing the Skill Value and/or giving additional Effect Dice. See 'Penalties and Bonuses', p.46.

	SKILL DICE ICONS		
ICON	ICON NAME	EFFECT	FULL DESCRIPTION
2 / 10	Numbered Face	The numerical result of the roll	The number faces, from 2 to 10, count as the number shown. See 'Skill Tests', p.42.
✱	Action Point	Allows some models to perform Quick Actions	This result counts as a result of 1. It also counts as 1 Action Point (AP). Some characters can use APs to carry out Quick Actions, extra minor activities, in addition to their main Actions. See 'Quick Actions', p.61.
!	Critical Point	Allows some models to use powerful, Critical weapon effects	This result counts as a result of 1. It also counts as 1 Critical Point (CP). Some characters can use the Critical Effects of weapons, which are powerful attacks available when enough CPs have been collected. Each Critical Point icon rolled gives the character 1 additional CP if their Skill Test is successful. See 'Criticals', p.66.
X / X	Fail	The Skill Test has not been successful	The X icon means the Skill Test has failed. As "X" is not a number, numerical bonuses cannot modify it into a success making this an automatic fail. One X bears an Action Point icon as well. It is an automatic fail, but it does grant an Action Point.

SECTION 4 – RULES OF PLAY

EFFECT DICE

The **Effect Dice** are twelve-sided dice of different colors, which are often rolled alongside the Skill Dice to determine extra effects. There are four colors (or types) of Effect Dice and which particular dice are rolled is usually determined by the equipment being used, circumstances, or the Overseer's rulings. Additional (bonus) Effect Dice may be awarded by the Overseer, or be gained from Skills and Abilities. Each color of dice represents a different type of detailed effect as shown in the Effect Dice table, below right.

The Effect Dice show various icons on their faces. Some icons make it more likely the Skill Test will be a success, and the others determine additional effects. The Effect Dice Icons table below lists these different icons. Two of the icons have a different name and effect depending on whether they are being used for a Combat or Expertise Skill Test (as explained later).

Some Effect Dice results (especially from the green Accuracy Effect Dice) modify the Skill Dice roll. Minus numbers on Effect Dice help achieve a lower (i.e. better) result and this modified total is compared to the adjusted Skill Value.

Example: A Paladin's adjusted **Skill Value** is **5**. The Paladin rolls the Skill Dice plus one Accuracy Effect Dice (due to their weapon). The Skill Dice shows a **6** and the Accuracy Effect Dice shows **-2**. The result of the **adjusted Skill Test** result is **6 – 2 = 4**, which is below the Paladin's Skill Value and, therefore, a success.

MAIN SOURCES OF EFFECT DICE

Effect Dice for skill rolls can come from several sources:

- Skills
- Equipment
- Assistance from other characters
- Luck
- Bonus dice awarded by the Overseer due to the situation, attributes, knowledge/experience, or other relevant factors.

(See 'Adjudicating Skill Tests', p.81 for more)

EFFECT DICE

DICE COLOR	DICE NAME	DICE EFFECT
⬟	Black (Damage) Effect Dice	More likely to have an increased effect. Primarily adds extra damage or Impact.
⬟	Yellow (Armor Reduction) Effect Dice	More likely to avoid an effect being blocked. Primarily reduces target's Armor or Resistance.
⬟	Green (Accuracy) Effect Dice	More likely to be a success. Primarily modifies the Skill Dice, making success more likely.
⬟	Blue Effect Dice	Used for determining all sorts of special effects.

EFFECT DICE ICONS

ICON	NAME	EFFECT FOR COMBAT SKILL TESTS	EFFECT FOR EXPERTISE SKILL TESTS
✦ ✦	Extra Damage / Impact	Each Damage icon adds 1 to the total damage before any armor is taken into account. See Damage, p.63.	Each Impact icon adds 1 to the total Impact before any Resistance is taken into account. See Impact, p.45.
🛡 🛡	Reduce Armor / Resistance	Each Reduce Armor icon reduces a target's Armor Rating by 1, making damage from this attack more likely to get through to whatever is behind the armor. See Armor, p.64.	Each Reduce Resistance icon reduces the target's Resistance Rating by 1, making Impact from this attack more likely to take effect. See Resistance, p.45.
-1 -2 -3	Bonus to Skill	These bonuses modify the number rolled on the Skill Dice during a Skill Test, making success more likely. See Skill Tests, p.42.	
🍾★☢	Special Effects	These three special icons are used to trigger effects specific to weapons, equipment and abilities. See Special Effects, p.50.	

BELOW: FALLOUT DICE INCLUDE A WHITE SKILL DICE, RED ARMOR DICE, AND FOUR EFFECT DICE.

Maximum Effect Dice

A single Skill Test cannot use more than 4 Effect Dice of the same color. Any dice over this limit go unused. For example, if a character's equipment and abilities total 5 black dice and 2 yellow dice, the Skill Test would consist of 4 black dice and 2 yellow dice, with the fifth black dice discarded before the roll.

RESOLVING EXPERTISE SKILL TESTS

Impact is the magnitude of success in a Skill Test. The greater the Impact, the greater the effect of a successful Skill Test. A success on the Skill Dice has an **Impact of 1** (just like a weapon in a Combat Skill Test with a base damage of 1), and **each ✺ adds one additional Impact**.

The greater the **Difficulty** of a test, the more Impact is needed to complete the task. Searching for a specific tool box in a small pile of garbage would have a low Difficulty compared to searching for the same toolbox in a large pile of garbage.

An Expertise Skill Test may have additional or other outcomes depending on the result, such as a Partial Resolution, or a failed roll causing a Complication (see page 46).

If the target has a Resistance Rating, roll the red **Resistance Dice** (also called the Armor Dice). If the result is equal to, or lower than, the target's Resistance Rating, the Impact is reduced by the Resistance result rolled. Each 🛡 rolled on other Effect Dice reduces the target's Resistance Rating by 1 to a minimum of zero. If the total Impact remaining **equals or exceeds** the target's Difficulty, the intended task has been achieved. The greater the Resistance Rating, the more likely that some Impact will be negated. Large amounts of Impact can potentially be negated, depending on Resistance.

If the Skill Test fails, none of the effect icons count apart from Action Point icons on the Skill Dice which are available to be used (see 'Action Points', p.61).

Strong Resistance

Strong Resistance is similar to Strong Armor (see page 64) and adds to the amount of Impact that can be resisted after the Resistance is rolled.

> **Example:** A high-security lock has a Resistance Rating of 2+1 versus Lockpick Skill Tests when trying to pick it. A Skill Test results in **2 Impact** and the lock rolls a **1** on the Resistance dice; therefore, it **reduces Impact by a total of 2** – one for the **1** rolled plus the **+1** due to its Strong Resistance. As a result, the attempt to pick the lock results in **zero Impact**. The lock remains locked!

Zero Impact

An Expertise Skill Test which has a total of zero Impact (most likely due to Resistance reducing the amount of Impact) has no effect. In the example above, the test is not a failure, it just didn't do anything: the bomb trap wasn't disarmed, but it wasn't accidentally set-off… this time.

THE RED RESISTANCE DICE (ALSO USED AS THE ARMOR DICE) REVEALS IF AND HOW MUCH IMPACT IS NEGATED.

PARTIAL RESOLUTION

For tests with a Difficulty greater than 1, the Overseer may allow some tasks to be achieved via multiple Skill Tests which produce enough total Impact through several successes.

> **Example:** The Overseer says breaking down a barricaded door requires 3 Impact, but this total can be from multiple attempts. One character tries breaking the door down and achieves 2 Impact, so it is partly broken but not down; another character tries and achieves 1 Impact, bringing the total to 3, and the door gives way as the total Impact equals its Difficulty.

In some cases, achieving some of the required Impact (but not enough to equal or exceed Difficulty) can deliver part of the intended effect.

> **Example 1:** The Gunner whacks a piece of rubble against the glass tank to release the water (Difficulty 2) but gets only 1 of the required 2 Impact. The Overseer decides the glass is cracked and leaking, but not smashed quite yet.
>
> **Example 2:** The Paladin tries using her Ripper to slash open a chain link fence and needs 2 Impact. The Paladin gains 1 Impact, so the Overseer decides that a hole was cut, but only some characters can fit through. This does not include the Paladin wearing Power Armor. Another option would be a small hole that any characters can squeeze through, taking longer to get through the fence.

In some cases, achieving less Impact than a Difficulty value can have a negative effect.

> **Example:** A computer with defensive programs has a Difficulty of 2. A character uses Computers skill and gets 1 Impact which is not enough to hack in. In this case, the Overseer decides the computer detects it is being hacked, sets off an alarm, and locks out the character, preventing further hacking attempts.

The Overseer may decide that the total Impact achieved via multiple Skill Tests may reduce over time.

> **Example:** A Raider tries scrambling up a ravine's steep sides to escape a Deathclaw. The Overseer determines this will require a successful **AGI Test** and 3 Impact in total to reach the top. The Raider gets 2 Impact on their test, but the Overseer rules that they lose 1 Impact sliding back before they can try again, and now requires 2 Impact to escape. Meanwhile, the Deathclaw gets nearer…

Partial Resolution During Free Play

When attempting an Expertise Skill Test during Free Play, it would be repetitive to roll the same Skill Test multiple times until enough Impact is garnered to equal or exceed the task's Difficulty. Therefore, the Overseer can compare the Impact result from a single roll to the Difficulty and then use that to determine the time taken to complete the task. This removes the need to make multiple Skill Tests when time is not an issue. This may not be appropriate to all tests that can be achieved by Partial Resolution, such as if there is a negative outcome if any Skill Test is a failure, e.g. traversing a narrow plank between buildings may require a lot of Impact, and a single failed test could mean falling.

PENALTIES AND BONUSES

The Overseer may apply various penalties and bonuses to a Skill Test. Penalties and bonuses can be a fixed amount that alters the Skill Value: these are in increments of 2 (see 'Awarding Bonuses and Penalties', p.81). A character may gain other bonuses and penalties for a Skill Test from their abilities, Perks, equipment, assistance from other characters, or even their approach to a Skill Test. For example, the Overseer should award bonuses for cunning solutions, as this is all part of great roleplaying.

Skills add **Effect Dice** to some Skill Tests. **Specialities** refine skills and give a **+2 bonus** to the relevant Skill Value when using a relevant item or ability (see 'Specialities', p.49).

Penalties

The Overseer allocates penalties by applying them to the Skill Value. The **situation** involving a Skill Test can make it more difficult and require a test penalty. For example, it might be more difficult than usual to:

- Pick a complex lock.
- Search in very poor light.
- Sneak past an alerted Brotherhood of Steel sentry.
- Triangulate the location of an emergency radio beacon in just a few seconds.
- Hack a computer while under fire.

As well as the situation, a Skill Test may need **specific knowledge** and/or **experience**. The Overseer may add a penalty to a test to represent a character's inexperience or ignorance. Some examples where these make a Skill Test more difficult are:

- Picking a lock of a type never seen before.
- Trying to bluff your way past a Brotherhood of Steel sentry with no knowledge of their methods.
- Trying to operate factory machinery with no experience of machinery.

Bonuses

The Overseer may give a bonus by adding to the Skill Value or adding Effect Dice, or both. The **situation** of the Skill Test can make it easier and result in a bonus to the test dice roll. Some examples of situations where tests are easier than usual are:

- Lockpicking a lock known to be easy to pick.
- Sneaking past a sleeping Brotherhood of Steel sentry.
- Tracking a person in open territory.
- Hacking a computer having watched someone enter a password beforehand.

As well as the situation, a Skill Test may benefit from **specific character knowledge or experience**, and the Overseer may add a bonus to the test to represent these factors. Some examples where knowledge or experience makes a Skill Test easier are:

- Lockpicking a very common type of lock.
- Trying to bluff your way past a Brotherhood of Steel sentry after serving with them for many years.
- Tracking a person in familiar territory.
- Trying to operate factory machinery that you know well.

The character's (**roleplaying**) **approach** to a Skill Test may also earn a bonus, such as a character pretending to be drunk to get close to their target before jumping them, or throwing a stone so a noise misdirects a guards' attention. The Overseer can even offer these bonuses to a character, but the cost of failure should be worse than usual. For example, if a character runs as fast as possible along a narrow plank connecting the two buildings over the alley, but with the downside of having no chance of grabbing on if they stumble.

COMPLICATIONS

The Overseer may decide an /X\ result on the Skill Dice is worse than a simple failure and results in a Complication as well as the failure.

Example 1: *Trying to hook the keys from a sleeping Raider without waking them may simply fail if the result is a number exceeding the Skill value. The Raider stays asleep and unaware of any risk to their keys. However, rolling /X\ means the failed attempt also wakes the Raider.*

Example 2: *While shooting, a Super Mutant rolls an /X\ so needs to re-load, or the weapon used jams or breaks.*

OPPOSED SKILL TESTS

An **Opposed Skill Test** occurs when a character tries to achieve something that is actively resisted by someone or something with its own skill, usually another character. To perform an Opposed Skill Test, all parties involved make Skill Tests against their own appropriate Skill Value. The **successful result with the most Impact wins**. (Impact is the quality of the result and will be explained in 'Expertise', p.45). A roll cannot win if it is not a success, even if the other parties involved do not have the requisite skill or all fail their rolls. ('Action Points' are not earned from Opposed Skill Tests, which will be explained in 'Action Points', p.61.)

Breaking Ties

In the case of a tie (because both characters succeeded with equal Impact), the **tied character with the highest roll wins**.

> *Example: During an **Opposed AGI Test**, a Super Mutant has a **skill of 5** and **rolls a 4**, and Piper has a **skill of 6** and **rolls a 2**. Both have succeeded and are tied (because they both have 1 Impact). They compare results: The Super Mutant's 4 and Piper's 2 are compared, so the Super Mutant wins.*

If a character's dice roll included Effect Dice results which reduced the result shown on the Skill Dice, the character uses the lowest of either:

A. their **Skill Value**; or
B. the **result shown on the Skill Dice** when comparing the highest successful result against their opponent.

> *Example: During an **Opposed Skill Test**, a Super Mutant has a **skill of 4** and **rolls a 4**, and Piper has a **skill of 6** and **rolls a 5** with a **-1** on a green dice making her **total 4**. Both have succeeded. They compare results: The Super Mutant's 4 and Piper's 5 are compared as she uses the lowest out of her **Skill Value (6)** and the result on the **Skill Dice (5)**, so Piper wins.*

> *If Piper had rolled an **8** with a **-3** on a green dice to make her **total 5**, then she would have used **6** for the comparison as that would be the **lowest** out of her **Skill Value (6)** and the result on her **Skill Dice (8)**.*

If still tied, resolution is at the Overseer's discretion.

THE AMMO'S ON THE FLOOR IN THE FRONT OF THE MUTANT HOUNDS? GREAT! SO A QUICK LEAP AND...?

INEVITABLE SUCCESSES

If a Skill Test would eventually be a success (given enough time and tests) where there is no downside to failure, the Player can declare this and automatically succeed after enough time has passed (as determined by the Overseer). The success only has an average outcome and is nothing special. For example, a character with the Lockpick skill who has as much time as they want (because no-one is trying to stop them), and a lock that will never get jammed, will eventually pick the lock.

EXCEEDING DIFFICULTY

If the Impact exceeds the needed Difficulty, the Overseer may award additional benefits from the outcome. The greater the excess of Impact, the greater the extra effect.

Example: A character makes a Skill Test using Search to find a key in a pile of robot parts. The Difficulty is 2, and the character gets a total of 3 Impact after taking account of Resistance. The Overseer may decide that they not only find the key, but also find two Stimpaks in the pile as well, or maybe the key was found straight away.

CRITICALS DURING EXPERTISE SKILL TESTS

CRITICAL ICON

In a similar way to what happens during combat, Player Characters and some Non-Player Characters with the **Critical icon** on their cards can gain additional benefit from **Critical Points** (**CPs**, see page 66). However, CPs are handled in a different way during Expertise Skill Tests than during combat.

If an Expertise Skill Test by a character is successful, a Critical Point icon () adds a beneficial effect as determined by the Overseer. This does not apply to an Outside Chance which already requires a Critical Icon simply to be successful with a limited effect. See 'Outside Chance', p.49.

The Overseer may determine if the CP counts as an extra Impact or another beneficial outcome.

Example: A Minuteman tries to persuade a farmer to tell her who has been burning their crops. The farmer is worried, so the Overseer decides that the Minuteman needs 2 Impact. The Minuteman rolls a  on the Skill Dice which counts as 1 Impact (for the success) plus the CP adds another Impact making 2 in total: a success! Alternatively, the Overseer could have decided that the roll only gained 1 Impact, so failed to convince the farmer to give the information. However, during the discussion the Minuteman noticed the farmer kept glancing at the barn: what is in there? Maybe it's incriminating evidence the farmers set fire to their own crops to hide that they are part of a local gang, or another secret the farmer would rather the Minuteman didn't discover.

NEAR SUCCESS

If the Skill Dice result of an Expertise Skill Test (and after bonuses and penalties) **fails by 1 greater than the required Skill Value**, the Overseer may decide that a **near success** has occurred, which has a reduced or lesser effect.

Example: A computer password is tough to crack. The Scientist rolls a near success and does not crack the code, but has a much better idea of what it might be. The Overseer will award them a bonus green dice if they try again.

UNSKILLED

Characters without a relevant skill for a Skill Test will find succeeding at tasks difficult compared to those with relevant skills. To make a Skill Test without the specific skill needed, the character uses the relevant attribute the skill uses (determined by the Overseer) for the Skill Value and suffers an **Unskilled penalty of -4** to the Skill Value.

Example: A Raider has no Track skill, but tries to track a fleeing Brotherhood of Steel scout anyway. The Overseer states Track is based on the PER attribute; the Raider's PER of 6 gives an **adjusted Skill Value** for this Skill Test of **6 – 4 = 2**.

An Unskilled success is always limited in its effect to the minimum required to succeed.

Skill Tests based on attributes are never treated as Unskilled because all characters have all attributes: For example, using an STR Test to see if a character can roll a vehicle over.

If a character's adjusted Skill Value is zero or lower, they may still accomplish a task; see 'Outside Chance', p.49. Success is impossible for some tasks without training or experience. See 'Impossible Tests', p.49.

OUTSIDE CHANCE

If the **adjusted Skill Value is 0**, the test only succeeds if a ⚠ is rolled. This is called an **Outside Chance** (a 15% chance of success).

If the adjusted **Skill Value is less than 0**, the Overseer can allow the character to have an Outside Chance or declare it an Impossible Test (see below).

A successful Outside Chance delivers a basic success for its effect, e.g. somehow a character manages to guess a password and access the computer with a Skill Value of 0, but can't access as many files as a trained hacker could if they succeed.

IMPOSSIBLE TESTS

An **Impossible Test** is one the Overseer decides has no realistic possibility of success regardless of character skills. This might be persuading a wily trader to buy an object they know full well is broken and useless, or a Human running and jumping across a 50-foot gap. If attempted, an Impossible Skill Test results in an automatic ⓧ on the Skill Dice.

SPECIALITIES

A **Speciality** refines a skill so it is an area in which a character is especially knowledgeable or gifted. Specialities are used for a very specific element within a skill: +2 to Rifle Skill when using a Bolt-Action Pipe Rifle, for example, or a specific subject area within the skill such as +2 to Track when tracking Super Mutants, or tracking in mountainous regions. Specialities are expertise that adds a reliable increase in capability: they always **add +2**. Note that the +2 is applied to Skill Value and *not* the underlying attribute. For example, a character's Melee skill is associated with their STR 6 and they have a Speciality in Pipe Wrench; as a result, they have a Skill Value of 8 when using a Pipe Wrench but STR remains 6.

ASSISTANCE

For Expertise Skill Tests, characters can work together to help improve their chances of success. One character makes the Skill Test (with any relevant Effect Dice) and the other characters involved (at the Overseer discretion) roll **1 black, yellow or green Effect Dice of their choice** and the result is added to the Skill Test. Assisting characters may not roll a blue Effect Dice. The Overseer always decides how many characters can help, or which dice they can add, and a wise Overseer at least listens to good arguments from the Players before making a decision! The Overseer may declare that only characters with an appropriate skill can assist. Maximum dice only applies to a single character, so the combined Effect Dice from assisting characters can be greater than the maximum Effect Dice (above).

Example: Three characters want to lift a large slab of rubble off a Wastelander. This requires a **STR Skill Test**. The strongest character has STR 8, another has STR 6 and the last STR 2.

The strongest character makes the Skill Test and the Overseer allows the character with STR 6 to help with the lifting, so they choose to **add a black dice to help the roll succeed**.

The Overseer decides the character with STR 2 is not strong enough to lift in any meaningful way, but does allow them to **roll a black dice** as they can pull the Wastelander out so that a **successful test may have a greater effect**.

"HEY, IRONCLAD, YOU WANNA HELP ME HACK THIS THING?"

FOWW RPG-001-111 — SECTION 4.2

SPECIAL EFFECTS

Some items and abilities include Special Effects which are activated by spending rolled icon results shown next to them. The icons – **Bottle**, **Star**, and **Blast** – are found primarily on the blue Special Effect Dice. On weapons and item cards, icons in white show requirements, and symbols in black next to them show the outcome. These outcomes often include conditions, as detailed on p.67.

- Each icon from a dice roll can only be used once.
- Gaining some Special Effects requires spending multiple icons.
- Special Effect icons that are not used during a Skill Test are discarded and are not carried over from one Skill Test to the next. They cannot be transferred to other characters or weapons.
- A Special Effect can be used multiple times during a character's activation.
- A number in a white circle limits the number of times a Special Effect can be used during a Skill Test.
- While some Special Effects can be used multiple times during the same attack, some cannot. The limits are shown by a circled number after the icons required. If there is no number, there is no limit to the uses.

Special Effects on Weapon Cards

The right-hand section of the weapon card is called the **Critical Meter**. Special Effects detailed outside the Critical Meter can be used with any attack, while those shown inside the weapon card's Critical Meter can only be used during a Critical Effect (see 'Critical Effects', p.66).

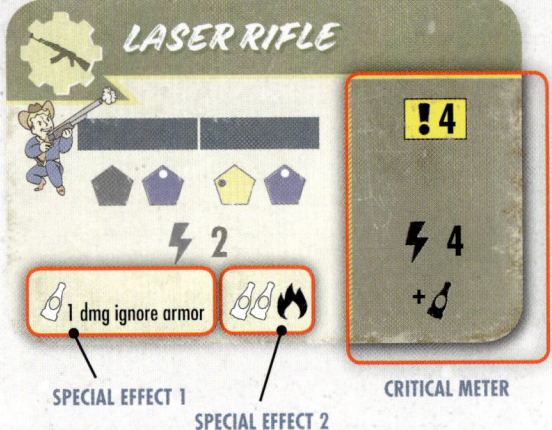

NUKA-COLA BOTTLE ICON

BLAST ICON

STAR ICON

SPECIAL EFFECT 1
SPECIAL EFFECT 2
CRITICAL METER

Example: The Laser Rifle has two Special Effects:

- **Effect A:** One Nuka-Cola Bottle icon can be used to change 1 point of damage to ignore armor.
- **Effect B:** Two Nuka-Cola Bottle results can be used to set the target On Fire.

The Laser Rifle is fired and the Skill Test results in 2 Nuka-Cola Bottle icons. If the Player uses 1 Bottle icon to use effect A, they do not have enough Bottle icons remaining to use effect B, but they could use effect A again with their remaining Nuka-Cola Bottle.

If an effect says 'If target takes damage', the effect happens if there is damage to be added to the character or target after any armor roll. Damage taken by other items first does not count. If a character's Power Armor takes damage the character inside does not. The same principle is true for non-combat tests but with Impact instead of damage and Resistance instead of armor.

For more details about Skills and Skills Tests, see 'Adjudicating Skill Tests', pp.81-85.

'ONCE PER ACTIVATION' MEANS ONCE DURING THE TIME FROM WHEN A CHARACTER IS ACTIVATED TO THE NEXT ACTIVATION OF THE SAME CHARACTER.

SAMPLE SPECIAL EFFECT ACTIVATIONS	
ICONS	REQUIREMENTS AND LIMITS
Blast + Star	Spend 1 Blast icon to cause Stun. No limit per Skill Test.
Bottle Bottle + Fire	Spend 2 Nuka-Cola Bottle icons to set target on fire. No limit per Skill Test.
Bottle + Star + Damage	Spend 1 Nuka-Cola Bottle icon plus 1 Star icon to cause 1 extra damage. No limit per Skill Test.
Bottle ③ + Armor	Spend 1 Nuka-Cola Bottle icon to add 1 Armor Reduction. Can be used a maximum of 3 times per Skill Test.
Star Star ① + Leg	Spend 2 Star icons to cause Injured Leg. Can be used a maximum of once per Skill Test.

EFFECT OR NO EFFECT?

If a Skill Test fails, all effect icons (apart from APs) are ignored (see 'Skill Dice', p.43). As a result, special effects do not always get triggered when a Skill Test fails, as a character would have no icons to spend to make them happen. However, some effects do take place if they do not need icons to make them happen: e.g. anyone caught in a Molotov Cocktail's area of effect is set On Fire. Some effects require damage in order for the effect to occur and these are mentioned on their cards, e.g. Radscorpion Pincers and Sting cards say a Bottle icon means Poison but only if damage is caused.

FOWW RPG-001-111 — SECTION 4.3

ACTION PLAY

When action occurs in the game it is broken into **rounds** which represent around 10 seconds each. During each round, the Players and the Overseer take alternating **turns** until every character has performed its **Actions**, and then a new round begins.

ADVANTAGE

At the start of each round, the Overseer determines whether the Players or the Overseer has the **Advantage** (see 'Advantage', p.86). Whoever has the Advantage decides if the Players or the Overseer take the first turn that round: they can act first or decide to let their adversaries make the first move.

TURNS

Every character is always in one of three states of **Readiness**: **Unready**, **Ready**, or **Used**. All characters start each round as Unready.

Players' Turn

When it is the Players' turn, they must choose ONE of their Unready characters to become **Ready**. This cannot be a character that is already Ready or Used. The Players then choose if:

A. **all** of their Ready characters will activate; or
B. **none** of their Ready characters will activate.

If all the Player Characters are Ready or Used, they must choose **A** and activate all Ready characters.

If the Players have no Unready characters remaining at the start of their turn, they take no more turns in the current round. The Overseer continues to take turns until all of their characters are Used.

Overseer's Turn

The Overseer's turn is exactly the same as a Players' turn: the Overseer makes characters Ready and uses characters they are controlling in the same fashion. If the Overseer has no Unready characters at the start of their turn, they take no more turns in the current round. The Players take turns until all of their characters are Used instead.

End of a Round

When every character (whether Player or Overseer-controlled) is Used, the round ends and a new round begins. The Advantage remains with whoever had it in the previous round unless the Overseer feels the situation has changed. See 'Advantage', p.86.

ACTIVATING AND PERFORMING ACTIONS

When the Players or Overseer decide that all of their Ready characters will act, Ready characters perform their Actions. Each character acts one after another in any order wished. When a character is chosen to perform their Actions, this is **activating**.

When activated, a character may perform **up to 2 main Actions** which can be any combination of those listed below, including performing the same Action twice. Character may also perform **Quick Actions** (see p.61) by spending Action Points if they have any. The different Actions listed below will be explained fully throughout this book. A new Action cannot be started until a current Action is complete (except during movement, see 'Using Actions During Moves, p.53). For the purposes of Actions, characters have Line of Sight in all directions.

The Actions a character may perform are shown in the table below.

TYPES OF ACTION		
ACTION	DESCRIPTION	SEE PAGE
Move	Moves the character	53
Charge	A movement that **engages** a target in combat (and usually longer than Move)	54
Shoot	Attack at range with a Pistol, Rifle, or Heavy Weapon	55
Throw	Use a Thrown Weapon (i.e. grenade)	57
Close Combat	The character attacks an **engaged** target	57
Use Expertise	Use a non-Combat skill	59
Prepare	Get ready to react to an opposing character's Action or Quick Action	59

After a character has completed their Actions, its Readiness changes from Ready to **Used**. A Used character cannot act again during the same round even if they did not use all of their Actions. Each character must complete their Actions before the next character is activated.

If the Players or Overseer chose to activate their Ready characters that round, once all the Ready characters have been activated and become Used, the turn is over. All Ready characters must act during a round and cannot remain Ready when the turn ends. A turn can be ended while characters are still Ready (and have taken no Actions) but those Ready characters still become Used.

COLOR RANGES

Fallout: Wasteland Warfare uses colors to signify distances. Icons on unit cards, ranges on weapon cards, and other items, are color-coded to show which distance is involved in each circumstance.

COLOR RANGES	
COLOR	FEET
Orange	6
Yellow	12
Red	18
Green	24
Blue	30
Black	36

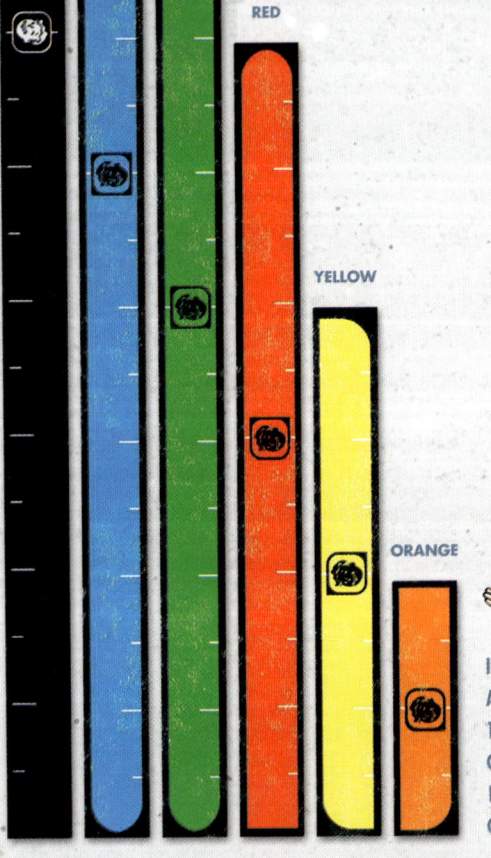

IF YOU USE MODELS WHILE ROLEPLAYING, AND YOU USE A MAP WHICH IS SCALED TO 1 INCH TO 1 YARD, YOU CAN USE THE COLORED RANGE RULERS FROM *FALLOUT: WASTELAND WARFARE* TO QUICKLY CALCULATE AND MEASURE DISTANCES.

TEST v USE

During Action Play, there is a difference between Testing a skill and Using a skill. Both require a Skill Test but testing a skill does not require an action, whereas using a skill does require an action.

For example, a character might Test First Aid to gain a first impression of an injured person's wounds. This does not require an action. They would need to Use First Aid to spend time tending to the wounds and this does require an action.

In the same way, a character might Test PER to notice some precarious rubble above the doorway of a ruined building. This does not require an action, but using PER to carefully study a distant person would require an action. If in doubt, the Overseer decides if a Skill Test requires focused activity and therefore uses an action.

During Free Play rather than Action Play, Test and Use are interchangeable so actions are not relevant (see 'Free Play', p.62).

While colors represent a specific distance in the game world, they are also useful for comparisons. A character who can Move Red is generally faster than a character that can Move Yellow.

Colour ranges are shown in the table, left, alongside the in-world distance they represent.

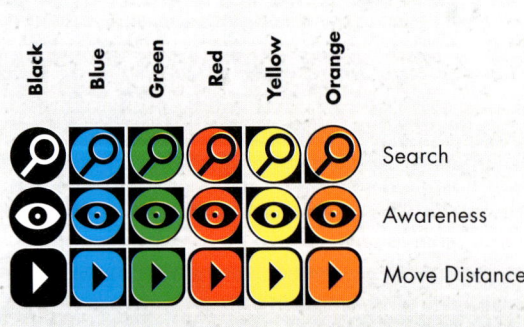

COLOR BLIND MARKERS

To help color-blind Players, colored icons have their own unique corner shapes. If using models and range rulers, find the matching range ruler by looking for the symbol with the same corner as shown on the icon. As a rule of thumb, from range Orange to range Blue, the more corners the longer the distance involved.

ACTION: MOVE

A **Move Action** allows a character to travel a distance equal to their **Move color**.

Characters may pass through other characters if the blocking character allows it (effectively gets out of the way). To pass a character who does not allow it and is actively blocking, both characters make an Opposed Skill Test each, using their highest value of either STR or AGI. The blocker character wins any ties. A character cannot make the test before they start their Move Action. They cannot make the test, fail and then decide not to use that Move Action. A character who fails stops when they reach the blocking character.

IF YOU OWN *FALLOUT: WASTELAND WARFARE* AND USE MODELS, THE RANGE RULERS ARE USED TO MEASURE MOVEMENT FROM FRONT OF THE MODEL'S BASE AT THE START OF MOVEMENT TO THE BACK OF THE REPOSITIONED MODEL'S BASE AT THE MOVEMENT END.

USING ACTIONS DURING MOVES

During a Move Action, a character may perform Shoot and/or Throw Actions, and other Actions allowed by the Overseer. Examples of Actions that cannot be used during a Move are lockpicking, examining tracks, Close Combat, reading a book, etc. Common sense should be the guiding principle. No penalty is automatically incurred for performing an Action whilst moving.

> *Example:* A vault dweller is under fire and wants to move from a doorway to the cover of a desk so they can search it. As a Player Character, they can use a Quick Action (see Heroic, p.21) to Move, and use one of their main Actions to return fire (Shoot) part-way along their movement. They then use their remaining Action to Search once they are behind the desk after the Move.

If using a Quick Action to move (see 'Quick Actions', p.61), the character may not perform another Action during the movement.

TERRAIN

Terrain falls into 3 main types: Normal, Difficult, Impassable.

Normal Terrain has no effect on movement.

Difficult Terrain impedes movement. Typical examples are marshy or rocky surfaces, or moving over obstacles that may be leaped like barriers and desks. Any Move that is partly in Difficult Terrain uses the next shortest color from the character's usual Move color. This is 6 feet shorter in game terms.

Some characters are unaffected by Difficult Terrain and Move and Charge over it as they would through Normal Terrain. This is indicated by the **Unimpeded** icon on their cards.

Impassable Terrain cannot be moved into or through.

UNIMPEDED ICON

CLIMBING AND FALLING

Characters can climb up or down climbable surfaces during their movement. Doing so counts as Difficult Terrain. When starting a climb, the character must make an **AGI Test.** If successful, the character climbs up or down the surface as Difficult Terrain. If the test fails, the character falls onto whatever is below. Falling damage is calculated from their start position (see below), and their Move or Charge Action ends.

A character can end an Action part-way through climbing and then continue the climb with a later Action. The Overseer determines if another AGI Test is required during a climb. When climbing, a character cannot attack, Use Expertise (see p.59), or use other skills unless the Overseer agrees this is possible.

Objects like ladders are easily climbable and do not require an AGI Test to succeed.

INABILITY TO CLIMB ICON

1 DAMAGE ICON =
+1 DAMAGE
WHEN ROLLING FALLING
DAMAGE

1 NUKA-COLA =
-1 ARMOR REDUCTION
WHEN ROLLING FALLING
DAMAGE

Falling Damage
The amount of falling damage taken by a character is the result of a black dice roll plus an amount based on the distance fallen. If a character suffers any damage (after an armor roll) from their fall, their Action ends where they land, unless they jumped down (see Jumping Down, below).

Inability to Climb
Characters with the Inability to Climb icon cannot climb or use ladders.

Jumping Down
A character that intentionally jumps down resolves falling damage but using a height one color (6 feet) less than the distance "fallen." Jumping down from Orange distance incurs no damage. If the character is undamaged from jumping down and still has movement left after the jump distance, they may use that remaining movement.

FALLING DAMAGE		
	DISTANCE UP TO	
COLOR	FEET	DAMAGE
Orange	6	
Yellow	12	+2
Red	18	+4
Green	24	+6
Blue	30	+8
Black	36	+10

Note: Overseer determines damage for any greater heights.

Power Armor
Characters in Power Armor ignore all falling damage from falling or jumping.

FOWW RPG-001-111 — SECTION 4.5

ACTION: CHARGE

When a character is in contact with an opponent, they are **engaged**. As well as a Move distance, each character has a **Charge distance** which can be used to engage an opposing character. Charge is similar to Move (and is not an attack) and is usually longer than the character's Move distance. To use a Charge Action, the following three requirements must all be fulfilled:

1. Charging must result in engaging an opposing character.
2. A character cannot start a Charge when already engaged with an opposing character.
3. At the start of a Charge, the Charging character must have Line of Sight to the enemy character they intend to engage.

A character's Charge ends as soon as they engage an opposing character.

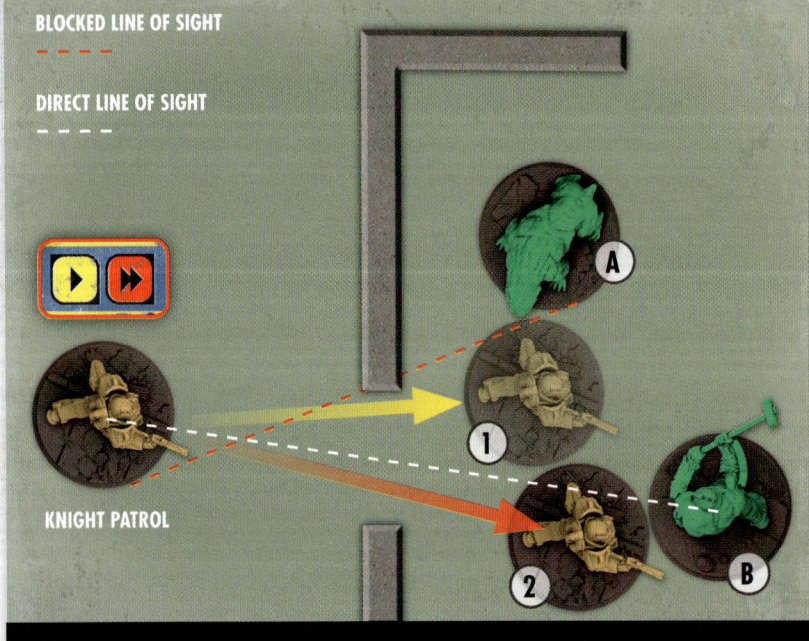

EXAMPLE: THIS KNIGHT PATROL CAN MOVE TO POSITION 1 TO ENGAGE TARGET A, BUT CANNOT CHARGE IT, BECAUSE THE KNIGHT PATROL DOES NOT HAVE LINE OF SIGHT FROM ANY PART OF ITS BASE. HOWEVER, THE KNIGHT PATROL HAS DIRECT LINE OF SIGHT TO TARGET B, WHICH IS WITHIN ITS RED CHARGE RANGE, SO IT MAY CHARGE.

MOVE DISTANCE — CHARGE DISTANCE, IN THIS CASE, RED

Charge Bonus
After completing a Charge, the Player selects a **Charge Bonus**, either a green dice or a black dice, to be added to their Skill Test as long as their next Action is a **Close Combat** attack against the now engaged opponent. This bonus only lasts one (the first) attack. If the character's next Action after a Charge (including Quick Actions) is anything other than Close Combat, the Charge Bonus is lost.

Using Skills During Charge
No other skills may be used during a Charge.

FOWW RPG-001-111 — SECTION 4.6

ACTION: SHOOT

To attack at range using a **Pistol**, **Rifle** or **Heavy Weapon**, a character makes a **Shoot Action** which can be attempted if the following are all true:

1. The attacking character must have a **relevant skill** that matches the weapon.
2. The target must be **within weapon range**.
3. The attacker must have **Line of Sight** to the target.
4. The attacker must not be engaged.

If all four requirements above are true, the character performs a Skill Test matching the weapon being used (Pistol, Rifle, or Heavy Weapon). If the Skill Test is a success, any damage effects are resolved (see 'Damage', p.63).

As well as characters, the target of a Shoot Action can be an object or a specific point on the landscape. Engaged characters can still use Pistols, Rifles and Heavy Weapons when engaged, but as a Close Combat Action (see 'Using Non-Melee Weapons In Close Combat', p.57).

> **COMBAT SUMMARY**
>
> 1. A character can use an **Action** (or Quick Action, see p.61) to make an attack.
> 2. Each weapon type has a skill icon in the top right of its weapon card. If the character has a **matching skill icon** next to one of their attributes then they may make an attack with that weapon (see example, below).
> 3. Attacks are resolved by making a **Skill Test** using the attribute's value and adding **Effect Dice** gained from the weapon, equipment, abilities, Perks, etc.
> 4. If a Skill Test for an attack is a success, **damage** is then resolved (see 'Damage', p.63), with a dice roll made to determine if the damage is reduced.

RANGE

Fallout: Wasteland Warfare RPG uses two weapon ranges: short and long. The distance of these ranges are shown by the colors on the weapon card (see below), with short range on the left and long range on the right. Long range starts where short range ends, but some weapons do not have a long range.

When a Player makes a Skill Test for shooting, they add all the Effect Dice shown beneath the relevant target range on the weapon card. If a target falls within both short and long range, the attacker chooses which range to use.

Example: Sole Survivor (1) is armed with an Assault Rifle. When shooting at Super Mutant A, the target will be at short range, so the Player rolls the Skill Dice plus 1 Accuracy (green) Effect Dice and 1 Damage (black) Effect Dice. If the Sole Survivor fires at Super Mutant B, the target will be at long range, requiring the roll of the Skill Dice plus 1 Damage (black) Effect Dice only.

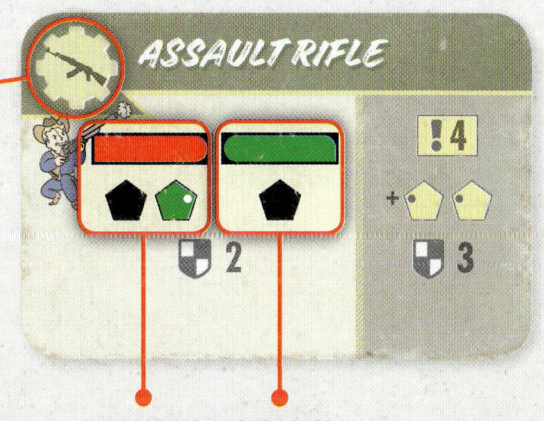

IF YOU OWN *FALLOUT: WASTELAND WARFARE* AND ARE USING MODELS, THE COLORED RANGE RULERS CAN BE USED TO MEASURE WEAPON RANGE BY SIMPLY PLACING THE TWO RELEVANT RULERS END TO END.

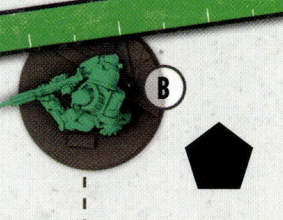

SECTION 4 – RULES OF PLAY   55

NO LINE OF SIGHT TO THE SECOND SUPER MUTANT, BUT THE SOLE SURVIVOR HAS COVER BETWEEN HER AND BOTH OF THEM

LINE OF SIGHT

An attacker has **Line of Sight** (**LoS**) if they can see ANY part of the target. Normal-sized characters do not block LoS, but may make it harder to hit the target (see Cover below).

COVER

While Line of Sight helps determine whether shooting a target is possible, objects between shooter and target are cover, making a shot more difficult. This can be due to items such as barrels between the shooter and target, or the target being only partially visible as they are hiding round the corner of a building. The effects of cover on shooting are:

- Each and every object that obscures part of the target gives a **-2 modifier on the Skill Value** of the attacker for the shot; and
- Any shot affected by cover also **increases the target's armor by 1**. This increase is only applied once no matter how many items of cover affect the shot.

Any cover in contact with the shooter is excluded, Leaning over a car roof, being behind a wall or around a corner doesn't give the target cover.

Example: The crate does not block Line of Sight so the Knight Patrol can shoot. The Line of Cover goes through the building and the crate but the Knight Patrol ignores the building as its base touches it. The value of the Knight Patrol's weapon skill is modified by **-2** and the Super Mutant's **Armor Rating increases by 1**. While they share LoS, any shot returned by the Super Mutant is resolved against a -4 modification of its weapon's Skill Value because of the crate and the building), but the Knight Patrol's Armor Rating still only increases by 1.

Normal-sized characters who are not friendly to the shooter also count as cover, Characters on the shooter's own side do not count as cover as they are working together.

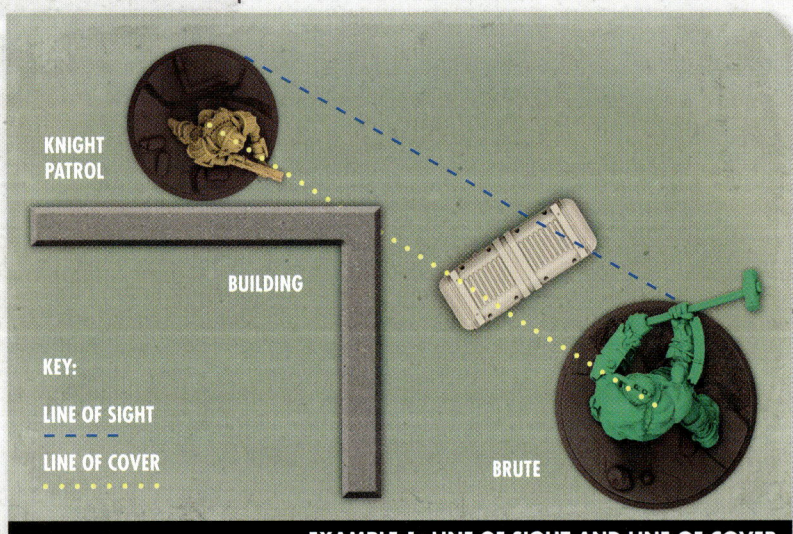

KNIGHT PATROL
BUILDING
KEY:
LINE OF SIGHT
LINE OF COVER
BRUTE

EXAMPLE 1: LINE OF SIGHT AND LINE OF COVER

HUGE CHARACTERS

Huge characters are significantly larger than most others, and the Overseer may decide that these add cover and/or block Line of Sight to smaller characters, even if the huge character is friendly.

MODEL BASE SIZES

32mm = Normal
40mm = Large
60mm or wider = Huge

FOWW RPG-001-111 — SECTION 4.7

ACTION: THROW

To launch a **Thrown Weapon**, the character performs a Throw Skill Test and then the damage effects are resolved (see 'Damage', p.63). A Thrown Weapon's range depends on the color of a character's **Throw Skill icon**. Thrown Weapon cards show a white range bar bearing the Throw Skill icon as a reminder. LoS and any target cover are determined in the same fashion as with Shooting (see p.55).

SCATTER

If a Throw Skill Test fails and the Thrown Weapon has a **Scatter icon**, scatter occurs before the weapon's effects are resolved. See 'Scatter', p.72.

THROWN WEAPONS AND CRITICALS

Thrown Weapons do not use Criticals (see pp.66-67), so no Critical Points can be gained when using a Thrown Weapon.

> **THROWING WITHOUT LINE OF SIGHT**
>
> Thrown weapons can be Thrown without having Line of Sight to their final intended target if the Overseer allows it (see 'Throwing Without Line of Sight', pp.86-87). For example, a character might want to toss a grenade or explosive over a wall to where they think enemies might be lurking.

UNSKILLED THROW

A character without the Throw skill who attempts a Throw suffers an Unskilled penalty as usual. The Overseer determines the maximum distance such character can throw something.

THROW SKILL ICON

THROWN WEAPON CARDS SHOW A WHITE RANGE BAR BEARING THE THROWN SKILL ICON ON IT

SCATTER ICON

SKILL ICONS ARE SHOWN TOP LEFT ON WEAPON CARDS

FOWW RPG-001-111 — SECTION 4.8

ACTION: CLOSE COMBAT

Engaged characters can only make Close Combat attacks. These have to be made against the opposing characters engaging them.

To make a Close Combat attack, a character makes a Skill Test using the skill matching the weapon they are using. Remember to add any dice gained from a Charge bonus (see 'Action: Charge', p.54). If the Skill Test is a success, the damage effects are resolved (see 'Damage', p.63).

Close Combat Strength Bonus

Any character with a total **STR 7 or more** that uses a **Melee Weapon** in Close Combat adds 1 bonus Damage (black) Effect Dice to the attack.

Super Mutant Close Combat Attacks

Super Mutants making a Close Combat attack with a pistol or rifle may use their Melee skill for the Skill Test (not Pistol or Rifle skill). The penalties for using a Ranged Weapon in Close Combat still apply (see below).

Using Non-Melee Weapons In Close Combat

A character can use a **Ranged Weapon** (Rifle, Pistol, Heavy Weapon, Thrown) for a Close Combat attack, but the attack is made as though one piece of cover is protecting the target: a **-2 Skill Value penalty** and the **target's Armor Rating is increased by 1**. If a weapon has a minimum short range greater than zero, it cannot be used for a Close Combat attack.

Outnumbered Characters In Close Combat

A character engaged with multiple opposing Characters is **outnumbered**. Any Close Combat attacks against an outnumbered character receive **1 bonus Accuracy (green) Effect Dice**. The outnumbered character must choose one target for their Close Combat attack.

Withdrawing From Being Engaged

An engaged character can Move out of engagement with an opposing character. A character cannot Charge out of engagement (see p.54). However, any opposed character gets an immediate **free Quick Action attack** on the disengaging character as they leave, providing that they are not themselves engaged with another character at the time. The free Quick Action suffers the usual **-2 Skill Value modifier** (see p.61). Free attacks Quick Action are made after the Player has committed to moving the character but before the character executes the Move.

Movement When Engaged

Close Combat is not a static affair. After performing a Close Combat attack, a character is allowed a special bonus movement, called a **Slide**, but only if this does not leave engagement with any opposing character(s). A character may Slide *around* the engaged opposing character and, as the Slide does not break engagement, it does not result in any free attacks. A Slide can move a character into engagement with another character with which it was not already

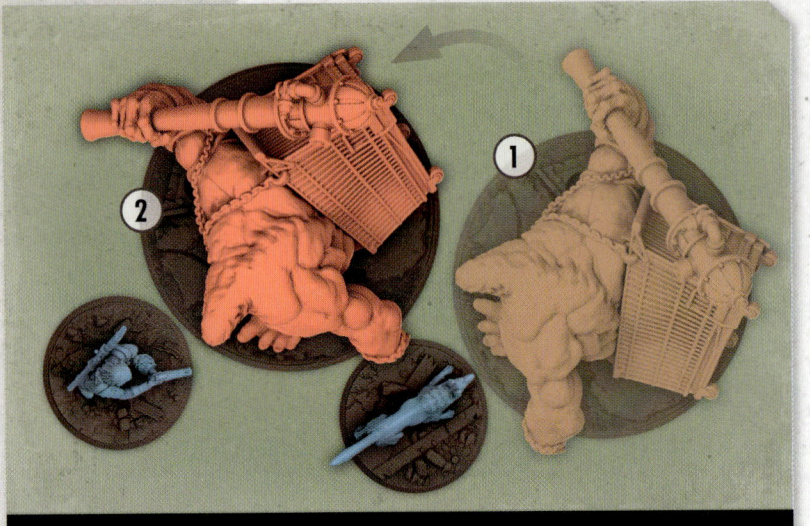

A BEHEMOTH BRUSHES OFF DOGMEAT AND SLIDES INTO ENGAGEMENT WITH THE SOLE SURVIVOR INSTEAD

to their Skill Value for the attack. Stunned engaged characters do not get a free attack on an engaged character who withdraws from engagement (see 'Withdrawing from Being Engaged' above).

Shooting Into Engaged Characters

A character can try to shoot at a character who is engaged with other character(s), but with little control over which of the engaged characters will be hit. The attacker determines their target as usual (this can be a friendly character) and rolls the attack as normal with a **+2 modifier to their Skill Value** because of the increased target size of the general melee. A failure is a miss, as usual. If the Skill Test is a success, decide on any special effects and then determine which of the engaged characters is hit:

1. The numbers 1-4 are allocated to the characters in the melee, starting with the target character as number 1. The numbers 2-4 are then allocated to any other characters in the melee which are both:
   - In **base-to-base contact** with the target; and
   - In the **attacker's LoS**.

2. If all characters have been assigned a number before all four numbers are allocated, a new circuit of number allocation occurs, again starting with the target.

3. Once all the numbers 1-4 are assigned, roll the red Armor Dice. The number rolled determines which character has the effect of the attack applied to it.

The same system is used for any area effect or Thrown Weapon (see pp.57, 71) targeting an engaged character. In those cases, if it hits, the character selected by the dice is where the effect is centered. If it misses, any scatter result is applied from the intended target.

engaged. A Slide is part of a Close Combat attack so any Triggers (see p.59) based on the Close Combat occur after the Slide has finished.

Example: A Behemoth has been intercepted by Dogmeat at position 1 (see above) and they are engaged. However, the massive mutant is more interested in getting to the Sole Survivor. After making a Close Combat attack against Dogmeat, the Behemoth takes a free Slide around Dogmeat's base to engage the Sole Survivor at position 2. As this Slide does not move him out of engagement with Dogmeat, Dogmeat does not get a free attack against the Behemoth.

Stunned While Engaged

Characters engaged with Stunned opposing characters (see Stunned, p.68) can perform Close Combat attacks on the Stunned characters, and gain a **+2 modifier**

A PLASMA GUN REMAINS EFFECTIVE, EVEN WHEN THE ENEMY IS BRINGING THE COMBAT UP CLOSE AND PERSONAL

FOWW RPG-001-111 — SECTION 4.9

ACTION: USE EXPERTISE

The **Use Expertise** Action allows a character to perform an Expertise Skill (which are any non-Combat Skills) that the Overseer determines must be an Action. Expertise covers the **Search**, **Computers**, **Lockpick**, **Presence**, as well as any other skills and including attribute tests (see 'Expertise' for more details, p.24). The character performs the relevant Skill Test and then the effect is resolved (see 'Skill Tests', p.42-44).

Interact
Some Expertise Skill Tests require a character to be **Interacting** with something. A character can 'Interact' with an object if they are next to it and they are not engaged. The "two arrows" icon is the **Interact icon**.

Engaged
Some Expertise Skill Tests require that the testing character is not engaged in order to use the skill.

COMPUTER SKILL ICON

LOCKPICK SKILL ICON

SEARCH SKILL ICON

PRESENCE SKILL ICON

INTERACT ICON

FOWW RPG-001-111 — SECTION 4.10

ACTION: PREPARE

A character may use an Action to **Prepare**, which gives the character a **Reaction**. A Reaction can be used later to perform an Action when the character becomes aware of a **Trigger** during an opponent's turn. For example, when a character notices an enemy move, the character could use a Reaction to shoot, pursue them, run away, lockpick, etc.

If a character uses an Action to Prepare and then performs other Actions during their activation, the Reaction is not lost. Prepare does not need to be the last Action a character takes during activation.

A character can only Prepare using an **Action Point** (see p.61) if they have the relevant Prepare Action Point Use icon.

PREPARE ACTION POINT USE ICON

TRIGGERS

A Trigger is an Action that may prompt other characters to make a Reaction (see below) if they are aware of it.

What Qualifies as a Trigger?
Except for Prepare, any Action by a character on the opposing side can count as a Trigger. A hit, whether it does damage or not, on any friendly character (including the character under consideration) is also a Trigger. Occasionally, special events during a game may also act as a Trigger. These are described in the scenario details.

Being Aware of a Trigger
Whether a character is aware of a Trigger or not depends upon (a) the Action, and (b) the color of the Reacting character's Awareness icon. Any Action (except Prepare) is a Trigger at up to one Awareness distance away. Only Attacks and Movement are Triggers at up to two Awareness distance away. All Triggers require Line of Sight except triggering Attacks as these can usually be heard.

Multiple Perceptions of a Single Trigger
When multiple characters are aware of the same Trigger, the Players must declare and commit to which characters will react, and how, before then resolving all the Reactions in the order the Players wish.

REACTIONS

A character is allowed only one Reaction at any time, so may never perform a Prepare Action if they already have a Reaction 'in stock.'

If a character has a Reaction and is aware of a Trigger (see p.59) they may spend the Reaction to make an immediate Quick Action (see p.61).

TRIGGER ACTIONS BY RANGE	
ONE LENGTH	TWO LENGTHS
Any Activity (except Prepare)	Movement
Friendly model hit by an attack	Attack

"DON'T SHOOT UNTIL YOU SEE THE WHITES OF THEIR EYES... OR THE GLOW OF THEIR TEETH"

The specific Action performed is chosen by the Player at the time of the Trigger and can be any Action usually available to the character within any restrictions that would normally apply. When a Reaction is complete, the Reaction is spent.

Note that because a Reaction is a Quick Action, there is a minor penalty to the Action being performed, and a character does not gain Action Points generated during a Reaction (see Quick Actions for full details, p.61).

Reaction Timing

Reactions are resolved after the triggering Action has been completed and before the next Action is started, whether by the same or a different character. Any part of an Action can be a Trigger but the Reaction is not assessed and resolved until the triggering Action is complete.

> **Example:** *A Super Mutant is in the Line of Sight of a Paladin with a Reaction. The Super Mutant uses an Action to move out of the Paladin's Line of Sight. The Super Mutant's movement is a Trigger and the Paladin can use their Reaction but, as the Super Mutant is out of sight at the end of the Paladin's Action, this Reaction cannot be used to shoot at it. However, the Paladin could use their Reaction to Move or Use Expertise.*

The Overseer may allow a Player that specifically states their character is waiting for a specific "something" to occur to use their Reaction before the related Trigger Action is complete.

Reactions that are Attacks

If a Reaction is an attack (Close Combat, Shoot, Throw), the attack can only target the triggering character, with the usual LoS conditions (as in the example above) applying after the Trigger Action has completed.

Reactions When Engaged

If a character with a Reaction is engaged with one or more opposing characters, the character can only use the Reaction to:

- Perform any Action in response to Triggers caused by engaged opposing characters; or
- Perform a Move only if they take damage from any source, not just from engaged opposing characters.

Reactions to Being Charged

If a character uses a Ranged weapon to shoot at a Charging character attempting to reach them, they react after the Action is complete: when the Charging character is engaged with them. They do not suffer the usual penalties for using a Ranged Weapon in Close Combat because the target is obviously growing bigger as it approaches. Someone being Charged gets a moment to shoot before the Charging character engages. This benefit only lasts for that Reaction. See 'Battle Cry', p.69, for one exception to this timing.

Limits to Reactions

In rare cases, a character is allowed multiple Reactions, but can only perform one Reaction for each triggering Action by others. A character can perform a Reaction to Move after being aware of a Trigger but cannot then immediately Shoot using another Reaction. Another Trigger is required for another Reaction.

Resetting Reactions

If a character has a Reaction when it is activated, it loses that Reaction. Reactions are not discarded automatically at the end of a round.

FOWW RPG-001-111 — SECTION 4.11

QUICK ACTIONS

Quick Actions are bursts of activity a character may perform in addition to their usual Actions but with a slight penalty. Quick Actions are mostly used when:

- Characters spend Action Points (see below).
- When making a Reaction to a Trigger (see 'Reactions', pp.59-60).

When a character performs a Quick Action, it is resolved the same way as the Action of the same name, but with a penalty that depends on the nature of the Action:

- Quick Actions that require a **Skill Test** suffer a **-2 modifier to the Skill Value**.
- Quick Actions that require **Movement** are **1 color shorter than usual** (6 feet less).

Characters can only perform specific Quick Actions if they have the relevant skill.

ACTION POINTS

Characters can gain and spend **Action Points** (**APs**) in order to perform Quick Actions. APs are shown on cards and dice by the **Action Point Icon**.

Gaining APs

A character may gain APs in two ways:

- APs may come from abilities, items, Perks, Boosts, V.A.T.S., etc.
- A character receives 1 AP if an AP icon is shown on the Skill dice result during a Skill Test which requires an Action.

APs are not gained:

- During a Quick Action.
- During an Opposed Skill Test.
- From Skill Tests which do not require an Action, e.g. testing AGI to avoid falling rubble as this does not require an Action that would generate APs.

V.A.T.S.

Some characters have the V.A.T.S. (Vault-Tec Assisted Targeting System) ability, which can generate APs for them each turn. When a character with the V.A.T.S. ability is activated, roll a Special (blue) Effect Dice and gain 1 AP for each Bottle, Star and/or Blast icon shown on the V.A.T.S. icons on their cards. In this example, the character gets 1 AP for each Nuka-Cola Bottle icon rolled. This roll is separate to any Test during the character's activation.

Using APs

When performing their regular Actions, a character can spend APs to perform Quick Actions. The Action Point Use Icons shown on the character's archetype or unit card shows exactly what APs can be spent on (see table, right).

It costs 1 AP for each Quick Action Point Use on the character's cards. Each Action Point Use icon can only be used once each during a character's activation.

> **OPTIONAL RULE**
>
> If you would prefer fewer dice rolls during Action Play and have characters with V.A.T.S., each Heroic character can receive 1 AP every time they activate instead of using the V.A.T.S. roll. Discuss this with your Overseer when you start Action Play.

Example: A character with 2 APs and only one icon could spend 1 AP to perform a Quick Action Movement but not 2 APs to perform two Quick Action Movements.

All Player Characters get 1 Movement, 1 Attack, 1 Expertise and 1 Prepare Action Point Use icon as shown on their Character Mat.

Unused Action Points

Unused APs are lost at the end of a character's activation. APs cannot be carried over to a new activation, transferred, or kept.

ACTION POINT ICON

A MODEL WITH THIS V.A.T.S. ABILITY GAINS 1 AP FOR EACH NUKA-COLA BOTTLE ICON ROLLED ON 1 SPECIAL (BLUE) EFFECT DICE.

ACTION POINT USE ICONS		
ICON	NAME	USAGE
◐	Movement	Character can spend 1 AP to perform a Move (Quick Action): Move or Charge
✦	Attack	Character can spend 1 AP to perform an Attack (Quick Action): Shoot, Close Combat, Thrown or Heavy Weapon
⚛	Expertise	Character can spend 1 AP to perform a Use Expertise (Quick Action): Any Expertise Skill or attribute test
◎	Prepare	Character can spend 1 AP to perform a Prepare Action

SECTION 4 – Rules of Play 61

FOWW RPG-001-111 — SECTION 4.12

MINOR ACTIVITIES

Some minor activities can be performed without requiring Actions. Picking up or dropping an item, switching weapons within easy reach, glancing at an object, and so on, do not require an Action. Usually, one of these minor activities can be performed before, after or during each Action. The Overseer will decide if more can be achieved during an Action, or if they are time-consuming enough to require spending an Action to achieve goals or require multiple minor activities to complete.

Example: Dropping a baseball bat at the end of one Action and drawing a 10mm Pistol from a holster at the start of the next Action is fine. Pulling out a 10mm pistol that is buried deep in your backpack would require an Action.

If an activity requires an Action not covered by the main Actions (such as the example of retrieving a 10mm Pistol buried deep in a backpack), the Overseer decides if a Move or Expertise Action must be performed to carry it out. This is important so that other characters' Reactions have a chance to happen in response to a Trigger.

> **FREE PLAY**
>
> During Free Play, timing is less important than in Action Play, so the game is not broken into rounds, and Players do not use Actions to perform tasks. Instead, Players tell the Overseer what they want to do in the order they wish. Skill Tests that are needed for Lockpicking, Shooting, Tracking, and the like are resolved in the same way as described in the Action Play section (without requiring Actions). For example, trying to hack a computer still requires a Computer Skill Test to see if a character is successful, and the character's Genius ability still means they cannot be locked out of computers.

PULLING OUT A GRENADE IS A VIABLE FIRST OPTION BEFORE THE FIREFIGHT BEGINS

FOWW RPG-001-111 — SECTION 4.13

DAMAGE

There are three types of damage in *Fallout*: **physical**, **energy** and **radiation**. Each weapon card shows the base damage done by a weapon on the left side of the card, with a damage type icon and the base damage value.

THIS ASSAULT RIFLE DOES A BASE DAMAGE OF 2 PHYSICAL DAMAGE

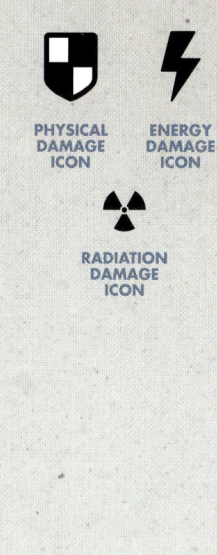

Applying Damage

Damage is recorded on the Health Track on the Player's Character Mat. The following process is used to apply damage:

1. Check the base damage shown on the weapon card.
2. Add 1 damage to the base damage for each ✸ on any Effect Dice results and relevant cards, etc.
3. Armor and other effects may block some or all damage from taking effect (see 'Armor', p.64).
4. Each remaining point of damage caused to a character is added to the Character Mat:

   A. **Physical Damage** 🛡 **and Energy Damage** ⚡

   Damage from physical and energy weapons cause **regular damage**. On the Character Mat, **place a cross** in the empty Health Track space furthest to the right. Do this once for each regular damage received. If there are no empty spaces, do not add any further regular damage.

   B. **Radiation Damage** ☢

   Damage from radiation weapons cause **radiation damage**. On the Character Mat, **fill in** the Health Track space furthest to the right which is not already filled-in *whether or not it has a cross in it*. Do this once for each radiation damage received. If all spaces are filled-in, do not add any further radiation damage.

Damage from a weapon is usually of a single type but, if more than one type of damage is caused at the same time, each type is resolved separately using any relevant armor to resist each type.

On the cards, the following symbols are used to show damage which is applied directly to the Health Track:

 Regular Damage   Radiation Damage

A BULLET IN JUST THE RIGHT PLACE

Example: *A character starts with* **Health 7**, *so the Player has already carefully filled in Health boxes* **8 and higher**. *The character then takes* **3 points of Energy Damage**, *so crosses out the right-most three of the remaining squares* (**5-7**)...

...*The character subsequently takes* **2 points of radiation damage**. *These are marked off by filling in the right-most squares not already filled-in – regardless of crossed squares* (**6-7**) – *as shown.*

FOWW RPG-001-111 — SECTION 4.14

ARMOR

Armor has the power to potentially block damage. If a character hit by an attack or other damage effect has armor that matches the type of damage inflict, they make an armor roll to see if the armor has blocked any damage.

Each character has an **Armor Rating** for each type of damage: physical, energy, and radiation. Most Armor Ratings are shown as a single number, which is the maximum damage that the armor can block.

To check if, and how much, damage has been blocked, roll the red 12-sided **Armor Dice**. The result will be a number between 1 and 4:

- If the result **is equal to or lower than the Armor Rating**, the damage is **reduced** by the number rolled.

- If the result is **greater than the Armor Rating**, no damage is blocked.

Example: A character with Armor Ratings of physical 3 and energy 2 is hit by an attack doing 3 physical damage. The character rolls the Armor Dice, and needs a result of 3 or less: their physical Armor Rating. The result is a 2, so 2 points of the 3 damage are blocked; the character takes 1 point of damage.

If the result had been a 4, no damage would have been blocked and the character would have taken all 3 damage. Ouch.

Higher Armor Ratings are better: they have the potential to block more damage, and will block damage more often than lower ratings. However, the Wasteland is a dangerous place, and even a minor attack can sometimes get past armor.

ARMOR REDUCTION ICONS

Some icons on the Effect Dice can reduce the effectiveness of armor. For each **Armor Reduction icon** (), the target's Armor Rating is **temporarily reduced by 1** when making the armor roll. Armor Reduction affects all armor types equally. If an Armor Rating is reduced to zero or lower, it is treated as zero and no armor roll is made.

Armor Reduction icons do not affect the Strong Armor bonus (see above) only the Armor Rating to the left of the plus sign.

BLOCKING DAMAGE
Using the Armor Dice roll your Armor Rating or lower to block some damage. If successful, what you roll is what you block.

A character's Armor Ratings are derived from one source which sets their values, plus one card (if available) of each card type that modifies those values, such as Armor, Clothing, etc. When a character is activated, the Player can choose which cards are used for its Armor Ratings. This decision cannot change at any time such as part-way through its activation or during another character's activation.

Immunity to Damage
Where a card shows Armor Rating as 'X', this indicates an immunity to that type of damage.

Strong Armor
Some Armor Ratings show two numbers separated by a plus sign, e.g. '3+1.' The second number is called the **Strong Armor bonus**. This is a fixed amount of damage that the armor will always block, in addition to the armor roll requirement indicated by the first number.

Example: A Paladin wearing Power Armor with a physical Armor Rating of 3+1 is hit by an attack dealing 3 physical damage. The Paladin rolls a 2 on the armor dice so the armor blocks 2+1, making a total of 3 damage blocked.

Had the roll been a 4, the armor would have blocked 0+1 for a total of 1 damage blocked.

Example: A Paladin with physical Armor Rating of 3+1 is hit by an attack that includes 2 Armor Reduction icons, reducing it to 1+1.

If the Paladin's physical Armor Rating had been 1+1, the 2 Armor Reduction icons would have reduced the armor to 0+1 for this attack. In this case the Armor Reduction icon would have reduced the 1 Armor Rating to -1 or effectively 0, and the Strong Armor bonus would have been unaffected by Armor Reduction icons.

Armor Reduction icons only reduce an Armor Rating for a relevant attack. Other attacks are considered separately.

ARMOR BOOST

Some effects temporarily offer extra protection which can wear off. An **Armor Boost** adds one Strong Armor bonus (see above) to the Armor Rating shown on a character's archetype or unit card. Each time a character with one or more Armor Boosts is hit by an attack, one Armor Boost is discarded after the attack is resolved regardless of whether damage is caused. A character can have multiple Armor Boosts, and they are in addition to (permanent) Strong Armor bonuses a character may already possess.

*Example: A Raider has an Armor Rating of **3 physical** and **2 energy**, plus **2 Armor Boosts**. Hit by an attack that would cause energy damage, the Raider resolves the armor as if they had a rating of **2+2**, after which one Armor Boost is removed. The Raider is then hit by another attack, but by a physical damage attack this time, and this time the armor has a rating of **3+1**. The second Armor Boost is then discarded.*

FOWW RPG-001-111 — SECTION 4.15

HEALTH

Each character has a **Health icon** next to one of the attributes on its unit card (see right). The attribute value next to the Health icon plus any additional Health due to abilities or equipment is the character's full Health. A character only uses the spaces on their Health Track up to this amount. Any effects that show increases or decreases for this Health icon affect the character's full Health.

HEALTH ICON

A character's current Health is equal to the number of empty spaces on their Health Track – that is, those not filled-in or containing a cross or another mark.

*Example: A character's Health is based on their END of **6**, so their full Health is **6**, and their Health Track uses spaces **1 to 6**. They take **2 regular damage**, so place **crosses** in spaces **6** then **5**. Their current Health is now **4**. Then, they take **3 radiation damage** so **fill-in spaces 6** then **5** then **4** which makes their current Health **3**. Later, they take **1 regular damage** and place a cross in space **3** which makes their current Health **2**.*

Incapacitated

A character is **incapacitated** when their current Health is 0: all spaces on their Health Track are either filled-in and/or contain a cross. A character that is incapacitated:

- Immediately becomes Used (if not already);
- Cannot perform Actions;
- Cannot be made Ready;
- Cannot have the Slow or Stunned conditions added to them;
- Cannot be fed food or drink;
- Can have Chems and First Aid used on them.

When incapacitated, regular damage that makes no change to the Health Track is not added. The Overseer may want the damage recorded to help work out what effects may be felt if the character stops being incapacitated. Radiation damage that changes regular damage into radiation damage is still recorded, as this changes a Health Track space from a cross to filled-in.

When an incapacitated character's current Health increases to more than 0, they are no longer incapacitated. The Overseer determines if there are any lasting effects from being incapacitated, and this is why it may be useful to record damage suffered while incapacitated.

At the end of the current scene, the Overseer determines the fate of those that were incapacitated at the end of that scene.

If a character that is Ready has their current Health reduced to 0, the Player make a Luck Roll (see Luck, p.35). If this is successful, the character gets to perform a single free Quick Action (see p.40) before becoming incapacitated. Healing during this free Quick Action has no effect and will not prevent the character's current Health being reduced to 0. This is a "last gasp" Action.

Non-Lethal Damage

An attacking character can choose a Melee Weapon's regular damage (physical or energy) to be **non-lethal**. The non-lethal damage is calculated, and counts as regular damage, and a character is incapacitated if their current Health reaches 0 as usual. However, non-lethal damage is removed over time without any healing required (see 'Healing', p.66). When recording non-lethal damage on a Health Track, mark '**NL**' below each space where the non-lethal damage is recorded in addition to the cross in the space.

Radiation damage can never be non-lethal. The Overseer may allow damage from a Ranged Weapon to be non-lethal with suitable circumstances or the right equipment.

Healing

Healing can remove regular, radiation or both types of damage as defined by the source of the healing.

For each point of regular damage healed, remove the leftmost cross on the character's Health Track. Healing regular damage doesn't cure radiation damage so does not remove filled in spaces. If 'NL' (non-lethal damage) is noted below any of these spaces, remove that too.

On cards, the **trash can symbol** means 'remove' and the number of regular damage icons is the quantity. For example, the symbols below mean remove (heal) 1 regular damage and 4 regular damage respectively:

For each point of radiation damage healed, erase the leftmost filled-in space on the character's Health Track. It does not matter if, when filled-in, the space was an empty space that was filled-in or a space that contained a cross. The damage is healed.

On the cards, the trash can symbol means 'remove' and the number of regular damage icons is the quantity. For example, the symbols below mean remove (heal) 1 regular damage and 4 regular damage respectively:

Rest

Resting for an hour in good conditions removes 1 regular damage, and a long rest (such as overnight) removes all regular damage. The Overseer may decide if any factors reduce or increase the amount of healing gained from rest. Rest can also remove the Injured Leg and Injured Arm conditions (see 'Conditions', p.67) if the Overseer decides they were temporary: a sprained ankle may be fine after resting, but a broken leg needs proper medical treatment.

Radiation damage is not healed due to rest.

All non-lethal regular damage is removed a few minutes after it was caused. The Overseer decides the time scale. If, after doing so, the spaces which are empty are not on the right-hand end of the Health Track, move them so that they are. This can happen if a character receives non-lethal damage as well as lethal regular damage.

Disease and Sickness

Disease and sickness are on-going conditions with various effects. Some diseases and sickness require an **END Test** to resist them. The Overseer determines the effects of disease and sickness and whether they can be cured via rest, healing or some other means. Finding a cure for some disease can even become an objective for characters to achieve.

Robots are immune to disease and sickness.

FOWW RPG-001-111 — SECTION 4.16

CRITICALS

Some weapons can be used to launch powerful attacks called **Critical Effects**, instead of their standard attacks. Player Characters, and some NPCs, with a **Critical icon** on their cards can gain **Critical Points** (**CPs**). These allow their weapons to use that as a Critical Effect. The details of any Critical Effect (if a weapon has one) are shown in a box on the right of the weapon card, called the **Critical Meter**.

GAINING CRITICAL POINTS

There are two ways a weapon can acquire CP necessary to unleash a Critical Effect:

- When a character who has a Critical icon on their cards and uses a weapon showing a Critical Meter successfully hits an opposing character with an Attack, the weapon gains 1 CP. No damage need be caused.
- Each Critical icon () rolled on a dice also adds 1 CP.

Hits on friendly characters or non-character items such as terrain do not generate any CPs.

If the number of CPs a weapon has accumulated equals the weapon's Critical Rating as shown on its card, the Critical Meter is **fully charged**. When fully charged, no further CPs can be gained on that Critical Meter; additional CPs gained are ignored.

CRITICAL EFFECTS

If a weapon's Critical Meter is fully charged at the *start* of an attack, the character can choose to use that weapon's Critical Effect instead of the weapon's standard effect. A character doesn't have to use the Critical Effect, which leaves the Critical Meter fully charged for later use. A weapon which becomes fully charged because of CPs gained from an attack roll cannot use its Critical Effect during that attack.

A character who declares a Critical Effect with a fully charged Critical Meter on the weapon, rolls the relevant Effect Dice shown on the card. However, the Skill Dice is not rolled; it is an automatic success regardless of other effects or modifiers. No CPs are gained when using a Critical Effect.

Instead of the weapon's standard effect, the effect described in the Critical Meter area is caused. The Critical Meter area shows new values, additional effects or both, which are on top of the standard effects. Additional effects have a **+** symbol in front of them.

> **Example:** The weapon's base damage of **2 energy** is replaced with **3 energy**, and **1 yellow Armor Reduction Effect Dice** is added to the standard number of Effect Dice (making a total of 2 yellow and 1 green at short range, or 1 black and 1 yellow at long range).

Note that an attack using a Critical Effect must still meet all the other usual attack requirements: Line of Sight, range, engaged status, and so forth. The attack is an automatic hit, but only if it is possible to hit the target. Note that some Critical Effects can only be used in certain situations (e.g. only at long range), and these restrictions are also described in the card's Critical Meter area.

Immediately after a weapon's Critical Effect has been resolved, CPs are removed from the weapon equal to the weapon's Critical Rating. In most cases, this will be all of them, and the weapon can then begin charging afresh.

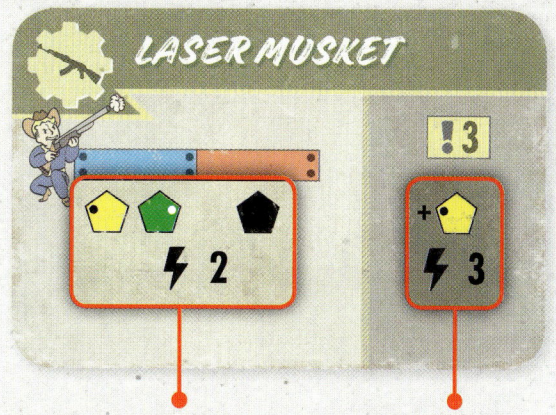

THIS WEAPON'S STANDARD DAMAGE IS 2 ENERGY DAMAGE, PLUS THE EFFECT DICE DEPENDING ON THE RANGE.

THIS WEAPON'S CRITICAL ATTACK DOES 3 ENERGY DAMAGE (INSTEAD OF THE STANDARD 2), AND ADDS 1 YELLOW DICE TO THE USUAL EFFECT DICE. THEREFORE AT SHORT RANGE THE DAMAGE WOULD BE 3 ENERGY PLUS 2 YELLOW AND 1 GREEN DICE.

If a Critical Effect is used to shoot at an engaged target, it automatically hits the engagement but the actual character affected by the Critical Effect is determined as usual. See 'Shooting into Engaged Characters', p.58.

THIS WEAPON'S CRITICAL ATTACK CAUSES 4 PHYSICAL DAMAGE BUT DOES NOT ADD ANY EXTRA EFFECT DICE. ALSO, THE CRITICAL ATTACK CAN ONLY BE USED AT LONG RANGE.

> **READING THE CARDS**
>
> If an item card has a condition icon on it, the condition applies when it's used. If this would cause Damage in any way, this damage is gained without an armor roll.

FOWW RPG-001-111 — SECTION 4.17

CONDITIONS

A character can be subject to one or more **conditions**, often as a result of weapon effects. A character cannot have duplicate identical conditions. When a character has a condition, circle the relevant icon on the Character Mat.

FROZEN

A character who is Frozen can perform Actions as normal but while Frozen:

- All Skill Values suffer a **-2 modifier**;
- All movement is **one color shorter**;
- The character **cannot use a Prepare Action**.

During Action Play, a Frozen condition ends when the character is next activated. During Free Play, the Frozen condition ends after 10 seconds. An On Fire condition (see below) replaces an existing Frozen condition.

INJURED ARM

A character with an Injured Arm suffers a **-2 modifier to all Skill Values**. Some items, such as a Stimpak or Robot Repair Kit (on Robots), can remove an Injured Arm if the Overseer decides it is not too serious. Rest also removes the condition.

INJURED LEG

A character with an Injured Leg suffers the **Slow** condition (see below). Some items such as a Stimpak or Robot Repair Kit (on Robots), can remove an Injured Leg if the Overseer decides it is not too serious. Rest also removes the condition.

ON FIRE

A character who is On Fire can perform Actions as normal. During Action Play, the On Fire condition is assessed when an On Fire character is activated.

FROZEN ICON

INJURED ARM ICON

INJURED LEG ICON

FIRE ICON

BLEEDING ICON

POISON ICON

SLOW ICON

STUN ICON

AURA ABILITY ICON

During Free Play, the On Fire condition is assessed every 10 seconds.

When assessed:

1. **Add 1 regular damage** to the character. There is no armor roll but Strong Armor still counts, then…

2. **Perform a 50:50 Test**. If successful the fire goes out and the On Fire condition is removed, otherwise, the character remains On Fire.

A character who is On Fire can attempt to put out the fire. This requires an **AGI Test**. If successful, the fire goes out and the condition is removed. During Action Play, putting out a fire out requires an Action or Quick Action. This is a Trigger like a Move, and can be a Reaction to a Trigger (see pp.59-60).

A Frozen condition (see above) replaces an existing On Fire condition.

POISONED

A character who is Poisoned can perform Actions normally, but suffers repeated regular damage over time. The Overseer determines the strength of the poison which determines how many minutes pass before the character suffers 1 point of regular damage with no armor roll to reduce it. Stronger poisons have shorter cycles of damage. During Action Play (and when enough minutes have passed), the damage is added when the Poisoned character is activated. A Poisoned character can use an item that cures poison to remove the condition.

Robots, and some creatures, are immune to poison.

SLOW

Characters can become Slow from various conditions, such as an Injured Leg. A Slow character's Moves are at **one color (6 feet) shorter**. This effect occurs before any other distance changes are applied such as a Quick Action for Move, or Charge, or Difficult Terrain. A Move distance cannot be shorter than Orange.

STUNNED

A character with the Stunned condition can do nothing except use an Action or Quick Action to remove the Stunned condition to "pull themselves together." This Action is a Trigger, and can also be a Reaction to a Trigger (see pp.59-60). Stunned characters do not block opposing characters' movement. Also see 'Stunned while Engaged', page 58.

BLEEDING

A character who is Bleeding can perform Actions as usual, but may suffer repeated regular damage over time. The Overseer determines the bleeding severity in terms of the minutes that pass before the character:

- **Adds 1 regular damage** to the character (no armor roll and Strong Armor does *not* count); then…

- **Perform a 50:50 Test**. If successful, the bleeding stops and the Bleeding condition is removed. otherwise, the condition remains.

Like poison, bleeding is more serious when the damage cycle is short.

The Bleeding condition can be removed by:

- Using a Stimpak or any other item the Overseer determines is suitable.

- A character may dress the bleeding wound of a character if they have some suitable materials. Both the "medic" and the bleeder must be unengaged. The character doing the treatment must make an **INT Test**; success removes the Bleeding condition. Bleeding characters can treat themselves, but must still make the **INT Test**.

During Action Play, an Action is needed to bind wounds; it is a Trigger (like a Move) and can be a Reaction to a Trigger (see pp.59-60). The Overseer may also decide that there are no appropriate materials to stop any bleeding or that the materials are insufficient. The Overseer should decide before the Action is declared. An appropriate skill (such as First Aid) may help improve the Test.

Robots are immune to Bleeding.

RESISTANT

If an effect makes a character 'Resistant' to something, make a 50:50 Test to see if resistance occurs or if it is ignored without effect.

AURA ABILITIES AND EFFECTS

Some abilities are described as Aura abilities shown by the Aura Ability icon after their name. A character's Aura abilities affect all eligible characters within the character's Presence skill range.

ADVANCED COMBAT AND WEAPONS

BATTLE CRY

Some characters have the **Battle Cry** skill. This can be used during a Charge Action to intimidate enemies.

 A colored Battle Cry Skill icon shows a character has the Battle Cry Skill (which includes the Resist Battle Cry Skill).

 A white Battle Cry Skill icon shows the character has only the Resist Battle Cry skill.

 This barred icon shows that a character is immune to Battle Cry.

A character may use Battle Cry after the movement of a Charge and prior to selecting the Charge Bonus. To use Battle Cry, resolve an Opposed Skill Test (see p.47) using the charger's Battle Cry skill versus the defender's **Resist Battle Cry** skill. The highest successful result wins. If tied, the Charging character wins.

If the charger wins the Battle Cry Test, they receive the following bonuses:

- The defender cannot use a Reaction in response to that Charge (see 'Reactions to Being Charged', p.60).
- The charger receives 1 black and 1 green dice as their Charge Bonus (instead of the usual 1 black or 1 green dice for the Charge).
- After engaging the defender, the charger may Push Back on the defender, which moves the defender away from the charger. This special move is up to a distance equal to the color of the charger's Battle Cry icon.
- If the defender wins the Battle Cry Test, the charger receives no benefit for the Charge, and this includes not receiving any Charge Bonus dice. The defender may immediately use a Reaction to Move their character out of engagement with the charger without giving the charger a free attack.

If both fail (i.e. no one wins), there is no Battle Cry effect; only the usual Charge Bonus is applied.

Battle Cry is part of a Charge Action, so triggers are resolved after the Battle Cry is resolved. This includes any Push Back. Note that a character must have the Battle Cry skill to use it; there is no Unskilled version.

AFTER A CHARGE OF GREEN (24 FEET) THIS BRUTE HAS A BATTLE CRY RANGE OF YELLOW (12 FEET), WITH A SKILL VALUE OF 8.

BATTLE CRY SKILL ICON (ORANGE RANGE)

RESIST BATTLE CRY ICON

BATTLE CRY IMMUNITY ICON

PUSH BACK

Push Back is a special movement which can be used when an ability or effect specifies it. A pushing character can move a target character a maximum distance equal to the Push Back color. This is usually the color of their **Battle Cry icon**. A character affected by a Push Back is moved away from the pushing character.

The pusher may follow the target so they remain in contact. Push Back movement stops if either pusher or target come into contact with anything substantial like a wall or other characters.

If the Push Back is part of an attack, any damage from the attack is resolved before the Push Back, otherwise Push Back does not allow a free attack on a character being pushed out of being engaged.

PUSH BACK ICON

BRUTE FORCE! A PUSH BACK OF 12 FEET

KNOCKDOWN

A character can try to **knockdown** another character whose STR is up to 2 greater than their own. To attempt this, the character first performs a Charge Action to engage the target and, as part of the Charge succeeds at an Opposed Skill Test using either STR or AGI (Charging character's choice). A STR Test pushes over the target, while an AGI Test trips them.

If the Charging character wins the Opposed Skill Test, the target is knocked down and is Stunned. If the target wins, the Charging character becomes Stunned but is not knocked down. If neither character wins, there is no effect from the Knockdown.

No Charge bonus is received for a Knockdown Charge. As Knockdown requires a Charge, it cannot be used once engaged. The Knockdown is part of the Charge, so Reactions occur after it has finished. Knockdown and Battle Cry cannot be used together. The Overseer may rule some characters cannot be knocked down in some situations: e.g. a Survivor couldn't Knockdown a Sentry Bot as the bot is very heavy and has wide tracks, but a Deathclaw or Behemoth could try to do it.

GRAPPLE

An engaged character may attempt to **grapple** their counterpart in the engagement. A character must use an Action to Grapple; this is a Move Action that doesn't move the character. The character attempting a Grapple is called the **grappler**.

Before attempting a Grapple, the grappler and their target compare both their STR and their AGI. If the grappler has both lower STR and lower AGI, they cannot attempt a Grapple. If the grappler has both higher STR and higher AGI, they receive a green dice for the resultant Opposed Skill Test (see below).

To attempt a Grapple, the grappler and target make an Opposed Skill Test based on STR or AGI:

- If the grappler has higher or equal STR to the target, the test is based on AGI.
- If the grappler has higher or equal AGI to the target, the test is based on STR.
- If both of the above are true, the grappler chooses which attribute to use.

If the grappler is unsuccessful, it has no effect. If the grappler is successful, the target is now being held and can do nothing other than an Action or Quick Action to perform a grapple against the character holding them.

A successful grapple ends when:

- the grappler stops grappling by performing any Action other than a Grapple. When the grappler activates, they must attempt a new Grapple to maintain their hold or the Grapple ends.
- the target performs a successful grapple on the grappler. If successful, this cancels the initial grapple so they are no longer held and allows the character to immediately Move Orange (6 feet) as they wriggle free. This movement does not result in a free attack for breaking engagement.

The Overseer determines if some characters cannot be grappled due to size differences, the circumstances are too difficult, etc.

MINES

MINE ICON

An unengaged character can use an Action to place a mine up to Orange (6 feet) away. This counts as a Move Action but does not move the character. It is also a Trigger and can be a Reaction to a Trigger (see pp.59-60). Mines have a proximity trigger area with a diameter equal to the color of their short-range bar on the mine weapon card. This is centered on the mine's location.

Mines become active once placed. During Action Play, a mine becomes active when the placing character is next activated. An active mine is triggered by opposing or unfriendly characters when:

- Such a character ends any Action within the proximity trigger area; or
- When a character enters, or moves within, the proximity trigger area. If a character Moves into the proximity trigger area, there is a pause to resolve the mine's effects before the Move is completed.

When an active mine is triggered, its effect is resolved immediately.

Blast Area of Effect

The diameter of the damage blast from a mine is an area effect (see below) centered on the mine's location. The mine's weapon card shows the size of the blast.

AREA EFFECT WEAPON DAMAGE

On a weapon card, the color of a damage value not only indicates that it is an area effect weapon, but also shows the diameter of that effect. Damage from an area effect weapon, centered on the target, is applied to every character – *friendly or not!* – who is wholly or partially in the area of the effect. A single roll is made to determine the weapon's effects and every affected character resolves that damage separately with each getting an armor roll, if relevant.

Objects between the area of effect's center and a character provide **cover** that increases the character's **Armor Rating by 1**. Objects blocking Line of Sight between the area of effect's center and a character may block the effect entirely (e.g. a thick wall), provide cover (e.g. a wooden fence) or have no affect (e.g. a curtain). The Overseer determines such protection.

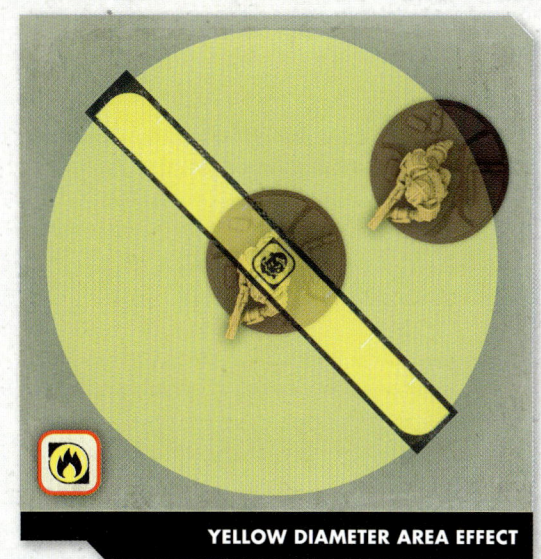

YELLOW DIAMETER AREA EFFECT

HEAVY WEAPONS

Firing Heavy Weapons uses a different skill icon to Pistols and Rifles. If a card does not show a **Heavy Weapon icon**, that character cannot use Heavy Weapons. A Heavy Weapon can only be fired if it is currently Loaded (see 'Slow Firing Weapons' below).

SLOW FIRING WEAPONS

During Action Play, Slow Firing Weapons can only be fired *once per activation*. If a character fires a Slow Firing weapon whilst performing their Actions, it cannot be used again even with a Reaction or by spending an Action Point.

Some weapons use their internal ammunition store each time they are fired, and need to be reloaded. Slow Firing weapons are marked with the **Slow Firing icon** at the top of their weapon card and are either **Loaded** or **Empty**. Such a weapon can only be used when it is Loaded; it only becomes Loaded if the character using it has the appropriate ammunition. The weapon becomes Empty after it is used.

Reloading does not require a specific Action, so when a character equipped with a Slow Firing weapon is activated, their Empty Heavy Weapon becomes Loaded, as long as they have ammunition available. The Overseer may rule that ammunition is limited, or is difficult to reach.

HEAVY WEAPON ICON

SLOW FIRING ICON

PRIMED WEAPONS

Some weapons need **Priming** before use. Primed Weapons can only be used once they have acquired a requisite number of **Primed points**: e.g. a Primed 3 weapon requires 3 points before it can be used.

The conditions under which weapons gain Primed points, and the procedure for activation, are detailed on the weapon or relevant unit card. Note activation may be detailed in the Critical Meter area of a weapon card, but Primed Weapon attacks are *not* Critical effects.

WALKED FIRE

Weapons with the **Walked Fire** ability fire multiple shots each time a Shoot Action is used. Each shot is resolved as a separate Skill Test. After a shot is resolved, the target of the next shot taken can be the same target, or any other nearby target within range (the color of the Walked Fire icon shown on the weapon card). Cover and LoS are calculated for each shot as usual. Remember that a target can also be a location, object or point on a battlefield.

WALKED FIRE ICON

THE WALKED FIRE ICON ABOVE SHOWS THAT THE WEAPON FIRES 5 TIMES, WITH A MAXIMUM DISTANCE BETWEEN TARGETS OF YELLOW.

ARMOR REDUCTION ICON

SCATTER ICON

GRENADE ICON

TARGET ICON

Walked Fire weapons can gain a maximum of 1 Critical Point during each Shoot Action, not per shot. They can also gain a maximum of 1 AP during each Shoot Action not per shot, excluding Quick Actions as usual.

A shot that hits a target gains **1 additional Armor Reduction icon for each repeated hit** by the weapon on the same target in the same Action. This is cumulative, and the Armor Reduction vanishes if a shot misses, the user changes target, and during a different, subsequent Action.

> *Example:* Three Walked Fire shots hit the same target. The armor roll for the first hit is standard; the Armor Rating for the second hit is reduced by 1, and the Armor Rating for the third hit is reduced by 2.

All shots fired are Triggers, but Reactions take place after the entire Shoot Action or Quick Action is completed, and a reacting character can only respond once to one of the Triggers.

SCATTER

When using a weapon whose card shows the **Scatter icon**, a failed Shoot or Throw Action Skill Test uses the Skill Dice result to determine how far the shot deviates from the intended target.

When a weapon effect needs scatter to be calculated, two factors are applied to the intended target location before resolving damage:

- The distance from the intended target.
- The direction from the intended target.

Scatter Distance

The scatter distance is based on how badly the modified Skill Dice result failed by. The weapon card shows the distance of the scatter based on this margin. If an [X] is rolled, the scatter distance used is always the largest scatter distance on the weapon card.

> *Example:* if an attack with the Missile Launcher failed by a margin of **3 or 4**, it would scatter **Yellow** distance. If an [X] was rolled, it would scatter **Red** distance.

Scatter Direction

The direction in which the scatter goes is random. To determine the direction, roll the armor dice:

1. Scatter directly away from the firer.
2. Scatter left of the target from the firer's point of view.
3. Scatter to the right of the target from the firer's point of view.
4. Scatter directly back toward the firer!

Scatter Collisions with Obstacles

If the weapon has a **Grenade icon**, check a straight line from the original target location to the new target location; otherwise check a straight line from the firer to the new target location. If this line passes through an obstacle, the weapon effect is resolved where the line first contacts an obstacle. The scatter stops there.

Target Effect

Any effect shown next to the **Target Icon** affects only the target. In the case of weapons that scatter, the Target effect does not apply if the weapon scatters.

UNIQUE WEAPONS

Some weapons are Unique. As the name literally suggests, there can be only one instance of a unique weapon between the Player Characters.

MULTIPLE EFFECTS

If a weapon shows multiple effects, these are accumulated and the combined effect resolved.

> *Example:* the Missile Launcher causes 2 damage to all characters in a Yellow area but also an additional damage to the intended target.

Therefore, the target would resolve 3 damage plus any icons from Effect Dice.

FOWW RPG-001-111 — SECTION 4.19

ITEMS

Characters can have one or more items, such as Weapons, Gear, Chems, Food and Drink, etc. and these cards are placed with their Character Mat.

Using Items

A character may use one accessible non-Weapon item immediately before or after they perform an Action. This can even be before or after a Reaction, see 'Prepare', p.59. Item effects have three types of duration: Instant, Fixed Effect, and Diminishing, as described below.

Items with a Fixed Effect can be identified by the **Fixed Effect Duration icon** (); Diminishing duration items can be identified by the columns and rows showing their varying effects over time; all other items are Instant duration and their effects happen immediately.

Items can have a set number of uses. Discard its card if that is its last remaining use after the item's effect ends.

If the item shows the Addictive icon, check for addiction just before discarding the card (see 'Addiction', page 74).

Fixed Effect Items

In Free Play, Fixed Effect items last for a period based on the duration number shown next to the Fixed Effect Duration icon: 3 minutes multiplied by the duration number. During Action Play, a Fixed Effect is discarded after the time has expired at the end of the final activation.

Limited Use Items

Limited Use items have a limit to the number of times they can be used, and are discarded after the final allowable use.

FIXED EFFECTS DURATION ICON

ITEM TYPES

TYPE	ICON	DESCRIPTION	LIMITED USE
Alcohol	🍸	Alcohol can have varied benefits, but can also result in the negative effects of addiction after use. See Diminishing Effects and Addiction, both p.74.	🗑
Armor	🛡	Armor offers protection against harm. A character's Armor Ratings are derived from one card that sets armor values. This may be their own card, plus another card of each type that alters those values. Characters can set which cards they are using for Armor Ratings at the start of activation. See Armor, p.64.	
Chems	💊	Chems can have powerful mind and body-altering effects, but can also result in addiction after use. See Diminishing Effects and Addiction, both p.74.	🗑
Clothing	👕	Clothing can increase attribute values and offer extra abilities. A character may equip no more than one clothing item.	
Food and Drink	🍜	Food and Drink items can heal damage, increase stats, increase resistances, and more. When cooked, some food and drink has increased effects and removes the harmful radiation gained from exposure to the Wasteland. Characters use the cooked effect if food has been cooked; otherwise, they use the uncooked affect. Super Mutants always use the cooked effect.	🗑
Gear	⚙	The Wasteland is full of all kinds of weird and useful items, from a Stealth Boy that renders the wearer temporarily invisible, to Stuffed Monkey toys which can be used to warn of enemy activity.	🗑
Junk	🛒	Many Wastelanders survive by scavenging junk and selling it for Caps.	
Mods	🔧	Mods are improvements to Weapons, Armor and Power Armor which change their capabilities. One Mod card can be attached to an item which is of the same type: e.g. Rifles can only be fitted with Mods showing the Rifle weapon type icon. Mods can only be fitted by characters with relevant Repair & Craft Skill, and need the appropriate Workbench for the job.	
Power Armor	🪖	Power Armor is amongst the toughest protection in the Wastelands. A character may equip 1 Power Armor item. See Power Armor, p.75.	
Weapons	(Various)	The main offensive power on the battlefield.	Grenades and Mines

SECTION 4 – RULES OF PLAY

DIMINISHING EFFECTS

Diminishing Effects items last for a while, but their effect changes over time. When made active, the item effect begins, and the card is placed underneath the Character Mat so that all green columns with dots at the bottom are showing. Some bonuses and penalties affect the character's S.P.E.C.I.A.L. attributes while some provide other effects, e.g. +1 AP, increased armor, Action Point Use icons, etc.

All bonuses and penalties that are visible are cumulative. All bonuses and penalties that affect S.P.E.C.I.A.L. attributes should be added together by reading across all the columns to give a new adjusted value of the attribute.

Example: a Paladin takes some Buffout. The initial effect is +3 STR and +3 END, giving them STR 9 and END 8.

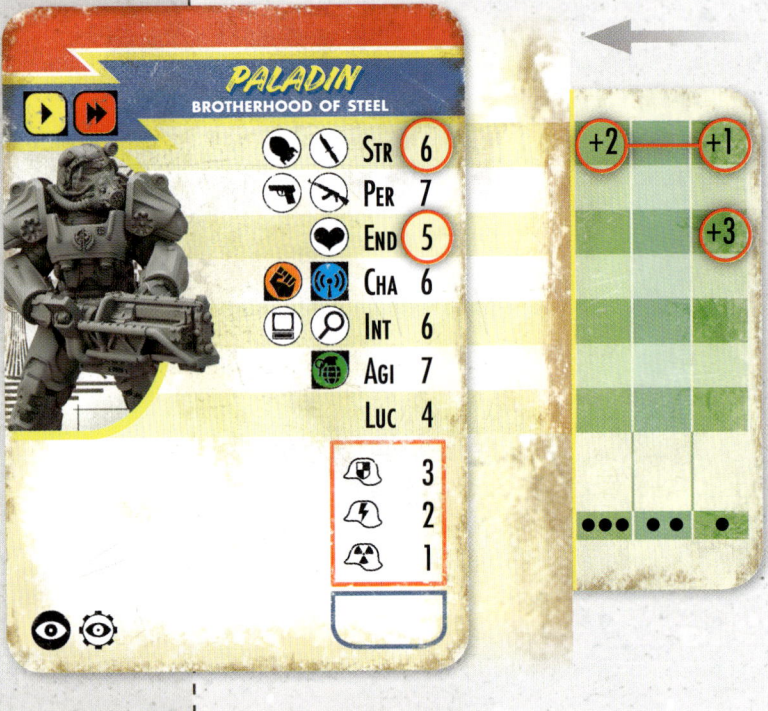

In Free Play, three minutes after the effect started, slide the item card under the Character Mat by one column. Any benefits or penalties that are covered by doing this no longer apply, reflecting the reducing or changing power of the item over time.

During Action Play, the item card is slid under the Mat the next time the character is activated after the three minutes, in the story, have passed.

Example: after three minutes have passed, the Paladin's item card slides one step under the Character Mat, which means the +2 STR benefit has gone, but the +1 STR and +3 END remain leaving the Paladin with STR 7 and END 8.

When 3 more minutes have passed, the item card slides beneath the Character Mat one step further. When 3 more minutes have passed, the item card will slide entirely underneath the Character Mat and all effects will end. The card is discarded.

ADDICTION

Some substances (such as Chems and Alcohol) can have a downside after use. When the effect of an item card with the **Addictive icon** (right) ends, place a cross in the relevant addiction box (Chem or Alcohol), top right on the Character Mat, if the box is empty. If the box already has a cross, a Special Effect Dice is rolled; the character becomes addicted if the result matches the icon shown next to the Addictive icon. Note that the Bottle and a Star dice result is treated as just a Star. If the dice result did not match the icon on the card, the item is discarded and there is no addiction effect, but the cross remains in the Character Mat box.

When a character is addicted, the card is not discard. Instead, it is turned 180 degrees and slid under the character's mat, so that the red section shows the addiction effects. These effects remain in force until the addiction is cured; addicted effects do not change over time. An addicted character can still use addictive items. The Overseer determines when an addiction box cross can be removed, which is usually overnight, after enough rest or after sufficient time has passed without using another one of the addictive item.

ADDICTIVE ICON

74 FALLOUT – WASTELAND WARFARE ROLEPLAYING GAME

Example: *the effect of Buffout ends, so the Paladin rolls a Special Effect Dice. The dice result is One Star, so the Paladin suffers the addiction effects which results in* **Str** *5 and* **End** *4.*

CHEM DURATION: JET

Jet's effects expire more quickly than those of other Chems. During Free Play, the effect of Jet lasts 30 in-game seconds, not 3 minutes. During Action Play, Jet lasts one round per column on the card: each time the character using Jet is activated, the Jet card is slid under the Character Mat by one column.

A character may only have one Diminishing Effect item in use at one time. For example, a character with an active Buffout would not be able to make another Chem active, or use an Alcohol item until the Buffout effects had completely finished. However, the character could still use items that have Instant effects or Fixed effects whilst a Diminishing Effect is in progress. A character cannot choose to end a Diminishing effect early; it must run its course.

HEALING ITEMS

Healing Regular Damage

Effects that heal regular damage remove the stated amount of regular damage only. Radiation damage is not healed. If the healing effect would remove more damage than the character has suffered, the excess is ignored.

Healing Radiation Damage

Effects that heal radiation damage only remove the stated amount of radiation damage. Regular damage is not healed. If the healing effect would remove more radiation damage than the character has suffered, the excess is ignored.

Healing Addiction

Addiction can be removed by using Chems called Addictol or Refreshing Beverage. Some foods and other items can cure addiction as well, such as a Radscorpion Egg Omelet. When addiction is healed, remove any addicted effects and remove any crosses from the the addiction boxes on the character's Mat.

POWER ARMOR

Power Armor is incredibly effective, usually providing good amounts of protection, a Strong Armor bonus (see p.64), and often other benefits such as increased Strength.

A character with Power Armor places the item card underneath the edge of their Character Mat so that its undamaged green side protrudes to the right, with attributes aligned to show the benefits. The Power Armor's Armor Ratings are shown at the bottom of the card.

> **Example 1**: *A Paladin is wearing T-60 Power Armor that offers* **+3 Str** *and* **+4 End** *bonuses. The character has a total of* **Str 9** *and* **End 9**. *However, the Armor Ratings* **do not** *stack.*

ABOVE: THE PALADIN'S POWER ARMOR HAS TAKEN 3 DAMAGE, BUT IS STILL FUNCTIOING AT FULL POWER, AND IS STILL GIVING A +3 STR BONUS AND A +4 END BONUS

RIGHT AND BELOW: A FOURTH DAMAGE EQUALS THE ENDURANCE BONUS OF THE GREEN SIDE OF THE POWER ARMOR CARD. IT IS NOW ROTATED TO THE YELLOW SIDE. THE ARMOR HAS NOW DEGRADED AND OFFERS ONLY A +3 STR BONUS.

A character wearing Power Armor only gets one armor roll when hit, regardless of any other armor worn beneath it. Before a character wearing Power Armor makes an armor roll, the Player can choose to use the Power Armor card instead of the character's usual Armor Ratings.

The Armor Ratings of Power Armor can only be increased by Power Armor Mods. Power Armor can only be repaired by items that specifically state they affect Power Armor.

Damage to Power Armor

When damage is applied to a character wearing undamaged Power Armor, the Power Armor accrues the damage until it equals the Power Armor's END bonus. It does not matter what attribute the character wearing the Power Armor uses for Health. When the total damage on the Power Armor equals the armor's END bonus, the Power Armor is **Degraded**: its card is rotated so that the green side is hidden and the yellow side now shows the reduced benefits and protection. Any remaining damage beyond the Power Armor's END is then applied to the character.

Even when Power Armor is Degraded, it gives benefits such as increased strength, negates falling damage, and may have other effects as shown on its card. Power Armor that is Degraded can be repaired so it becomes undamaged. Power Armor can only be repaired at a Power Armor Station.

Example 2 (top left): A Paladin with T-60 Power Armor has taken **3 damage** on their Power Armor card. The player notes this damage on the Character Mat, next to the Power Armor card. With an **END bonus of +4**, the Power Armor is not yet degraded.

Example 3 (left): The Paladin takes **2 more damage**. The first point of damage is added to the Power Armor which has now taken **4 damage**, equaling the **+END bonus**. The Power Armor is now **degraded**. The Player rotates the card 180 degrees to show its degraded side. It still gives **+3 STR**, but there is no more END bonus and the Armor Ratings are lower (although still better than the Paladin's unit card). The second of the 2 points of amage is taken by the Paladin.

Falling Damage and Power Armor

Power Armor always negates all damage from falling (including jumping) regardless of its condition.

MODS

Only one Mod may be added to one item at a time. Mods can only be added to and/or removed from an item by a character with the relevant Perk. Mods can only be added to and/or removed from an item at an appropriate Workbench.

REPAIR

Items that are broken can be repaired by a character using the relevant Workbench or materials, e.g. weapons can only be repaired with a Weapons Workbench. The Overseer determines what materials are required, and may require a character to make a Skill Test to repair an item.

COOKING

Food can be cooked using a Cooking Station. Cooked food allows the cooked effect at the bottom of the card to be used instead of the uncooked effect at the top of the card. Once cooked, the cooked food can be consumed at a later time.

ENCUMBRANCE

A character carrying too much equipment suffers restrictions. A character's load is calculated by adding up the 'load' value of the items they are carrying which are listed below:

ENCUMBRANCE LOADS	
ITEM	LOAD
Heavy Weapon	3
Rifle	2
Pistol	1
Melee Weapon	1 (excluding Improvised Melee Weapon)
Grenades	Every 4th grenade is 1
Ammo Loads	Every 4th ammo load is 1
Junk	Overseer will determine, based on where has been scavenged.

Items not listed above are not considered in a character's total load, unless an excessive amount is carried. The Overseer will specify a load value for other items, such as carrying 3 hot plates, or a large quantity of Chems and/or Food.

Encumbered

A character is **Encumbered** if their total load is **greater than their STR + 4**. An Encumbered character gains the 'Slow' condition, and loses the condition when enough load is dropped to become Unencumbered.

Over-Encumbered

A character is **Over-Encumbered** if their total load is **twice their (STR + 4)**. An Over-Encumbered character cannot move, and can only move again when they stop being Over-Encumbered.

> **STRONG BACK?**
>
> The encumbrance rules are about the total burden on a character due to the weight rather than storage capacity. A backpack or other such container does not increase the total load a character can carry before becoming Encumbered or Over-Encumbered. Rather, a backpack allows a character to carry many items at once and is less able to carry stuff without one.

WEAPONS

Ammunition

Weapons in the Wasteland are one thing. Having the ammunition to use in them is quite another. Rather than track every round of ammunition, *Fallout: Wasteland Warfare RPG* records ammo loads for most weapons that require ammunition. Each load is enough ammunition to last for a while, certainly the duration of a battle in Action Play unless the Overseer rules otherwise.

Weapons need ammunition of one of three types: physical, energy and radiation. A weapon may only be fired if the character has at least one ammo load that matches the weapon's damage type.

When a character fires an odd shot here and there, the current ammo load is unaffected. When a character uses a significant amount of ammo, one ammo load of the matching type is used. The Overseer determines when a significant amount of ammo has been used, such as in a noteworthy combat.

When a Complication occurs as a result of firing a weapon, usually by rolling a ⚠ on the Skill Dice, the Overseer can declare that an ammo load has been used. In this case, the Player may only continue using the weapon if they have another appropriate ammo load available.

> *Example:* a Lancer has a Laser Rifle (energy damage) and a 10mm Pistol (physical damage) and 2 loads of Energy ammunition and 1 load of physical ammunition. During a firefight, the Lancer rolls a ⚠ on the Skill Dice while using their Laser Rifle so the Overseer determines the weapon's ammo load runs out. The Lancer deducts 1 energy ammunition leaving 1 energy ammo left; after reloading they can continue to use the Laser Rifle. After a few more rounds, the combat comes to an end and the Overseer says the Lancer has used up another load of energy ammo. With no energy ammunition, the Lancer cannot use their Laser

Rifle until they gain some more, but can use their 10mm Pistol for now.

During Action Play, reloading does not require an Action unless the new ammunition is hard to reach, such as being stored deep in a backpack.

The Missile Launcher and Fat Man do not use ammo loads. These weapons record Missile and Mini Nuke rounds individually.

Overseers should remember that ammunition is one of those things some Players want to track and others do not care about. If your group prefers a simpler system, don't track ammunition at all. If your group prefers a more detailed system, track each shot used. Agree this with your Players at the start of the game. Ammunition can add to the tension of a game as well and create minor objectives in finding some more on the way to a main plot objective.

Weapon Breakages and Jams

If a Complication occurs when firing a weapon (usually by rolling a ⟨X⟩ on the Skill Dice), the Overseer may determine that the weapon has jammed or is broken. A jammed weapon can be cleared with an Action or Quick Action; a broken weapon must be repaired by someone with the right skills and Workbench before it can be used further.

OBJECTS

Characters can attack objects in order to damage or destroy them. Objects have Health and Armor values, and are destroyed when reduced to 0 Health. Examples with Health and Armor values are shown in the table, right.

If there is no pressure on the character (e.g. they are not currently in combat) or they are very close to the target object, the Overseer may award a bonus to an attack. If the target object is small, moving, far away, or some combination of those factors, the Overseer may penalize the attack.

OBJECT HEALTH AND ARMOR VALUES				
OBJECT	♥	👤	⚡	☢
Light Wooden Door	2	1	3	X
Heavy Wooden Door	3	2	4	X
Heavy Steel Door	4	2+1	3+1	X
Filing Cabinet	2	1	2	X
Mirelurk Egg	1	-	-	X
Computer Terminal	2	2	1	X
Heavy Console	4	3	3	X
Nuka-Cola Machine	6	2	2	X
Fuel Pump	3	2	1	X
Padlock	2	1	1	X
Chains	2	2+1	3+1	X
Rope	1	1	1	X

TURRETS AND FIXED DEFENSES

Turrets are automated defenses whose details are shown on their weapon card. Turrets have additional rules:

- Unlike characters, turrets can have multiple Reactions. Turrets start each round with the total number of Reactions shown on their card, regardless of any remaining from a previous round; i.e. the number of Reactions always resets to this standard value.
- Turrets use a Reaction to shoot using the skill shown on their card. A turret can only use one Reaction per Trigger as usual.
- Double the Awareness range of turrets for all Triggers.
- Turrets react to every Trigger of which they are aware.
- All Actions (including Prepare) are Triggers for turrets. In addition, if the character decides not to take any Actions, the turret is triggered at the end of their turn.
- Being hit by an attack is not a Trigger for turrets.
- A turret engaged by a character cannot target other characters who are not engaged with it. However, a turret will react to any Triggers it is aware of including those by characters not engaged with it. In such a case, the turret will react by shooting at one of its engaged characters. Randomize the target choice if there is one to be made.
- If engaged, a turret receives the usual penalties for using a Ranged Weapon in Close Combat.
- By default, turrets have 360-degree Awareness, but some turrets may be limited in their Awareness arc for Triggers. They may also be limited in firing arcs as well.

SECTION 05
THE OVERSEER

FOWW RPG-001-111

FOWW RPG-001-111 — SECTION 5.1

THE ROLE OF THE OVERSEER

Given the importance of the Overseer's role, it is vital that you prepare for a *Fallout: Wasteland Warfare RPG* game, and that you are comfortable with the responsibility:

- **Know the Rules:** You should be as familiar with the rules as possible. This doesn't mean knowing the rules inside and out, but you should at least know the core rules and the common tests and character attributes well enough to run the game. Knowing where to look up rules is fine to start with, and you'll soon get the hang of play.

- **Know the Plot:** The Player Characters are the focus of the stories you tell in the Wasteland. It is essential that you provide exciting stories to give Players something for their characters to do. You should include interesting locations from the *Fallout* universe, as well as recognizable characters as companions – and enemies with dangerous agendas. Roleplaying games are a group effort, so you should always let Players interact with the world, and be ready to adapt to decisions they make. Don't panic if Players go "off script" and want to do things that are not part of the story. They're exploring, and that's fine.

- **Be Prepared:** The Overseer is responsible for making the game run smoothly; in many groups, this may include providing pencils and paper, dice, or other useful gaming aids. Some Overseers prefer to hold onto the Character Mats and related cards between sessions, ensuring that they're all in one place. Keeping track of the little details helps keep the game moving.

THE OVERSEER'S ROLE AND RESPONSIBILITIES

Being the Overseer requires a different approach to taking part from that of a Player. These pointers should help you run your *Fallout: Wasteland Warfare RPG* sessions.

Presenting Dramatic Problems

It is the Overseer's first responsibility to present the challenges that the Player Characters encounter. These problems can be all kinds of things: a battle, a malfunctioning machine, or a caravan trader running a hard bargain. Problems provide the Player Characters with something to overcome, and provides dramatic tension to the story.

Decide How NPCs Respond and Interact

Just like the Players and their characters, you decide how Non-Player Characters (NPCs) in a scene act and respond to the PCs. NPCs are people too, and they behave according to who they are and what they want – a Super Mutant will behave very differently from a Brotherhood of Steel Paladin.

Using the Rules

An important part of your role is deciding which rules apply in what circumstances. The combat rules apply if someone is shooting a gun, but what happens if the Players want to force open a hatch on an old, wrecked tank? The rules in this book give you and your Players ways of resolving character actions. They can handle a wide range of circumstances when used with common sense and imagination.

RUNNING THE GAME

During Free Play and at the start of Action Play, you and your Players all have an opportunity to push the action and story forwards, so scenes usually play out like this:

- **The Overseer sets up the action:** You describe the scene. Who is present? What is happening? Where and when is the scene occurring? Why are these events happening? Your description should be informed by – and might include – answers to those questions.

- **The Players act:** The Players decide what they want their characters to do. This might be resolved as the scene evolves through discussion during Free Play, or it might be structured into rounds and turns during Action Play.

- **Resolve Action:** You and the Players determine the outcome of characters' actions, by rolling dice if there's a chance of something dramatic happening, or by judging their competence, and describing what happens as a result.

- **Repeat:** A scene may be complete with just one action, or the Players may want to carry out more actions in response to consequences of what just happened.

- **Wrap-up:** Once a scene is complete, you, as Overseer, provide any narration needed to wrap things up and move onto the next scene.

ADJUDICATING SKILL TESTS

AWARDING BONUSES AND PENALTIES

Awarding bonuses and penalties to Skill Tests is where you, as Overseer, can make the in-game situation really bring a scene to life. The Skill Tests section (see pp.42-47) mentions some ways that you can interpret the result of a Skill Test, and this section offers further advice.

MAKING SKILL TESTS EASIER

Skill Tests can be made easier by awarding a fixed bonus to the Skill Value, or by awarding bonus Effect Dice. It is important to make Skill Tests easier for characters who are not experienced, such as frail locks, or easily hacked computers, so the characters have a decent chance of success. This doesn't mean making everything a walkover; things should still be challenging. For starting characters, you may want to reduce the Unskilled penalty to -2.

Fixed Skill Value Bonuses

A fixed bonus is a guaranteed effect: it has no randomness so these are good to represent definite simplicity. Fixed bonuses are usually added in multiples of +2. For a frame of reference, a bonus of +2 increases the chances of success by +10% or +20% depending on the skill value.

Effect Dice

The different color Effect Dice have a mix of Effect icons on them but each has a different main focus.

The effect of the Effect Dice is random, so reflects bonuses which are uncertain. Note that there is some overlap of effects on the Effect Dice as they all share some icons.

MAKING SKILL TESTS HARDER

Skill Tests can be made harder by awarding a fixed penalty to the Skill Value. It is important to make Skill Tests harder for Players and characters who are experienced, so sturdy locks, or protected computers should be the norm so that success isn't too easy, though it should not be an impossible challenge. Effect Dice should not be taken away from characters.

Fixed Skill Value Penalties

A fixed penalty has no randomness, so these are good to represent defined difficulty factors such as a complex lock. Fixed penalties are usually added in multiples of -2. For a frame of reference, a penalty of -2 decreases the chances of success by -10% or -20% depending on the skill value.

MODIFIERS

Make A Skill Test Easier
Bonus to Skill Value (in multiples of +2)
Bonus Effect Dice

Make A Skill Test Harder
Penalty to Skill Value (in multiples of -2)
Increased Difficulty
Increased Resistance

EFFECT DICE

DICE COLOR	DICE EFFECT
+	Primarily cause more Impact: if successful, an effect will probably be greater. *Average increase damage/Impact per dice: 0.6. (Range: 0 to 2)*
+	Primarily reduce the chance of an effect being reduced or blocked. *Average increase armor/Resistance reduction per dice: 0.6 (Range: 0 to 2)*
+	The chances of success are likely to be greater. *Average improvement to Skill Test result per dice: 1.1 (Range: 0 to -3)*

EFFECTS EXPLAINED

Black Dice	Bigger effect
Yellow Dice	Overcome uncertainties
Green Dice	Better chance of success (Uncertain)
+2	Better chance of success (Definite)

Resistance

An Expertise Skill Test can be made harder by adding or increasing the Resistance. Resistance represents an uncertainty or unknown difficulty, as they are reliant on a Resistance dice roll.

Difficulty

An Expertise Skill Test can be made harder by increasing the difficulty, though this should be done with caution. Expertise Skill Tests with a Difficulty greater than 1, which therefore require multiple Impact to complete, can be difficult to achieve without bonus dice, etc. This is particularly the case if all the required Impact is required in a single roll and Partial Resolution is not allowed. Assistance, skills, Luck and equipment are some ways Players can gain extra dice to achieve multiple Impact in a single roll, and the ⚠ can add 1 Impact if you allow it. However, be careful not to set a Difficulty too high, and consider other ways of making a test harder instead.

DIFFICULTY MODIFIERS	
Resistance	Lower chance of success (Uncertain)
-2	Lower chance of success (Definite)
Difficulty	Greater effect required

FACTORS AFFECTING SKILL TESTS

There are many factors that can influence a Skill Test, including the in-story situation, character attributes, character knowledge, and equipment.

Situation

The in-game circumstances of a Skill Test can make it easier or harder.

Examples: Sneaking past a guard is easier when the sound of the heavy rain adds a lot of background noise or the guard is sleepy, and harder if the guard is already alert or suspicious. Searching is easier when there is lots of light, and harder in the dark. Tracking is easier on the open plain, and harder in a dense forest. Hacking a computer is more difficult if under fire.

Attributes

Some bonuses and penalties can be influenced by Attributes, so one character may be better at a test than another with the same skill.

*Example: Firing a rifle from a moving vehicle may use PER for the Rifle skill with a **-4 penalty** due to the unstable platform, but for a character with high AGI the penalty could be **-2** instead.*

Knowledge and Experience

Previous knowledge or experience may make a Skill Test easier or give a character a bonus for a test.

Example: It is easier to hack a computer having previously seen someone enter part of a password, or to pick a very common, simple lock, or to bluff your way past a Brotherhood of Steel sentry if you have served with them for years, and so on. It is harder to pick a difficult lock of a design never encountered before, or bluff the Brotherhood of Steel sentry if you know nothing about the group.

Approach

A character's approach to a Skill Test may also earn a bonus or penalty. Effectively, if the Player has a good idea, give them a bonus; if they rush in where angels fear to tread, hit them with a penalty.

Examples: Bonuses could be awarded for throwing a piece of rubble to distract a Feral Ghoul's attention just before trying to sneak past, or pretending to be drunk when closing on a target before attacking. A penalty might be awarded for crashing through an area known to contain traps.

Equipment

Having appropriate equipment can make a Skill Test easier by providing a bonus, adding Effect Dice, or both:

Example: Using an advanced lockpick kit could add a green dice to a Skill Test.

Suggestions

As Overseer, you can suggest bonuses to Players if they wish to do something specific:

Example: The Overseer suggests the character could have an extra black dice to put out a fire if they take off their jacket and use it to beat the flames.

Some of these suggestions may give a bonus, but at the cost of a failure being worse than usual outcome:

Example: The Overseer suggests a character could run along a narrow plank connecting two buildings over the alley to add a green dice. If they stumble, however, there is no chance of grabbing the plank to stop a fall.

Examples for Adjusting Some Common Expertise Skill Tests

The Expertise Skill Tests of Computers, Lockpick, Search and Presence are commonly used during games. This section provides some context on how each type of bonus could affect different types of dice rolls.

Computers: Multiple Impact can be required to hack difficult systems. Sometimes this is needed from a single Skill Test, and sometimes hacking just takes time, and the Impact can be garnered over multiple tests. Some computers have defenses, and so get to roll Resistance Dice, which may reduce Impact. A character may have hacking gear which gives them green dice to make success more likely; or special programs that add black dice that may increase Impact; or intrusion subroutines which add yellow dice that reduce the system's Resistance.

Dice examples:

 + *Training, a fast typist; Knowledge of subject being queried*

 + *Knowledge of the system's weak points*

 + *Hacking kit*

Lockpick: Multiple Impact can be required to open complex locks either from a single Skill Test, or built up over multiple attempts. Some locks have mechanisms to protect against picking and get to roll the Resistance Dice to reduce the Impact. Characters may have lockpick tools to give them green dice to make success more likely; advanced tools which add a black dice that may increase Impact; or they may have specialist knowledge that adds yellow dice to reduce the lock's Resistance.

Dice examples:

 Understanding of the lock type; Special lockpick tools

 Oil to ease corrosion

 Calm and quiet surroundings

Search: Multiple Impact can be required to find objects due to being in dark or confined areas; when hunting for small objects; or even for being the proverbial "needle in a haystack." Sometimes Impact is needed from a single Skill Test, and sometimes it just takes time to build up Impact to locate something. A search may require finding one item amongst many similar items, and therefore there would be a Resistance roll. A character could have a flashlight that gives them green dice to make success more likely; good eyesight which adds a black dice that may increase Impact; or additional information on what is to be found and where which adds yellow dice to reduce the search's Resistance.

Dice examples:

 Good eyesight

 Knowledge of the item being searched for

 Flashlight; Quiet whilst searching for a beeping bomb

Multiple Bonuses & Penalties

Any mixture of bonuses and penalties can be awarded on any test, depending on circumstances as described above.

Impossible

Sometimes you may decide a Skill Test is impossible if there is no realistic chance of success.

Example: Even with the Tracking skill, rain has washed out all useful traces of a character's prey.

SETTING EXPERTISE SKILL TESTS

When setting an Expertise Skill Test, you must set the Difficulty, often 1, and Resistance, often zero. If the Difficult is greater than 1, consider if all the Impact needs to be achieved in one Skill Test or if the task can be achieved over several tests, i.e. if Partial Resolution is allowed.

If the Difficulty is greater than 1, consider:

- **Can the Impact be accrued over several rolls or is it all needed in one go?**

  Several rolls: breaking toughened glass to access a laboratory requires 3 Impact which can be accrued via multiple attempts as each Impact causes lasting damage to the glass.

  Single roll: pushing a pile of junk to make it fall requires 3 Impact. If less than 3 Impact is achieved, it wobbles but does not fall. Further attempts are no easier despite some Impact on previous attempts.

- **What happens if only some of the Impact required is achieved?**

  When breaking down a door, parts of the door give way as Impact is achieved; a computer, on the other hand, will not be accessible until all of the Impact required to hack it is achieved.

- **Is there any negative effect if only some of the Impact required is achieved rather than all at once?**

  Example: Trap A is a complex, interlinked trap and requires 2 Impact to disable, it but it will activate if only 1 Impact is achieved.

  Trap B is a complex trap requiring 2 Impact to fully disable, but its trigger mechanisms are not linked and achieving 1 Impact will disable part of the trap without activating it.

- **Does the Impact achieved reduce over time?**

  Example: The boat has a leak. Each Impact achieved bails out some water but, each round, the Difficult increases by 2 as water continues to flood in, undoing the good work of bailing.

COMPLICATIONS

When a **Complication** occurs due to an ⚀, you can decide on the negative effect. This effect does not need to be large, because Complications can happen quite often (15% chance), but a Complication is a worse outcome than just a normal failure. A Complication could have: a direct negative effect on the character; a negative effect on the target if that would be bad for the character; a negative effect on the situation;

or could be an advantage for the character's opponents. For Lockpick and Computer tests, a Complication often causes the Player to be locked out for a while (see 'Complications', p.46).

Some examples of Complications:

Effect on character

- When shooting a weapon, the ammo load is used or the weapon jams.
- Whilst trying to get the vault lift working, the character suffers a minor electric shock and takes 1 non-lethal damage.
- During a chase, the character not only fails to slip through the crowd but gets tangled up with someone causing a delay.
- Whilst shooting round a corner, the character strays out of cover to get the shot needed.
- A sonic pulse device to deter the Deathclaws has overheated and needs fixing, or it has run out of power.

Effect on target

- Whilst lifting a heavy prototype bot, the character drops it and it is now broken.

Effect on situation

- As the character tries to sneak quietly through the cave, they make some noise thanks to the failure, but this small noise is due to knocking against a pile of junk which topples over in spectacular fashion causing a much more noticeable crash!
- The character accidentally trips an alarm.

Advantage for opponents

- The character fails to hack into a computer to open the exit, but another door opens instead, allowing the guards chasing the character to enter the room.
- The character's headlight gets switched on, making it easier to see them; opponents get a green dice on their next attack.

Sometimes, you can have the character make a test to see if the Complication occurs, e.g. testing Luck or Intelligence, or a skill. This reduces the frequency of complications and also allows the Player to feel that character Attributes and abilities make a difference.

EXTRA IMPACT

If a character's Expertise Skill Test results in more Impact than required, this can have a beneficial effect: almost the opposite of a Complication. The more extra Impact beyond the required Difficulty, the better or more numerous the benefits. The benefits are usually directly linked to the test, but can be of a more general nature, e.g. a wandering Radstag distracts one of the Radscorpions attacking the characters.

Some examples of extra Impact:

- As well as finding some Sugar Bombs in the old kitchen, there's some Cram found as well.
- Binding a wound not only stops the bleeding, but also restores 1 Health.
- The character not only finds messages showing the name of a gang leader, but realizes they know where that individual lives.
- The character hides so well from a Deathclaw that it gives up searching and wanders off rather than hunting them further.
- The trader reduces the price for a Combat Shotgun and also throws in some extra ammo loads.

SIMULTANEOUSLY SUCCESSFUL OPPOSED SKILL TESTS

When two characters' Skill Tests are both successful during an Opposed Skill Test, the relative amount of Impact should be taken into consideration when determining the final outcome. For example, if a Knight achieved 1 Impact and a Raider achieved 4 Impact, then the Impact is more in the Raider's favor than if they had only gained 2 Impact.

FASTER SKILL TEST ROLLS

To speed up dice rolls, the red dice for Armor or Resistance can be added to the Skill Test roll, as it doesn't make a difference who rolls it. Remember, however, that many Players prefer rolling the red dice for their own character, and it can keep Players involved in all the action. You can ask Players to roll the red dice when making Skill Tests against NPCs or objects – equally you can get the Players to roll red dice when you perform Skill Tests as an NPC. This not only reduces the number of rolls, but it also frees you from some details when you could be doing other things to keep the game flowing.

DESCRIBING THE OUTCOME OF A SKILL TEST

Success or failure may happen because of all sorts of reasons. As an Overseer, you can describe any reason you wish, but the dice can help guide you. For example, an attack that hits and does little damage may be because the Armor Dice blocked all the damage, or because the Effect Dice added no extra damage. If a shot misses out on hitting the target by 1 or 2 due to the penalty added due to cover, maybe the shot hits the cover without penetrating it, or zings off into the distance. Did a Lockpick Skill Test succeed because the result was below their Skill Value and the lock opened due to pure talent, or was it only successful because the Effect Dice provided by the special lockpick kit reduced the Skill Dice result?

As well as the dice results, many different interpretations can be created to describe the action.

For example, Sturges attempts to Lockpick the door to access the basement of the harbor master's office whilst a Mirelurk is asleep on the other side of the office. If Sturges fails a Manual Dexterity Skill and awakens the Mirelurk, it might be due to the sound of the lock springing open with a loud click, or perhaps Sturges dropped his tools, broke something, or slipped on the wet planking of the dockside and knocked something over, etc.

Opposed Skill Tests can be especially descriptive as the dice result can be used to understand who succeeded and who failed. For example, a character being noticed whilst using Stealth may have failed to move quietly whilst the Radscorpion succeeded at noticing them, or maybe the character successfully moved quietly, but the Radscorpion's senses were just too finely honed.

UNSKILLED TESTS

When a character does not possess a required skill for a Skill Test, they can still attempt the Skill Test but with the **Unskilled** penalty. Battle Cry is an exception which cannot be used Unskilled. When this occurs, the Overseer needs to pick the attribute on which the character will base the Skill Value. This can vary, depending on the character concerned: e.g. most characters use STR for Close Combat but some use their AGI. The situation may also determine the attribute to use: e.g. a Search that requires looking for a physical item may be PER-based, whereas finding information in a library of books could be based on INT. The decision is the Overseer's to make, based on what feels relevant to the situation. There is, however, a default attribute for every skill. Default attributes for Expertise Skills without specific icons are described in the table of Expertise Skills on p.24. Default attributes for all Combat Skills and Expertise Skills with specific icons are shown below:

UNSKILLED TEST ATTRIBUTES	
SKILL	DEFAULT ATTRIBUTE
	PER
	PER (or AGI for some Humans)
	AGI
	STR (or AGI for some Humans)
	STR
	PER (or INT for some Human and Super Mutants)
	INT or AGI
	INT (or LUC for the occasional Super Mutant and Human)
	CHA (or STR for some Super Mutants)

JUST A CRATE AND SOME NUKA-COLA BOTTLE. NO TRAPS... RIGHT?

FOWW RPG-001-111 — SECTION 5.3

OTHER ADJUDICATIONS

ADVANTAGE

When the game is being played in rounds, either the Players or the Overseer have Advantage. At the start of a round, the side with Advantage decides which side takes the first turn.

Deciding Who Gets Advantage First

Usually the Overseer decides on **Advantage**. If one side has surprise over the other, Advantage goes to the side with the element of surprise. If a situation is uncertain or fluid, give Advantage to the Players.

If one or more characters have been completely caught off-guard, they are **Used** for the current (first) round and so will not act. If **partially caught off guard**, characters can be given the **penalty of -2** to tests for that round. If one or more characters are lying in wait, they can start **Ready** for the first round. More than one of these can apply to a situation depending on its circumstances.

> **OPTIONAL ADVANTAGE RULES**
>
> If you prefer a random allocation of Advantage, the Overseer can select an attribute, such as PER if the two sides could detect the other's presence, or AGI if the two sides are already facing each other down and who "draws first" is an issue. The Player Character and Overseer's character with the highest relevant attribute values make an Opposed Skill Test, and the winner gains Advantage for their side.

Advantage During Action Play

At the end of a round, the Advantage usually remains with whoever had it at the start of the round unless the Overseer feels the situation has changed. If the side with the Advantage is taking heavy losses or not making progress, then the other side can be given Advantage as they have gained the upper hand. Remember: Advantage does not always mean acting first in a round!

PREPARE WITH A PURPOSE

When a character Prepares (see p.59), you can allow that character to state specifically what they are waiting for, and what their reaction will be if that thing happens. In such a case, the character may use their Reaction as soon as they are aware of the specified Trigger and before the Trigger Action is completed. The Reaction cannot be used for any other Trigger, and the character may only perform the action they declared. A character doesn't have to use Reaction of this type, but it can't be used for anything else.

Example: a Raider hears a Survivor moving around inside the Super Duper Mart and getting nearer. The Raider uses their Action to Prepare, stating they will use their Reaction to shoot at the Survivor as soon as they appear from around the corner. The Survivor walks into view and, before it gets to complete its move, the Raider takes the shot. If the Survivor had appeared from a different direction, thrown a grenade over the racks into the Raider's aisle, or done anything else, the Raider could not have used their Prepared Reaction.

THROWING WITHOUT LINE OF SIGHT

Throw can be used to toss items to places without a Line of Sight from the character if you allow it, such as posting a grenade down a vent, throwing one into a room without looking, lobbing a bomb over a high wall without knowledge of what's behind it, etc.

Penalties (or bonuses) should be added to the roll to reflect the difficulty of hitting the intended target. Whilst the character may not be able to see the weapon's final destination, they are still trying to throw an item to a specific point which they can see in order for it to reach its final destination. For example, a trick throw to bounce a grenade around a corner needs to be done so that the grenade hits the right spot to deflect to its intended target; throwing something over a wall needs to be done so it passes through a high enough point to arc over the barrier. Trying to hit a small, specific point makes a throw more difficult. Dropping a grenade down a vent right next to the character is easy. When deciding bonuses and penalties consider how accurate the character needs to be to achieve a desired effect. Does the amount of power in the throw help accurate execution? Is the target area small? Are there any other factors involved like wind, a moving target, or the like?

You might also take into account if the character knows where a thrown item needs to end up. Throwing a grenade over a wall is easy, but not knowing the location of an intended target behind the wall may make it very difficult to hit them. In some cases, it's just blind luck if a successful throw over a wall hits an intended target, so the character could make a Throw Skill Test and then roll the Special (blue) Effect Dice to see if the throw hits the intended target with whatever suitable chance you see fit. Potentially, you could have a character make a Notice Skill Test to try to estimate the position of a target from sounds, shadows, or other clues, which could then increase their chances with the Special Effect Dice.

ZERO HEALTH AND INCAPACITATED

Damage taken at zero Health needs to be recorded so the total damage shows the true magnitude of character injuries. A character who takes a lot of additional damage after becoming incapacitated will feel it for longer – if they survive – than a character who didn't take any further damage. As Overseer, you should feel free to determine suitable lasting conditions, such as an Injured Arm or Injured Leg, or create ailments like feeling dizzy with a -2 to Skill Tests, being temporarily deaf, or unable to carry heavy burdens.

If all characters are incapacitated simultaneously with no immediate salvation, you decide what happens to them: For example, did the Super Mutants haul them away somewhere, leave them to the Radroaches, or put them in a meat bag? This decision may include how much damage the characters have when they recover. Do they come round with a current Health of 1, or do they wake up in bed back at the Settlement with all their Health restored? Perhaps there was no saving them and they all perished. Resist the temptation to punish Players: you want them to have an exciting adventure, not repeatedly die in new and horrible ways!

DISEASE AND SICKNESS

The Wasteland is home to many types of disease and sickness. The **Resilience** skill is used when resisting illness. You can create any disease and sickness you want for your games, but you need to consider how it is contracted, how it is healed, and its effects. If you can fill in a list like the one shown in the example, your disease is defined enough for play. Details such as its appearance are there for descriptive flavor only.

For example:

MOLE RAT DISEASE
Source: *Bite of an Infected Mole Rat which does damage after an armor roll.*

Test Resilience to resist: *Yes. No effect if passed.*
Gestation: *Effect starts after 1 hour from being infected.*
Effect: *-1 full Health.*
Cure: *Cured only via a special and rare medication*. Rest, time and normal healing have no effect.*
Description: *An infected person develops bloodshot eyes and their hair, if any, falls out.*

* *This may turn out to be a useful objective for further adventures in the Wasteland, tracking down the needed ingredients for a cure.*

LUCK POINTS

Luck can be used to nudge situations in a character's favor, giving them opportunities to beat difficult odds, get out of a jam, or turn a sticky situation from bad to good. Luck Points should always be a limited and scarce resource so should never become a major influence, but gaining them regularly means Players are more comfortable with spending them, rather than clinging on for use only on special occasions.

Luck Points can be given to Players at any time, but it is best to time the acquisition of Luck Points with fitting moments in the game, and not grant them if there is no valid context. You can award Luck Points as a reward and incentive for good roleplaying, clever thinking, noticing clues, etc. All else being equal, characters go back up to their **maximum Luck Points after a long rest**, or **gain 1 Luck Point after a short rest**, but you can vary this as you see fit.

In addition to the ways in which Luck Points can be spent (see 'Luck', p.35), you may occasionally allow Players to spend Luck for other reasons such as turning an **Impossible Skill Test** into an **Outside Chance** (see p.49), or to remove the Unskilled penalty, or for any other reason that manipulates the game rules to a similar extent. Characters shouldn't rely on Luck Points as spending them should only "tweak" events and be a limited resource.

FOWW RPG-001-111 — SECTION 5.4

NON-PLAYER CHARACTERS

Major NPCs

Major NPCs are the main characters and bosses the Players will meet during an adventure. They are like Player Characters, so **they are Heroic** and can have Skills and other abilities too. They **can use Criticals**.

Character consists of: *Unit card + Heroic.*

Regular NPCs

Regular NPCs are the general run-of-the-mill characters the Players encounter in the world. They are generally capable people, such as the leader of a local settlement. They are like Player Characters and have skills and other abilities too but they **do not count as Heroic**. As a result, they do not have access to the Action Point Use Icons so, when they do gain an Action Point (usually from a Skill Test), often their only option is to use it to **Prepare**. They **cannot use Criticals**.

Character consists of: *Unit card.*

Minor NPCs

Minor NPCs are the background crowd in a story, or the least capable. They are the "extras" in the movie of the characters' lives, e.g. the mass of inexperienced Raiders, the crowd in a market, and so forth. These characters are **not Heroic** and **do not usually have skills or other abilities**. They have limitations on the Actions they can take, and **always have to use one of their two Actions to Move or Charge**. They **do not use Action Points** and **cannot use Criticals**.

Character consists of: *Unit card (and one Action must be a Move or Charge).*

FOWW RPG-001-111 — SECTION 5.5

THE COVERT APPROACH

A quiet and subtle approach can often get better results than going in all guns blazing. Players are, of course, free to use either strategy.

STEALTH

A character can attempt to move unnoticed by making as little sound as possible or remaining unseen. Other nearby characters may notice them. An **Opposed Skill Test** is performed to determine if the sneaking characters will be noticed, with the character attempting to use stealth using their **Stealth** skill and any opposing character who could spot the movement using their **Notice** skill. As mentioned in 'Opposed Skill Tests' (p.47), the **success with most Impact wins**; ties are broken by the highest Skill Dice result.

If the character attempting stealth wins the Opposed Skill Test, they pass unnoticed. If a spotting character wins, they are aware of the movement and this counts as a Trigger (see 'Triggers', p.59).

Normally, if neither character wins an Opposed Skill Test there is no effect, but this is slightly different in the case of stealth. If neither character wins because they both failed, or it is a tied result, the character has not been stealthy enough to go completely unnoticed, but has also not been properly detected. In such a case, the spotting character notices only the slightest of activity, so their state of alertness (see page 89) is raised slightly – they think they heard something but cannot be entirely sure.

If several spotting characters are close enough to detect a stealthy character, the stealthy individual makes a single Stealth Skill Test, and each spotting character makes their own individual Notice Skill Test separately. One result is compared against many in a set of Opposed Skill Tests. It is possible that one character may notice the use of Stealth while another does not.

Example: *Ronnie Shaw tries to move quietly along a rocky canyon ledge. There is a Super Mutant on a path above her and Mutant Hound on the ground below. Ronnie rolls a* **6 for her Stealth Skill Test** *(a* **success***) with* **1 Impact***. The Overseer has decided that the Mutant Hound has the Notice skill, but making a Notice Skill Test, the Super Mutant rolls a* **9** *(***fail***) with* **1 Impact** *and the Mutant Hound rolls a* **3** *(***success***) with* **2 Impact***. Ronnie won the test versus the Super Mutant who does not notice her but lost versus the Mutant Hound (it succeeded, but with more Impact). Therefore, the Mutant Hound is alerted to Ronnie's movement.*

If the Mutant Hound had rolled **1 Impact** *instead of 2, Ronnie would have won the tests and been completely unnoticed as they would have had the* same Impact. The tie-break would have been based on the highest Skill Dice roll. Now Ronnie must hope the Super Mutant above her does not work out why the Mutant Hound has started barking!

To avoid making many multiple rolls if there are lots of potential spotters, the Overseer can make a single roll on behalf of several characters instead but, perhaps, add a bonus (like a green Effect Dice) to their Notice Skill Test. Sneaking past multiple characters is harder than sneaking past just one.

If a character moves to engage a target using Stealth and does not win the Opposed Notice Skill Test, (a) the target will be aware of them even if this was due to both failing their tests; and (b) the target may React, and this includes a Move away. This does not allow a free attack for disengaging.

Performing actions unnoticed has limits, so you may declare some Stealth Skill Tests impossible. A character may not use Stealth against a target if they are clearly noticeable at any time during their Move, or the target knows where they are. A character can only Move their usual distance using Stealth; it cannot be used for a Charge.

Impact

As with all Expertise Skill Tests, the amount of Impact from a successful Stealth Skill Test shows the magnitude of the success. For example, a character that succeeds with 1 Impact moves unseen but with 3 Impact they may have moved a bit faster, only stepped on hard ground and so leaving no tracks, or avoiding stepping in puddles that would then cause wet footprints later, etc.

A success with zero Impact is still considered a success, but as the character did not move more stealthily than usual, their skill use had no effect. A success with zero Impact still wins and a character doing so would go unnoticed versus a failed Notice Skill Test.

Bonuses and Penalties During Stealth

When Stealth is used, bonuses and penalties can be awarded to the Stealth Skill Test and the Notice Skill Test based on different factors. Keep in mind that a Stealth Skill Test is about if, and how well, the character executed their activity in a stealthy fashion regardless of who or what is watching. The Notice Skill Test is about whether an opposing character was aware of the activity.

STEALTH SKILL TEST BONUSES AND PENALTIES DURING OPPOSED SKILL TEST FOR STEALTH

BONUS	+ ⬟	Greater effect	▪ Equipment such as Stealth Boy, Camouflage ▪ Hard ground leaving no sign of passage
	+ ⬟	Overcome uncertain difficulties	▪ Things that reduce Resistance factors
	+ ⬟	Uncertain better chance of success	▪ Equipment such as camouflage ▪ Intermittent background noise ▪ Quiet terrain such as short grass ▪ Cloudy night providing shadows from passing clouds
	Fixed +2	Definite better chance of success	▪ Guard in distance ▪ Short distance to cover ▪ Continuous background noise or darkness ▪ Equipment like Stealth Boy
PENALTY	Resistance ⬟	Uncertain difficulty	▪ Crossing a narrow plank or rusted walkway ▪ Precarious objects that could be knocked over ▪ Noisy/slippery terrain ▪ Rusty door handle to open, or wearing noisy armor
	Fixed -2	Definite difficulty	▪ Lack of shadow and/or cover ▪ Long distance to be covered

NOTICE SKILL TEST BONUSES AND PENALTIES DURING OPPOSED SKILL TEST FOR STEALTH

BONUS	+ ⬟	Greater effect	▪ Equipment such as a torch ▪ Twigs, leaves and branches on the ground, magnifying the effect of movement
	+ ⬟	Overcome uncertain difficulties	▪ Trained ▪ Familiar with the area
	+ ⬟	Uncertain better chance of success	▪ Guard randomly looking in the character's direction ▪ Spotlight sweeping the area occasionally
	Fixed +2	Definite better chance of success	▪ Guard already alert or expecting someone ▪ Guard solely focused in character's direction ▪ Still night
PENALTY	Resistance ⬟	Uncertain difficulty	▪ Intermittent background noise ▪ Distractions ▪ Sleepy
	Fixed -2	Definite difficulty	▪ Constant background noise ▪ Can only see part of the relevant area ▪ Guard distracted, not suspicious or asleep

The examples above are suggestions rather than a definitive list of bonuses and penalties, and show the ways the Stealth and Notice Skill Tests could be adjusted.

ALERTNESS FOR NON-PLAYER CHARACTERS

NPCs are usually in one of the following alertness states: **Unaware**, **Suspicious**, **Investigative** and **Alerted**. Winning an Opposed Stealth v Notice Skill Test will usually raise a level of alertness, and the greater the Impact, the more it is likely to rise. The amount of change in alertness depends on the NPC, their status, the current situation, and the like: are they scared, or have they heard there could be an attack tonight? Only in a few circumstances will an NPC go from being completely unaware to full alert just due to a single, successful Notice Skill Test. This is especially true if only 1 Impact was rolled.

*Example: a Brotherhood of Steel Knight on guard duty on their own and expecting an attack is likely to be **Suspicious** and go to **Alerted** at the first real sign of trouble. In contrast, a drunk Raider, who is not expecting any activity will probably start **Unaware** and become **Suspicious** the first time they hear or see something. They may go to **Investigate** the next time they hear something, or even ignore it if apparently unimportant.*

> **NPC ALERTNESS**
>
> Having NPCs go from Unaware to Alerted immediately leaves no room for error by the Player Characters. Sneaking around becomes almost impossible, and so unforgiving that they may not even consider it as a tactic.

NPCs' alertness may also go down over time if they notice no further suspicious activity.

SURPRISE ATTACKS

If a character performs an attack on a target who is unaware of their presence (due to attacking from hiding, using Stealth to get close undetected, or firing unobserved from a distance), they gain a green and black Effect Dice on the Skill Test for their attack. As a character cannot use Stealth whilst Charging, a character cannot simultaneously receive a surprise attack and a Charge Bonus.

Example: The Raider watches the Feral Ghoul shamble past from inside the doorway of the building. The Raider uses Stealth to move to engage the Feral Ghoul and wins the Opposed Notice Skill Test. With their next Action, the Raider swings at the Feral Ghoul with their Lead Pipe and chooses to add a green and black Effect Dice to their attack. If the Raider had lost the Opposed Notice Skill Test, they would have Moved and engaged with the Feral Ghoul, but the Feral Ghoul would have been aware of them so the Raider would not add the green and black Effect Dice to their attack.

A surprise attack is a Trigger even if it misses, as is the effect of the attack, e.g. a bullet hitting a character other than the target, or an object nearby, would be a Trigger. A gunshot from far away which misses the target and has no effect on the surrounding area might not cause a Trigger if the noise is lost in the distance.

If a character engages a target which is unaware of them, the character must make a new Stealth Skill Test. If the attack is Close Combat and it incapacitates the target, you determine if the attack effect is a Trigger or not. Possibly it might be unseen and quiet enough to go unnoticed by others.

COVERT MANUAL DEXTERITY

Manual Dexterity covers many activities which are covert by their very nature, such as pickpocketing and sleight of hand. It can be used to perform an activity covertly. However, nearby characters may notice. An Opposed Skill Test is performed to determine if the covert activity succeeds or if it is noticed. The covert character uses their **Manual Dexterity** skill, and any character that may notice activity uses their **Notice** skill. As mentioned in 'Opposed Skill Tests' (p.47), the success with most Impact wins, and ties are broken by the highest Skill Dice result.

The Overseer can make the Manual Dexterity Skill Test easier or harder depending on how much subtlety is required to be covert.

If the character covertly attempting to use Manual Dexterity wins the Opposed Skill Test, they succeed unnoticed. If a character that may have noticed the covert use of Manual Dexterity wins, they are aware of the attempt. This counts as a 'Trigger' (see Triggers, p.59); usually this occurs before the activity is complete (e.g. the pickpocketing fails before anything is taken). However, you may decide an activity is noticed after completion, when partially complete, or even as it starts, depending on the results of the Manual Dexterity Skill Test if both succeed in their rolls and generate Impact.

If several characters are close enough to notice an activity, the covert character makes a single Manual Dexterity Skill Test and each detecting character makes and compares their own Notice Skill Test results separately. It's quite possible one character may notice the use of Manual Dexterity when another does not.

To save making a lot of rolls if there are many potential observers, you can make a single roll and apply it to several characters instead, but perhaps add a bonus (like a green Effect Dice) to their collective Notice Skill Test.

Performing unnoticed actions has limits, so you may declare some Manual Dexterity Skill Tests to be impossible. A character may not covertly use Manual Dexterity if they would be watched at any point during the activity, or if the target of their activity is already fully aware of them. For example, a target cannot be pickpocketed if they are aware of, and suspicious of, the character attempting the pickpocketing.

Impact

As with all Expertise Skill Tests, the amount of Impact from a successful Manual Dexterity Skill Test shows the magnitude of the success. For example, a successful character with 1 Impact may take the first thing they find in a target's pocket but with 3 Impact they may have been able to take something else or just better.

A success with zero Impact is still considered a success but the character did not complete their task, as their skill use had no effect: e.g. they picked the pocket but got nothing from it. A success with zero Impact would still win and go unnoticed against a failed Notice Skill Test.

Bonuses and Penalties During Covert Manual Dexterity

You can award bonuses and penalties based on the situation, such as a target being animate or inanimate, the armor or clothing worn by the covert character, the condition and position of the item being used or taken, and so on.

Example: a Railroad operative is undercover inside the Brotherhood of Steel's outpost. They need to covertly slip a note into a contact's foot locker, but there are other Brotherhood members present. Opening the catch is relatively easy but the catch is very rusty, so has a Resistance Rating; a good Skill Test may still be neutralized by the creak of the hinge...

Other examples are a Resistance Rating when pickpocketing if a target keeps moving around. Achieving multiple Impact (and therefore a higher result quality) would be more likely to overcome such unpredictable circumstances. For example, you could award green dice if a required key is poking out from a guard's belt; you could award black Effect Dice when using sleight of hand to take a watch laying on a bar if its owner is preoccupied looking at a (staged) brawl across the room.

NOTICE

A covert activity that is noticed is a Trigger. As a result, characters using Notice can potentially detect stealthy activity at a distance double their Awareness for Movement and anything noisy, and normal Awareness distance for more subtle activities like lockpicking or computer hacking. Various factors can increase or decrease these distances such as the light levels, background noise, Line of Sight, etc.

OTHER COVERT ACTIVITIES

Skills other than Stealth and Manual Dexterity can be attempted covertly. An Opposed Skill Test is made versus any potential observers' Notice. The Overseer may make the activity's Skill Test harder because pickpocketing and moving stealthily are innately covert but other activities like searching through trash or climbing are harder to achieve.

COVERT ACTIVITIES DURING ACTION PLAY

During Action Play, Stealth can be used on Move Actions and Quick Actions. Characters who are unaware of a stealthy character cannot draw a Line of Sight or use a Reaction. Successful covert activities are not Triggers.

A character can become aware of someone else they didn't know was there between the activations of the covert character.

> **Example:** a Raider uses their remaining Action to Move using Stealth to engage an Eyebot from behind, to be ready to capture it next round. Before the Raider can activate the next time (either in the current round or start of the next), the Eyebot activates, happens to turn in the Raider's direction, and sees the electrified net in their hand. They Eyebot is now aware of the Raider just before the Raider could act, and it flees as fast as it can. The Overseer gives the Raider a free attack as the Eyebot breaks engagement. If the Eyebot had just moved away while still being unaware of the Raider, the Raider would have had a free attack, but could have had the green and black dice bonus for the surprise attack too if the Overseer has so ruled.

FOWW RPG-001-111 — **SECTION 5.6**

CHASE SCENES

Giving a visual element to a chase can really help you and the Players keep track of everyone's relative positions. This can be achieved using the range rulers. To start, place the range rulers so they are all side-by-side in order of length with their ends aligned at one end. Where they all line up represents the chase target for the characters or something that is chasing the characters. The Players each place their models – or a token – at the end of the range ruler that matches their starting distance to the target (or chaser).

A chase is broken into **moments** and, during each moment, give the characters a choice which could move them to a shorter range ruler (if the gap between them and the target narrows), to a longer range ruler (if the gap widens), or leave them where they are. If a character reaches the target it is caught. When a chaser is after them, if it reaches the characters they are caught.

Each moment presents the characters with a test or choice carried out individually by all of them. Players need to make a choice or make the appropriate dice roll quickly, so the situation feels fast and tense. Hesitation or any discussion more than a few words means the gap to the target will automatically extend if they are chasing a target, or close if they are being pursued. This "hesitation factor" is in addition to the result of their eventual choices. After as many chase moments as you wish, the result of the chase can be judged.

If a character has a higher Move or Charge distance than the target (or vice versa for a chaser pursuing the characters), you can occasionally increase or reduce the gap distance for those characters to reflect this, as you feel appropriate.

An example will make this clearer. Below are a few moments of a chase where the characters are pursuing a trader through the alleyways of Diamond City in order to question him. 'Gain 1 Distance' means move one range ruler closer to the target, e.g. from Green to Red, and 'Lose 1 Distance' means move one range ruler further from the target, e.g. from Orange to Yellow.

A cart is pushed out from a side alley. The target goes around just as it emerges.

Choice: *Slide under or go around?*

- Slide: **Test Acrobatics**.
  - ✓ Gain 1 Distance.
  - ✗ Lose 1 Distance.
- Go around: No change.

A large group of ill-looking people stand arguing about who is next to see the Doc.

Choice: *Shout at them to get out of the way or go around where it's clear?*

- Shout and go through: **Test Presence**
  - ✓ They step aside. Gain 1 Distance.
  - ✗ The shout merely confuses them. No change in Distance but you press up against some of them as you pass (-2 on END Test below).
- Either way: Characters **Test END** after the chase and failure means catching Mole Rat disease.
- Go around: No change.

The trader weaves around a large wooden roofing panel that blocks much of the alleyway. It looks fairly lightweight.

In order of distance from the trader (closest first)…

Choice: *Ram through the panel or weave around?*

- Ram panel: **Test STR**
  - ✓ Character smashes through it. Gain 1 Distance and all Players yet to choose can automatically move through the same gap and Gain 1 Distance too.
  - ✗ Character bounces off the panel. Lose 1 Distance. Next character gets +2 to their STR Test (which is accumulative) if they choose to ram.
- Weave around: No change.

Chase Result
If any Player is now at:

Yellow or Orange: The trader can't shake the characters and gives up.

Red or longer: The trader rounds a corner and is gone by the time the characters reach it. Perhaps it's time for the characters to find someone who might know where he'll go to ground…

SCAVENGING

Many items can be found lying around in the Wasteland but others need to be sought out, or need other work to gain them. When characters scavenge for items, Overseers can present them with an opportunity to use their Search, Lockpick and Computers skills to gain "stuff", plus apply Knowhow and other skills too.

Some items (or even just locations) may be booby-trapped, or involve other dangers like gas leaks, a concealed and resting Feral Ghoul, or a precarious pile of rubble. These could be triggered immediately, but it is always best to give characters a chance to avoid, or at least mitigate, some negative effects through appropriate tests. That way Players will feel like they have some control over their destinies, are actively involved, and their capabilities and good roleplaying make a difference: all things that make for a more interesting game. For example, if some rubble falls, have the character perform an AGI Test to try to get out of the way. A success might avoid all or most of the damage. This is better gameplay rather than simply giving the full damage amount automatically.

As well as immediate tests, dangers can require characters to act cleverly to attempt to avoid a situation: disable a trap, move slowly so as not to disturb a Stingwing resting by a useful item, or throw food to distract a mongrel for long enough to grab something, and the like.

Having plenty of opportunity to make choices about their characters' actions will engage your Players. A prime way to do this is to give them a minor negative-seeming option plus a test which could give a much better or worse outcome depending on their success or failure.

Example: A character notices too late that a tripwire has pulled a pin from a baseball grenade. The character could immediately duck into cover so they have some protection and still take some damage, or they could try to find the pin. If they succeed, they will take no damage, but if they fail they won't even have cover and will take the full force of the explosion. The Player must decide immediately on a course of action…

> IF YOU OWN *FALLOUT: WASTELAND WARFARE*, ITEM CARDS CAN BE GIVEN TO THE PLAYERS. YOU, AS OVERSEER, CAN CREATE A DECK OF ITEM CARDS TO REPRESENT WHAT MIGHT BE FOUND IN AN AREA.
>
> THIS CAN BE THEMED, SUCH AS FOOD & DRINK IN A SUPER DUPER MART, STIMPAKS IN A HOSPITAL, JUNK IN A JUNK YARD, ETC.
>
> THE DANGER AND CREATURE CARDS ARE ALSO A GOOD SOURCE OF INCIDENTS THAT CAN BE FOUND IN THE WASTELAND.

"SOMETHING IN THE DUCT… AND WHEN I SAY 'DUCT', I MEAN THE BARREL OF THAT BIG GUN WE'RE PLANNING"

FOWW RPG-001-111 — **SECTION 5.8**

ITEMS AND COSTS

In *Fallout*, bottlecaps ('Caps' for short) are used for currency. The base values of items are listed in the table below as a guide. The actual sale price of items can vary from the base value, depending on the comparative Persuasion skills of the buyer and seller, the seller's pricing in general, the current supply and demand in that part of the Wasteland, and even the reputation of the character. All prices are for the basic version of an item, so any Mods or extra capabilities would increase the cost.

RIFLES

ITEM	COST
Assault Rifle	108
Bolt-Action Pipe Rifle	60
Combat Rifle	100
Combat Shotgun	82
Double-Barrel Shotgun	93
Hunting Rifle	95
Institute Laser Rifle	77
Laser Musket	66
Laser Rifle	180
Plasma Rifle	144
Pipe Rifle	45

PISTOLS

ITEM	COST
.44 Revolver	56
10mm Pistol	48
Alien Blaster	550
Gamma Gun	174
Indy's Freezing .44	146
Laser Pistol	56
Pipe Pistol	40
Thirst Zapper Cola	132

HEAVY WEAPONS

ITEM	COST
Broadsider	275
Gatling Laser	428
Minigun	330
Missile Launcher	314

MINES

ITEM	COST
Bottlecap Mine	80
Fragmentation Mine	40

THROWN WEAPONS

ITEM	COST
Baseball Grenade	42
Cryo Grenade	49
Fragmentation Grenade	49
Molotov Cocktail	32
Pulse Grenade	75

AMMUNITION

AMMO TYPE	COST
Physical	5 per load
Energy	8 per load
Radiation	20 per load
Missile	50 per shot
Mini Nuke	200 per shot

MELEE WEAPONS

ITEM	COST
Baseball Bat	18
Baton	28
Board	10
Fire Hydrant Bat	144
Huge Club	103
Improvised Weapon	5
Lead Pipe	33
Machete	18
Pipe Wrench	25
Ripper	50
Sledgehammer	42
Stun Baton	85
Super Sledge	118
Tire Iron	36

GEAR

ITEM	COST
Artillery Smoke Grenade	10
Climbing Spikes	34
Fire Extinguisher	21
Flashlight	16
Fusion Core	250
Mr Handy Fuel	16
Robot Repair Kit	75
Skeleton Key	32
Stealth Boy	112
Stuffed Monkey	24
Turret Inhibitors	49
Vertibird Signal Grenade	15

ARMOR

ITEM	COST
Armored Pads	36
Army Helmet	45
Chain Dog Collar	34
Chains	24
Combat Armor	184
Damaged Hazmat Suit	45
Freefall Leg Armor	50
Hazmat Suit	70
Heavy Gauntlets	50
Power Armor Frame	150
Rock's Bladed Helm	69
Sturdy Combat Armor	390
Sturdy Leather Armor	277
T-45 Power Armor	528
T-51 Power Armor	762
T-60 Power Armor	3600

CHEMS

ITEM	COST
Addictol	98
Berry Mentats	60
Buffout	75
Calmex	85
Day Tripper	43
Fury	85
Jet	75
Med-X	63
Mentats	50
Mysterious Serum	57
Orange Mentats	64
Overdrive	55
Psycho	50
Radaway	70
Rad-X	45
Refreshing Beverage	155
Stimpak	80
X-Cell	108

MODS

ITEM	COST
Arm Breaker	20
Armor Piercing Receiver	20
Balanced	30
Ballistic Weave	14
Bayonet	24
Biocom Mesh	13
Boosted Servos	14
Comfort Grip	25
Dissipating	14
Emergency Protocols	31
Hardened Receiver	36
Headlamp	12
Heavy	37
Hot Rod Shark Paint	12
Improved Flexibility	12
Lead Lined	13
Lightweight	17
Long Barrel	20
Multi-Calibre	14
Multi-Purpose	14
Re-Bored	31
Refined	17
Reflex Sights	30
Silenced	19
Spiked	23
Stun Pack	15
Superior Materials	30
Thicker Plating	30
Venomous	32

CLOTHING

ITEM	COST
Aviator Cap	42
Atom Cats Jacket & Jeans	21
Bowler Hat	32
Camouflage	39
Dirty Postman Uniform	22
Dog Bandana	11
Eyeglasses	8
Military Fatigues	29
Patched Three-Piece Suit	17
Road Goggles	12
Robotic Bits	9
Sea Captain's Hat	24
Vault 111 Jumpsuit	21

ALCOHOL

ITEM	COST
Bourbon	15
Ice Cold Gwinett Ale	25
Rum	29
Vodka	20
Whiskey	24

FOOD & DRINK

ITEM	COST
Bloatfly Meat	20
Blood Pack	25
Brahmin Meat	33
Cram	20
Deathclaw Meat	85
Fresh Melon	15
Iguana Bits	26
Iguana on a Stick	25
Mole Rat Meat	28
Mutant Hound Meat	40
Nuka-Cola	30
Nuka-Cherry	55
Nuka-Cola Quantum	90
Radroach Meat	9
Radscorpion Egg	54
Radstag Meat	57
Squirrel Bits	10
Squirrel on a Stick	23
Squirrel Stew	33
Yao Guai Meat	80
Yao Guai Rib Meat	85

N.B. FOR REASONS OF GAME BALANCE, ITEM COSTS ARE DIFFERENT BETWEEN *FALLOUT WASTELAND WARFARE* AND THE ROLEPLAYING GAME EXPANSION.

FOWW RPG-001-111 — SECTION 5.9

SETTLEMENTS

Characters may want to remain in an area and build up a settlement to serve as their base of operations. At other times, characters wandering in the Wasteland may come across Settlements that need assisting, investigating, controlling, attacking... Whatever their personal reasons, a Settlement is the main homestead or camp for many Wasteland inhabitants. Settlements come in many different forms and the following section provides some advice on what they could contain, and what characters may want to include when building one of their own.

LOCATION

The Wasteland often appears to be an empty place, but it can be surprising how many people and creatures lay claim to it. If the characters wish to start an entirely new Settlement, they will need a suitable location and this may require "negotiation" with any existing inhabitants or claimants. Using an existing Settlement gives characters a head-start and requires less set-up resources, but sometimes characters will want to clear a piece of land of existing structures, trees, junk, etc., and build their new Settlement by recycling resources from the clearance.

TYPE

Settlements are often re-purposed houses or farms, but can be factories, city buildings, water treatment plants, beached ships, or anything else with enough space or security. The Brotherhood of Steel develop military-style camps with a perimeter barrier and gates, whilst Super Mutants take a much more organic approach focused on room for their meat bags and little thought for defenses.

DEFENSES

Settlements are a source of security but can are also be targets. Many see little reason to hunt through the Wasteland for resources when others have already done it. Even better, Settlements are collections of all those wonderful things in one easily raided location! Defenses, then, become important in fending off troublesome visitors.

Fencing can consume a lot of resources but it delays or deters unwanted visitors from approaching along some routes. Even if not a complete ring, fences across some approaches can allow the settlers to focus their defenses in fewer directions. Going further than fencing, there are barricades, usually made out of barbed wire, planks, and sandbags, which provide fighting positions for defenders, as well as maybe chairs, lights, and perhaps a table for long sessions of guard duty.

Turrets on tripods are not an uncommon sight in a Settlement, and add extra and constant firepower with the soft chug of a turret motor giving comfort to those defended by them, and deterring would-be attackers. Coming in various shapes and capabilities, turrets run from simple machine gun turrets to laser turrets and missile turrets. Some turrets can be wall-mounted; others come with their own spotlights and react to anything entering their illuminated patch. Laser turrets and spotlight turrets require power to run, and taking out their power supply will stop the turrets from working.

Mines are also an option for defense, though placing signs to alert people to their presence is required if they are to be a deterrent prior to someone standing on one. Sometimes a minefield sign alone can work wonders in making attackers think twice. A wandering Brahmin or Radstag can be a problem, though.

POWER AND WATER

Generators come in various sizes and are an essential for a good standard of living in a Settlement. Power is required for water purifiers, lighting, computer terminals, radio beacons, laser and spotlight turrets, and even simpler cookers. All of those need wiring up too.

GENERATORS	
GENERATOR TYPE	**PRODUCTION**
Generator – Small	3 power
Generator – Medium	7 power
Generator – Large	12 power
Generator – Windmill	3 power
Generator – Fusion*	100 power
*Requires fusion core to run	

Water pumps provide essential, untainted water for settlers, animals, and crops. These can be simple hand pumps to draw up ground water, or can be machines that draw and filter water from a river. Having some way to store water is advantageous to provide lots of water for irrigating crops, as a contingency against drought, and for emergency uses, such as putting out fires.

Each settler uses 1 unit of water every 24 hours, regardless of any other water needs.

WATER PUMPS & PURIFIERS		
EQUIPMENT	PRODUCTION	POWER REQUIRED
Water Pump	3 water/day	
Water Purifier	12 water/day	1 Power
Water Purifier – Industrial	40 water/day	1 Power

LIVING

Settlers need rest. **Beds** and bunk rooms are usually the first items to be built, but chairs, tables, lights, and other "luxuries" also make Wasteland living easier.

Food is essential, and Cooking Stations can be used to cook up recipes using the required ingredients. Settlers may gather ready-to-eat food from the surrounding area, or buy it from traders. Alternatively, they may find or buy raw foods to cook, folowing recipes. Settlers can also have fields in which to grow their own crops as raw food, though these require water and tending.

FOOD SUPPLY		
ITEM	PURPOSE	REQUIREMENT
Crop Fields	Grow Food	1 water per day
Cooking Station	Convert Food from Uncooked to Cooked	

Computer Terminals can be used to automate some tasks, such as switching turrets and lights on and off from a central location. If a Settlement has valuables, then a well-hidden **safe** may also be important.

MAINTENANCE, CRAFTING, AND SCRAPPING

A Settlement is only as good as its maintenance, so **Workbenches** and **Workstations** are important to fix weapons and armor, as well as create new items and mods too. The heart of any Settlement is the **Workshop** which is required to build other Settlement elements such as beds, lighting, generators, Water Pumps, Workbenches, barricades, etc.

For most maintenance work, **parts and materials** are required. Anything collected in the Wasteland can be salvaged for some usable materials: wood from trees, aluminum from surgical trays, screws from desk fans, etc.

Rather than track specific quantities, you can have the construction or repair work require a rough amount of junk from which the characters can draw materials. If they have a varied supply, they can carry out maintenance or craft new items. If there are not enough supplies, or the settlement is missing one or more key types of resource, such as having no metal when trying to build armor or a generator, you may require the characters to go on a junk run to gather more.

COMMON CRAFTING RESOURCES

Acid	Copper	Nuclear Material
Adhesive	Cork	Oil
Aluminum	Crystal	Plastic
Antiseptic	Fertilizer	Rubber
Asbestos	Fiber Optics	Screw
Ballistic Fiber	Fiberglass	Spring
Bone	Gears	Steel
Ceramic	Glass	Wood
Circuitry	Gold	
Cloth	Lead	
Concrete	Leather	

WORKSTATIONS	
ITEM	PURPOSE
Workshop	Creating items for the Settlement such as barricades, turrets, etc.
Weapons Workbench	Repair and modify Weapons
Armor Workstation	Repair and modify Armor
Power Armor Station	Repair and modify Power Armor
Chemistry Station	Make Chems, Grenades, Mines and Medical

THE MYSTERIOUS STRANGER HAS A SUITCASE FULL OF RARE OBJECTS TO SELL. BUT HE COMES WITH PROTECTION.

TRADERS AND SUPPLY ROUTES

Why gather resources when they could come to you? Many traders wander the Wasteland gaining, and then keeping, good relationships with travelers who can bring many items to a Settlement as part of regular visits. Of course, such convenience comes at a cost, so items can sometimes be expensive. Traders will often accept other goods, instead of Caps, as payment because they will make a profit on them later elsewhere.

Some traders set up stalls in Settlements, and while some deal in a wide range of goods, others specialize in weapons, food and drink, clothing, armor or medical treatments. For the right number of Caps, nearly anything should be available, eventually, but never cheaply.

NEW RECRUITS

A Settlement could just be the home of the Player Characters, but having more people often means safety in numbers and a wider range of skill sets.

The Players' characters could be part of an existing Settlement, but are not in charge. They may be in charge with other settlers inhabiting it and relying on them. Having other settlers in addition to the PCs gives the Players (and you) the chance to allocate some tasks to the other NPC settlers. This can free up the Player Characters to focus on the more exciting tasks of a scenario, or bring in valuable information.

NPC settlers can also be a source of adventure hooks to get the Player Characters involved in even more action out in the Wasteland. Such NPCs will have needs for specific salvage, may ask for help, may get lost and require rescue, and much else besides.

> ### SETTLEMENT STORYLINE HOOKS
> Settlements can be a great base of operations for characters and can also provide an opportunity for new storylines. Creating and establishing a settlement is a good background task fraught with many challenges that require finding items, repulsing raids by envious gangs and wandering creatures. Other, surrounding settlements may require help too.

If looking for a boost in population, a Settlement can send out a message using a Radio Beacon to tell people they are welcome. Of course, more settlers means more mouths to feed, and more people needing a place to sleep and work.

FOWW RPG-001-111 — SECTION 5.10

CRAFTING

During Free Play, characters with the right skills, tools, and resources can make, modify and repair items. In the Wasteland, a character often needs to find an item and then fix or improve it. Some can also be created from scratch.

CREATING ITEMS

Some items can be created by characters with the right skills and resources. The categories of items that can be created are described below:

CAN BE CREATED VIA CRAFTING	CANNOT BE CREATED VIA CRAFTING
Basic Melee Weapons	Advanced Melee Weapons
Basic Gear	Advanced Gear
Mods	Non-melee Weapons
Chems	Ammunition
Food and Drink	Armor
	Power Armor

IF YOU OWN *FALLOUT: WASTELAND WARFARE*, THE GUN NUT, BLACKSMITH AND ARMORER PERKS ARE NOT USED IN THE RPG. INSTEAD, CRAFTING AND REPAIRING WEAPONS AND ARMOR IS COVERED BY THE REPAIR & CRAFT SKILLS.

In addition to the items on cards, you can allow a character to create bespoke items.

To create an item, the character must have the appropriate Repair and Craft skill, resources, and Workbench or Workstation (see 'Maintenance, Crafting, and Scrapping', p.98). Many resources come from scrapping items, including Junk: e.g. a desk fan can provide screws, gears, and steel, and some resources can be bought from traders too. You may require a character to have other Skills, such as Knowhow: Science if the item uses advanced tech. A character might even be required to purchase a skill more than once for especially advanced items. Most items do not require any plans or recipes, but some special items, usually advanced ones, may require schematics before creating them can be attempted.

Once a character has gathered all the prerequisites, determine which Skill Test is required to create an item. The more advanced the item, the more difficult the Skill Test (see 'Skill Tests', p.42-49). A character may need to accumulate enough Impact to complete an item.

Creating items can take time and the Overseer should allow one Skill Test every "x" period of time. This time depends on the item. For example, cooking food is quite fast, so maybe one test per 30 minutes compared to creating an advanced Power Armor Mod which may be one test per 8 hours. The amount of time may also depend on the item's complexity: simple food is faster to make than creating complex recipes.

A failed roll just represents time spent without making progress, whereas a /x\ is a potential complication. This may mean an item will take longer to create (additional difficulty); may require more resources (as some have been damaged); or may even have a flaw. The character may not even be aware of the flaw, which may come into effect later, perhaps after a number of /x\ have been rolled. The exact nature of the complication will depend on what is being created, and the abilities of the character.

REPAIRING ITEMS

A broken item cannot operate or provide any of its usual benefits.

There are no rules for tracking wear and tear on equipment, but you may rule that a Complication during a Skill Test, or any other incident you feel is appropriate, causes an item to break. Scavenged items may be broken when they are first found.

Repairing an item is handled in the same way as creating an item. The character needs the requisite Repair & Craft skill, a Workbench or Workstation, resources, and perhaps other skills. Repairing an item is easier than creating the same item, and requires less time. When a repair is complete, a broken item becomes fixed and operates normally.

WEAR AND TEAR

After an item has had a prolonged period of use, you may require characters to make a roll of the blue Special Effect Dice to see if their weapons are now unusable or less efficient. If they are, they will need Repair to bring them back to full effectiveness. How far you go in having breakdowns, wear and tear, maintenance, and rugged environmental conditions wear out equipment is entirely up to you and your Players. Some like the flavor, others dislike the record keeping.

MODIFYING ITEMS

Characters use Mods to improve items. Mods can be added and removed from items using the appropriate Workbench or Workstation by a character with the appropriate Repair & Craft Skill. Only one Mod may be attached to an item at a time. Mods may be found in the Wasteland but characters can create Mods too (see 'Creating Items', above).

FOWW RPG-001-111 — SECTION 5.11

REFERENCE: SPECIAL EFFECT DICE

The blue Special Effect Dice can be used to determine many random outcomes. The information below shows the dice icons and the chances of them occurring after a single roll; knowing this can help when deciding what results you expect for a successful roll.

The most useful statistics are the chances of gaining at least one Bottle – 7/12 (58%) – at least one Star – 4/12 (33%), and one Blast – 2/12 (17%).

The following list shows ways to use the Special Effect Dice to achieve different probabilities, including those mentioned above. All the results that fulfill the requirements are shown on the right-hand side. The different requirements are shown in order of probability:

ICONS	RESULT	PROBABILITY		QUALIFYING RESULTS
★★	Two Stars	1/12	8%	★
🍾★	Exactly one Bottle and one Star	1/12	8%	🍾★
💥	One Blast	2/12	17%	💥
🍾🍾	Two Bottles	2/12	17%	🍾🍾
★	Exactly one Star	3/12	25%	★
★	At least one Star	4/12	33%	★ ★★ 🍾★
★/💥	At least one Star OR Blast	5/12	42%	★ ★★ 🍾★ 💥
🍾	At least one Bottle	7/12	58%	🍾 🍾🍾 🍾★
🍾/💥	At least one Bottle OR Blast	9/12	75%	🍾 🍾🍾 🍾★ 💥
🍾/★	At least one Bottle OR Star	10/12	83%	🍾 🍾🍾 🍾★ ★ ★★

SOME OPPONENTS JUST AREN'T EASY TO INTIMIDATE, WHATEVER THE NUMBERS

FOWW RPG-001-111 — SECTION 5.12
PLAYING IN CONJUNCTION WITH F:WW

If you own the *Fallout: Wasteland Warfare* tabletop game, many of the components can be used with the *Fallout: Wasteland Warfare RPG*.

CARDS

The cards in *Fallout: Wasteland Warfare* can be used in conjunction with the *Fallout: Wasteland Warfare RPG*.

TOKENS

The tokens in *Fallout: Wasteland Warfare* can be used on archetype or unit cards, or next to models, to show the related effects rather than tracking those effects by other means.

Searchable tokens can be drawn to randomly determine items a character searches, e.g. if a Player wants to examine a found suitcase, draw a Searchable marker and resolve what it says, such as gain an Item, draw a Danger, Use Expertise to unlock it, etc.

\multicolumn{2}{l}{**FALLOUT: WASTELAND WARFARE CARDS IN F:WW RPG**}
TYPE	**USAGE**
Unit	Use for NPCs; Players can use them for their character at the Overseer's discretion.
Items	Use as is. The Overseer may need to interpret a few details.
Danger	These can be used to generate random dangers when required, such as when a test to open a trapped lock fails.
Creature	Can be used to generate random creatures when required, such as when investigating some bushes, as well as for Dangers.
Stranger	Can be used to add random strangers to a situation.
Explore	Can be used as minor encounters during a journey. For example, it takes 2 days to reach the outpost, during which time 3 Explore cards are drawn and resolved.
Quest	Players can attempt to achieve these if appropriate and if the Overseer allows them. The Overseer may award Experience Points for achieving them in addition to, or instead of, the Quest card's reward.
Boost	Especially good ideas or rolls can be rewarded with Boost cards which the Players can use at any time. The Overseer could give Players several of these cards at the start of each session, or at a suitable point in the adventure's storyline.
Events	Can be used to generate random circumstances.
Heroic	All Player Characters and Major NPCs count as 'Heroic' by default. Therefore, the Heroic card cannot be added to a Player Character or Major NPC. The bar of icons above the character card on the Character Mat already show the icons from being Heroic.

SECTION 06

INTRODUCTORY CAMPAIGN: PARZIVAL AND THE WASTELAND KNIGHTS

FOWW RPG-001-111

FOWW RPG-001-111 — SECTION 6.1

SUMMARY

'Parzival and the Wasteland Knights' is a three-part campaign for the *Fallout: Wasteland Warfare RPG*. It was written for an Overseer and **4-6 Players**, though it can be adjusted to be used for larger or smaller groups. As written, it is set within the *Fallout 4* era, though Overseers familiar with the setting and lore should have no problem adjusting the contents to fit a different campaign framework.

> **WARNING: OVERSEERS ONLY!**
>
> Players interested in working through this campaign should not read the contents of this document, as even a quick glance may spoil the surprises!

Part One: Mister Parzival

In the first part of the campaign, a group of Player Characters get involved in a Raider attack on a caravan navigating the Wastelands outside what remains of Boston. After the skirmish, the Player Characters meet one of the survivors, a garishly painted, old-generation Mr. Handy robot that calls itself Mister Parzival. Mister Parzival reveals that he is on a quest to find something called Kameloth. The Player Characters investigate Mister Parzival's story and his eroding memory banks, and gather data through research and social interactions while in Diamond City. By the end of Part One, the Player Characters will have sufficient data about Kameloth to embark on Mister Parzival's quest if they so choose.

Part Two: The Quest

In the second part, the Player Characters leave Diamond City and re-enter the Wasteland, using the information they have gathered to track down clues to the location and contents of Mister Parzival's Kameloth. During their quest, the Player Characters encounter a number of Wasteland challenges, and cross paths with Yawen, a Behemoth who leads a force of Super Mutants. Yawen, a former connection of Mister Parzival, also seeks Kameloth, but for entirely different reasons. The Player Characters will have the opportunity to engage Yawen in a battle of wits or, failing that, a battle of arms.

Part Three: Kameloth

In the third and final part, the story comes to a dramatic conclusion as the Player Characters and Mister Parzival race to reach Kameloth before Yawen and his minions. The Player Characters will endure combat challenges and social challenges from various Wasteland dwellers and creatures. After a climactic pitched battle with Yawen and his force of Super Mutants, the surviving Player Characters enter Kameloth and discover the secrets contained within its glittering walls.

> **OVERSEER NOTE**
>
> This campaign assumes the Players will want to follow the heroic storyline largely as written, barring any major changes by you, the Overseer. However, given that this is *Fallout* and that the setting is based on characters having a strong independent will and a tendency to make their own way in the world, you should be prepared for Players not choosing to take the heroic or honorable path through this campaign.
>
> Should that occur, you should adjust the events accordingly, and be flexible and willing to veer far off the rails should the Players decide to take matters in a very different direction than the developers of this campaign intended. Guidance is provided throughout this campaign booklet to provide you with options, though it's simply not possible to predict every possible Player choice or brainstorm idea that may arise during play.
>
> Similarly, choose adversaries and weapon loadouts for them that fit with the encounters and abilities of your players – examples are provided, but feel free to change things as you see fit.

> **OVERSEER NOTE**
>
> While most of the combat encounters in this campaign can be played without miniatures or battle maps, you and your Players are strongly encouraged to make use of the contents of the *Fallout: Wasteland Warfare* Two-Player Starter Set, especially its miniatures, character cards, and gear cards. Having these physical props on the table during the campaign will help your Players visualize the fast-paced combat of the game and enhance the post-apocalyptic feel of the game setting.

PART ONE: MISTER PARZIVAL

SYNOPSIS

While roaming the Wasteland for supplies, the Player Characters hear a pitched battle nearby and investigate. A caravan traveling to Diamond City is being ambushed by Raiders, and the PCs can get involved as they see fit. When picking up the pieces after the Raiders retreat, the Player Characters encounter an old, badly damaged Mr. Handy robot that introduces itself as Mister Parzival. The robot is eccentric, but intriguing. The Player Characters escort the remains of the caravan through the Wasteland to Diamond City. Along the way, Mister Parzival reveals that he is on a quest for something special, and takes the PCs into his confidence.

Mister Parzival reveals that he has been following clues gathered from an ancient book he refers to as "Malory Morte." He has this stored on a Pip-Boy integrated into his hardware. The Pip-Boy is old and damaged, and the text contained within it looks corrupted and in places nonsensical. With effort, Player Characters can tease out some clues from the text, which suggest a location somewhere in the Wasteland. Mister Parzival insists the location is the legendary Kameloth, and that there are treasures contained within its confines. He thinks.

Over the course of Part One, the Players will have the opportunity to:

- Get involved in a Raider attack on a caravan, and interact with any survivors, including Mister Parzival.
- Escort the survivors through the Wasteland to the relative safety of Diamond City.
- Learn about the quest for Kameloth from Mister Parzival.
- Gather additional information about Kameloth.
- Learn more about Mister Parzival and his history.

LENDING A HAND... OR SEVERAL. MISTER PARZIVAL JOINS THE PARTY

SCENE 1

Open this adventure by reading or paraphrasing the following text:

> *Another day navigating the Wasteland, another day closer to Diamond City, one of the few beacons of light in the devastated landscape all around you. You're looking forward to entering the city, and finding time and space for a drink, a half-way decent meal, maybe some companionship – any break from staring at devastation and debris all day long. Steady rainfall has been a constant companion the last two days. As you work your way through the blistered ruins of a small town, its name long lost through time and war, the pattering of raindrops changes to the staccato beats of a frenzied firefight somewhere nearby.*
>
> *What do you do?*

The Player Characters have **two options**: avoid the battle or investigate further.

- **Attempt to avoid the battle:** If they want to try and avoid the battle, they must make **Stealth Skill Tests** to avoid being detected. The terrain and heavy rain give the test a **-4 penalty**.

  Three successful attempts will enable the group to carefully sidestep the battle among the ruins, and then they'll be able to make their way toward Diamond City unmolested. Proceed to Part 1, Scene 2, and adjust how the Player Characters meet with Mister Parzival (e.g., he's slowly making his way toward Diamond City alone, he's slouching along the path toward the city, he's evading a Radscorpion, etc.).

  A test failure by any of the PCs on any one of the tests to avoid being detected will result in a Raider rushing out of a nearby building, seeing the group, calling out, and then opening fire on them. The Players are now engaged in the battle – and most likely should not have Advantage! (Use any selection of the Unit Cards, left, for the Raiders.)

- **Investigate the battle:** If the Player Characters want to investigate further, they may each attempt an **AGI Test** to sneak into position to observe the battle.

  Success at the tests means the Player Characters find a good position within the ruins and see that a caravan of settlers and survivors are fighting a pitched battle with a band of Raiders. Depending on their allegiance and desires, the Player Characters can join the fight on one side or the other, enter as a third party in a no-holds-barred melee, or sit back, watch, and wait it out.

  Failing an AGI Test results in the Player Characters being detected by either the settlers or the Raiders. Roll the black **Damage Dice**: any Damage result (✸ or ✸) means the Raiders discover the Player Characters; any other result means the settlers discover them. If the settlers detect the PCs first, they'll call for help. If the Raiders detect the PCs first, they'll warn them off from what is 'their prize.'

If the Player Characters enter the combat, you may want to declare that they have not been detected by anyone as yet, and have the Advantage as the encounter begins.

By the time the Player Characters are in position to join the battle, there are as many active NPCs left in the caravan as there are PCs, and as many Raiders as there are opponents; i.e., if there are four Player Characters, there are four NPC caravan fighters and therefore eight Raiders. If you want an easier or more

> ### LEVELING UP OR EASING OFF
>
> Overseers may not always have the right creature or unit card for the level of the party; you may want to have a super-powered Radroach swarm, or an immature Radscorpion instead of the exact unit card you have. Overseers should feel free to increase or reduce the attribute values or dice these adversaries use against the Player Characters to even things out.

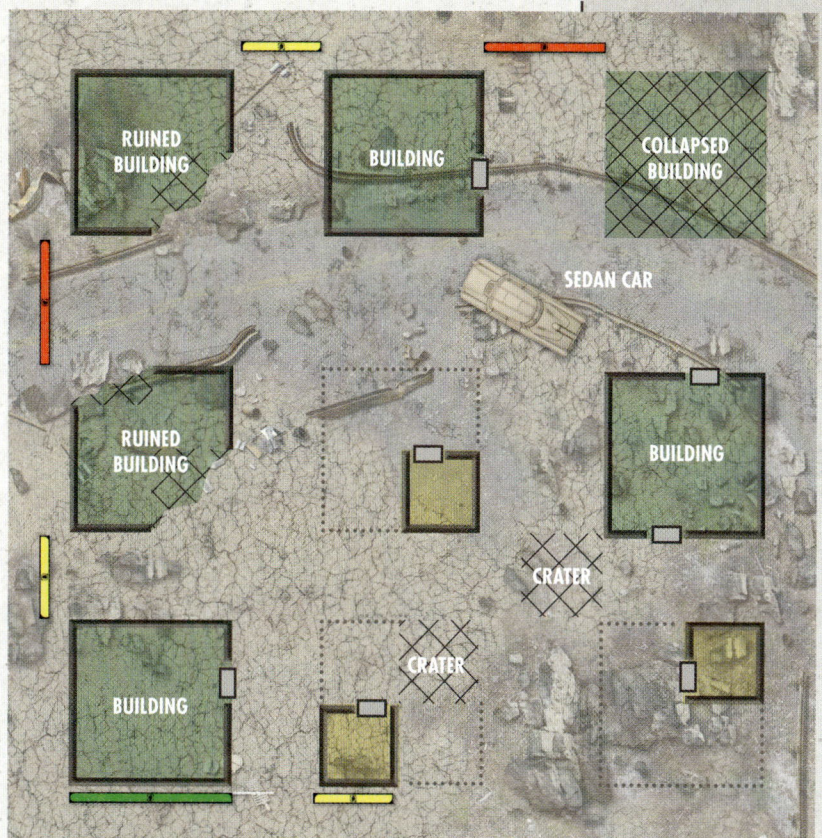

challenging encounter for your Players, change the number of NPCs.

The steady downpour provides a **-2 modifier** to any test made during this battle. Terrain modifiers, and any other relevant features, such as potential areas of cover, are noted on the battle map. This is an urban battle, from ruined building to ruined building. You should encourage the Player Characters to make use of cover where possible, and should make sure the NPCs do likewise (just because they are NPCs doesn't mean they are stupid).

The caravan fighters have nothing to lose and will fight to the death. The more cowardly Raiders will retreat once they have lost half their numbers. The Player Characters are free to chase down any survivors and deal with them as they see fit. If they let any of the Raiders go, the Raiders will disappear into the Wasteland and could be used as part of an encounter later in this campaign, if you want.

 IF USING THE *FALLOUT: WASTELAND WARFARE* RANGE RULERS, THE LAYOUT ABOVE IS ONE POSSIBLE ARRANGEMENT FOR SCENE 1. HOWEVER, OVERSEERS SHOULD FEEL FREE TO ARRANGE THE ENCOUNTER ACCORDING TO THEIR PREFERENCE AND AVAILABLE SCENERY.

KEY:
▭ = DOORWAY
⋮⋮⋮ = FENCE
▬ = WALL
CROSSHATCHED AREAS = DIFFICULT TERRAIN

SCENE 2

After the battle, the Player Characters may engage in conversation with the caravan survivors and gather information, or scavenge gear off the fallen Raiders and maybe the fallen caravan fighters, although this may spark some outrage from any survivors.

The Player Characters also encounter an old-generation Mr. Handy robot, painted in a garish blue and orange checkerboard pattern superimposed by faded images of unidentifiable creatures. One of its three eyes hangs limply against its body and one of its three appendages drags in the dirt, encrusted with debris and the wear and tear of time.

Read or paraphrase the following:

> *The Mr. Handy robot swivels its two working eyes toward you as you approach. From somewhere within its metal casing, you hear something that sounds like someone clearing their throat, and then in a gravelly voice it says, "Good day, fellow travelers. We seem to have hit a spot of trouble and woe betimes. Thank you for your assistance. My name is Mister Parzival."*

Player Characters may attempt a **Knowhow (Robots) Skill Test** to glean extra information about the robot's name from their memories.

A successful test indicates that the name sounds familiar, though hard to place: it's most likely from a history book or an old story about knights.

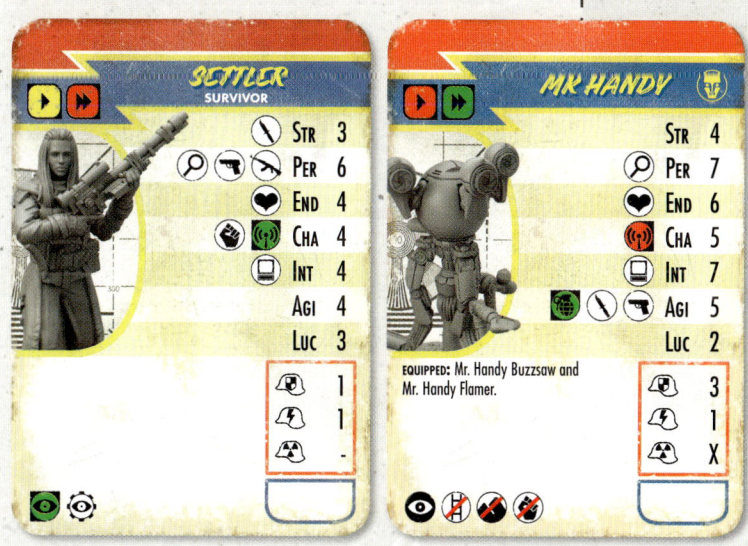

Failing the test means that the Player Characters don't note anything particular about the name, other than it being an odd name for a Mr. Handy to adopt.

Examining the robot with a **Repair/Craft (Robots) Skill Test** reveals that it was shot during the recent battle, though the damage appears to be minor in comparison to the wear and tear Mister Parzival has endured over decades of service. He will graciously accept any Player Character's offer of assistance if there is someone mechanically inclined in the group. If a Player Character does attempt to repair Mister Parzival's recent damage (a **Repair/Craft (Robots)** or **Repair/Craft (Machinery) Skill Test**), they'll also note that there is an old-style Pip-Boy hard-wired into Mister Parzival's chassis, only visible on a close inspection. Mister Parzival will avoid discussing the Pip-Boy if the Player Character brings it up, and will rapidly attempt to change the subject.

If asked, Mister Parzival will state that he has traveled the Wasteland for years, and a week ago joined this particular caravan on their journey toward **Diamond City**. He seems like he wants to say more, but any prodding from curious Player Characters will have him demur and mutter, "Not yet… cannot trust others… not just yet."

Some of the other caravan survivors may be available to speak with as well, depending on how friendly or chatty the Player Characters decide to be. Use standard character cards as noted above for the combat encounter, and pick from the following list of names to use as needed. Gender of the character is at the Overseer's discretion, and the Overseer is encouraged to assign some character traits to each survivor to add some flavor; use the Gifts, Scars and Perks tables on pages 28-33 of the *Fallout: Wasteland Warfare RPG* rulebook as the basis for these traits.

Caravan survivor names: Brogan, Delilah, Edwin, Gary, Jericho, Ophelia, Shytei, Zappie.

The survivors note that the caravan originated in **Hagerstown**, a demolished town outside the ruins of Washington, D.C., which at its height numbered almost a hundred people and animals. The long trip overland from Hagerstown toward Diamond City was brutal, and the caravan now numbers less than a dozen survivors, including Mister Parzival and the named survivors above. They're grateful for any help the Player Characters provide, and accept any offer of assistance in traveling the remaining distance to Diamond City. This will take a week at a steady pace. Of course, if the PCs have acted aggressively toward the caravan survivors, this interaction may play out very differently.

Assuming the Player Characters choose to travel to Diamond City with the survivors of the caravan, the group will depart the ruins once their dead have been attended to, and relieved of their useful supplies and weapons. The caravan then resumes travel into the Wasteland toward Diamond City. Mister Parzival will ask the Player Characters to travel with him if it seems like they need encouragement to accompany the caravan.

MISTER PARZIVAL AND HIS QUEST

This sidebar contains key information about Mister Parzival, his backstory, and his quest. Feel free to use these contents as you see fit, and sprinkle them into any discussions **Mister Parzival** has with the PCs during their time together. A PC who befriends Mister Parzival may be able to hear some of the following information as well, either through conversations with Mister Parzival, or during attempts to repair or upgrade the robot.

Mister Parzival is one of several Mr. Handy robots once assigned to staff the **Graygarden**, a greenhouse. At some point in his years of service there, he was damaged in an accident and wandered off the property and into the Wasteland. He bore the wear and tear of his journeys, but somewhere along the way, a possibly insane Ghoul calling itself **Maerlyn** fitted this particular Mr. Handy with an old Pip-Boy. This was loaded with a significantly corrupted text edition of Sir Thomas Malory's *Le Morte D'Arthur*, the classic edition of the Arthurian legend from ancient Great Britain.

Maerlyn eventually died or disappeared, and left Mr. Handy on his own once again. As he continued to roam the devastated countryside, he delved into the ancient text and read it over and over until the contents were seared into his memory banks. Various glitches and damage sustained over the years further scrambled the poor robot's circuits, to the extent that he now believes that his name is Mister Parzival, and that various individuals from his past are characters from the tale, including Guinevere, Arthur, Lancelot, Galahad, and so on.

Elements of his original programming still exist, though they are buried deep within his memory core and circuitry. He has a yearning to return home to Graygarden, though he cannot recall the name and has conflated the quest for the Grail with the founding of **Kameloth**. He believes he is seeking out Kameloth and the "gray garden" he was meant to tend and help grow. In essence, he is a machine with a burning desire to find something green and alive out in the Wasteland, and he wants to find good people, good knights, to join him on his quest.

He speaks in standard English with the occasional archaic word dropped in here and there. He is unaware of any language lapses and will act confused if anyone points out this verbal quirk. When pressed, he will grow frustrated at feeling like he knows something but that his damaged memory core circuits have rendered the information unrecoverable.

If forced to fight, Mister Parzival will defend himself, but his need to complete his quest will compel him to retreat and run more than endure a battle. If a Player Character befriends him and repairs some of the damage to his chassis, particularly repairing his damaged eye and broken third appendage, he will be more grateful than a robot perhaps should be able to do, and will ally himself with that Player Character.

SCENE 3

The journey from the battle site to Diamond City takes approximately a week on foot, though the Player Characters may choose to push the pace, and either scout ahead in advance of the caravan or push the members of the caravan at a faster pace. You should feel free to incorporate a **-1 to -3 penalty** to all tests attempted during the trek to Diamond City if the Player Characters are pushing the pace. This represents the additional level of exertion used to move more quickly.

The terrain between the battle site and Diamond City is generally easy to navigate, though there are occasional stretches of challenging terrain where the Player Characters and the caravan survivors will need to step carefully through debris fields, impact craters, wrecked buildings, and the like. The rain is steady for two more days, then becomes a miserable drizzle, and finally intermittent sunlight by the time the Player Characters reach Diamond City.

Over the course of the journey, Mister Parzival will spend time chatting with the Player Characters, paying particular attention to any character who is mechanically gifted, or shows interest in what Mister Parzival has to say. He regales the Player Character(s) with tales of heroism and bravery, chatting about some of his long-lost companions, such as Bors, Ector, Galahad, and Pellinore. If a Player Character engages Mister Parzival in conversation, the robot might let slip a mention of somewhere called "Kameloth", though he will quickly divert any subsequent questions with a mechanical cough and a string of high-pitched whines suggesting something is wrong with his speaker system or voice software.

A Player Character may attempt a **Talk Skill Test** to gain more information about Kameloth from Mister Parzival.

If a PC succeeds, Mister Parzival will note that Kameloth was "his home, a shining beacon of light and joy in the Wasteland, home to treasures uncounted and unmatched in all the world." Then Mister Parzival coughs electronically and shrugs as best he can, and adds, "Or at least I think it was. It's hard to remember these days."

Failing the test means that Mister Parzival changes the subject and avoids chatting about Kameloth any further.

Optional Encounters

You can narrate the journey to Diamond City to move the story along, but feel free to add one or more of the encounters presented below to add more action and excitement to the adventure and the campaign. These can be presented to the Players in any order, or may be omitted if you want. To use one of the following encounters, select it outright. If you want to leave it to chance, roll the blue **Special Effect Dice** and use the following result:

Encounter A
Encounter B
Encounter C

Encounter 3A: Radroaches!

During the trek toward Diamond City, the PCs notice a strange heap of debris in a crater field. The craters are all partly filled with rainwater from the recent storms. Upon close inspection of the debris, the PCs discover that it is a crashed Vertibird. The wreckage is mangled

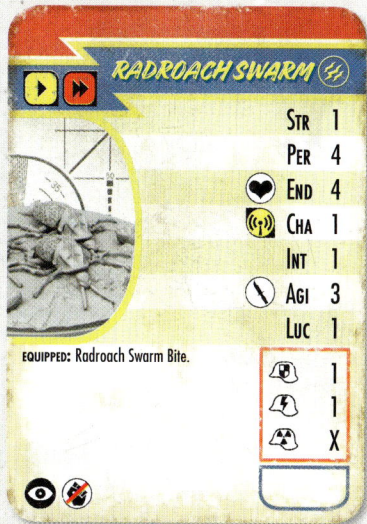

IF USING THE *FALLOUT: WASTELAND WARFARE* RANGE RULERS, THE LAYOUT BELOW IS ONE POSSIBLE ARRANGEMENT FOR ENCOUNTER 3A.

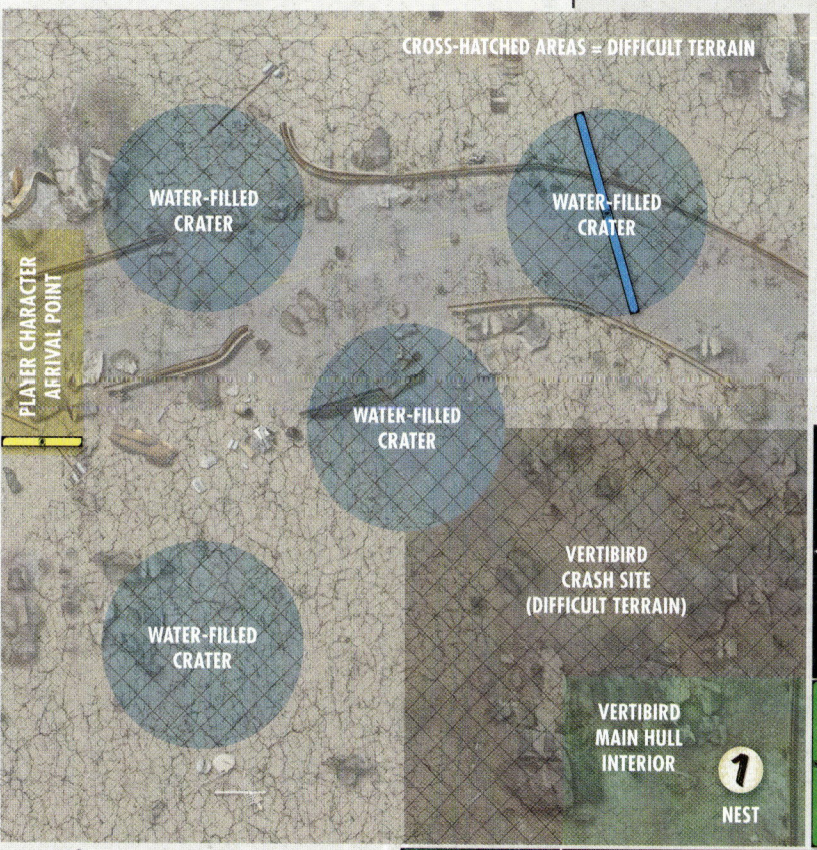

and barely recognizable, but the open hatch and the faded hull insignia confirm its origin. There are strange chittering sounds within the rusting hulk and, if anyone gets close, a swarm of Radroaches will attack. There are three separate swarms of Radroaches, though you are welcome to add more to the battle if the Players want more of a challenge for the group.

The Radroaches, defending their nest within the crashed Vertibird, fight to the death. If the Player Characters search the nest, they find **12 Caps**, a **FLASHLIGHT**, and **a pair of EYEGLASSES**. A Player Character may attempt a **Search** or **Notice Skill Test**, with success enabling them to scavenge various parts and wiring worth **50 Caps**.

Encounter 3B: Radscorpion Nest

As the PCs and caravan survivors work their way through an old parking lot pockmarked with craters, the cracked asphalt beneath their feet gives way. Each PC and NPC must make a **Acrobatics Skill Test** to avoid falling into a void beneath the asphalt.

Success means that Player Character steps away from the crumbling edge of the hollow.

Failure means that Player Character falls in and is considered prone when this encounter begins. Prone characters must spend their first Action in their turn standing up. Until a character spends an Action standing up they should be considered to have the Slow condition.

Within the hollow are several intact Radscorpion eggs, a couple of eggs that were crushed by any character who fell in, and a pair of immature Radscorpions! The small Radscorpions emit fearsome chitters of alarm before they attack.

Two rounds after the encounter begins, an adult Radscorpion some distance away cries out a challenge and rushes toward the hollow. It will defend its offspring to the death and will fight in a frenzy (**-2 modifier** to all dice rolls) if it discovers any of its offspring have been injured or killed.

PCs who search after the battle will find the three intact **RADSCORPION EGGs**, and a battered but still functional **ARMY HELMET** with a blue camouflage pattern..

IF USING THE *FALLOUT: WASTELAND WARFARE* RANGE RULERS, THE LAYOUT BELOW IS ONE POSSIBLE ARRANGEMENT FOR ENCOUNTER 3B.

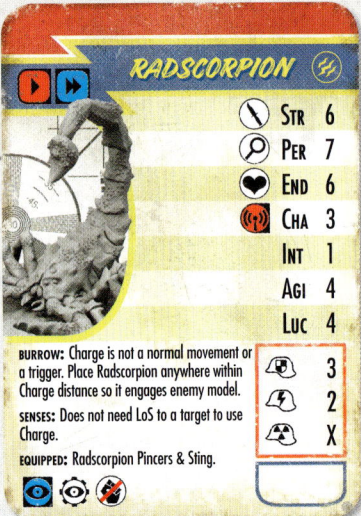

Encounter 3C: Madrighoul

One evening during the journey toward Diamond City, the PCs and the caravan find shelter in an abandoned barn that has somehow withstood the ravages of war and time. Most of the roof is intact, and the barn is empty save for a couple of broken stall doors and one defiant black rat. The nearby farmhouse did not last so well and has been flattened to little more than debris.

The Player Characters may search the barn, though doing so is an **Impossible Test**. They will find nothing of interest. That evening, while the PCs are talking with Mister Parzival or the caravan survivors, they hear the faintest sound of mechanical gears turning, and then they can hear someone singing loudly and off-key some distance away.

If the PCs investigate, Mister Parzival will join them. They will discover that part of the barn flooring has shifted aside to reveal a narrow ladder going down 10 feet to a tunnel. The tunnel, lined with a long string of flickering holiday lights, some long-since burned out, leads straight toward the ruined farmhouse. The tunnel opens into one large chamber and then narrows into a tunnel again, the closer it gets to the farmhouse. The far end of the tunnel is choked with rubble and debris from the crushed farmhouse and the exit there is inaccessible.

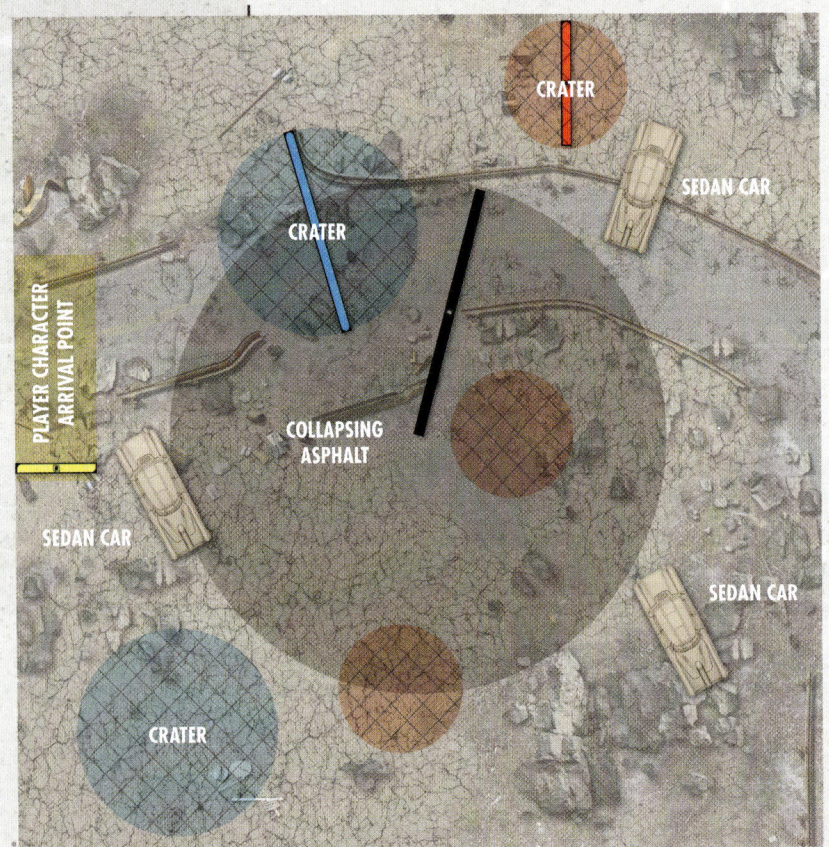

108 FALLOUT — WASTELAND WARFARE ROLEPLAYING GAME

In the large chamber is a cozy-looking futon with a tacky green cover, a small stove, a small table, a narrow bookshelf with two books on it, and a few other knick-knacks. A ghoul is seated on the futon, with an old red book in his hands, the cover and spine cracked with age and hard use, and dozens of pages missing or mouldering. He's wearing a faded set of blue overalls and a paisley shirt underneath. His wrinkled and aged feet are bare, and he has a moth-eaten gray wool beret perched on his bald head.

He continues to sing off-key as the PCs approach, and then stops and closes his book. "I hoped you would join me. My name is Palam and I welcome you into my home."

Mister Parzival reacts to the ghoul's name. When asked, Palam looks mystified and studies Mister Parzival closely. After a long pause, he shrugs. "I don't recall ever knowing a Mr. Handy, much less one adorned as you."

Mister Parzival replies, "Your name is familiar, though I'm unable to place it." He rotates his eyes toward the PCs (especially if he's taken at least one of them into his confidence) and then turns back to Palam. "Do you know of Kameloth?"

Palam looks confused and asks Mister Parzival to clarify. Mister Parzival says, "Kameloth. A… a wondrous realm, a center of peace in the Wasteland."

Palam's blank face and lack of reaction suggests that he does not know of Kameloth, which he soon confirms by putting voice to the statement. He'll apologize and then invite everyone to join him for dinner, moving the small table to the center of the room. He's more than happy to share his cram casserole: "Best not to think too closely on what it contains," he warns.

If asked why he opened the secret door in the barn that led to his quarters, Palam shrugs. "I observed you all moving toward the barn and I was fairly confident you meant no harm. I expect, given your numbers, that you're heading toward Diamond City. Consider me a pause in the journey, a haven in the Wasteland."

He'll pause, then add, "But not for long. Too many Raiders moving around of late. This barn won't stand for long." If the Player Characters have been polite and have treated him well, he'll add, "I expect to leave soon, and when I do, I'll lock up this tunnel and demolish the barn. No sense letting some malcontents come in and ruin it."

If the PCs have gotten along well with him, he'll finish dinner and accept help to clean up. He'll produce a half-filled bottle of rum to share with anyone who wants it and then, in the post-dinner conversation, will slide a **key card** across the table and toward the PCs (and one character in particular if anyone has stepped up during this scene). "I'll lock it up tight before I go. If you ever find yourself coming this way again and could use a safe space for a little while, feel free to use this. You look clever enough to find the key slot, in time."

After the bottle is empty, Palam will say his goodnights and encourage his guests and Mister Parzival to sleep in the barn. The secret door closes and locks behind him. The PCs enjoy a quiet night in the barn before venturing back into the Wasteland in the morning.

Once you have completed all the optional encounters you wish and the PCs are ready to approach Diamond City, read or paraphrase the following:

> *The rainstorm that has been a constant, unwelcome companion these last several days tapers off as you approach Diamond City's border. Beyond a Commonwealth Minutemen checkpoint lies the rubble of buildings that once stood around Diamond City. Just beyond is Diamond City itself. Mister Parzival stares at the massive fortified city, largely painted in shades of green, and says, "A fine fair realm, this. May we find rest and resources here to guide us on our way to Kameloth."*

BELOW: THE CHAMBER BENEATH THE FARM (ENCOUNTER 3C)

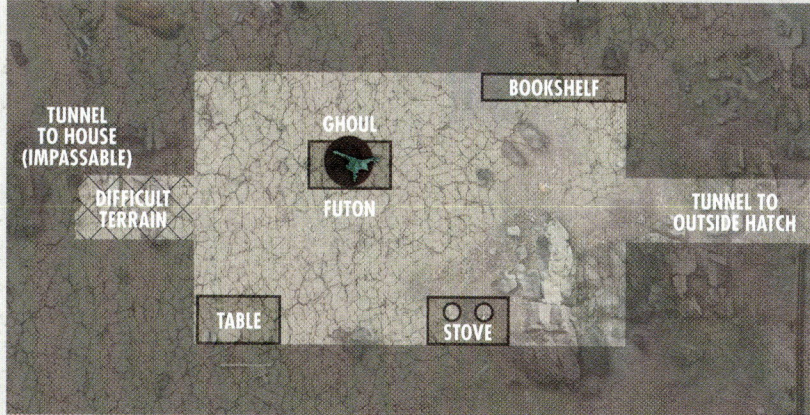

OVERSEER NOTE

If the Players decide to attack Palam or otherwise commit mayhem, he won't put up much of a fight, being unarmed. If they kill him before he has a chance to interact with them and share the information presented above, they find a leather-bound journal tucked under the futon that contains Palam's diary. You can summarize the contents and include the information from discussion in it. The key card is tucked into the journal.

SECTION 6 – INTRODUCTORY CAMPAIGN 109

SCENE 4

The Player Characters, Mister Parzival, and the remaining caravan survivors are stopped at a checkpoint by a Commonwealth Minutemen patrol, who listen to the group's story, check their belongings, and only then allow them to pass into Diamond City.

The Minutemen are well-armed and ready for a fight. They specifically ask the PCs if they've run into any Raider bands recently, and listen to any news with open interest. Clearly there has been an uptick of Raider activity lately and most are on edge about it.

> **OVERSEER NOTE**
>
> If the Players decide they want to attack the Minutemen, by all means prepare a combat encounter. Use an overwhelming force of Minutemen along with armored reinforcements arriving every couple of rounds. It is a foolish endeavor to attack these troops near their stronghold, but sometimes Players make unexpected choices. It's easy to create new characters for this game…

Read or paraphrase the following:

Diamond City, better known to residents and locals as the Great Green Jewel, is a fortified city and well-protected against external threats. It is built on an old baseball stadium, with the lower levels being reserved for the lower tiers of society and the upper levels for high society. The city contains shops, pubs, hotels, hostels, and people of all shapes and sizes. A wide variety of gear, supplies, and distractions can be had for the right price or the right trade goods.

Once in Diamond City, the caravan survivors thank the PCs for helping them reach the city, and then make their way inside to get on with their lives. If any of the NPCs have interacted well with one or more of the Characters, you are encouraged to make them companions to the PC group and keep them around for the course of the campaign. Barring that, any of the named NPCs from the caravan could pop up while the PCs explore the location in the following selection of optional encounters.

DIAMOND CITY LOCATIONS

This list details just some of the locations within Diamond City that PCs may visit during their stay there.

1. **All Faiths Chapel**
   A non-denominational religious building within the city, open to all faiths.

2. **Chem-I-Care**
   A store specializing in first aid gear.

3. **Colonial Taphouse**
   A bar serving food and drinks.

4. **Commonwealth Weaponry**
   A store specializing in weaponry and armor.

5. **Diamond City Surplus**
   A store selling and trading assorted basic goods and supplies.

6. **Dugout Inn**
   A bar and hotel with modestly priced rooms and food.

7. **Kathy & John's Super Salon**
   Beauty salon and barbershop.

8. **Power Noodles**
   The city's power reactor and best noodle dishes around.

9. **Science! Center**
   A well-appointed workshop and chemlab rolled into one.

10. **Valentine Detective Agency**
    Nick Valentine's office.

You should encourage the Players to spend some time exploring the city in search of supplies or clues to help with Mister Parzival and his Kameloth. Use any or all of the following encounters. They are presented in no particular order and may be run as best fits the needs of your group and campaign.

Encounter 4A: Hitting the Books

Some PCs may decide to seek out a terminal likely to have access to information related to Kameloth and Mister Parzival. There is a schoolhouse, an old library, and various government buildings in Diamond City, though the access to some of these is in areas of higher society levels than the Player Characters are less likely able to reach. They can access terminals at the schoolhouse or at the old library, and clever or socially-focused PCs might be able to sweet-talk their way to a terminal situated at a high-class building.

Once at a terminal, a Player Character may attempt a **Computers Skill Test** to hack into the terminal and dig for any information on Kameloth or Mister Parzival. Hacking into a secured terminal gives the test a **penalty of -2**. Failing to hack into the terminal alerts the Diamond City police, who will arrive in **3 rounds** to investigate the hacking attempt.

Success means the Player Character has hacked in. They'll need another **Computers Skill Test** with a **penalty of -2** to run a search for the keywords or data they're interested in. **Failure** this time means that the Player Character spent an hour or more searching through the city's databases, but turned up nothing useful.

If the Player Character succeeds at the test to search for information, they find the following pieces of information:

```
ROBCO INDUSTRIES UNIFIED OPERATING SYSTEM
    COPYRIGHT 2075-2077 ROBCO INDUSTRIES

From Commonwealth Minuteman field report
[15 years ago]
Prisoner revealed location some distance
to the north/northwest of Diamond City,
referred to alternately as Camelot
(Kameloth?) or Cibola. Prisoner was
wounded and not lucid and was then
neutralized.

From an children's book [title unknown]
Sir Parzival, one of many knights of
King Arthur's Round Table, quested for
the Holy Grail for many years before
eventually finding it, and love.
```

Once the PC closes down the terminal and heads back to meet their allies, they may attempt a **Presence Skill Test**. **Failure** means they return to their allies unmolested, and never notice the hooded form observing them from the alleyways. **Success** means the Player Character notes someone following them from wherever they accessed the terminal.

DIAMOND CITY SECURITY

Diamond City has its own police force, created by the locals after the war to enforce laws and protect the city, its inhabitants, and visitors from external threats as well as any criminals or would-be criminals inside the walls.

Security officers are armed with **PIPE RIFLEs** and **BASEBALL BATs**, and wear armor fashioned from old baseball masks and vests. They will be friendly or neutral toward the PCs unless the PCs give them reason to act otherwise. If the PCs get into an altercation while in Diamond City, roll the red dice. A squad of three Diamond City security officers will arrive in a number of rounds equal to result. An engaged squad of Diamond City officers can call for backup that will also arrive after a number of rounds equal to the red dice result.

The hooded form waves them over (or nudges them in the street), and says, "You are not the only ones seeking the Grail. Be wary."

The hooded form will attempt to slip away, and the Player Character may attempt an **Opposed Test** using **Sneak** (or **AGI**) to catch up to them.

Failure at the test means that the Player Character loses the hooded form in the crowds and alleyways.

Success means that the Player Character can grab hold of the hooded form, which is revealed to be a sad-eyed Ghoul, something of a rare sight in Diamond City. The Ghoul refuses to name herself, and, when pressed, looks fearful and says, "The Lord Yawen of the Super Mutants hunts for the Grail for himself. I... I am old and weary, but... I would see someone else find it first. Know that you are not the only ones seeking it." She then pulls away from the Player Character and escapes into the crowds and alleyways of the city.

USE THE MINUTEMAN CARD FOR THE DIAMOND CITY SECURITY, AND IGNORE THEIR ABILITIES.

Encounter 4B: Parts for Mister Parzival

Mister Parzival wants to take advantage of the time in Diamond City to secure parts and repairs for himself. If he has befriended a Player Character by this point, he will ask them to accompany him to the market to barter or buy items. If he has yet to befriend anyone, this is an opportunity to have him do so. He'll approach the group and ask if anyone is available to accompany him to the market.

Mister Parzival has **96 Caps** in a storage tray built into his chassis, which he will use to buy parts and materials for his upkeep. He'll be chatty with the Player Character who accompanies him. You should make use of this opportunity to add in any detail from the Mister Parzival sidebar presented on page 106.

Mister Parzival will come across as a gentle soul (at least for a robot) and it should be made clear that his yearning for finding Kameloth is strong. At one point in the trip to the market or at the market, Mister Parzival will nudge the Player Character to observe a couple buying food together and holding hands. Mister Parzival sighs and says, "Oh, were I ever to win knightly fame, may I be worthy to ask someone for love." The PC is free to react as appropriate on hearing such a sentiment from a robot.

Encounter 4C: The Supplier

If the Player Characters treated the caravan survivors well and helped them to Diamond City, one of the survivors (see the names on page 106) will seek out the PCs, and indicate that they are the second cousin of one of the employees of **Diamond City Surplus**. They'll also tell the PCs that, for their kindness and for escorting the caravan to Diamond City, the survivor worked with their second cousin to arrange a **20% discount** that they can use at the surplus store to buy reasonable supplies and equipment.

The survivor accompanies the PCs to Diamond City Surplus, then introduces them to store employee **Filora**. She welcomes the PCs, thanks them for helping her cousin reach Diamond City, then encourages them to shop and ask for whatever they may need.

A PC may attempt a **Persuade Skill Test** to chat up Filora. **Failure** results in lousy customer service. **Success** means that Filora takes a liking to the PC and she will say that she can probably persuade one of her friends, an employee at **Commonwealth Weaponry**, to give the Player Characters a similar discount there.

> **OVERSEER NOTE**
>
> If the Player Characters treated the caravan survivors poorly or arrived at Diamond City without the caravan, do not use Encounter 4C.

WHAT IS IT YOU NEED? A FRESH DELIVERY FOR DIAMOND CITY SURPLUS

CHASING OR JUST FOLLOWING? GHOULS AREN'T ALWAYS MINDLESS CANNON-FODDER

SCENE 5

The Player Characters return to their temporary housing to discuss their findings from the encounters above. Allow the PCs time to share what they found, and use Mister Parzival, and any other allied companion the PCs have, to move the conversation along as needed. The PCs have two leads for things within the Wasteland: Kameloth itself, and the Super Mutant Yawen. They may also have an idea or two as to who can supply them for their quest.

In addition, Mister Parzival may have been repaired or upgraded during their time in Diamond City, especially if there is a technically inclined PC in the group. This particular character may be given special treatment by Mister Parzival, and may even be looked upon as something of a friend or close ally, depending on how the PC has approached their interactions with Mister Parzival. If so, the PC may have learned some of the content contained within the Mister Parzival sidebar on page 106.

Mister Parzival will be an eager participant in the information-sharing and discussion, and will do all he can to encourage his companions to embark on the quest with him. He promises no payment other than sharing the riches he is confident will be found in Kameloth.

However, if the PCs encountered the mysterious Ghoul in Encounter 4A, Mister Parzival will be evasive when asked about the Super Mutant Yawen. They may attempt an **Opposed Test** using **CHA** to talk or threaten Mister Parzival into revealing what he knows.

Failure means that Mister Parzival remains tight-lipped, other than to say that he ran into Yawen years ago, and that he's confident the Super Mutant will have forgotten all about him and his "silly quest."

Success means that Mister Parzival will reveal that, during his wanderings in the Wasteland, he was once badly damaged in a chance encounter with a Mirelurk. He was "saved" by Yawen and his company of soldiers, who took Mister Parzival in and repaired him. In "payment", they scoured his memory banks for any useful data. They were less than gentle and soon discarded him among the other debris within the Wasteland, leaving him rather than dismantle or destroy him, thanks to Mister Parzival's entertaining way of telling ridiculous stories.

Mister Parzival notes that it's entirely possible he told Yawen more about Kameloth than he remembers, since he has endured much hardship in the years since his capture. It's possible that tracking down Yawen and questioning him might be more effective than wandering the Wasteland to the north and west of Diamond City, hoping to stumble upon Kameloth.

Conclusion

At this point, the Player Characters should have gathered enough information to leave Diamond City and begin the quest for Kameloth or to track down Yawen. You should either proceed directly to Part Two of this campaign, or feel free to run other scenarios and adventures between Part One and Part Two if your Players wish to explore other parts of the story, the campaign, or the setting.

FOWW RPG-001-111 — SECTION 6.3

PART TWO: THE QUEST

SYNOPSIS

The Player Characters have met Mister Parzival, learned of his quest for a location he calls Kameloth, and learned that at least one other individual, a Super Mutant Behemoth named **Yawen**, may also be seeking Kameloth and its secrets. Mister Parzival encourages the PCs to take up the quest and he is eager to join them as they head out into the Wasteland.

Over the course of Part Two, the Players will have the opportunity to:

- Head out into the Wasteland in search of clues as to what Kameloth is and where it might be found.
- Encounter various Wasteland dwellers, creatures, and hazards.
- Find the trail of the Super Mutant Yawen and track him down.
- Encounter Yawen and his company.

> **OVERSEER NOTE**
>
> The Player Characters likely have two paths to pursue in Part Two: search for Kameloth by traveling north and west from Diamond City (Path One); or seek out clues to the whereabouts of the Super Mutant Yawen and his company (Path Two). No matter which path they take, the story will eventually lead them to Scene 3 and the rest of this campaign's sections. After Scene 3, it proceeds as written, no matter which previous path the Players chose.
>
> Path One is slightly more focused on social encounters and roleplaying, though there are some combat encounters. Path Two is slightly more focused on combat, though there are some social encounters and opportunities for roleplaying. The encounters are unique to each path, which means that a group of Players playing through this campaign more than once may experience different events over the course of the campaign.

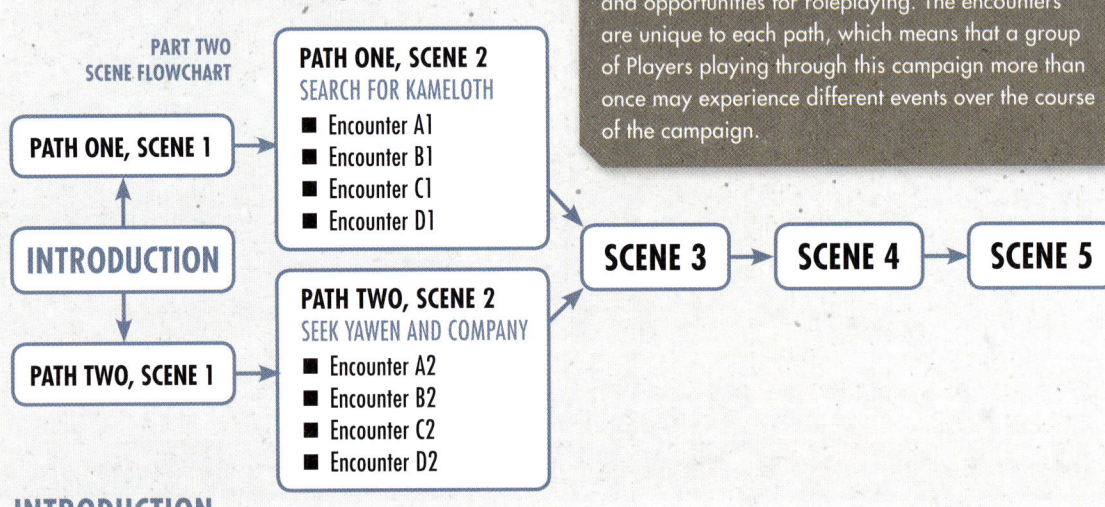

INTRODUCTION

Encourage the Player Characters to open this part of the campaign with a roleplaying scene amongst themselves and any companions they've gathered so far, including Mister Parzival, to determine which path they want to pursue. Once the Players have made a decision, proceed to either Path One: Scene 1 or Path Two: Scene 1, as appropriate.

If the Players come up with an option outside the scope of either Path One or Path Two, adjust the material of this campaign accordingly and have fun!

PATH ONE: SCENE 1

This path assumes that the Player Characters have decided to travel north and west from Diamond City in an effort to locate Kameloth itself. Give the PCs the opportunity to gather gear or talk to contacts as they wish while in Diamond City, and then encourage them to leave the city and head out into the Wasteland.

It takes around two hours for the Player Characters to reach the northern outskirts of Diamond City's borders, and the area they travel

> **OVERSEER NOTE**
>
> Should one or more of the PCs be a member of the Raiders faction, you have a couple of options. You could assume that the Raiders are a collection of disparate clans, bands, and companies, and that one band of Raiders doesn't necessarily owe allegiance or friendship to another. This could be used to explain why some Raiders are attacking settlers and scavengers and threatening Diamond City, while others, such as any PC Raiders, are not (at least, not yet).
>
> Alternatively, if you don't want to deal with the whole Raiders-as-different-groups issue, simply replace any Raider encounter in this campaign with another faction. Perhaps the Institute has roving bands of operatives in the Wasteland around Diamond City, or maybe the Brotherhood of Steel has sent out squads to cleanse or pacify the area.

is well-patrolled by alert units of Commonwealth Minutemen. The PCs are essentially free to discuss matters amongst themselves, and this is an opportunity for you to have Mister Parzival add more commentary about his life and experiences, using the sidebar on page 106. It's also an opportunity for roleplaying with any companions the PCs may have accumulated to date.

During the travels to the northern border, the Player Characters will occasionally encounter travelers heading toward Diamond City singly, in pairs, or in small groups. These various and sundry stragglers pause long enough to share a little of their story, and their story is the same one: these are settlers, scavengers, and the like who have been pushed out of their enclaves, homes and regular routines by heightened Raider activity all around Diamond City. None of them know why the Raiders are on the warpath. Each of these encounters should leave the Player Characters with the feeling that something strange may be occurring in the Wasteland to get the Raiders amped up for their attacks.

NOTE THAT THE CARDS BELOW ARE NOT COMPATIBLE WITH *FALLOUT: WASTELAND WARFARE*.

PATH ONE: SCENE 2

The Player Characters reach a border checkpoint and the squad of Minutemen on watch see them on their way, with an encouragement to keep a sharp eye out for bands of Raiders. If the PCs pause to question or interact with the Minutemen, they may attempt a **Talk Skill Test**.

Success means that one of the Minutemen tells the Player Characters that most of the stragglers coming into Diamond City's protection have been coming from the northwest, so they should prepare for trouble if they're heading in that direction.

Failure at the test provides nothing of value other than the Minutemen offering the group a half-hearted "Good luck."

Once past the Minuteman checkpoint, the PCs enter the Wasteland and begin their search for Kameloth. Granted, they don't have a lot of information to go on, other than knowing it may lie to the north or northwest of Diamond City. PCs who wish to question Mister Parzival further may make a **Cha Test**.

Failure at the test reveals no new information.

Success with additional Impact means that Mister Parzival studies the blasted landscape all around them, and soon focuses on the remains of a nearby major highway. Most of the concrete supports still stand, but there are piles of asphalt and concrete rubble, twisted guardrails, and the like.

Mister Parzival stares at the ruined highway, then makes an excited sound. "Perhaps, yes! Kameloth was located near one of the main thoroughfares of its day. Perhaps by following the king's high road, we may come across it, or more guidance to get us there." If questioned, Mister Parzival has no idea why he used the word "king."

Once the Player Characters decide on a direction, provide appropriate narration as they head out into the Wasteland under an overcast sky. Use as many of the optional encounters below as desired to fill out the travel time for the PCs to get to Scene 3, and to provide entertainment for your group.

Encounter A1: Stingwings

One day during their quest to find Kameloth, Mister Parzival excitedly leads the Player Characters toward a twisted overpass along the highway, gesturing toward crumbled buildings beneath it. Thinking this might be Kameloth, Mister Parzival leads the group into the clutter beneath the overpass and upsets a large nest of glowing Stingwings. The PCs must battle these creatures or beat a hasty retreat. Should they successfully eliminate the stingwings, they can attempt a **Search Skill Test** to search the Stingwing nest.

Success means they find **STURDY COMBAT ARMOR**.

Failure means they find little more than Stingwing carcasses, spoiled yellow sap, and disappointment for Mister Parzival.

Encounter B1: The Brotherhood

One afternoon during their travels, the Player Characters cross paths with a pair of Brotherhood soldiers: **Margo**, a Field Scribe, and **Merchad**,

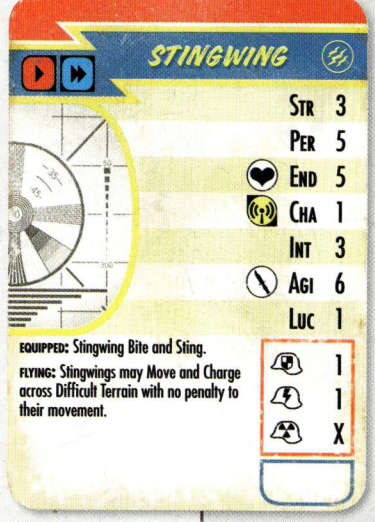

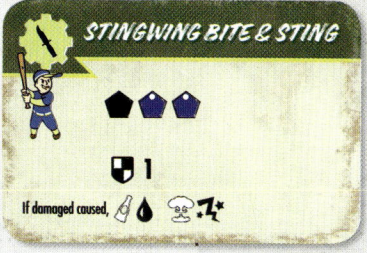

THE MAP BELOW CAN BE REUSED FOR ENCOUNTERS A1, B1, AND C1.

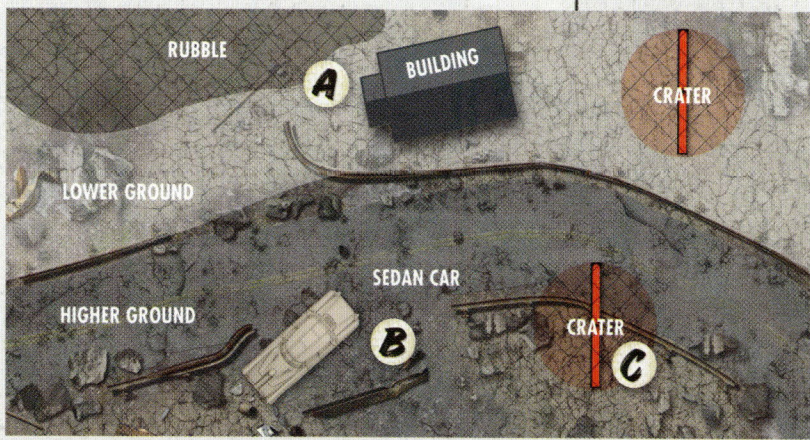

a Paladin wearing Power Armor. The two are initially wary of the PCs, especially if there are any mutants among the group, but social **Talk Skill Tests** should keep them friendly enough.

Mister Parzival is very excited upon hearing their names and, noticing the Paladin's armor, asks if they are also on the quest for Kameloth. Merchad is stone-faced, but Margo is quite curious and asks questions of the PCs and Mister Parzival about Kameloth. Once it's clear that Kameloth is a place, Margo will shrug and point out that many of the overpasses along the highway have ruined buildings in and near them: the group may be looking for the proverbial rock amongst a big pile of rocks.

If asked what their mission is out in the Wasteland, the two soldiers will be cagey. With some encouragement, Margo will say that they were sent out to survey some ruins in search of a site for a new Brotherhood base of operations. He'll also say that, over the last two weeks, they've seen a few roaming Raider bands, as well as settlers and survivors heading toward Diamond City. This is an opportunity for the PCs to share information and roleplay with a pair of potential allies. If the Characters happen to mention they might encounter Super Mutants, this will pique the Brothers' curiosity. The two will have a private conversation loud enough for the PCs to hear, along the lines of wanting to join the expedition but being duty-bound to follow orders.

If any of the Player Characters are members of the Brotherhood of Steel, or if the PCs are in clear need of medical assistance, or somehow endear themselves to the two soldiers with effective roleplaying, Merchad will wish them the best on their journey. He will offer the group a **pair of STIMPAKs** and a **VERTIBIRD SIGNAL GRENADE**, on the off-chance that the PCs run into any mutants or other trouble they can't handle and have need of the Brotherhood's help.

The two will then make their farewells and head off southwest into the Wasteland.

Encounter C1: Mole Rats

One cloudy evening, the group is attacked by a ravenous horde of Mole Rats desperate for a meal! No loot is associated with this encounter save for the irradiated **MOLE RAT MEAT** of one of the corpses, once the PCs are done with them.

Encounter D1: Happy Freeze

During their travels through the Wasteland, the Player Characters hear strange electronic music echoing on the wind. Upon investigation, they discover a large square robot wandering around, its white and blue finish pockmarked with rust and grime. There are faded images of ice cream cones and sweets on the sides of the robot, and tinny, tinkling music coming out of small hidden speakers. It is almost like a music box that has run down but is stuck on repeat. There are dispenser slots on two sides of the robot.

The nest of eyes set into the robot's front focus on the Player Characters, and then the robot turns toward them. In a metallic voice it says, "Happy Freeze is he-he-here! Treats for the l-l-little ones! Treats for them all! Cold and fresh and dee-dee-delicious!"

As the robot approaches, the PCs may attempt a **Persuade** or **Search Skill Test**. Success reveals that there are strange wires hooked into the dispenser slots, and what looks like explosives are tucked inside! The Player Characters may take **one action** to dive for cover, or otherwise prepare themselves, before the robot explodes, causing **2 damage +** 🔺🔺 (area of effect 🔥). If the Player Characters failed the test, they take the full brunt of the damage without having had a chance to prepare or duck.

Alternatively, the PCs may decide to shoot the robot before it gets too close, in which case it will explode and inflict **2 damage +** 🔺, area of effect 🔥.

Somehow, the explosion does not affect the machinery attached to the speakers, which continues to bleat out the tinny music. The scrap from the explosion, if gathered up, is worth **25 Caps**.

PATH TWO: SCENE 1

This path assumes that the Player Characters have decided to head into the Wasteland and hunt down Yawen and his Super Mutant group. Give the PCs the opportunity to gather gear or talk to contacts while in Diamond City, and then encourage them to leave the city and head out into the wastes.

If the Player Characters made any friends among the settlers in Part One, one or more of them may approach the PCs and ask to accompany them on their hunt for Yawen. They want payback for the harm the Super Mutants did to them and their dead friends. The PCs can accept their company, or not, depending on how much help the Players think they'll need.

After around two hours, the Player Characters will reach the outskirts of Diamond City's borders, whichever direction they decided to travel. The area is well-patrolled by alert units of Commonwealth Minutemen. The PCs are essentially free to discuss matters amongst themselves, and this is an opportunity for you to have Mister Parzival speak more about his life and experiences (see sidebar, p.106).

During their travels toward the border, the PCs occasionally encounter travelers heading to Diamond City, sometimes in small groups. These sad and pathetic refugees pause long enough to share their stories, and the tales are largely the same: settlers, scavengers, and the like who have been pushed out of their enclaves and homes by the Raider activity all around Diamond City.

Provide the PCs with an opportunity to attempt **Talk Skill Tests** to encourage travelers to provide extra detail.

A successful test means that one of the travelers will say that their village was attacked by Super Mutants and Mutant Hounds, and that they managed to escape only because they could run faster than their friends. These encounters should leave the PCs with a sense that Super Mutant activities in the Wasteland are having an effect on the Raider clans, and encouraging the Raiders to strike at the settlers and scavengers.

PATH TWO: SCENE 2

The Player Characters reach the border checkpoint and the Minutemen on watch there see them on their way with an encouragement to keep a sharp eye out for Raiders. If the PCs question the Minutemen, they may make a **Talk Skill Test**.

Success means a Minuteman tells the Player Characters that most refugees and stragglers have been coming from the northwest, so they should watch out if they're headed in that direction.

Failure results in a half-hearted "Good luck…" from the Minutemen.

Once past the Minuteman checkpoint, the PCs enter the Wasteland proper and can begin the hunt for Yawen and his company. Granted, they don't have much to go on, other than knowing Yawen may be somewhere to the north or northwest of Diamond City.

Once the Player Characters choose a direction, provide narration as they head out under an overcast sky. Use the following optional encounters as desired to make the journey interesting for the PCs as they head toward Scene 3.

Encounter A2: Minutemen Ambush

Soon after leaving the borders of Diamond City, the PCs accidentally stumble into the path of a squad of six Commonwealth Minutemen advancing on a ramshackle shack built up against the remains of a twisted overpass. The Minutemen encourage the Player Characters to either step back out of the line of fire, or join the battle against a trio of Raiders they've been chasing for the last few hours. If the PCs want to join the Minutemen, they will take part in a battle. You could simply narrate this, since the Minutemen plus the Player Characters present an overwhelming force against the Raiders, or you may choose to conduct the battle using miniatures and a map, as with other battles in this campaign. The Minutemen

IF USING THE *FALLOUT: WASTELAND WARFARE* RANGE RULERS AND BATTLE MATS, THE LAYOUT BELOW IS ONE POSSIBLE ARRANGEMENT FOR ENCOUNTER A2: MINUTEMAN AMBUSH. HOWEVER, OVERSEERS SHOULD FEEL FREE TO ARRANGE THE ENCOUNTER ACCORDING TO THEIR PREFERENCE AND AVAILABLE SCENERY.

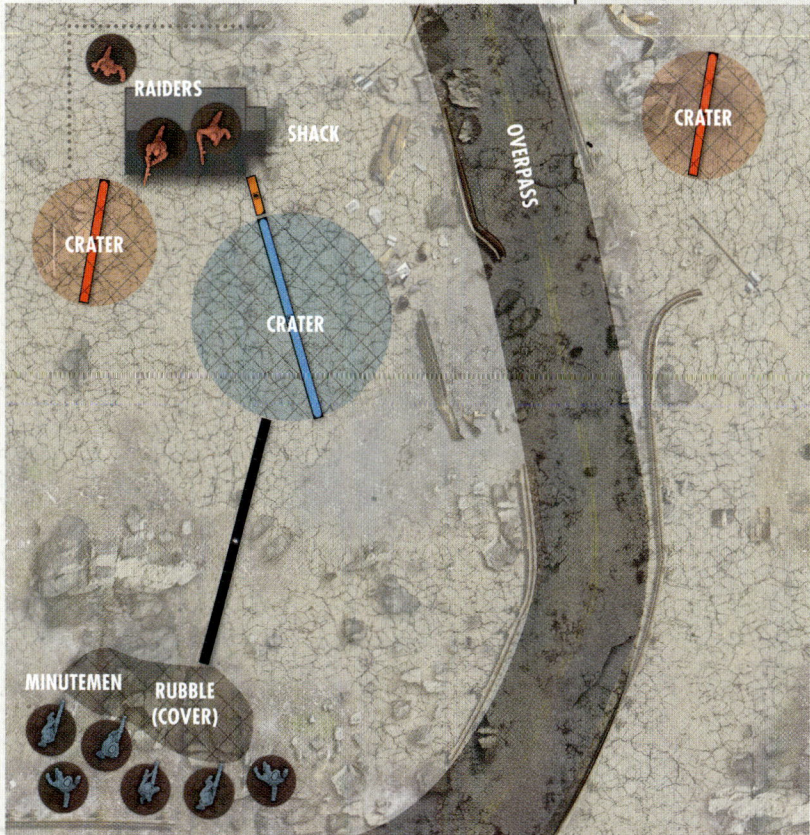

Encounter B2: Crazed Raider

One afternoon while the PCs are traveling, they stumble upon a critically wounded Raider slumped inside the rusted-out shell of a car. There is an empty medical kit nearby, along with the partly eaten carcass of a mole rat. When he sees the characters approach, he raises one hand weakly as if to ward them off, but then drops his hand back to his lap and lets his head loll back with a chilling giggle. A PC may attempt a **Medical Skill Test** to determine the health of the Raider. **Success** reveals that the Raider is mortally wounded and that there is nothing that can be done in the field other than to make him comfortable.

The Player Characters may question the Raider by attempting a **Talk Skill Test**, but with a **penalty of -2** to Charisma due to the Raider being doped up on strong medication and badly wounded. **With a success**, the Raider reveals that he was part of a war band, but that his group was ambushed by Super Mutants two days ago and wiped out. He gestures toward the northwest and says that the fight took place in that direction. The PCs may choose to stay with him until he passes, help him to his final rest, leave, or whatever other action they feel appropriate.

If the PCs choose to attack the Raider, he will not – cannot – put up a fight. He has no gear save for his blood-stained clothes, a **PIPE PISTOL** with no ammunition, and a small, silver, half-heart charm on a broken chain tucked into his left boot, worth 17 Caps.

Encounter C2: Freaky Farmers

During one day of their travels, the Player Characters discover a small farmstead carved out of the Wasteland. There are a pair of emaciated Brahmin hooked to a plow working a field. It's unclear what crop has been planted, if any. A pair of Ghoul farmers, wearing dingy clothing and wielding shotguns, encourage the brahmin in their work. Upon seeing the PCs, the farmers loudly demand that they get away from the farm and off their property.

If the PCs linger, the ghoul farmers will shoot with the intent to drive them off the farm or, if they don't go, simply kill them all. If the PCs move on without engaging the farmers, one farmer will hurl a few insults their way and then go back to their work.

The Player Characters may be able to talk with the Ghouls, though attempting to do so without being shot will require the PCs to make a **Persuade Skill Test** with a **penalty of -4** due to the inherent suspicious natures of the Ghouls.

With a success, the Ghoul brothers introduce themselves as **Ede** and **Nud**. They offer the PCs a share of their meal. If the PCs also inflict **additional Impact** during the test, the brothers will allow them to sleep in the barn with their

want at least one prisoner for questioning, so they encourage the PCs to be careful when shooting.

Any surviving Raider is disarmed and bound. The Minutemen squad's leader, Corporal Gates, takes the lead in questioning them, though a PC is welcome to step up and join in by attempting a **Persuade** or **Presence Skill Test**.

With a successful test by the PC or Corporal Gates, the Raider reveals that they had been attacking outlying farms and settlements, because they had been pushed out of their own fortifications by a company of Super Mutants. If the PC gets **additional Impact**, a Raider also reveals that the Super Mutants stripped the Raider camp for supplies and ammunition, so it wasn't a territory grab as much as it was a stockpiling raid for resources. They have no idea why the Super Mutants would attack many Raider outposts and fortifications.

A failed test means the Raiders reveal nothing, and refuse to cooperate. More dire threats and a **Presence** or **Intimidate Skill Test** may be attempted, at a **penalty of -4**. Failure at this second test means that the Raider will simply not give up any more information, and will die, if necessary, before talking.

118 FALLOUT – WASTELAND WARFARE ROLEPLAYING GAME

Brahmin overnight, if that'll help them with their journey. They are clear that they expect the PCs to be on their way in the morning.

With a failure of the test by the Player Characters, the Ghoul brothers simply open fire and will defend their farm to the last.

Should the PCs defeat the Ghoul farmers, they may search the modest farmhouse. Within, they'll find the place to be decently maintained. Some **MUTANT HOUND MEAT** is cooking in the oven, and assorted gear stored in the house: **MILITARY FATIGUES**, some ammunition, two bottles of **NUKA-COLA**, and a sealed bottle of **VODKA**.

Encounter D2: Rabid Radstag

One evening, a rabid Radstag brays out a challenge and rushes the Player Characters' camp, attracted by the sounds of people in its territory. If they kill the Radstag, the Player Characters will discover **6 Caps** in its stomach, and gain **RADSTAG MEAT**, should they choose to clean and dress the carcass. If you wish to make this a harder encounter, feel free to make it a small herd of Radstags charging into the camp.

NOTE: RADSTAG AND RADSTAG GORE CARDS ARE NOT COMPATIBLE WITH *FALLOUT: WASTELAND WARFARE* PLAY.

THE WASTELAND CONTAINS ALL MANNER OF STRANGE CREATURES... INCLUDING SCAVENGING ADVENTURERS

BOTH PATHS: SCENE 3

After a few days of traveling and enduring some or all of the encounters presented above, one brisk afternoon the Player Characters hear high-powered gunshots somewhere ahead of them. Anyone wishing to investigate should attempt a **Stealth Skill Test** to sneak up to a nearby pile of debris overlooking a valley.

Success gets them there without being detected.

Failure means that they have been spotted by lookouts, though the PCs will not know this until later in the scene.

Looking down into the valley reveals a gruesome sight. A large reinforced wagon, built out of scavenged Vertibird parts, sheet metal, and other elements stands in the valley, a team of four Brahmin hooked up to it. Inside the wagon are several Humans, all of whom appear to be wounded and bound. About a dozen well-armed Super Mutants stand around the wagon. One is a Behemoth in size, and clearly the leader of the band. There are several temporary shelters built up around the wagon; the overall look of the encampment is that this is a temporary, traveling company. There is also a second wagon built out of scrap metal and chitin, though this one is uncovered and packed with various supplies, weapons, and scrap, all of which look to be scavenged materials. From a distance they may well be the product of the raids the Super Mutants have conducted on Raider enclaves and settlers.

A pair of makeshift poles have been planted into the ground a dozen feet away from the wagon, and there is a body hanging from each pole. One body is missing most of its limbs, including its head. The other person is still alive, and frantically wriggling in their bonds to try and escape. The Behemoth bellows an order and one of the Super Mutants, holding a rifle, takes aim and shoots at the bound prisoner, hitting her arm. The prisoner cries out in pain while the Super Mutants laugh. It seems clear that the Super Mutants are having some sport with their prisoners, and it looks likely that they'll continue until they're all dead.

The Player Characters may decide to attack the camp outright, or move in to speak with the group, or another option the Players may come up with. There is no one right path here: it depends entirely on the morals of your particular PC group and how they want to approach interacting with Yawen and his company. Mister Parzival, on seeing the situation and the number of opponents, will note that, "The odds are not in our favor. I suggest we move toward the camp slowly and parlay."

If the PCs decide to shoot it out, use the Encounter Map on page 121 and proceed with the battle. The Super Mutants will attempt to wound the Player Characters so that they can take them captive and torture them for information and sport. Their larger numbers and tactical advantages should prove enough to defeat the PCs, though this is by no means a certain victory. Any characters wounded or incapacitated and then captured during the battle are bound and thrown into the prison wagon. The more PCs that are wounded, the more likely it will be for Yawen to demand the others surrender. With no good

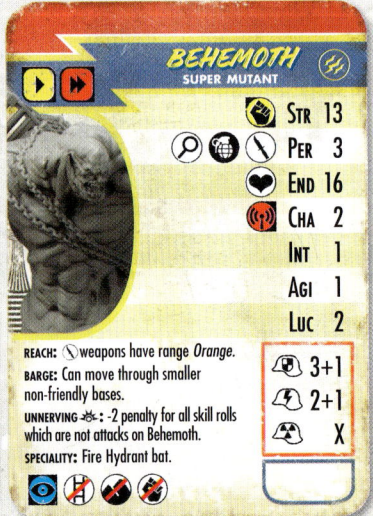

alternatives, the PCs will likely need to admit defeat, at least for now.

If the Player Characters decide to walk toward the encampment, they should do so without ready weapons in their hands and be clear about their peaceful intentions. A pair of wary Super Mutants will move toward them with weapons at the ready, and escort them into the camp.

Whether the Player Characters are all taken captive or are escorted into the camp, proceed to Scene 4.

SCENE 4

> **OVERSEER NOTE**
>
> Adjust the opening of this scene depending on whether the PCs enter the camp under their own power escorted by guards, or they are visited by Yawen while they sit captive in the prison wagon.

The Player Characters are escorted through the camp toward the Super Mutant Behemoth. Yawen looms over the Player Characters, his massive bulk and presence dwarfing most other beings. In a deep, gravelly voice, he says, "Who dares enter my domain?"

The Player Characters may speak up, but if none do after a few moments, Mister Parzival will. The robot says, "Yawen! I remember you! Dost remember me? I am Parzival, knight and seeker of Kameloth!"

Yawen stares at Mister Parzival while another, smaller Super Mutant, wearing a satchel over one shoulder and with an old Pip-Boy in the other hand, whispers into Yawen's ear. Yawen listens, then shrugs him away. "Away from me, scribe."

The PCs may attempt a **Notice Skill Test**. **With success** at the test, they note that the Pip-Boy in the scribe's hand is displaying a map, though it's not legible enough at distance to make out details.

Yawen focuses on Mister Parzival. "I do not remember you, scrap metal. But I do know the name Kameloth. What do you know of that place?"

The PCs may attempt a **Presence** or **Persuade Skill Test** (or another appropriate Skill) if they wish to converse with Yawen. He is belligerent and knows he has the advantage, and is content to speak from a position of power. He knows the likely location of Kameloth, and has more soldiers and weapons than the PCs. During the conversation, find a good place to drop in the following statement from Yawen. "We will take Kameloth, strip it of its treasures, and then raze it to the ground. Or… I may use it as my new stronghold. None can oppose me."

Yawen seeks additional information about Kameloth and its surrounding environment. The PCs may

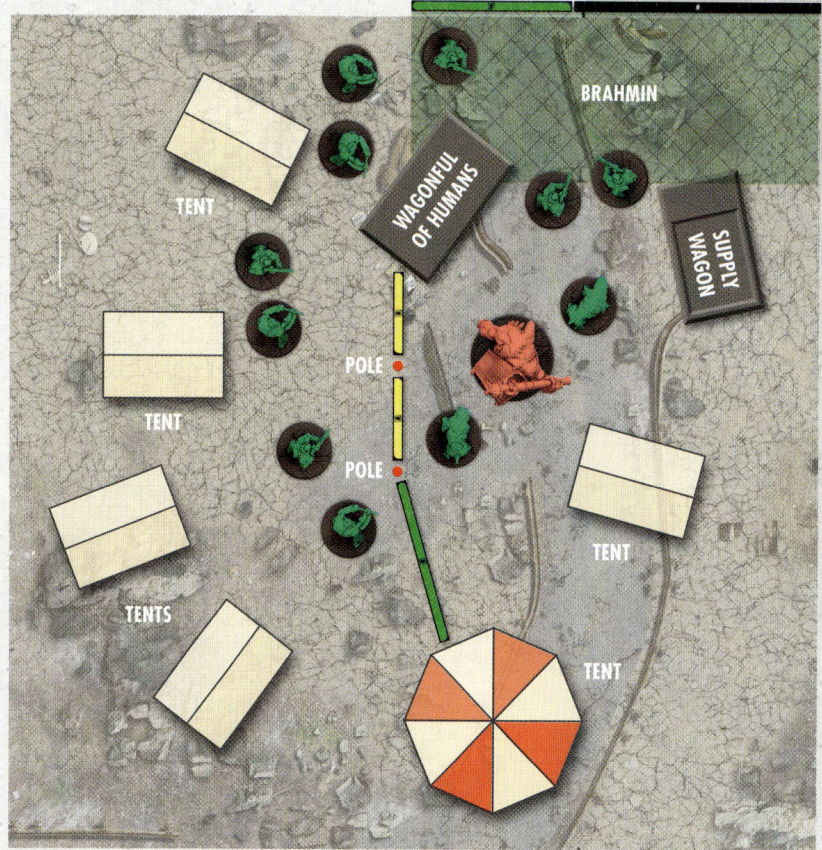

attempt to bluff their way through the conversation or choose to be honest. In either case, Yawen will soon realize they have nothing to offer him and his company. Mister Parzival is not much help, as much of his original memory and programming were wiped. He'll go on about wanting to find the place, and how important it is to return there, but he can't offer specifics on where to find it or what to expect when they get there.

If the Player Characters were escorted into the camp under their own power and conducted themselves appropriately while talking to Yawen, he will allow them to leave the camp as long as they go and never return to this area of the Wasteland. If the Player Characters were wounded and thrown into the prison wagon, Yawen is likely to keep them as prisoners, though PCs may attempt **Talk Skill Tests** to talk their way out, at a **-4 penalty** to the test.

If the Player Characters decide to fight their way out of the camp, they are welcome to do so, though it will be a very hard fight against overwhelming odds. The PCs might attempt to grab the **Pip-Boy** from Yawen's scribe as they make their escape. You should feel free to either let the dice fall as they may and wipe out the PCs here, or give them opportunities to split the party. Perhaps some are able to escape while others are wounded, captured, and dragged back to the prison wagon. Keep the action moving and reinforce the brutality of life in the Wasteland. See Part 3, Scene 1 for more details on how this fight might be conducted.

IF USING THE *FALLOUT: WASTELAND WARFARE* RANGE RULERS, THE LAYOUT ABOVE IS ONE POSSIBLE ARRANGEMENT FOR SCENES 3-5. HOWEVER, OVERSEERS SHOULD FEEL FREE TO ARRANGE THE ENCOUNTER ACCORDING TO THEIR PREFERENCE AND AVAILABLE SCENERY.

FIRE AWAY, BUT DON'T EXPECT SUPER MUTANTS TO STAY BACK AND PLAY FAIR

SCENE 5

Despite their best efforts, some or all of the PCs, and Mister Parzival, have been wounded or beaten into submission. They are stripped of their gear, placed in chains, and stuffed into the makeshift mobile prison wagon made from scrap metal, Mirelurk shell parts, and weathered rope. When asked why Yawen just doesn't kill them outright, the guards or perhaps Yawen himself will state that it is a five-day journey to where he believes Kameloth can be found, and that the company will need additional feed along the journey.

The prison wagon is guarded by a trio of well-armed Super Mutants and a pair of Mutant Hounds. Their orders are to wound, not kill, but they will not pull their punches if the PCs are clearly earnest about trying to escape or do them harm. "Dead taste as good as the living," is their philosophy. If the PCs engage their guards, use the NPC cards presented previously.

Faced with imprisonment and the likelihood of being somebody's brunch, the imprisoned PCs are left to ponder their fate. Mister Parzival, resting upon the rough flooring of the makeshift prison, rotates his eyes from companion to companion. He says "The questing knights faced many challenges in their quest… We will face this one as well, together as friends." Whether this will cheer up any of the PCs is matter for them.

If any Characters evaded capture and escaped Yawen's camp, give them the opportunity for a roleplaying scene, and emphasize the bleakness of their situation. Their party is split, some are imprisoned, some wounded or perhaps dead, and there is little hope of allies or support from any

> **OVERSEER NOTE**
>
> Adjust the opening of this scene depending on the results of the conversation with Yawen in the previous scene. PCs may have left the camp empty-handed but wait outside the valley to discuss options, may have fought their way out but left some wounded allies behind, or all may be prisoners of Yawen. The flow of this campaign is based on the idea that the PCs are either all prisoners of Yawen by this point, or that some of them have been taken captive while others escaped, and are outside the camp, determining their next steps.

direction. The howls of some fearsome creature echo in the night, and the braying of Yawen's Brahmin and the rough laughter of his cohorts are dreadful music across the broken landscape.

Conclusion

This should be presented as the low point of the campaign. The PCs have met or engaged all the key NPCs and have a good knowledge about the location of Kameloth. They also know that Yawen is ready to lead his company to take Kameloth for himself. However, they are now largely powerless to do anything about it. You should proceed directly to Part Three of this campaign, but feel free to run other adventures between Part Two and Part Three as desired.

PART THREE: KAMELOTH

SYNOPSIS

Armed with sufficient intelligence, the Player Characters travel through the Wasteland in search of Kameloth, racing against Yawen and other characters, with the encouragement of Mister Parzival. As they approach what they believe is Kameloth, Yawen and his allies attack the Player Characters and there is a desperate battle for survival. The Player Characters come to the location of Kameloth, a battered but operative seedfarm revealed to be **Graygarden**.

Should they survive the battle, the Player Characters meet Graygarden's caretakers, a trio of Mr. Handy robots that Mister Parzival refers to as **Guinevere**, **Arthur**, and **Galahad**. They introduce themselves as Supervisors **Greene**, **White**, and **Brown**, and welcome Mister Parzival home, though they call him **Supervisor Orange**. Mister Parzival is mystified at this name for him, the memory of it having been wiped from his circuits long ago. Mister Parzival eagerly escorts the Player Characters into the greenhouse, and shows them the treasure he had been seeking all this time.

Over the course of Part Three, the Players will have the opportunity to:

- Race toward Kameloth against Yawen and his company and any other Non-Player Characters that have been caught up in the quest.
- Battle Wasteland creatures and the Super Mutant company led by Yawen.
- Discover Kameloth and its secrets.

SCENE 1

Coming out of Part Two, the Player Characters are either all imprisoned by Yawen and his company, or some are imprisoned, with a few PCs on the outside looking in, and left to determine what to do. Give the PCs some roleplaying opportunities to note their situation and to brainstorm ideas on what to do next.

> **OVERSEER NOTE**
>
> Part Three picks up where Part Two left off, with the Player Characters in a bad situation. They have to decide how to get out of the mess they're in, with a number of options in front of them. Clever and creative Players may come up with additional options. You are encouraged to use or modify any option that works best for your group of Players.

If all of the PCs were imprisoned at the end of Part Two, then a **jailbreak** is a clear solution to their situation. The guards are alert-ish but complacent, and clever PCs may be able to talk their way out of the prison wagon, or otherwise manage an escape. They should then figure out how to get their gear and the Pip-Boy from the scribe, and leave the camp without attracting additional attention. Running the scene in this manner may give you the opportunity to focus on stealth skills and subterfuge rather than direct physical combat, perhaps even using social Skill Tests to persuade or intimidate guards into helping the PCs.

If some of the Player Characters were captured and others are thinking about breaking their fellows out of prison, you are encouraged to switch between groups in a dynamic fashion, keeping the action moving. Perhaps the imprisoned group can attempt to sneak their way out of the prison wagon while those outside the camp attempt a rescue or otherwise attempt to help their friends stuck in the prison wagon.

If the Player Characters have not yet attempted to steal the Pip-Boy from Yawen's scribe, they have a golden opportunity to do so if they manage to escape the prison wagon or try to sneak around the camp. PCs may attempt a **Notice Skill Test** to single out the scribe and identify where he rests at night. The Player Characters may attempt **Stealth Skill Tests** to slip into the scribe's tent.

Success means that they enter it unnoticed, and may attempt further **Stealth Skill Tests** to take the Pip-Boy off the scribe's arm, either by stealthily killing him first, or by using a **Manual Dexterity Skill Test** to remove it without waking the scribe.

Failure in a **Stealth Skill Test** to get into the tent means that one or more Super Mutant guards or a hound detect the PCs and raise the alarm. The Characters have one round to take an Action before the camp erupts, as angry Super Mutants wake and a general melee follows.

If the Player Characters end up in a fight with the bulk of the Super Mutants, it will be a very hard struggle against overwhelming odds. You should feel free to either let the dice fall as they may and potentially wipe out the Player Characters, or you can give them opportunities to escape. It's possible some of the Player Characters might get wounded and captured again, or that they all may be able to get away, with or without the Pip-Boy containing the map to Kameloth. Keep the action moving and reinforce, once more, the brutality of Wasteland life.

SCENE 2

Once the Player Characters escape from Yawen's camp, you may narrate a chase across the Wasteland toward Kameloth, interspersing moments of narration with combat encounters with the Super Mutants as they attempt to catch up, or with any of the encounters below. The intent is to keep up the action as the Player Characters work their way through toward Kameloth, pursued by Yawen and his company, and any other adversaries they've managed to generate (or annoy) over the course of the campaign.

This scene also presents the opportunity for any NPCs encountered during the campaign to show up and provide assistance to the PCs, depending on how you want to present events, and how well or poorly the PCs interacted with people during previous events. Some options for potential assistance include:

- **If the PCs encountered Margo and Merchad** of the Brotherhood of Steel earlier, the PCs might be able to signal for their help using the signal grenade that was given to them. Margo and Merchad could arrive out of the Wasteland and lend assistance to the PCs, and can even call in additional support, though any additional Brotherhood of Steel support could arrive too late to be relevant for the purposes of this campaign.

- **If the PCs didn't encounter Margo and Merchad**, now might be a good time for them to turn up. The Brotherhood of Steel soldiers are roaming the Wasteland, hunting down Super Mutants, and they have tracked Yawen and his company for some time. They'll encounter the PCs and offer to help them rescue their imprisoned friends or attack the Super Mutants. If the PCs are unclear about what they want to do, Merchad and Margo will announce that they're going to attack, and will leave the PCs behind as they conduct an attack on the Super Mutants.

- **If the Player Characters encountered Palam the Ghoul** earlier in the campaign, he could show up at to provide assistance. He's not much use

> **OVERSEER NOTE**
>
> It's also possible to run this scene as the Player Characters chasing Yawen and his company, especially if some of the Player Characters are wounded and still prisoners. The PCs might have escaped, in which case they might be able to follow the Super Mutants toward Kameloth and ambush them at some other time during the journey. You could even rotate it back and forth, by having the pursuers becoming the pursued, and then flip the situation as one group or another forges ahead, depending on the dynamics you wish to present to your Players.

BEHEMOTH OR NOT, YAWEN IS A MUCH-RESPECTED LEADER, AND FEAR GOES A LONG WAY IN THE WASTELAND

with a weapon – he will fight if asked – but could provide medical assistance or act as a runner if the PCs wanted to send him ahead to Kameloth, or back toward Diamond City, for assistance. Kameloth has no aid to provide, and Diamond City is too far away for any help to arrive in time.

- **If the PCs weren't difficult during their time in and around Diamond City**, a patrol of Commonwealth Minutemen might arrive to lend support. Their leader could say that they chose to follow the Player Characters into the Wasteland, or perhaps they were tipped off by caravan survivors that the Player Characters escorted to Diamond City.

Encounter A: Mole Rats

If you need to, you can use the Mole Rat encounter from p.106, under Path One, Scene 2.

Encounter B: Minefield

During their rush toward Kameloth, running from Yawen and his company, or chasing after them, the PCs stumble into a large patch of land peppered with active land mines. Mister Parzival, any of the PCs, or their companions must attempt a **Notice Skill Test**.

Any successful character notices a partly uncovered mine in the ground, and is able to warn others away from it.

Any PC failing the test triggers a mine and suffers its effects accordingly.

A Player Character may attempt a **Repair/Craft (Weapons)** or **Manual Dexterity Test** to disable a mine.

Success means the Player Character successfully deactivates the **FRAGMENTATION MINE** and may remove it from the ground and reuse it if desired.

Failure means the PC triggers the mine. Boom!

Encounter C: Raider Revenge

The Player Characters encounter a rag-tag group of Raiders trailing the Super Mutants. The Raider group clearly looks to be a mix of individuals from different Raider factions, suggesting that they have banded together for a common purpose. There are twice as many Raiders as there are PCs and companions, and the Raiders have a good mix of weapons and armor: enough to pose a stiff challenge if the PCs seek a fight. The Characters may choose to approach the Raiders carefully, or the Raiders themselves may approach the PCs under a flag of truce.

The Player Characters may attempt a **Persuade Test** or a relevant skill depending on how they want to approach a social encounter with the Raiders. The PCs get a **bonus of +2** to any social-focused Skill Test, because the Raiders intend only to attack the Super Mutants. It is clear that the Raiders are tired of being

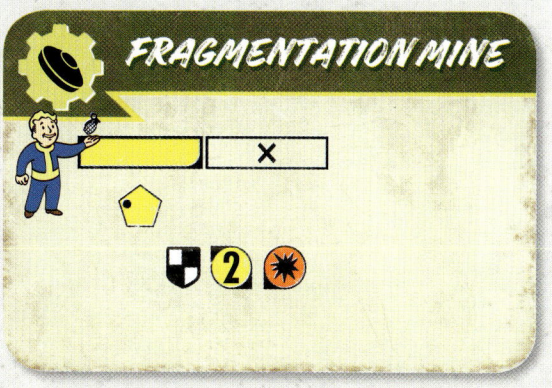

beaten down by the Super Mutants, and are desperate for revenge against the Mutants that wiped out their homes and slaughtered their allies.

Whether the PCs go along with this shift in Raider morality and targeting is up to the Players. This is an example of how political tides shift and change in the Wasteland, and an enemy can become an ally depending on circumstances. Mister Parzival may join in the conversation, suggesting something along the lines of "The enemy of our enemy could become our friend, for a time…" if an opportunity presents itself.

With effective test rolling and roleplaying, the Characters may be invited to join the Raider faction in an attack against the Super Mutants, or they may be asked to take the lead in planning an attack.

The Raiders are not especially gifted at planning, and might be willing to let a PC take the lead if one does well at a social Skill Test.

IF USING THE *FALLOUT: WASTELAND WARFARE* BATTLE MAP, THE LAYOUT ABOVE IS ONE POSSIBLE ARRANGEMENT FOR ENCOUNTER 2B. OVERSEERS MAY ARRANGE SCENERY ACCORDING TO WHAT THEY HAVE AVAILABLE, AND SHOULD FEEL FREE TO INCREASE OR DECREASE THE NUMBER OF MINES ACCORDING TO THEIR BLOODTHIRSTINESS!

IF USING THE *FALLOUT: WASTELAND WARFARE* RANGE RULERS AND BATTLE MAP, THE LAYOUT BELOW IS ONE POSSIBLE ARRANGEMENT FOR SCENE 3. HOWEVER THE OVERSEER CHOOSES TO ARRANGE SCENERY, ENSURE THE SUPER MUTANT START FROM RAISED GROUND, AND THAT THERE IS SUFFICIENT TOPOGRAPHICAL REASON FOR THE PLAYERS TO ENGAGE THEM. SOME COVER WILL OFFER TACTICAL COMPLEXITY. THE RED-DIAMETER CRATERS ARE POSSIBLE LOCATIONS FROM WHICH RADSCORPIONS, MOLE RATS, OR RADROACHES MAY EMERGE, IF YOU WISH TO USE ADDITIONAL ADVERSARIES.

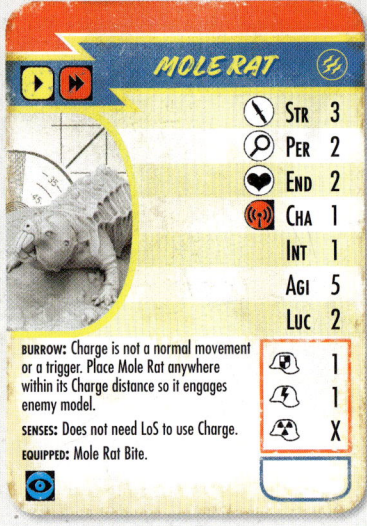
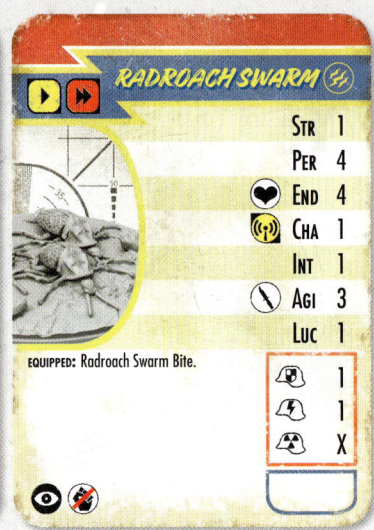

SCENE 3

Once it's clear that Kameloth is less than a mile away, the PCs hear a loud bellowing sound. It's the same war horn Yawen and his company have used over the last several days as part of their race (or chase) toward Kameloth. This blast sounds close and, sure enough, a quick look shows Yawen and his surviving allies atop a nearby hill and charging toward the characters.

As the Player Characters and any allies prepare to enter the final climatic battle with Yawen and the Super Mutants, Mister Parzival (if he is still with the company and able to move and speak) makes a strange little gesture over his chassis with his appendages and says, "We shall now seek that which we shall not find." After a moment of perhaps confused silence, Mister Parzival glances at the PCs and any companions and makes a shrugging gesture. He then produces a **10MM PISTOL** from a storage drawer built into his chassis and joins the PCs in the fight against the advancing Super Mutants.

Yawen and his company want blood and will not leave the battlefield. They will fight to the death, as they consider they have nothing left to lose and Kameloth is nearby. Companions traveling with the PCs will fight to the last, unless you feel that they would perform a token effort, then cut and run. This might fit better with some personality types and reflect how the PCs treated their allies over the course of the campaign.

If the Overseer desires to make this an even more challenging fight with additional adversaries for the Player Characters, roll a **Special (blue) Effect Dice** every round and use the following result:

Add a pair of Radscorpions. Only use this result once over the course of the battle.

Add a horde of mole rats.

Add a swarm of Radroaches.

These extra creatures will be willing to attack either side, concentrating on wounded characters or creatures in the hope of getting an easy meal.

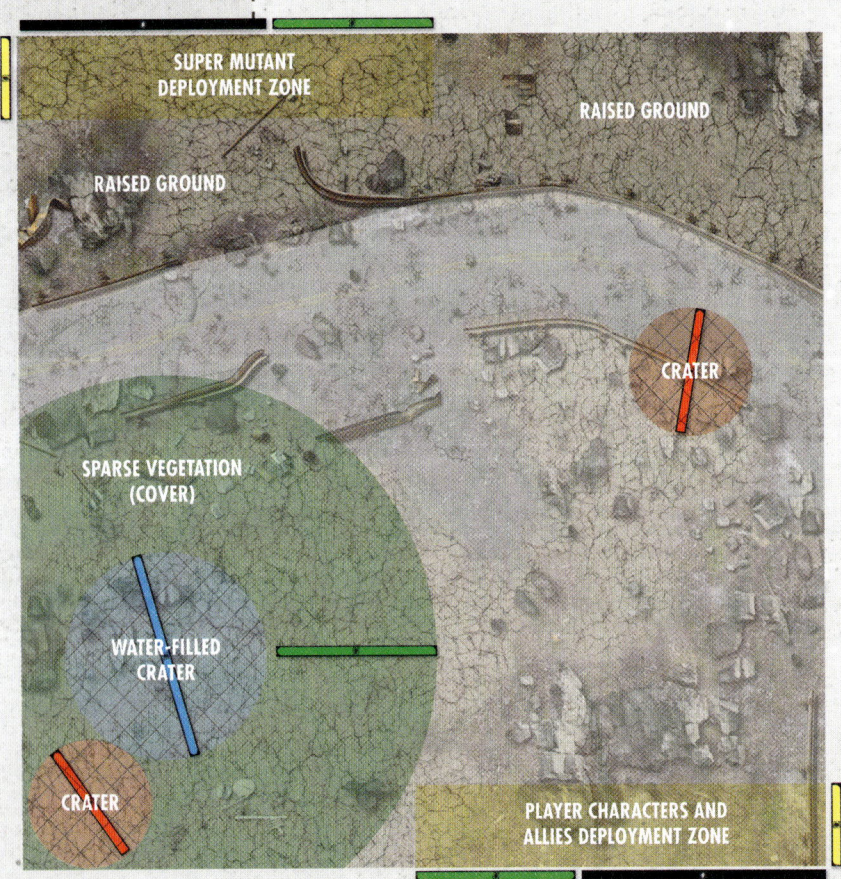

OVERSEER NOTE

This large battle has many participants, so you are strongly encouraged to use miniatures and a battle map if you haven't already been doing so. Make use of as many NPC cards, tokens, and miniatures as needed to make sure each participant is visible on the map. This will make your Overseeing job easier, and boost immersion for your group.

SCENE 4

Should any of them survive, the Player Characters may pilfer the battlefield and any fallen for equipment and supplies, then regroup and finally move toward Kameloth.

Read or paraphrase the following:

> *Near a crumbled concrete and asphalt overpass lies the realm of Kameloth, its gleaming walls and roof panels sparkling in a sudden sunbeam that breaks through the overcast sky. A long rectangular building with a peaked roof dominates the scene with smaller outbuildings scattered around it. One of the outbuildings appears to be a toolshed, while another is a partially collapsed two-story homestead. Several Mr. Handy robots work here and there, some in a large mutfruit field, and others in additional crop fields that appear to be well-tended and maintained. There are a couple of ancient, rusted-out vehicles parked haphazardly in the crop fields.*

The Player Characters see no opposition moving toward them from Kameloth, and are free to move forward. If he is still functional and able to move, Mister Parzival will make a delighted electronic squeal and move toward the large central building at his best possible speed. The unnamed Mr. Handy robots tending the fields ignore the PCs and only glance at Mister Parzival before resuming work.

Kameloth's caretakers, a trio of Mr. Handy robots that Mister Parzival refers to as **Guinevere**, **Arthur**, and **Galahad**, soon emerge from the central building. They introduce themselves as **Supervisors Greene**, **White**, and **Brown**, and welcome Mister Parzival home, though they call him **Supervisor Orange** (see sidebar for more information). Mister Parzival is mystified by their name for him, the memory of his early days here having been wiped long ago.

Mister Parzival exclaims that he is delighted to be home at Kameloth, which confuses the supervisors. They will correct him and say that this facility is actually called **Graygarden**. Mister Parzival shrugs off the name, convinced that the place is, in fact, the Kameloth of the quest he has pursued for the last many years.

Mister Parzival ignores the welcome from the three supervisors and eagerly escorts the Player Characters into the greenhouse. He shows them the plants being tended to there, including corn, carrots, gourds, mutfruit, and tatos. He leads the Player Characters past the crops to a large flower bed set against one of the long walls, and stops suddenly at the sight of a freshly blooming yellow rose. Mister Parzival sighs in almost Human-fashion and presents this treasure to the Characters, before making his very best attempt at shedding a tear.

He says, "To have traveled so far, and to have endured so much, that our quest should end here is truly a sign of providence." He looks hard at the Player Characters. "Can you ken such joy?"

OVERSEER NOTE

If Mister Parzival met his end before the Player Characters arrive at Kameloth or Graygarden, the three supervisors will have a similar reaction if the PCs refer to the place as Kameloth. They will correct the Player Characters, calling the place Graygarden. The PCs may attempt an **INT** or **Knowledge Skill Test**. If the Player Characters succeed at the test, they'll recall a rumor they unearthed during their earlier research that an ancient scientist named Doctor Edward Gray built a self-sufficient hydroponics greenhouse out in the Wasteland. Graygarden or Kameloth would appear to prove that particular rumor true.

If they fail at the test, no additional information is recalled, and the name "Graygarden" carries no extra meaning for them.

THE THREE SUPERVISORS

The three supervisors in charge of operations at Graygarden are Mr. Handy model robots, programmed to manage the facility to the full extent of their capabilities. They have worked at Graygarden for more than two hundred years, maintaining the facility and its crop fields. They are each very proud of their personalities and the fact that Doctor Gray programmed them to be something different from the other Mr. Handy robots working at Graygarden.

Supervisor Brown: Brown has a male voice with a decidedly British tone of voice, is painted in shades of brown, and sounds like a soldier from ancient Great Britain. He keeps the unnamed Mr. Handy robots in good repair, and orders them around the grounds with military-like orders. In conversation, he'll often drop in a "Jolly good!" or "Cheerio!" or "I say, chaps!" or the like into his speeches.

Supervisor Greene: Greene has a male voice, is painted in shades of green, and sounds like every game show host ever conceived rolled into one identity. He is friendly and gregarious, and doesn't hesitate to make deals with PCs, offering them successively larger sums of Caps if they take greater risks at challenges or even just as part of a conversation. He'll often drop in something like "You can choose from one of these fabulous prizes!" as a conversation ender, though no such prizes are to be found except, perhaps, a few Caps or fresh mutfruit.

Supervisor White: White has a female voice, is painted bright white (something of a surprise given the general dirtiness of the Wasteland), and sounds like an ancient cinema ingénue, sprinkling every comment with the Player Characters with archaic language such as "Dreadful!" and "Ghastly!" Whether she learns any of the PCs' names or not, she refers to everyone as "Darling."

The Player Characters are free to explore the greenhouse and surrounding buildings so long as they don't damage anything or act aggressively toward the Mr. Handy robots. The storage building contains some **scrap metal** and **old tools**. The two-story homestead has a partially collapsed kitchen that is inaccessible, an empty living area, and a locked door leading to a basement. A Player Character may attempt a **Lockpick Skill Test** to open the lock.

Should any Player Character ask the three supervisors questions about the facility or their history, they will be happy to answer questions. Graygarden was built before the Great War by Doctor Edward Gray, who intended the facility to be self-sufficient. The facility is, indeed, self-sufficient, entirely automated under the guidance of the three supervisor Mr. Handy robots. There is very little in the way of construction materials in the area, but much of the surrounding land is arable and can be converted into additional crop fields should the PCs or other characters deliver crop samples to the Mr. Handy robots.

If the Player Characters ask any of the supervisors about Mister Parzival, they will be confused but curious. They'll note that Doctor Gray had programmed just the three of them with advanced cognition processors, giving them the ability to conduct complex decision-making and reasoning. That a Mr. Handy originally programmed to work the greenhouse somehow developed a similar level of programming is a curiosity to them, and perhaps also to any PC with a mechanical background or interests. Where and how Mister Parzival got his programming, however, is a mystery for the ages, or another campaign for you to develop for your Players.

The supervisors note that, due to their isolated location, Graygarden is rarely visited and hasn't been attacked by Raiders for a very long time. As long as word doesn't get out about Graygarden's location, the facility and the PCs should be relatively safe, if they need a base of operations or a stable place to return to between their excursions into the Wasteland.

MISTER PARZIVAL… OR SHOULD WE ADDRESS YOU AS SUPERVISOR ORANGE?

FOWW RPG-001-111 — SECTION 6.5

CONCLUSION

The Overseer should provide time for the PCs and any remaining companions to react to the resolution of the quest. The three supervisors and Mister Parzival are present to answer questions and to give the Player Characters a tour of the facility.

Mister Parzival will settle back into a working role at Graygarden, though he'll continue to refer to it as Kameloth, and will call his three robot friends by his names for them rather than their actual identitites. He'll be full of gratitude toward the PCs for helping him complete his quest, and his gratitude is honest and heartfelt, something of a rarity in the Wasteland.

The three supervisors make it clear that the PCs and their companions are welcome to stay at Graygarden for as long as they wish, so long as they don't abuse their hospitality, don't damage anything, and don't get in the way. If any PCs offer to help, the supervisors will put them to work on modest tasks first, and then give them more involved jobs should the characters prove capable.

If any Brotherhood of Steel members are with the Player Characters, they will remain with them at Graygarden for a day or two before moving on. They will say that they'll include Graygarden in their reports but will not encourage any of their brethren to visit the site unless an emergency arises.

The Player Characters have a number of possibilities to pursue following the events of this campaign, should they or the Overseer wish to continue with this particular group. You and your Players should feel free to expand on the plot hooks below, or head off through the Wasteland in entirely new directions!

- The PCs could align themselves with Mister Parzival and his allies at Graygarden/Kameloth and use the site as a base for exploring nearby regions, or perhaps use it as a staging area for mounting cleansing operations against the Raider bands.

- The Player Characters could eliminate Mister Parzival and his allies and claim the location for themselves, then fortify it for whatever intentions spark their interest.

> **OVERSEER NOTE**
>
> Players expecting a large payoff may be disappointed that the end result of the quest is Mister Parzival finding and presenting a rose to the Player Characters. Some Players may appreciate a robot seeking out love and joy and finding some of both by the end of his quest, while other Players will be more interested in what gear and supplies they can loot. If your Players are more slanted toward the latter end of the spectrum, feel free to add some useful supplies, Caps, and the like to the final battle with Yawen and his company. This gives the Player Characters a large reward at the end of the fight, before they get to the end of the quest's story element.

- The PCs could offer to search the Wasteland for crop samples to return to Graygarden in exchange for food or Caps. This might give them a sustainable source of food for export to Diamond City, the settlers, or perhaps even Raider factions willing to pay for food.

- The Player Characters could spend some time at Graygarden recovering from their wounds and then head out into the Wasteland once again, bound for whatever adventure next awaits them.

- If the PCs have Brotherhood of Steel companions, Raider companions, or allies who might travel back to Diamond City, it's possible that word of Graygarden's existence might spread. Is this something the three supervisors or the PCs want? Do the characters work with the NPCs and keep quiet about the location's existence? Do they quietly eliminate anyone who might spread the word about Graygarden? A subsequent adventure or campaign could focus on the Player Characters defending Graygarden from all kinds of external threats if news about the place gets out into the Wasteland and beyond.

FOWW RPG-001-111 — APPENDIX A1

MINIATURES GALLERY

The next few pages display some of the miniatures available for *Fallout: Wasteland Warfare*. They are designed to be usable with this RPG expansion, adding depth and flavour to your encounters and utilising the combat and encounter rules as they are designed to be used.

There is a tick box next to each set, helping you collect all the possible miniatures to expand your roleplaying experience. For more weapons, items, NPCs, and characters to play as, there are also card expansion sets. All of these are available from **www.modiphius.net** and your favourite local gaming store, and advice for building and painting your collection can be found at **www.modiphius.com**.

SURVIVORS — CORE SET

SURVIVORS — MINUTEMEN POSSE

BROTHERHOOD OF STEEL — CORE SET

SUPER MUTANTS — CORE SET

RAIDERS — CORE SET

BROTHERHOOD OF STEEL – FRONTLINE KNIGHTS

BOSTON COMPANIONS

HEROES OF SANCTUARY HILLS

SUPER MUTANTS – SUICIDERS

RAIDERS – ACK ACK, SINJIN, AND AVERY

BROTHERHOOD OF STEEL – PALADIN DANSE AND KNIGHT CAPTAIN CADE

X01-POWER ARMOR AND DOGMEAT

RAIDERS – RAIDERS, SCAVVERS, AND PSYCHOS

SUPER MUTANTS – HAMMER

INDEX OF ICONS

SOME ICONS SHOWN ON FALLOUT: WASTELAND WARFARE CARDS ARE NOT USED IN THE FALLOUT: WASTELAND WARFARE RPG. WHERE THEY APPEAR IN THE INDEX BELOW, THEIR PAGE REFERENCE IS GIVEN SIMPLY AS 'F:WW'.

Action Point	61
Addictive	74
Alcohol	73
Armor	73
Armor, Energy	64
Armor, Physical	64
Armor, Radiation	64
Armor Reduction	44, 64
Attack (Quick Action)	59
Attack Response (AI)	F:WW
Aura	68
Awareness / Prepare	20, 52
Awareness (Orange Range)	20, 52
Awareness (Yellow Range)	20, 52
Awareness (Red Range)	20, 52
Awareness (Green Range)	20, 52
Awareness (Blue Range)	20, 52
Awareness (Black Range)	20, 52
Resist Battle Cry	69
Battle Cry (Orange Range)	69
Battle Cry (Yellow Range)	69
Battle Cry (Red Range)	69
Battle Cry (Green Range)	69
Battle Cry (Blue Range)	69
Bleeding (Condition)	68
Immunity to Battle Cry	69
Inability To Climb	54
Caps / Counting Tokens	94
Charge (Orange Range)	69
Charge (Yellow Range)	69
Charge (Red Range)	69
Charge (Green Range)	69
Charge (Blue Range)	69
Chems	73
Clothing	73
Computers (Expertise)	25, 56
Creature (Type)	34
Critical Point	48, 66
Damage	44, 54
Damage, Energy	63
Damage, Physical	63
Damage, Radiation	63
Defend Response (AI)	F:WW
Dice, Armor	64, 89
Dice, Damage Effect	31, 44, 81
Dice, Special Effect	31, 44, 81
Dice, Accuracy Effect	31, 44, 81
Dice, Armor Reduction	31, 44, 81
Limited Use / Discard Card	73
Dog (Type)	34
Dog Handler (Aura Ability)	34
Duration, Fixed Effects	73
Effect, Blast	44, 50, 99
Effect, Nuka-Cola Bottle	44, 50, 99
Effect, Star	44, 50, 99
Expertise	59
Expertise (Quick Action)	59
Fall Back Response (AI)	F:WW
Fail / Failure	92
Fire	68
Flip Card	F:WW
Food and Drink	73
Frozen	67
Gear	73
Health	65
Heavy Weapon	71
Heroic	21
Injured Arm (Condition)	67
Injured Leg (Condition)	67
Interact	59
Junk	73
Leader Card	34
Lockpick (Expertise)	25, 59
Lowest	64
Luck	35
Maximum Uses	50
Melee	57
Close Combat Method (AI)	F:WW
Mine	70
Mods	73
Move (Orange Range)	53
Move (Yellow Range)	53
Move (Red Range)	53
Move (Green Range)	53
Move (Blue Range)	53
Move Response (AI)	F:WW
Movement	40
Movement (Quick Action)	59
Objective Response (AI)	F:WW
Pistol	55
Poisoned (Condition)	68
Power Armor	73
Push Back	69
Prepare (Quick Action)	59
Presence (Expertise)	26, 59
Presence (Orange Range)	26, 59
Presence (Yellow Range)	26, 59
Presence (Red Range)	26, 59
Presence (Green Range)	26, 59
Presence (Blue Range)	26, 59
Presence (Black Range)	26, 59
Remove	F:WW
Rifle	55
Robot (Type)	21, 34
Scatter	57, 72
Search (Expertise)	27, 52, 59
Search (Orange Range)	27, 52, 59
Search (Yellow Range)	27, 52, 59
Search (Red Range)	27, 52, 59
Search (Green Range)	27, 52, 59
Search (Blue Range)	27, 52, 59
Ranged Combat Method (AI)	F:WW
Slow Firing	71
Slow	68
Stun	68
Success	92
Target	72
Throw / Thrown Weapon	57, 72
Throw (Orange Range)	57
Throw (Yellow Range)	57
Throw (Red Range)	57
Throw (Green Range)	57
Throw (Blue Range)	57
Throw (Black Range)	57
Unimpeded	53
Unique Unit	20
Weapon Range, Orange	52
Weapon Range, Yellow	52
Weapon Range, Red	52
Weapon Range, Green	52
Weapon Range, Blue	52

INDEX

KEY: ^{X} = EXPERTISE SKILL ^{G} = GIFT ^{S} = SCAR ^{P} = PERK ^{CP} = CHARACTER PROFILE

A

Acadia 8
Accuracy Effect Dice 44
Acrobatic Dodge^P........... 30
Acrobatics^X...................... 25
Action 51
    Action: Close Combat 57-58
    Action: Move 53-54
    Action: Prepare 59, 86
    Action: Shoot 55-56
    Action: Throw 57
    Action: Use Expertise ... 59
Action Boy/Girl^P 30
Action Play......................... 51
Action Point (AP) 43, 59, 61, 88
Action Point Use ... 21, 59, 88
Activating 51
Addiction/Addictive 73, 74, 75
Addiction^S 29
Addiction Boxes 22
Advanced Combat and
    Weapons 69-72
Advanced Systems Division 18
Advantage 51, 84, 86
Agile^P 30
Agility (AGI) 20
Alcohol 73, 94
Alert^G 28
Alerted 89
Alertness for NPCs 89-90
Ally^G 28
Ambidextrous^G 28
Ammunition 77-78
Amputee^S 29
Aqua Boy/Girl^P 30
Archetype cards 20-21, 38, 61
Area (of) Effect 70, 71
Armor 64, 73, 94
Armor Boost 65
Armor Dice.................. 45, 64
Armor Knowledge^P 30
Armor Rating 45, 64, 75, 76
Armor Reduction 64, 72
Arrogant^S 29
Artillerist^P 30
Assaultrons 6
Assistance 49
Athletics^X 25
Attack Dog^P 31
Attribute 20, 24, 42, 82
Aura Ability 68
Automatons 6
Average Joe/Jane^G 28
Awarding Bonuses and
    Penalties 81
Awareness 20, 59, 78, 91
Ayo, Justin 18

B

Bandit^{CP} 22
Base Damage 63
Base Sizes 56
Base-to-base Contact 58
Basher^P 31
Battle Cry 69
Battle Experience^P 31
Behavior^X 25
Benefactor^G 28
Big-Boned^G 28
Big-Brained^G 28
Big Leagues^P 31
Bioscience Division 18
Black Effect Dice............... 24
Bleeding (condition) 68
Blends In^G 28
Blitz^P 31
Blocking Damage 64
Bloody Mess^P 31
Bold^G 28
Boneyard, The 4
Bonuses 46, 81
    Fixed Bonuses 81
    Multiple Bonuses &
    Penalties 83
Brahmin 5
Brave^P 31
Breaking ties 47
Bright-Eyed^G 28
Broken Hills 8, 13
Brotherhood of Steel 9
Bug Free^G 28
Bushcraft^P 31

C

Cannibal^P 31
Cap Collector^P 31
Caps (bottlecaps)........ 4, 94
Capital Wasteland   4, 10, 12
Cards 42, 100
Careful^P 31
Centaurs 14
Character Mat 22, 63, 67, 74-76
Charge (Action) 54, 57, 69, 70
Charge Bonus 54, 90
Charge weapon ... see Criticals
Charisma (CHA) 20
Charismatic^P 31
Charmed Life^G 28
Chase Scenes 92
Chem Duration: Jet........... 75
Chemist^P 31
Chem Maker^{CP} 22
Chem Resistant^P 31
Chems 73, 75, 94
Climbing 53
    Inability to Climb 54
Close Combat 57
    Close Combat Strength
    Bonus 57
Clothing................... 73, 94
Color Ranges 52
Combat 80
Combat Skills 42
Combat Summary 55
Crafting Resources 96
Commonwealth 5, 10, 11, 12
Commonwealth Institute of
    Technology (CIT) 17
Competitive^G 28
Complication 27, 46,
    .... 77-78, 83-84
Computers^X 25, 59, 82, 93
Concentrated Fire^P 31
Condition 67-68
Confident^G 28
Contact^G 28
Cooking 77, 96
Courser 18
Cover 56
Covert Activities 91
Crafting/Creating Items ... 98
Creatures 34
Critical Banker^P 31
Critical Effect (Criticals)
    .... 21, 48, 57, 66, 67, 88
Critical Meter..... 50, 66-67, 71
Critical Point (CP) 35, 43, 48, 66
Cursed^S 29

D

Damage 63, 65
    Non-Lethal (NL) damage 65
    Radiation damage ......
    .... 63, 64-65, 75, 77
Damage Effect Dice........... 44
Dead Aim^G 28
Deaf^S 29
Death-Hand, Garl 12
Deathclaw 5
Deception^X 25
Defender^{CP} 22
Defenses, Settlement 95
Degraded 76
Demolition Expert^P 31
Department of the Army .. 16
Devotion^S 29
Diamond City 5, 8, 17, 110
Difficulty 45, 48, 81
Diminishing Effects........... 74
Disciples 11
Diseased^S 29
Disease and Sickness 66, 87
Distracting^P 31
Dodge^G 28
Dog Handler^P 31, 34
Dog 34
Dullard^S 29

E

East Coast Brotherhood ... 9
East Coast Mutants 13
Eden, John Henry 6, 16
Effect Dice ... 42, 44, 64, 67, 81
Effect Dice icons 50
Eidetic Memory^G 28
Enclave 6, 9, 15
Encumbrance/encumbered 77
Endurance (END) 20
Enduring^P 31
Energy damage 63, 64, 77
Engaged 54, 55, 57-58, 59, 70
Exodus, the....................... 9
Experience 36
Experience Points (XP) 21, 36
Expertise 24, 36
Expertise Skills ... 22, 24, 36
Eyebots 6
Eyes like a Radowl^G 28

F

Faction 20, 34
Facilities Division 18
Falling 53-54
Famous^G 28
Far-sighted^G 28
Fast Healer^G 28
Favor Owed/Indebted^S ... 29
Filmore, Allie 18
Fist^P 31
Fixed Effect Items 73
Fixer^{CP} 23
Flat-footed^S 29
Fleet of Foot^G 28
Food and Drink (item) ... 73, 94
Forager 23
Forced Evolutionary Virus
    (FEV) 9, 13, 14, 18
Forged 11
Fortune Finder^P 31
Fragile^S 29
Free Play 2, 62, 74, 80
Frozen (condition) 67
Fumble-fingered^S 29

G

Gear (item)................. 73, 94
Generators 95
Genius^P 31, 62
Ghoul 5, 7, 22
Ghoulish^P 31
Gift of Gab^G 28
Gifts 28-29
Go for the Vitals^G 28
Grapple 70
Great War 4, 7, 9
Grenade 72
Grey, Richard 13
Gullible^S 29
Gunslinger^P 31

H

Hacker^P 32
Hammer Time^P 32
Handyman^{CP} 23
Hatred^S 29
Healing 66, 75
    Healing Addiction 75
    Healing Items 75
Health 65, 87
Health Track 21, 22, 63, 65, 66
Healthy^G 28
Heavy Gunner^P 32
Heavy (Super Mutant)^{CP} ... 23
Hemophiliac^S 29
Heroic 21, 88
Hidden Shame^S 29
Hit Every Branch on the Way
    Down^S 29
Holdren, Clayton 13
Hub, The 4, 7, 8
Hunted^S 29
Hunter (Super Mutant)^{CP} ... 23
Huntsman^P...................... 32

I

I Know Something^S 29
Impact 44, 45, 47, 81-82,
    .... 83, 88-89, 91
Incapacitated 65, 87
Indifferent^S..................... 30
Infamous^S 30
Infantry 23
Inheritance^G 28
Initiate 10
Injured Arm/Leg 67, 87
Instant Duration............... 73
Institute 10, 17

Intelligence (INT) 20
Intelligent^P 32
Interact 26, 59
Intimidate^X 25
Intolerant^S 30
Investigative 89
Iron Stomach^G 29
Items 73, 94
    Limited Use items 73

J
Jumping Down 54
Junction City 8
Junk (item) 73

K
Knights 10
Knockdown 70
Knowhow^X 25

L
Lead Belly^P 22, 32
Leaders 34
Lead Skin^G 29
Life Giver^P 32, 37
Li, Madison 18
Line of Sight (LoS) ...54, 56, 86
Loaded 71
Lockpick^X 25-26, 59, 62, 83, 93
Locksmith^P 32
Lone Wanderer^P 32
Look Out!^P 32
Lost Hills 9
Luck (LUC) 20, 21, 35
Luck Points (LP) 35, 87
Lucky^P 32
Lungs like a Brahmin^G ... 29
Lyons, Owyn 12

M
Manual Dexterity^X ... 26, 90-91
Mariposa 9, 13, 16
Medic^P 32
Medical^X 26
Megaton 7, 8
Midwest Brotherhood 9
Mines 70, 94, 95
Miniatures 130
Minor Activities 62
Mirelurk 5
Miss Nanny 6
Mod/Modifying Items 73, 76, 98
Modifiers 81-82
Molecular Ray 17
Mole rat 6
Move Color 53
Moving Target^P 32
Mr. Gutsy 6
Mr. Handy 6, 23
Mute^S 30
Myopic^S 30
Mysterious Stranger^P ... 32

N
Narrow Vision^S 30
Natural Leader^G 29
Near-sighted^S 30
Near Success 48
Necropolis 5
Nerd Rage^P 32
New California Republic (NCR)
    .... 4, 7, 8, 9, 10, 12
New Khans 12
New Recruits 97

Newshound^P 32
Night Blind^S 30
Nimble^P 32
Ninja^P 32
Non-Player Characters (NPCs)
    .... 80, 88
    NPC Awareness 90
Notice^X 26, 88, 89, 90, 91
Nuka-World 11, 12

O
Objects 78
One-eyed^S 30
On Fire (condition) 67-68
Operators 12
Opposed Skill Test
    .... 47, 53, 84, 88, 90
Orders^P 33
Outside Chance 49
Over-Encumbered 77
Overseer 2, 80

P
Pack Leader^P 33
Pack, the 12
Pain Train^P 33
Paladin 10
Partial Resolution 45, 81
Party Boy/Party Girl^P 33
Patron^G 29
Peacekeeping and Recovery 16
Penalties 46, 81
    Fixed Penalties 81
    Multiple Bonuses &
    Penalties 83
Perception (PER) 20
Perceptive^P 33
Perk 22, 30, 36
Persuade^X 25
Physical Damage ... 63, 64, 77
Pilot^{CP} 23
Pilot^X 26
Pistol 55, 94
Pitt, The (Pittsburgh) 9, 12
Player Character (PC) 2, 80
Poisoned (condition) 68
Power and Water 95
Power Armor 10, 16, 54,
    .... 73, 75-76
Presence^X 27, 59
Protectrons 6
Prydwen 9, 10
Purpose^P 33
Push Back 69

Q
Quick Action 59, 61
Quick Draw^G 29

R
Rad Resistant^P 33
Radroaches 6
Radscorpions 6
Raider 7, 11, 12
Railroad 17
Randomizing 35
Ranges 52, 55
Reaction 59-60, 78, 86
Readiness 51, 52
Ready 51, 52, 86
Reduce Resistance 44
Refractor^P 33
Regular damage 63, 75
Repair 77

Repair & Craft^X 26
Repair and Craft 98
Repairing Items 98
Research and Development 16
Researcher^{CP} 23
Resilience^X 27
Resistance 44, 45, 81
Resistance Dice 45
Resistant 68
Rest 66
Rifle 55, 94
Rifleman^P 33
Rival^S 30
Rivet City 5, 7, 8
RobCo 6
Robotics Expert^P 33
Robots 34
    Maxson, Roger 9, 13
Rooted^P 33
Rounds 51
Rousing^P 33
Rust Devils 12

S
Sandy Shores/Shady Sands ...8
Scars 28-29
Scatter 72
Scavenging 93
Scourge 12
Scout^{CP} 23
Scrapper^P 33
Scribe 10
Scrounger^P 33
Search^X 27, 59, 83, 93
Secretly a Synth^S 30
Sense of Direction^G 29
Sense of Time^G 29
Sentry Bots 6
Settlements 22, 95-97
Sharpshoot^P 33
Sickness 66
Sigma Squad 16
Situational Awareness^G ... 29
Skill Dice 42-43, 45
Skill Test 24, 35, 42, 45, 46, 59,
    .... 81, 82, 98
    Faster Skill Test Rolls ... 84
    Impossible Skill Test 49, 83
Skill Value 42, 46, 81
Slide 57, 58
Slow (condition) 68
Sneak^P 33
Sniper^{CP} 23
S.P.E.C.I.A.L. 20, 74
Special Effect Dice 99
Special Effects 50
Specialities 20, 25, 36, 49
Starting Character Profiles 22
Steady Aim^P 33
Stealth^X 26, 88-89, 91
Strength (STR) 20
Strong^P 33
Strong Armor 45, 64, 65, 75
Strong Back^P 33
Strong Resistance 45
Stunned (condition) 58, 68
Super Mutants 13, 34
    Basic Super Mutants ... 15
    Behemoth Super Mutants 15
    Mariposa Super Mutants 15
    Huntersville Super
        Mutants 15
    Initiate Super Mutants 15
Super Mutant Close Combat
    Attacks 57

Surprise Attacks 90
Survivors 7
Suspicious 89
Synth 5, 10, 17
Synth Retention Bureau (SRB)
    18

T
Talk^X 27
Target Effect 72
Technician^{CP} 23
Tech Wizard / Gearhead^G ... 29
Terrain 53
Thrown Weapon 57, 94
Thug^{CP} 23
Tokens 100
Toughness^P 33
Track^X 27
Traders and Supply Routes 97
Trigger 59-60, 78, 86, 88, 90, 91
Turn 51
Turret 78, 95
Two Left Feet^S 30
Type 34

U
Unarmed^P 33
Unaware 89
Underworld, The 5, 8
Unique 20, 72
Unit 20
Unready 51
Unskilled 24, 42, 48, 81, 85
Unskilled Throw 57
Urban^P 33
Used 51-52, 86
Utility Robots 6

V
V.A.T.S. 21, 61
Vault 7, 8, 12, 15
Vault-Tec™ 4, 8, 15
Vertibird 10, 16

W
Wanted^S 30
Wasteland 4, 7
Wasteland Whisperer^P 33
Watchers 18
Water Pumps & Purifiers ... 96
Weak Lungs^S 30
Weak Point^P 33
Wealthy^G 29
Weapon Cards 50, 66
Weapons 77-78
    Heavy Weapon ...55, 71, 94
    Improvised Weapon 22
    Jammed Weapon 78
    Melee Weapon ...57, 65, 94
    Primed Weapons 71
    Slow Firing Weapons ... 71
    Using Non-Melee Weapons
        in Close Combat 57
    Walked Fire Weapons 71-72
West Coast Brotherhood 9, 10
West Coast Mutants 13
Wild^P 33
Withdrawing 57
Workbench 26, 76, 77, 96
Workstation 26, 96

Z
ZAX 16
Zero Health 87

To claim your free PDF's simply select the Fallout: Wasteland Warfare RPG (Expansion book) PDF and check out using the promo code below:
https://www.modiphius.net/collections/fallout-wasteland-warfare

FWW-4jfu7n